DOMESTIC ALLEGORIES
OF POLITICAL DESIRE

True understanding in literature and in literary studies is always historical and personal.

TZVETAN TODOROV, *Mikhail Bakhtin: The Dialogical Principle* (1984)

Recognizing the power of the erotic within our lives can give us the energy to pursue genuine change within our world, rather than merely settling for a shift of characters in the same weary drama.

AUDRE LORDE, "Uses of the Erotic: The Erotic as Power" (1978)

"You haven't learned our language yet. We don't just blurt into the Negro Problem; that's voted bad form. We leave that to our white friends. We saunter to it sideways, touch it delicately because"—her face became a little graver—"because, you see, it hurts."

WILLIAM E. B. DU BOIS, *The Quest of the Silver Fleece* (1911)

Domestic Allegories of Political Desire

The Black Heroine's Text at the Turn of the Century

CLAUDIA TATE

New York   Oxford
OXFORD UNIVERSITY PRESS
1992

Oxford University Press

Oxford   New York   Toronto
Delhi   Bombay   Calcutta   Madras   Karachi
Kuala Lumpur   Singapore   Hong Kong   Tokyo
Nairobi   Dar es Salaam   Cape Town
Melbourne   Auckland   Madrid

and associated companies in
Berlin   Ibadan

Copyright © 1992 by Oxford University Press, Inc.

Published by Oxford University Press, Inc.,
200 Madison Avenue, New York, New York 10016

Oxford is a registered trademark of Oxford University Press

Library of Congress Cataloging-in-Publication Data
Tate, Claudia.
Domestic allegories of political desire : the Black heroine's text
at the turn of the century / Claudia Tate.
p. cm.   Includes bibliographical references and index.
ISBN 0-19-507389-4
1. Domestic fiction, American—History and criticism.
2. American fiction—Afro-American authors—History and criticism.
3. American fiction—Women authors—History and criticism.
4. Politics and literature—United States.
5. Afro-American women—Intellectual life.
6. Afro-American women in literature.
7. Heroines in literature. 8. Marriage in literature.
9. Desire in literature. 10. Allegory. I. Title.
PS374.D57T38   1992
813.009′352042—dc20   91-46931

9 8 7 6 5 4 3 2 1

Printed in the United States of America
on acid-free paper

For Ma, Daddy, Gramps
Read, Jay, and Harold

ACKNOWLEDGMENTS

This work has been greatly enriched by the support of many people. I extend a special thanks to Skip Gates; the Staff of the Moorland-Spingarn Research Center of Howard University, especially Esme Bhan, Karen Jefferson, and Janet Sims-Woods; E. Ethelbert Miller of the Afro-American Studies Resource Center of Howard University; Betty Culpepper of the Library of Congress; and Elizabeth Maguire and Susan Chang of Oxford University Press.

I am especially grateful to the following scholars who critiqued chapters of my manuscript at various stages and/or wrote letters to funding agencies in support of my work: Vicki Arana, Don Bacon, Carolyn Brown, Hazel Carby, Eve Hawthorne, Sue Houchins, Barbara Johnson, Jennifer Jordan, Ann Kelly, Debbie McDowell, Nellie McKay, Marilyn Mobley, Judith Plotz, Hortense Spillers, Chris Sten, Cheryl Wall, Tara Wallace, and my anonymous readers. I thank David Levering Lewis for his consultation on William E. B. Du Bois. Their assistance, comments, and criticism greatly enhanced this book. However, all excesses of critical zeal, speculation, and overdetermined reading are mine.

My expression of gratitude would be incomplete were I not to mention my parents Harold and Mary Tate, my grandmother Mozella Austin, my sons Read Hubbard and Jerome (Jay) Lindsey, III, and my brother Harold Tate.

This project was supported, in part, by George Washington University, the American Council of Learned Societies, the Ford Foundation, and Howard University, with which I was professionally affiliated 1977–89.

Portions of this book appeared in my essay "Allegories of Black Female Desire; or, Rereading Nineteenth-Century Sentimental Narratives of Black Female Authority" in *Changing Our Own Words: Essays on Criticism, Theory, and Writing by Black Women* edited by Cheryl A. Wall. Copyright © 1989 by Rutgers, The State University. Reprinted by permission of Rutgers University Press. I am grateful to Oxford University Press for permission to reprint the photograph of Gertrude B. Mossell that appears as the frontispiece to *The Work of the Afro-American Woman*.

CONTENTS

DOMESTIC ALLEGORIES OF POLITICAL DESIRE

INTRODUCTION
A Highway through
the Wilderness of
Post-Reconstruction

> This book will, therefore, fill a two-fold mission, coming as it has at this
> most critical period in the existence of the colored American. It brings to
> my people the golden thoughts on how to perfect themselves in all things
> social, economical, physical, political and financial; it also proves to those
> who are inclined to think otherwise that some good thing can come out of
> Ethiopia. Not only to those, but to all lovers of advanced thoughts and
> seekers after truth and light, do I most heartily introduce "Golden
> Thoughts."
>
> > HENRY R. BUTLER, *Golden Thoughts on Chastity and
> > Procreation* (1903)

> Ah was born back due in slavery so it wasn't for me to fulfill my dreams of
> whut a woman oughta be and to do. Dat's one of de hold-backs of slav-
> ery. But nothing can stop you from wishin'. You can't beat nobody down
> so low till you can rob 'em of they will. Ah didn't want to be used for a
> work-ox and a brood-sow and Ah didn't want mah daughter used dat way
> neither. . . . Ah wanted to preach a great sermon about colored women
> sittin' on high, but they wasn't no pulpit for me. Freedom found me wid a
> baby daughter in mah arms, so Ah said Ah'd take a broom and a cook-pot
> and throw up a highway through de wilderness for her. She would ex-
> pound what Ah felt.
>
> > ZORA NEALE HURSTON, *Their Eyes Were Watching God* (1937)

In the above passage from Zora Neale Hurston's novel *Their Eyes Were
Watching God*, "Nanny" explains the material conditions of the lives of hundreds of thousands of women who were Hurston's figurative foremothers.
According to Nanny, they had to postpone "[their] stand on high ground lak
[they] dreamed."[1] Holding onto dreams for prosperous futures, they returned
to their brooms, cook pots, laundry tubs, and hoes to eke out a living during
the Reconstruction era—the years immediately following the Civil War from
1863 to 1877. Rapid resurgence of racial oppression soon shattered those
dreams, forcing them reluctantly to reclaim the demeanor as well as the imple-

3

ments of servility in order to survive what was probably one of the most violent periods of white/black race relations. This period spans the end of Reconstruction in 1877 (marked by the withdrawal of federal troops from the South and the Hayes Compromise that sanctioned the revival of Southern states rights) to 1915, the year of Booker T. Washington's death and the end point of what many historians have termed the "Era of Compromise" or the "Progressive Era."[2]

I refer to this period by its historical label—*post-Reconstruction*—and use that term to designate the eleven extant domestic novels—about courtship, marriage, and family formation—written by African-American women during the decade of the 1890s and the first years of the twentieth century that are the focus of this study. These novels are *Iola Leroy, or Shadows Uplifted* (1892) by Frances Watkins Harper (1825–1911); *Contending Forces: A Romance Illustrative of Negro Life North and South* (1900), *Hagar's Daughter: A Story of Southern Caste Prejudice* (1901), *Winona: A Tale of Negro Life in the South and Southwest* (1902), and *Of One Blood: Or, the Hidden Self* (1903) by Pauline E. Hopkins (1859–1930); *Clarence and Corinne; or God's Way* (1890) and *The Hazeley Family* (1894) by Amelia E. Johnson (1859–1907)[3]; *Megda* (1891) and *Four Girls at Cottage City* (1898) by Emma Dunham Kelley-Hawkins (n.d.–n.d.); and *Beryl Weston's Ambition: The Story of an Afro-American Girl's Life* (1893) and *Clancy Street* (1898) by Katherine D. Tillman (1870–n.d.).[4]

These novels of "genteel domestic feminism"[5] are direct precursors of *Their Eyes Were Watching God*, and their authors, Hurston's literary predecessors. These works also reflect the viewpoint widely held among turn-of-the-century African Americans that the acquisition of their full citizenship would result as much or more from demonstrating their adoption of the "genteel standard of Victorian sexual conduct" as from protesting racial injustice (Moses, p. 964). *Golden Thoughts*, referenced in the first epigraph, is one of several book-length conduct manuals written by and for black people at the turn of the century that, like the domestic novels, regarded bourgeois decorum as an important emancipatory cultural discourse.[6]

Without a doubt, the vigorous activity among black women's clubs during the decade of the 1890s made this proliferation of novels possible, by stimulating their production and by creating an audience for them. As journalist Paula Giddings explains, "The breakthroughs of the N[ational] A[ssociation of] C[olored] W[omen] women were also reflected in the artistic and social achievements of Black women generally."[7] Indeed, "the emergence by the turn of the century of a vigorous, self-defined, middle-class women's movement in the black community . . . " adds Elizabeth Ammons, "simultaneously reflected and fostered the sense of powerfulness, mission, and possibility necessary to the emergence of art not simply by scattered individuals . . . but by women as a group."[8] But while the literary production of black women at that time was impressive, until the recent publication of *The Schomburg Library of Nineteenth-Century Black Women Writers*, edited by Henry Louis Gates, Jr., all that productivity with the exception of Harper's 1892 novel *Iola Leroy* had slipped through the cracks of African-American literary scholarship and fallen into oblivion, leaving *Iola Leroy* to stand alone as if it were unique.[9]

My discussion of these eleven novels and the cultural contexts that influenced them, and which they in turn influenced, addresses how this body of fictions participated in late-nineteenth- and early-twentieth-century dialogues about racial justice and sexual equality by novelizing these ambitions within the diverse social attitudes of that era. Hence I read these novels against the cultural history of the epoch of their production. By doing so, I attempt to recover much of the cultural meaning, values, expectations, and rituals of African Americans of that era, which are symbolically embedded in these black Victorian love stories. While I repeatedly perform close textual readings of the domestic novels, my intention is not to provide a comprehensive analysis of each work but to read the novels against the cultural history of their first readers—middle- and working-class black men and women.[10] It is also not my intention to focus on exposing the myths of wedded bliss that maintain the illusion of the harmonious conjugal symmetry of husbands and wives in these novels, for I contend that their authors did not intend for the novels to be read as mimetic representations of courtship and marriage among African Americans.

By drawing on the works of many writers, literary scholars and theorists, historians, and critics of culture, I endeavor to illustrate how black women authors of the post-Reconstruction era used domestic novels, as did other politically excluded writers, as entry points into the "literary and intellectual world and as a means of access to social and political events from which [they as black women were] . . . largely excluded."[11] By subjecting these eleven novels to close textual readings, cultural critique, and discourse analysis, I demonstrate how these writers specifically used their stories—"female texts"—of ideal domesticity to promote, in the words of one black writer of the post-Reconstruction period, "the steady growth, development and advancement of the colored American in the very teeth of all kinds of obstacles."[12] At the same time I offer explanations for how these stories novelize what Mikhail M. Bakhtin has called "a zone of direct contact with developing reality" in order to mediate the conflicting viewpoints about the participation of black Americans in general and black women in particular in public enterprise at the turn of the century, a time and place when the politics of race, gender, and class were particularly volatile.[13] Thus my intention is to identify the idealized domesticity in these novels as a fundamental cultural symbol of the Victorian era for representing civil ambition and prosperity as a nineteenth-century "metonym for proper social order," a symbol that black women writers in particular used to promote the social advancement of African Americans.[14]

The post-Reconstruction domestic novels of black women, most of which cluster in the 1890s, constitute a specific category of African-American fiction in which a virtuous heroine generally undergoes a series of adventures en route to marriage, family happiness, and prosperity. In fact, according to critic of popular culture John G. Cawelti, many writers and readers have contended that "[t]he feminine equivalent of the adventure story is the romance."[15] However, these fictions also sustain another discursive category of adventure, namely, the story of female self-development. Such recurring features invite the designation of what Cawelti has identified as the formula story of social melodrama, and suggest as well that these works must have repeatedly gratified their first audience in ways that are no longer compelling to contemporary readers (p. 260). Clearly, their first readers were not seeking originality. Neither do they seem to have been seeking explicit expressions of their outrage at racial oppression. Nor do they seem to have been attracted to participatory reading, engrossed, according to Nina Baym, "in the text as construer[s] of meanings, interpreter[s] of value systems, or supplier[s] of bridges over gaps in signification"; for as she contends in discussing the expectations of the prior generation of white readers, "These concepts of reader behavior lay far in the future, and they imply a profoundly different kind of activity."[16] The popularity of the formulaic domestic plots of black women's post-Reconstruction novels, as evidenced by their preponderance during the decade of the 1890s, suggests that their first readers found emphatically confirmed in them personal and social meaning with which they had decided affinity.[17] That first audience undoubtedly found pleasurable self-affirmation that reflected their racial and gender aspirations to live in a world where such stories were possible.

While Baym's work assists me in identifying the expectations of the first readers of these domestic novels, the aesthetic reception theory of Hans Robert Jauss provides a methodology for reconstructing the cultural value of these works. He argues that "[t]he way in which a literary work, at the historical moment of its appearance, satisfies, surpasses, disappoints, or refutes the expectations of its first audience obviously provides a criterion for the determination of its aesthetic value."[18] The spate of domestic novels written by black women at the turn of the century therefore suggests that these novels

> precisely fulfill[ed] the expectations prescribed by a ruling standard of taste, in that [they] satisfie[d] the desire for the reproduction of the familiarly beautiful; confirm[ed] familiar sentiments; sanction[ed] wishful notions, ma[de] unusual experiences enjoyable as "sensations"; or even raise[d] moral problems, but only to "solve" them in an edifying manner as predecided questions. (Jauss, p. 25)

In short, the post-Reconstruction domestic novels of African-American women fulfilled the expectations of their first public audience for pleasurable reading in plots affirming the social meaning to which it generally subscribed. By recovering what Cathy N. Davidson has called "the interpretative grid," or what I might call the community of assumptions among black post-Reconstruction readers, I suggest in this study why these novels were especially satisfying during an era of intense interracial violence (Davidson, p. 4).[19] In doing so, I read them as products "of a complex set of generic, stylistic, thematic, cultural, ideological, and literary expectations that readers bring to texts and that authors (themselves readers of the works that they are writing) play with and around in the creation of texts" (Davidson, p. 4). Moreover, by recovering the aesthetic value of these novels I suggest ways in which gender influences symbolic representation throughout African-American literary culture.

The aesthetic value of these novels initially resided in their ability to gratify a distinct audience of ambitious black Americans who sought to live fully, despite their commonly experienced racial oppression. For that first public audience, reading these stories probably incited pleasure because they enabled these readers temporarily to escape oppression and gain access to a collective racial desire for enlarged social opportunity as full-fledged American citizens. The story of ideal family formation was especially well suited to this first audience because its formulaic plot line encoded bourgeois constructions of the successful individual, community, and society to which that audience subscribed. In the words of one very popular, mid-nineteenth-century white woman writer by way of a contemporary critic, for Victorian readers marriage was "'the most sacred tie on earth' because it secures not only 'the peace of families, [but] the social welfare of the whole community.'"[20] In responding to black people's assumptions about racial advancement and the family as the basis of self-definition and social mobility, the formula stories about family prosperity were to "become collective cultural products because they successfully articulate a pattern of fantasy that [was] at least acceptable if not preferred by the cultural groups who enjoy[ed] them. Formulas enable[d] the members of a group to share the same fantasies" (Cawelti, p. 34). These domestic stories, then, allowed black people of the post-Reconstruction period "to identify imaginatively with actions they would like to perform but [could] not in the ordinary course of events," given their exclusion from civil political participation (Cawelti, p. 22).[21] Moreover, because formula stories in general tend to harmonize group tensions, conflicts, and ambiguities, the black domestic melodramas provided their first readers with opportunities "to explore in fantasy the boundary between the permitted and the forbidden and to experience in a carefully controlled way the possibility of stepping across this boundary" (Cawelti, p. 35). What is especially important to observe is that such exploration was not simply gratuitous escapism; it offered the recently emancipated an occasion for exercising political self-definition in fiction at a time when the civil rights of African Americans were constitutionally sanctioned but socially prohibited.

Cawelti's description of the popular format of social melodrama, which I quote below at length, fits all eleven domestic novels and especially those by Hopkins, due to the fact that her novels consistently portray "the murky melodramatic triangle of virtuous heroine, noble hero, and dastardly villain [as] a drama of providence" (Cawelti, p. 270).

> Instead of a particular formula, social melodrama is a type defined by the combination of melodramatic structure and character with something that passes for a "realistic" social or historical setting. The appeal of this synthesis combines the escapist satisfactions of melodrama—in particular, its fantasy of a moral universe following conventional social values—with the

> pleasurable feeling that we are learning something important about real-
> ity. . . . [T]he social melodramatist tends to take advantage of anything
> that can give his tale the appearance of deep social significance and truth.
> If the novel's setting is historical, there is usually a parade of important and
> well-known personalities, issues, and events. . . . [T]he social melodrama
> seems to be the most time-bound of all the major formulas. I suspect this
> is because this formulaic type depends to such a great extent on the outlook
> and values of a particular era. (Cawelti, pp. 261, 263)

Applying this description to the eleven domestic novels, we see that they repeatedly, in Cawelti's words, "dramatized the congruence between the social ideals of domesticity, romantic love, and respectable mobility and the religious faith in the divine governance of the world" (p. 270). Thus each of the black domestic novels presents a heroine who is an exemplar of feminine purity, piety, and the work ethic as well as outlines a plot that confirms bourgeois social objectives of domesticity and respectability. Together these ideals sustain the integrity of the formulaic plot that culminates in poetic justice. If these ideals did not accurately reflect the social and moral parameters of the novels' first community of readers, then the story of ideal domesticity would possess little aesthetic and cultural value for that audience. These works were, however, inordinately appealing to their first readers, and thus there must have been a very strong congruence between the ideals revered in the works and those the audience endorsed.

The aesthetic value of these works for contemporary readers lies in our ability to recuperate the bases of their appeal to their first readers. To do this we must recover the inscription of those readers' political desire. Whereas contemporary readers frequently regard politics as simply an exercise of power over others, the political desire in these black female texts is the acquisition of authority for the self both in the home and in the world. By categorizing these texts as "female" I am not referring to the female identity of the author, narrator, or principal character of the work, though female figures predominate in the *female text*. Rather, a *female text* is one in which the dominant discourses and their interpretations arise from woman-centered values, agency, indeed authority that seek distinctly female principles of narrative pleasure.[22] While *male texts* often center a female figure or recall a marriage story, the text itself is governed by male expectations, privilege, and proprietary authority. In other words, the text is regulated by a dominant masculine ideological narrative—a patriarchal "master narrative."[23]

What probably made the female-centered domestic story of post-Reconstruction black women compelling to its first readers, and should inform our reading of it now, is not simply the promised happy ending but the story's interior plotting or "thick description" (referring to cultural anthropologist Clifford Geertz's term[24]) of the cultural indices and political contingencies necessary to support the surface story. The interior political matrix permits the prosperous marriage story to move forward to its consummation, while implicitly constructing an external, fictive world in which marriage as the sign of private prosperity is also the sign of civil justice. The post-Reconstruction domestic novels not only presented fictions of connubial happiness to the community of their first readers, but more importantly they also offered histories of racial prosperity within a matrix of sanctioned Victorian social, political, and economic viewpoints. These domestic formula novels chronicle the heroines' successful lives and simultaneously reflect the political ambitions of the authors' constituency. As the central insight of the second wave of the feminist movement—"The personal is political"—reminds us, "the seemingly most intimate details of private existence are actually structured by larger social relations."[25] Hence the social equation between personal and political or private and public works in two directions: not only do public and political social constructions shape the details of intimate lives; those personal details also form comprehensive social practices and institutions. Black women's post-Reconstruction domestic novels aspired to intervene in the racial and sexual schemes of the public world of the turn-of-the-century United States by plotting new stories about the personal lives of black women and men.

Pleasurable reading, however, is just one side of an equation of aesthetic reception. As the first private audience for these novels, the authors themselves must have experienced gratification in producing their novels. Recognizing these authors' and their first readers' textual pleasure prompts another question in determining the cultural meaning and aesthetic value of this body of fictions: What social factors made the idealized story of family formation a form of vicarious delight among African Americans at this particular historical moment?

During post-Reconstruction, advocates for Southern states' rights effectively undermined the meager social, political, and economic progress that African Americans had achieved during Reconstruction. Southern and Northern state legislatures, in addition to local governments, increasingly ignored the Fourteenth Amendment that granted black people equal protection under the law. As during slavery, blacks lost their civil rights to the point where they possessed no legal claims that white people were bound to respect. Southern state legislatures had practically rescinded the Fifteenth Amendment, which enfranchised black men, by implementing prejudicial voting requirements such as literacy tests, poll taxes, and grandfather clauses. In 1883 the U.S. Supreme Court ruled the Civil Rights Act of 1875 unconstitutional, thereby laying the groundwork for each state to legalize de facto segregation. By 1896 state-sanctioned de facto segregation gained national authorization with the Supreme Court case of *Plessy v. Ferguson*. As a consequence, segregation abounded in housing, public transportation, and accommodations, matched only by exploitative employment discrimination, as signs—"for whites only," "for coloreds only"—dotted the South and the North with increasing frequency. White people of both regions generally condoned mob rule and civil subterfuge to enforce new racialist laws and covenants.

The justification for this oppressive racial regime was founded, as historian Herbert G. Gutman has explained, on the "retrogressionist" arguments of "southern Bourbon political rhetoric that promised to redeem the South and save the nation from political corruption, economic extravagance, and racial and sexual 'irregularities'. . . ."[26] This white Southern redemption would occur as a consequence of its "reimposing dominance over a race and a class that disclosed in the years following the emancipation an incapacity to 'restrain' itself and thereby adapt decently to its changed status" (Gutman, p. 532). In short, *white radical conservatives*[27] — Southern and Northern — contended that the (alleged) sexual excesses of the recently emancipated were the result of their unrestrained retrogression into savagery, and the social theory accounting for this transition was termed "retrogressionism" (also "regressionism"). It formed the basis of the racist ideology that ultimately disenfranchised black people and segregated them in all aspects of social exchange as well as reaped on them the terrorism of lynching and rape.[28] As a consequence of the wide dissemination of retrogressionism (a viewpoint remaining with us still), racial prejudice permeated all areas of U.S. social culture, transforming black people's recent entitlement to the American dream into a nightmare from which they could not awaken. So intense were the revival of racist politics and the subsequent interracial hostility that historian Rayford W. Logan was compelled to coin his own terms — *the nadir* and *the Dark Ages of recent American history* — for characterizing this period.[29] What is important to point out here is that repudiating the racist sexual discourse of retrogressionism at the heart of white Southern ideology was crucial to black people's changing their subjugated social status, and repudiating that discourse was a main objective of black women's post-Reconstruction domestic novels.

Academic scholarship, print media, plastic arts, manufactured goods, and colloquial speech of the post-Reconstruction era all reflected the ideology of retrogressionism and characterized black people not merely as intellectually inferior but as lazy, ugly, intemperate, slothful, lascivious, and violent, indeed bestial. Racist delineations of coons, mammies, and sambos were so heavily interwoven into the texture of American life during this era that they became stock decorative features of the mass-produced items that the Industrial Revolution efficiently furnished for broad consumption. Coons and their figurative relatives were not only seen on minstrel stages but materialized as bric-a-brac and leered from common household items like calendars, framed prints, potholders, and playing cards. Ironically, we now refer to these turn-of-the-century artifacts of racial denigration as black memorabilia. Their scarcity in the contemporary marketplace indicates the success of generations of social activists who worked to eliminate the racist images from the public realm. However, this racist ideology so broadly informed all social constructions of good and bad in relationship to white and black that its vestiges remain with us today.

As a distinct population, African Americans of the post-Reconstruction era had yet to secure the civil rights of U.S. citizenship that the Constitution should have guaranteed and had yet to escape the extreme penury that their labor ought to have relieved. Indeed, the malevolent racial climate of that era made achievement of those goals increasingly difficult. Black people did not passively accept the deterioration of their status, but made repeated attempts to exercise their constitutional rights. In doing so they met hostility, litigious circumventions of the law, race riots, and lynch mobs. Central to the survival of African Americans, to the preservation of black culture and community, was finding strategies to withstand the persistent physical and psychological racial assaults. To mount a sustained struggle, black social activists and artists alike formulated strategies for fortifying the resolve of black Americans to continue the battle for freedom.

Just as in the antebellum period it had been essential for African Americans to celebrate the desire for freedom to sustain that ambition,[30] so too during the periods of Reconstruction and post-Reconstruction did it become essential for them to glorify an industrious black citizenry to retain their faith in hard work, education, and frugality as practical means for attaining social and economic prosperity, indeed for demonstrating their worthiness as full U.S. citizens. In addition, like the dominant society, late-nineteenth-century black culture regarded happiness and economic prosperity as mutually dependent, thus the culture's early and virtually unquestioned appropriation of bourgeois professional and familial values.

Many of the black women writers of the post-Reconstruction period complemented their literary interventionism with activism in specific reform movements (temperance, women's suffrage, the nullification of segregation laws, the reform of convict-lease systems, and antilynching legislation), activism that was an expression of conviction in the ultimate power of Christian virtue to advance human society. Without that faith, their dream "too long deferred" (to invoke Langston Hughes) would have become, as it now has for many, transfigured into the living nightmare of domestic and street violence repeatedly described in our contemporary newspapers. To fight back, the black women authors of the post-Reconstruction domestic novels nurtured, exalted, and disseminated by means of ideal heroines their faith in the inevitability of their freedom. However, these constructions of black female virtue did not arise simply from Christian piety, moral rectitude, intellectual talent, and personal commitment; gentility, skin color, and class status also qualified portrayals of the exemplary heroines (discussed in Chapter 2).

These writers repeatedly wrote novels about the moral development, spiritual maturation, professional aspirations, and economic advancement of and of course social justice for black Americans. They inscribed these pursuits within the familiar marriage plot of nineteenth-century white women's sentimental fiction, transforming that plot into the story of racialized, ideal-family (re)formation. Even in those instances when the racial designation of the characters was effaced to some degree, the author's racial identity or black cultural markers indirectly racialized the story. Like their white female British and American counterparts, these black women writers repeatedly relied on what Nancy K. Miller has termed the "heroine's text" to discuss the possibility not simply of a woman's entry into society but of society's reform through her successful marriage.[31] No doubt the sustained prominence of "heroine's text[s]" throughout particularly the nineteenth century, their didacticism and attendant sentimental conventions, influenced black women writers to appropriate the marriage story in order to address social issues bearing on African-American women, especially the resurgence of racism and the encroachment of intraracial male privilege. For, as Molly Hite has explained, "one reason that 'heroine's texts' written by women remained vital for so long and can still engage reader expectations may well be that in revealing ['the constrictions of the romance plot' or] the 'other side' of an apparently simple and familiar story, female novelists embedded a cultural critique that introduced complication and novelty."[32] This familiar story also contoured the domestic novels of black women writers of the post-Reconstruction era, serving as a ready vehicle for contesting, mediating, and disseminating changing cultural values about the process of self-definition within culturally diverse reading communities of African Americans of that era.

The recurring sentimental courtships in these domestic novels all reflect excessive moralizing (by late-twentieth-century standards), an ambience of gentility, hyperbolic representation of emotion, tightly circumscribed household settings, and the development of an exemplary heroine. Yet these novels are not ideologically identical. They dramatize decidedly different racial and gender discourses as well as varying intensities of female piety, an essential element of the sentimental novel. The reformist discourses range from being explicitly racial and militantly agitating for social equality to being racially indefinite and generally affirming the meritorious consequences of hard work, frugality, and an equitable distribution of political justice. The explicitly black contextual novels of Harper and Tillman are optimistic—their investment in the ethic of hard work reflects faith in black people's inevitable acquisition of their civil rights. By contrast, those of Hopkins increasingly depict the tragic consequences of persistent racism and the deferral of equal justice. Consequently, only the first of Hopkins's four novels—Contending Forces—has the traditional happy ending. All of her novels advocate the political rights and personal autonomy of black people. In her three serial novels (which I discuss in detail in Chapter 7), Hopkins used the courtship story to frame the then-popular formulaic plot lines of the detective story, the western, and the psychological ghost story to repudiate the resurgence of racial prejudice and discrimination during the post-Reconstruction period. In comparison, the novels of Johnson and Kelley-Hawkins avoid racial despair by suppressing entirely or partially the discourse of race, thus sustaining racially nonspecific, reformist viewpoints of social justice under the general auspices of equal opportunity in a meritocracy.[33] Like the novels of Hopkins, though, Johnson's do not extend that framework to assert what late-twentieth-century readers would recognize as even a relative assertion of sexual equality.

Hence another important and related area of ideological difference in these novels concerns gender. They present fictionalized mediations of increasing conservatism in female gender roles in African-American society at the turn of the century and the decreasing importance of the family as both a site of political change and a trope for reformist discourse in African-American culture in the twentieth century. At the one extreme are Johnson's racially indefinite (and thus presumed white) heroines who regard the ideal woman as the competent housewife who cheerfully maintains an efficient home so that her husband (or other males in the household) can direct his (or their) full attention to getting ahead in the marketplace. Johnson's heroines, particularly Flora Hazeley of *The Hazeley Family*, encode the more conservative gender role for the ideal woman as wife, by dramatizing her acquisition of domestic skills concerning frugal and effective home decoration, the preparation of savory meals, and provision of home entertainment so that the males of the household "would not be lured away to less seemly recreations."[34] At the other extreme are the novels of Harper and Tillman who decidedly racialize the "heroine's text" and liberate it so as to advance beyond the wedding ceremony. As a result the reader witnesses the heroines' continued reliance on their own intellectual ability, forbearance, piety, and moral rectitude as well as their domestic skill in nurturance, compassion, and efficient management for cultivating (and reforming, if need be) the self, family, and community.[35]

Harper and Tillman decidedly politicized their heroines' lives by correlating their roles as wives, mothers, and teachers to their performance as and training of African-American citizens, to the acquisition of their collective civil rights, and to the general advancement of their race. As a consequence, their heroines are not simply well groomed and well behaved; by standards of that day they are well educated and community-minded in the dedication of their labor to the inseparable progress of the self and race, particularly as principals and instructors at all levels of secular and religious educational institutions.

The novels of Hopkins and Kelley-Hawkins are ideologically situated between the restricted domesticity of Johnson on one end and the enlarged domestic realm of Harper and Tillman on the other. The latter two writers represent the virtual marriage of private and public female ambitions, whereas Johnson confined the public ambition of her heroines. Hopkins's novels stand forthright in their militant agitation for racial equality, but they rely on heroes, rather than heroines, to voice its public expression. While Hopkins's heroines are courageous, independent, and outspoken in private settings, marriage curtails the public expression of these virtues, thereby offering the heroines little opportunity to redefine a woman's social ambitions in a civil arena. The novels of Kelley-Hawkins, like those of Hopkins, present heroines who express professional ambitions, but only while single. Whereas public activity complemented the domestic duty of the heroines of Harper and Tillman, enhancing their social value, modest public activity seems to be a respectable substitute for ideally sanctioned domesticity for the heroines of Kelley-Hawkins and Hopkins. Once these latter heroines become wives and mothers, they focus on the home and family with only discreet activities of social benevolence temporarily enlarging that focus. Thus these heroines preserve their exclusive, ideal role as wife and mother rather than becoming a "civilizer of the race" (Wills, p. 178).

The novels of Harper, Johnson, Kelley-Hawkins, Tillman, and to some extent Hopkins are concerned with using spiritual piety and temperance to shape character development and incite social activism. These works dramatize earthly rewards for a pious life, and rely on the moral authority granted to the converted heroine to enlarge the discourse of feminine propriety so as to reform the lives of those within her community. Moreover, the advocacy of temperance in these novels should not be read as the authors' vigilant endorsement of prudery. Rather, we should recall that the temperance movement provided women activists of the post-Reconstruction era with an entry into the public arena of social reform as well as an active role in safeguarding the economic and emotional bases of the family.[36] While Johnson's *The Hazeley Family* and *Clarence and Corinne* as well as Kelley-Hawkins's *Four Girls at Cottage City* center evangelical stories, we should be mindful that these novels fundamentally are female Christian *Bildungsromans*.[37]

Whether conservative or liberal, the domestic plots rely on a tradition of politicized motherhood that views mothers and the cultural rhetoric of maternity as instruments of social reform. This tradition held sway from the late eighteenth through most of the nineteenth century, from the ideology of republican motherhood that designated white American mothers responsible for "instructing children in and keeping spouses true to republican principles" to "the cult of true womanhood" that defined white women as the arbiters of moral virtues as well.[38] As fictions in the tradition of the "politicization of domesticity,"[39] black women's post-Reconstruction domestic novels kept the distressed ambitions of African Americans for racial justice alive, not as abstract desires but as courtship stories in which the might of true love, like vigilant self-will, frees the individual from dominant racist constructions and conventions. The popular discursive mode of bourgeois domestic romance in these fictions, then, provided both a ready formula for liberal black self-construction and relief for black readers from direct encounters with racism and a reinforcement of the viewpoint that prosperity, which they understood as middle-class aspirations, was largely a product of one's tenacity. Hence in amazing opposition to the violent resurgence of racial oppression that marked this period, these novels focus by and large on happy domestic settings without directly addressing interracial turmoil. The settings are suggestive of the civil accord that black people of the prior Reconstruction era had optimistically anticipated. Even in those works that explicitly agitate for social equality outside of the domestic setting, namely those of Hopkins, the racial discourse complements the romantic story, and the conflict between justice and oppression is staged as the contest of true love in which the black heroine and her suitor (who is black in the first and last of Hopkins's novels and white in the remaining two) succeed or fail in sustaining their moral integrity, physical forbearance, and mutual emotional commitment.[40] Their union in marriage reflects their success; their separation reflects their failure. By preserving these noble attributes, Hopkins's heroic couples execute liberational self-construction rather than succumb to racist, social conventions. While the nobility of Hopkins's couples does not empower them to change the racial codes of their societies, the successful couples resist the corruption of racist oppression often by removing themselves from the sites of racial hostility.

Two important questions immediately arise in exploring the politicization of black domesticity, or—put another way—the domestic ideation of black political desire in African-American literature. First, why was this a prominent discursive pattern in black women's writing of the post-Reconstruction period? And second, why does this pattern wane throughout the twentieth century? The explanations I offer arise from a theoretical reconstruction of the cultural milieu of these authors in which the novel, as Cathy Davidson has argued, had already been for more than half a century "a form of education, especially for women" (p. 10). No doubt black girls and women of the post-Reconstruction era, who were excluded from agency in U.S. social rituals due to race and in the intraracial institutions of church and school due to gender, would find writing and reading stories that presented their "versions of emerging definitions of America," black communities, and female advocacy particularly appealing. Moreover, I suspect that the post-Civil War optimism among black people and their endorsement of bourgeois individuation in the form of discrete acts of racial uplift would find alignment with these ideal domestic plots.[41] For they reaffirm a resilient faith in the political ambitions of the Reconstruction by keeping those goals alive as the story of the happy marriage, during what they probably assumed to be a difficult, temporary period of interracial social adjustment.

However, by the second decade of the twentieth century, when Angelina Weld Grimké (1880–1959) wrote her stories and plays about black domestic life (discussed in the last chapter of this book), the backlash had proven most persistent. This chronic entrenchment of institutionalized racism in the United States further suggested the futility of sustaining indirect arguments about social parity in the tropology of idealized domesticity. The frustrated optimism among African Americans of the post-Reconstruction era rapidly became chronic despair, as degenerating race relations descended deeper into "the nadir" with the advance of the twentieth century.[42] "African-American cultural grief"[43] became especially graphic in all forms of black cultural production during the first two decades of the twentieth century, as Figures 1 and 2 from *The Crisis* of 1911 clearly reveal.[44] In addition, by the early twentieth century the myth of the happy marriage was becoming more and more contested as newer generations of women increasingly challenged the patriarchal family. For both reasons, modern black readers no longer regarded the repetitive stories of civil optimism framed by requited love as strategic displacements and repudiations of racial conflict. No doubt the harsh social climate made the discourse of domestic optimism seem delusory to writers and readers alike. Therefore, the fictive affirmations of political and sexual desire in the post-Reconstruction domestic novels ceased to gratify new audiences, and these novels became increasingly obscure with succeeding decades. In this inhospitable terrain it was not long before the ideal "heroine's text" became subject to deformation during the first three decades of the twentieth century, as stories of domestic affirmation became domestic tragedies in the works of Grimké and domestic parodies and tragic satires in those of her contemporaries Jessie Fauset and Nella Larsen.[45]

Therefore, by the 1920s the allegorical link between idealized domestic tropes, on the one hand, and liberational racial and sexual desire, on the

Figure 1. "The colored man that saves his money and buys a brick house will be universally respected by his neighbors." Illustration from *The Crisis,* 1911. Courtesy of the Moorland-Spingarn Research Center, Howard University.

other, had become disengaged. Furthermore, the sentimental conventions of "heroine's text" were no longer pedagogically effective for modern readers. This is the period in which Grimké wrote her stories and plays. I refer to her writing because she seems to have written more by 1920 than her black female contemporaries and because her works repeatedly appropriate and revise, indeed deform, the idealism of the prior domestic plot.[46] Like the novels of her black female predecessors, Grimké's stories present noble heroines and inscribe sentimental conventions, especially pathos; however, the successful marriage is not possible because of racial conflict. In fact the nullification and often the repudiation of the marriage plot in Grimké's writings transform them

Figure 2. "New and dangerous species of Negro criminal lately discovered in Baltimore. He will be segregated in order to avoid lynching." Illustration from *The Crisis,* 1911. Courtesy of the Moorland-Spingarn Research Center, Howard University.

into domestic tragedies in which racial *protest* displaces racial affirmation. Moreover, the domestic domain in her works no longer sustains a political discourse of desire, namely the nineteenth-century polity of domesticity, but becomes a dramatic site for plotting out intraracial despair, interracial hostility, and violence (usually lynching and rape[47]), which repeatedly either renders her black families dysfunctional or totally devastates them. Unable to preserve faith in idealized domestic figuration of racial desire, Grimké's stories and plays repeatedly and emphatically voice racial protest that arises from aversion to racial insults, employment discrimination, and especially interracial violence. Grimké's writings, then, locate one point in African-American literary culture when a "new horizon of expectations has achieved more general currency" (Jauss, p. 26), specifically when the formerly successful and optimistic domestic plots of social uplift become outmoded and explicit depictions of racial protest start satisfying the expectations of twentieth-century black readers.

Speculating about the effects of chronic racial despair is also particularly revealing when directed to Grimké's black female predecessors. For when they encountered the persistent racist entrenchment, they seem to have stopped writing idealized domestic fiction altogether. For example, Tillman was in her 30s during the first decade of the twentieth century. I refer to her "writing career" because she continued to write and her works are less obscure than those of the other black women writers of the period due to the fact that she continued to rely on the sponsorship of the A.M.E. Church to publish her works. Though Tillman continued to write, she apparently stopped writing female-centered, idealized domestic novels like *Beryl Weston's Ambition* and *Clancy Street*. She turned instead to short stories and Sunday School dramas, primarily for intraracial dissemination.[48] While Tillman's domestic novels, published in the 1890s, adhere to what Joan R. Sherman has described as an integrationist imperative (because she "propagandiz[ed] . . . America's cherished habits of hard work, self-reliance, and Christian idealism"[49]), Tillman's Sunday School dramas and short stories, published in the next decade, place the ethic of hard work not into an idealized domestic context but into a decidedly racist social setting that typified the late post-Reconstruction era in which civil politics became the dominant consideration of her writings.

To illustrate this shift in perspective I refer to two of her Sunday School dramas and a short story, the three published in chronological sequence. In *Thirty Years of Freedom*, published in 1902, the character Aunt Savannah describes the institutionalization of mob violence in her comparison of the North with the South:[50] "But one 'ing I do no, dey nebber has no Klu-Klux nor lynching' ob cullud men fer white men's meanness" (p. 5). In "Preacher at Hill Station," published in 1903,[51] Tillman wrote about a race riot resulting from "a party of young white men, considerably the worse for drink, . . . trying to drive the Negro voters from the polls. . . . [As a result a] large number of both black and white men were coming upon the scene, and the situation grew more serious each moment" (p. 641). Last, in Tillman's 1910 play *Fifty Years of Freedom; or from Cabin to Congress*,[52] discrimination in education is a principal subject, as illustrated by a white character's proclaimed racist viewpoint about the black male hero: "I say, it's a beastly shame to have that nigger here in the university with us. We don't stand for anything like that in Texas, I tell you" (p. 33). Although the title of this dramatic work suggests optimism in that the hero moves from a lowly cabin to congress, Tillman's placement of the action into a self-contradictory time frame undermines that optimism.[53]

Given the fact that Tillman relied on the A.M.E. Church to publish and disseminate practically all of her work, we can safely assume that she directed her works primarily to a black audience. In addition to fiction and plays, she wrote subtle though mild-mannered racial protest poetry as well as pious integrationist and dialect poetry. As Sherman has explained, integrationist and dialect poetry were the products of black people's inability to fight racism directly; thus these forms of black poetry sought to "whitewash" the black social milieu while "educating and up-lifting [its] people" (Sherman, p. xxix). While integrationist poetry "justifies the race to white society," dialect poetry depicts black people as harmless, "a defensive response to the images of blacks as demonic, murderous savages" (Sherman, p. xxix). By 1902 Tillman had written virtually all the poetry that she would publish. Although domestic ideation of black political ambition is decidedly absent in her later works, Tillman continued to inscribe in her short stories and dramas a strong desire for racial equality and prosperity, supported by education, hard work, and self-sacrifice. Despite her vigilance in preserving these ideals, female agency and domestic settings were decidedly displaced in Tillman's writing as the proponents of social advancement became increasingly male, the terrain for their performance public, and the racial protest more explicit.

Not only did Tillman apparently write no more idealized domestic novels (or even employ domestic imagery for expressing political desire) after 1898, but Kelley-Hawkins and Johnson—who wrote two and three domestic novels during the decade of the 1890s, respectively—seem to have abandoned not only the genre but writing for publication in general. At the turn of the century Harper was in her 70s; thus it was unrealistic to expect another novel from her. However, this was precisely the period in which Hopkins wrote her four novels, although she too seems to have deserted the domestic novel of ideal black family formation. After writing one such story in *Contending Forces*, she wrote three serial novels—*Hagar's Daughter, Winona,* and *Of One Blood*—which continued to sustain explicit racial protest but set their arguments in the white social milieu and marginalized their stories of courtship and family development. These serials depict growing racial frustration and imply that the prosperity of African Americans is more likely to be secured outside the boundaries of the United States.[54]

The literary response of these writers to the entrenchment of racism in post-Reconstruction politics as well as the diminished political significance of the home in a post-Victorian society appears to have made it impossible for any of these writers to maintain even an allegorical equation in their fictions between idealized black domesticity and fulfilled political desire. Yet for roughly a decade—the 1890s—black women writers of the post-Reconstruction era reaffirmed in novels their belief that virtuous women like themselves could reform their society by domesticating it.

Without an historicized interpretative model, the black domestic novels seen maudlin, inconsequential, even vacuous. But by regarding these texts from a reconstituted cultural perspective of African Americans of the post-Reconstruction era, that is, by reducing the "aesthetic distance" between our contemporary "horizon of expectations" and that of the novels' first readership, I attempt to discern the efficacy of the domestic genre for expressing the social desire and despair, the personal and political dreams and frustrations of late-nineteenth-century black people (Jauss, p. 25). In so doing I attempt to recover in large measure their reformist strategies of social intervention that arise from manipulating the well-established abolitionist equation between domesticity and civil polity (which I shall discuss in more detail in the next chapter). Like the general population of the nineteenth century, as Gillian Brown has explained, the black subset of American readers and writers were also well imbued with politicization of domesticity as a basis for reformist political discourse (p. 8). They understood that "the domestic values celebrated in *Uncle Tom's Cabin* and popular domestic novels represent[ed] an alternative, moral, feminine organization of life which could radically reform American society" (Brown, p. 17). By appreciating this viewpoint, I reclaim the emphatic belief of late-nineteenth-century Americans—black and white—in the powers of disciplined domestic management, true love, and self-willed personal aspiration for changing the quality of individual lives and whole communities.

Thus by reducing the "aesthetic distance" between that first audience and ourselves, I argue that we late-twentieth-century readers can recognize the cultural interventionism inscribed in the post-Reconstruction domestic novels that has been ironically obscured from our view by the writers themselves. For in fictionalizing their gratification of black civil impartiality, these African-American women writers of the post-Reconstruction era centered their narratives on one half of the abolitionist equation—ideal domesticity—while marginalizing, even erasing, the other half—racial subjugation—that compelled them to write. The first audience to whom these writers directed their works required no elaboration of racist conditions or justification that authorial political intentions did in fact condition the works. Like the authors, the audience to whom they directed their writings shared the same hostile social climate. Brief, even indirect allusion was enough to give the racist context of their lives distressing immediacy, and the black writer who sought a public audience was acknowledged by her or his constituency as an agent of racial progress.

This study attempts to reconstruct a cultural network upon which intersect turn-of-the-century social values about black female and male identity, personal aspirations, family formation, racial prosperity, and racial and sexual reform, all within the context of a politicized domesticity and literacy. It is against this network that I read the eleven post-Reconstruction novels, not as their apologist but as their decoder, empowered by a late-twentieth-century black feminist reading protocol. What I am particularly interested in examining is the symbolic representation of the political desire—collective and personal—of the heroines of these novels; for the heroines' desires are reflections of the aspirations of their creators and first readers at a time when the social optimism of all African Americans was rapidly waning.

In Chapter 1 I begin constructing my cultural network in the early tradition of African-American women writers by looking back to the mid-nineteenth-century works of two such antebellum writers—Harriet A. Jacobs and Harriet E. Wilson. My focus is their manipulation of the reformist discourse of domesticity to construct their protests of racial and sexual oppression. Placed into the historical context of that discourse, the objective of black women's post-

Reconstruction domestic novels becomes discernible not so much as ideal depictions of domesticity but as deployments of what Jane Tompkins has termed "the sentimental power,"[55] already invested in the domestic genre. "Sentimental power" recuperates political desire from the emplotted domestic ambitions in the antebellum and post-Reconstruction works.

Chapter 2 augments my cultural grid. By delineating many of the expectations of the first readers of the domestic novels, I intersect three tracts of dominant cultural conventions of the post-Reconstruction era, which I term "legacies." They concern antebellum constructions of gender particularly for black women; the interrelationships among gentility, skin color, and social mobility; the pedagogy of sentimentality; and the generic differences between late-nineteenth-century male and female narratives of racial protest.

Chapter 3 begins by highlighting the antagonistic discourses of marriage and freedom in two modern black novels. By comparing the axioms of twentieth-century "black aesthetics" to the nineteenth-century critical imperatives of race literature, I postulate an historicized reading model that recovers the politicization of the heroine's desire as an unequivocal discourse in the post-Reconstruction domestic fictions. Three recent critical studies, all published in 1987, are particularly instructive to my formulation of that model because each postulates a reading model for retrieving the masked political intentionality from beneath the sentimental domestic cover-plots. These studies are *Reconstructing Womanhood: The Emergence of the Afro-American Woman Novelist* by Hazel V. Carby; *Desire and Domestic Fiction: A Political History of the Novel* by Nancy Armstrong; and *Sensational Designs: The Cultural Work of American Fiction, 1790–1860* by Jane Tompkins.[56]

Chapter 4 begins by characterizing the intended readers of the domestic novels. I recuperate the politics of desire in these novels by reading the gendered discourses of domestic civility as allegorical discourses of citizenship, which were inherently gendered until the ratification of the Twenty-second Amendment in 1920.[57] Thus by placing the domestic novels into their historical context of racially contested and gender-restricted civil agency, I recover woman-centered political agency in the novels of Frances Harper, Pauline Hopkins, Amelia Johnson, Emma Kelley-Hawkins, and Katherine Tillman.

In Chapters 5 through 7 I discuss various strategies that black women writers of the post-Reconstruction period used to critique the social affairs of their communities. Chapter 5 analyzes the racialized discourse of manhood in selected writings of Frederick Douglass, Booker T. Washington, and William E. B. Du Bois and the corresponding discourse of womanhood in the books of Anna Cooper and Gertrude Mossell as gendered literary strategies of social intervention. By referring to the latter discourse as one specifically about responsible feminized citizenship, and by placing the exemplary heroines of the domestic novels into this discourse, domesticity becomes a site of female political negotiation, and the heroine a self-authorized political agent. Chapter 6 examines late-nineteenth-century gender rites and the higher education of black women as an introduction to a discussion about the mediation of liberal and conservative gender roles for wives and husbands in the domestic novels.

Chapter 7 addresses the growing impact of literary realism on the character portrayal of Tillman's heroines and charts the descent of Hopkins's serial heroines from domestic happiness to racial despair. While collective and assertive social intervention was the strategy of racial reform in the domestic novels of the 1890s, racial despair transforms that program into individual efforts of personal transformation in Hopkins's serial novels. In summary, in these three chapters I argue that the domestic novels of post-Reconstruction black women were emphatic expressive forces for authorizing the collective dream of African Americans about freedom, either transforming that dream into a veritable consummation of civil liberty (the novels of the 1890s) or displacing that dream for safekeeping (those of the early twentieth century).

Last, Chapter 8 focuses on selected works of Angelina Weld Grimké in order to illustrate three important sites in the tradition of black writing. The first marks a point when the plot of ideal domesticity became tragic, thereby empowering the domestic story to express explicit and unreserved racial protest. The second marks a point when African-American literature in general increasingly directed its attention to civil discourses to address racial grievances. And the third records early appearances of what twentieth-century readers would later term modern anxiety and modernist discursive strategies.

1

Maternal Discourse as Antebellum Social Protest

"Come, cousin, don't stand there looking like one of the Fates; you've only seen a peep through the curtain, — a specimen of what is going on, the world over, in some shape or other. If we are to be prying and spying into all the dismals of life, we should have no heart to anything. 'T is like looking too close into the details of Dinah's kitchen."

HARRIET BEECHER STOWE, *Uncle Tom's Cabin* (1851)

Reader, my story ends with freedom; not in the usual way, with marriage. I and my children are now free! . . . The dream of my life is not yet realized. I do not sit with my children in a home of my own. I still long for a hearthstone of my own, however humble.

HARRIET A. JACOBS, *Incidents in the Life of a Slave Girl* (1861)

"O, aunt Jane —, I have at last found a home, *— and not only a home, but a* mother.*"*

HARRIET E. WILSON, *Our Nig*, Appendix (1859)

The Kitchen Politics of Abolitionism

Nineteenth-century abolitionism provides the historical context for recovering the cultural formula used by black women writers to align domestic ideology, reformist politics, and female agency from the mid-nineteenth century to the present (though granted the formula has lost most of its political power along the way).[1] As Barbara Welter has notably argued in her classic study on the "cult of true womanhood," the relationship between the moral stability of society and women/domesticity as a sign of morality was in place by the early decades of the nineteenth century: "a stable order of society depended upon [the true woman's] maintaining her traditional place in it."[2] Thus when Harriet Beecher Stowe drew upon the cultural power of the "true woman" to condemn slavery's invasion into the sanctity of the domestic sphere in her 1851–52 serial novel *Uncle Tom's Cabin*, her audience readily discerned the parallel between a disorderly house and an immoral nation.[3] But Stowe's ambition was not just to duplicate the symbolic, moral function of true wom-

23

anhood; she attempted to transform the virtuous woman into the arbiter of national morality.

Uncle Tom's Cabin, in the section on Dinah's kitchen, provides a striking dramatization of this ideological equation. Stowe's parody on domestic disorderliness extenuates the degree of social corruption occasioned by slavery and clearly indicates that reformation of the private sphere will infuse the public domain with honesty, integrity, moral justice:

> "Shif'less!" said Miss Ophelia to herself, proceeding to tumble over the drawer, where she found a nutmeg-grater and two or three nutmegs, a Methodist hymn-book, a couple of soiled Madras handkerchiefs, some yarn and knitting-work, a paper of tobacco and a pipe, a few crackers, one or two gilded china saucers with some pomade in them, one or two thin old shoes, a piece of flannel carefully pinned up inclosing some small white onions, several damask table-napkins, some coarse crash towels, some twine and darning-needles, and several broken papers, from which sundry sweet herbs were sifting into the drawer.[4]

Cultural critic Gillian Brown makes explicit the connection between the economies of the private and public spheres by arguing that "slavery, according to *Uncle Tom's Cabin*, undermines women's housework by bringing the confusion of the marketplace into the kitchen, the center of the family shelter. . . . The chaos in Dinah's kitchen signifies the immanence of the dissolution of domesticity's difference from the marketplace" (Brown, p. 16). "The real horror that slavery holds for the mothers of America to whom Stowe addressed her anti-slavery appeal," Brown contends, "is the suggestion that the family life nurtured by women is not immune to the economic life outside it" (p. 16). To avert this contamination it was necessary to extend the ideal domestic values of women into the civil affairs of men. This was precisely the mission of *Uncle Tom's Cabin* and nineteenth-century politicized domestic novels—to "represent an alternative, moral, feminine organization of life which could radically reform American society," to the extent that good housekeeping became the exemplar of political providence and "ideal maternal practices merge motherhood with Christianity" (Brown, pp. 17, 28). Obviously a woman had to be white to have access to the ideologies of true womanhood and Christian motherhood. By contrast, the relationship of black antebellum women—freeborn and enslaved—to these ideologies was one of desire, indeed a feminized black political desire.

When Harriet E. Wilson and Harriet A. Jacobs voiced their black *and* female desire for self-authorized households for themselves and their children in their respective works *Our Nig; or, Sketches from the Life of a Free Black* (1859) and *Incidents in the Life of a Slave Girl* (1861), they simultaneously gave voice to their desire for an equitable society. The equation between the nurturing household and a morally productive national polity was not only pervasive in mid-nineteenth-century writings of white and black women but also repeatedly empowered the link between the domestic and political discourses in the post-Reconstruction domestic novels of black women.

While the oppressive domestic situations in *Incidents* and *Our Nig* represent that desire unfulfilled, the desire is depicted as ideally realized in the post-Reconstruction novels, a depiction that emphasizes the absence of realization in the world outside the texts.

That the economy of slavery demanded slave women to be bearers of human chattel and that slave families existed outside legally secure and institutional constructions of marriage, motherhood, family, and household or home hardly requires stating. Domestic groups among slaves often did not correspond to the typical white family household of husband and wife, children, and kin.[5] However, the implications of the slave economy on the dominant society's antebellum social construction of female slave identity require some elaboration for us to discern how fictive participation in these institutions constitutes a political discourse of desire, particularly for black bondwomen. They, like bondmen, were categorically restricted to the market economy of cash crops and the slave-labor force. Although slave mothers might appropriate for themselves the role of motherhood, white society regarded them as breeders, like farm livestock. Hence female slaves had only slight biological claim on the institution of motherhood and about as much social claim on that of womanhood as a brood mare, sow, ewe, or cow.[6] Slave women had no claim on the institution of marriage at all, as the parodic ceremonies on matrimonial solemnity—"to jump the broom" or "marry in blankets"—suggest.[7] By contrast, as Welter has explained, white womanhood was a formidable social construction of absolute purity, piety, domesticity, and gentle submissiveness[8] that matrimony and subsequent motherhood enhanced. Together, these institutions elevated the patriarchal esteem for white women. All of this is to say that slave women, although compelled to be mothers, existed not only outside institutions of womanhood, marriage, motherhood, and family; they also existed outside all four institutions' social constructions of female respectability. Black women were public commodities of exchange whose market value was exclusively indexed as the production of material wealth, whereas white women were private individuals who circulated in patriarchal society for producing heirs and regulating moral, spiritual, and emotional values. Black women had expendable value as base items of consumption; white women had exalted cultural value.

While free black people could marry, their participation in the institutions of parenthood and family were severely compromised by their impaired civil status. But even more threatening to their survival was employment discrimination, which made economic maintenance of the black family extremely difficult even with the incomes from a working wife and husband as well as adolescent children. For those free black women who found themselves single parents, economic maintenance was especially difficult. "[F]or freedwomen with children found that economic necessity bred its own kind of slavery," explains historian Jacqueline Jones.[9] "By every demographic measurement," historian Dorothy Sterling adds, "free blacks were at the bottom rung of the ladder. Disenfranchised, denied employment, excluded from schools, they had the lowest incomes and the highest mortality rates in the [North]. Yet, somehow, many of them survived."[10] Often the children of single black mothers of the antebellum period, Sterling continues, "were bound out as indentured servants" (p. 87), because the extreme hardship of trying to support themselves made it impossible to support their children as well.[11]

Possessing no political rights or broadly sanctioned social status, black women—slave and free—usually petitioned religious morality to justify their rights as mothers and to solicit public sympathy for their plight. Going public, however, demanded a vehicle. Some, like Sojourner Truth, lectured at public gatherings; others, like Wilson and Jacobs, used the written word as the means to transform their private and personal struggles into public testimony; their writing violated gender conventions as well as crossed social boundaries between white and black, free and slave, public and private. By making their individual lives publicly visible for moral scrutiny, Jacobs and Wilson dared to change not only their own personal, social, and material conditions but those for all black people.

Politicizing the Black Mother's Voice

Jacobs's *Incidents in the Life of a Slave Girl* (1861) and Wilson's *Our Nig* (1859) utilize maternal discourses of desire as a particularly black *and* female politicization of domestic ideology.[12] Hence the white women's antebellum narratives of feminized polity, like *Uncle Tom's Cabin*, celebrate the consummation of the orderly household as a sign of a moral society, while the corresponding black texts—*Incidents* and *Our Nig*—distinctly mourn the persistent violation of black womanhood, maternity, family, and home.[13] Domestic defilement informs these latter discourses of racial protest.

Although *Incidents* undoubtedly contributed to the abolitionist cause, this book ironically fell into disrepute for more than one-hundred years.[14] *Our Nig* was even less fortunate. That book's appeal for patronage failed, and immediately after publication it languished, becoming obscure for more than a century.[15] Jean Fagan Yellin speculates that the scholarly disrepute for *Incidents* was probably due to the fact that the narrative does not adhere to the general format of well-known slave narratives, like Douglass's 1845 narrative.[16] For *Incidents* does not focus on the traditional abolitionist argument about the general inhumanity of slavery and its onerous effects on white people but rather on what male consensus has presumed to be the somewhat marginal complaint about sexual abuse of female slaves by masters and overseers. Jacobs rendered that abuse in the particularity and authenticity of self-revelation, although in the guise of Linda Brent, the novelization of her autobiographical voice.[17] By portraying her experience of sexual molestation, Jacobs dared to breech social and literary convention as well as to make the sexual oppression of an adolescent black female a symmetrical paradigm to that of the brutally whipped bondman for the institution's depravity. "Rare indeed," Valerie Smith asserts, "is the account that provides glimpses of the interior lives or survival strategies of women so victimized."[18]

Incidents specifically seeks a sympathetic white female audience, thus Jacobs's deliberate appropriation of the conventions of sentimental fiction and constructions of pious womanhood, which were popular among that readership.[19] Smith provides yet another explanation for the sentimental form of the narrative other than audience appeal: "[I]n order to tell of Jacobs's sexual vulnerability, a condition that the techniques and conventions of the slave narrative could not adequately represent, Jacobs employed the techniques of the sentimental novel" (p. xxxi).[20] The disparity between the representations of freedom in *Incidents* and male slave narratives, like Douglass's narrative, illustrates how the goal of freedom becomes problematic in a female text. Freedom in *Incidents* is less a region—North—than a place that sustains an opportunity for Jacobs to grant herself the authority of personal inviolability, in short, black female self-authority. For, as Smith further explains,

> Jacobs inscribes a subversive plot of empowerment beneath the more orthodox, public plot of vulnerability. . . . From her garret, she is able to secure Sands's promise to help free her children. In hiding, she prevents her own capture not merely by remaining concealed but, more importantly, by embroiling her master in an elaborate plot that deflects his attention. (pp. xxxiv–xxxv)

Additionally, the text characterizes freedom not so much as a political condition as the domestic desire for the nurturance of free black children. Whereas *The Narrative of the Life of Frederick Douglass* depicts psychological freedom as the consequences of a successful, physical contest against those who hold Douglass in bondage and depicts physical escape as well, as a consequence of a successful largely linear departure, *Incidents* portrays "Jacobs's journey from slavery to freedom [as] a series of similar structures of confinement" (Smith, p. xxxiv). Hence freedom in *Incidents* is the result of a highly compromised, largely passive, psychological battle that is not won without considerable self-sacrifice.

Jacobs wrote that she managed to escape the sexual abuse of her licentious master Dr. Flint and ultimately slavery not as the result of physical strength. Rather, she transformed herself into a less desirable sexual object by exchanging her virginity for a sexual relationship with a neighboring white planter, Mr. Sands. In becoming sexually experienced she devalued Flint's estimation of herself as a sexual object, and she also deflated his ego by displacing him with the younger, more virile Sands. According to Victorian gender constructions, the dynamics of Jacobs's struggle make her a compromised (fallen) woman, which jeopardizes her position as a heroic character in the eyes of her intended white female readership. In sharp contrast, Douglass's battle with slavery and specifically with the slave breaker Covey reproduces the conventions of heroic conquest so as to underscore Douglass's full claim to the role of hero.

Incidents, then, evolves from a feminized version of the abolitionist racial discourse of the inhumanity of slavery. However, instead of focusing her petition for the abolition of slavery on moral and religious hypocrisy, as Douglass did,

> If [religious conversion] had any effect on his character, it made him more cruel and hateful in all his ways; for I believe him to have been a much worse man after his conversion than before. Prior to his conversion, he relied upon his own depravity to shield and sustain him in his savage barbarity; but after his conversion, he found religious sanction and support for his slaveholding cruelty. He made the greatest pretensions to piety. He prayed morning, noon, and night.[21]

Jacobs embedded the discourse of moral hypocrisy within her text in the form of one black woman's moral outrage at the sexual abuses of slavery. Thus, rather than employ the abstract, polemical rhetoric of civil protest to mount an argument on slavery as an inhumane social institution that victimizes black and white people alike, as did Douglass, Jacobs feminized the presumably gender-free abolitionist polemics of the slave narrative by situating her argument in the personal and individuated context of the sexually violated female slave and the morally outraged slave mother.[22]

Douglass provided examples of both types of sexual abuse early in his narrative. First he referred to the violation of his mother by her master as a typical event:

> The whisper that my master was my father, may or may not be true; and, true or false, it is of but little consequence to my purpose whilst the fact remains, in all its glaring odiousness, that slaveholders have ordained, by law established, that the children of slave women shall in all cases follow the condition of their mothers; and this is done too obviously to administer to their own lusts, and make a gratification of their wicked desires profitable as well as pleasurable. (p. 2)

A few pages later he elaborated on the pervasiveness of the sexual oppression of female slaves by describing the whipping that his master gives to his Aunt Hester because she was "absent when master desired her presence. . . . Why master was so careful of her," Douglass continued, "may be safely left to conjecture" (p. 51). Not only was Douglass reticent about the particular physical character of those abuses, he also reserved the role of sexual object for slave women alone. Like other male authors of slave narratives, he relied on the absolute silencing of homosexuality and the possibility of unrestrained sexuality of the slave mistress to mute, indeed erase, all traces of the implication that a male slave might also be subject to sexual violation, viewpoints that Sherley Anne Williams and Toni Morrison present respectively in their 1986 and 1987 slave novels *Dessa Rose* and *Beloved*.[23] As a consequence of the erasure of male sexual exploitation and victimization in the slave narratives of men, as well as male writers' literary prominence compared with female writers, the reader has cause to believe that sexual abuse of slaves was categorically a condition of female oppression. In contrast, the general protest of the exploitation of black people in chattel slavery seems to be a masculine discourse.

Once Douglass had sympathetically ascribed the female "other" as the object of sexual abuse, he abandoned that topic in favor of abstract humanistic abolitionist arguments that drew heavily on the republican discourses of the American revolution.[24] By comparison, in *Incidents* Jacobs had the novelized self—Linda Brent—define her entire text as one about sexual abuse. From her early and repeated allusions to her master's verbal harassment as "whisper[ing] foul words in [her] ear" (p. 27) to her realization that his words were imminent deeds, she plots a way to elude him by attracting the attention of an unmarried neighboring white planter, Mr. Sands. In recalling the interlude with Sands, Jacobs had Brent explain reflectively that "I will not try to screen myself behind the plea of compulsion from a master, for it was not so. . . . Neither can I plead ignorance or thoughtlessness . . . I knew what I did, and I did it with deliberate calculation" (p. 54). Brent exercises freedom of choice outside the master's compulsion, and willfully becomes a free agent in her sexual battle with Flint for her own mind and body. However, her offensive strategy is sexual and its expression is prohibited by the nineteenth-century gender codes of feminine propriety that demanded female sexual obsequiousness and silence. Although Jacobs had Brent appropriate an oblique disclaimer of sexual submission for her aggression—"It seems less degrading to give oneself, than to submit to compulsion. There is something akin to freedom in having a lover who has no control over you, except that which he gains by kindness and attachment" (p. 55)—she could not mask Brent's deliberate violation of feminine decorum.

On one level we know precisely what the act of "giving herself" is, but on another level the text seeks to obscure the agent of this act. The text implies but does not explicitly state that Jacobs either initiated or, at the very least, encouraged the attention of Sands, who until the moment of his utility in her design had not appeared in the narrative. At the moment of his appearance, the text switches from the rhetorical conventions for sentimental fiction to those for the novel of seduction in order to requalify the sexual character of the heroine from innocence to experience. Brent assumes the role of the typical male center and deliberately enacts the seduction ritual.

Brent cannot physically overpower the liberational object (Sands), as does the male protagonist Mr. B of Samuel Richardson's well-known eighteenth-century novel of seduction *Pamela*; rather, she deliberately uses her knowledge of what she refers to as "evil ways" (p. 54) to entice Sands. The text transforms the novelized Brent from one man's object of seduction to the seducer of another, as she becomes the free agent who chooses to exchange her already challenged virginity for psychological leverage. Brent elects to play the only offensive and efficacious role available to her, that of the seductress instead of the seduced victim.

Brent's role of seductress, though liberational, is nevertheless problematic, due to her willful violation of the Victorian prescriptive for female sexual innocence. That she deliberately exposes such sexual behavior makes her story doubly onerous by Victorian standards. Consequently, her two decisions have the potential for alienating Jacobs's intended readership. To mitigate that possibility Jacobs had Brent apologize profusely throughout *Incidents* and suffer her grandmother's rebuke as well. I excerpt two instances of her frequent apologies, which both ameliorate her guilt and challenge the standards of virtue of those who have been protected by law or custom:

> But, O, ye happy women, whose purity has been sheltered from childhood, who have been free to choose the objects of your affection, whose homes are protected by law, do not judge the poor desolate slave girl too severely. (p. 54)

> Pity me, and pardon me, O virtuous reader! You never knew what it is to be a slave; to be entirely unprotected by law or custom. . . . (p. 55)

By demanding extravagant apologies from Brent and by characterizing her grandmother as unrealistically hardhearted, given the circumstances, Jacobs constructed a textual censure of Brent's conduct. Her grandmother exhorts,

> "O Linda! has it come to this? I had rather see you dead than to see you as you now are. You are a disgrace to your dead mother." . . . "Go away!" she exclaimed, "and never come to my house, again." (pp. 56–57)

The grandmother's excessively insensitive and punitive response is also an index of Jacobs's desire to make feminine sexual propriety unconditionally available to black women. That is, the more extreme the grandmother's censure, the more Jacobs sought to sanction absolute sexual autonomy and continence for black women, conditions that could only exist if black women were free political subjects.

With the issue of her sexual immorality attended to, Jacobs could maintain her abolitionist appeal and grant herself the traditional male prerogative of sexual agency by participating in the market of sexual exchange. This is her strategy for securing a degree of freedom from bondage rather than merely being an enslaved object of that exchange. The willful exchange of female sexual experience for the preservation of psychological autonomy and the assertion of political freedom were radical, indeed revolutionary acts for a woman, white or black, to execute, let alone to record in a public document. Nevertheless, Jacobs pragmatically abandoned what was an impractical claim to the Victorian virtue of sexual innocence for bondwomen inasmuch as slavery already negated such claim. Adamantly refusing to erase this socially forbidden story from her narrative, she did, however, recount it with indirection by utilizing the conventional ellipses and circuitous narration found in sentimental fiction for relating prohibited content. Thus Jacobs revised the presumably nongendered humanistic petition for black civil liberty, located in texts like Douglass's 1845 narrative; set that petition into a sexual discourse; and expanded the conventions of the slave narrative as well.

Jacobs girded her protest on heroic maternal discourse by emphatically evoking natural and divine law to affirm the rights of black women to be respected as mothers and by repeatedly repudiating their ill treatment as "brood-sows[s]," to use Nanny's term in Zora Neale Hurston's *Their Eyes Were Watching God*.[25] Jacobs insisted that the slave mother "may be an ignorant creature, degraded by the system that has brutalized her from childhood; but she has a mother's instincts, and is capable of feeling a mother's agonies" (p. 16). Although she was ultimately successful in claiming her own children, many other slave women were not, and their stories form the tragic countertext to her personal triumph.

One particular story runs throughout the narrative and reiterates the oppression of slavery as that particularly experienced by black mothers. The first part of that story concerns Jacobs's grandmother's refusal to allow slavery to destroy her hope, integrity, and human compassion. Indeed *Incidents* especially underscores her grandmother's struggle to preserve her compassion for her female oppressors with repeated references to the fact that she had to wean her own three month-old daughter, Brent's mother, in order to suckle the woman who was (in the narrative) Mrs. Flint's sister. Moreover, the grandmother has to take another of her babies "from her breast to nourish [Mrs. Flint]" (p. 85). Mrs. Flint's sister is depicted as a kindly woman who promises the grandmother freedom, but on that woman's death the grandmother becomes an asset in an insolvent estate and Brent becomes a bequest to her young niece, Mrs. Flint's daughter. The Flints are embarrassed into freeing the grandmother, but Brent remains enslaved. Clearly, the so-called kindly woman's action indicates her inability to extend compassion to her slaves and implicates what is presumed to be her noble feminine character. This woman's failure is exacerbated by Mrs. Flint who wreaks deliberate cruelty on Brent's grandmother, the woman who nourished her. Nevertheless, the tie of physical nurturance prevents the grandmother from holding any malice toward either white woman because she had fed them both at her breast. The text juxtaposes this ideal image of the nurturing mother with an ungrateful Mrs. Flint, who returns maternal care with coldheartedness and cruelty. Mrs. Flint is not only an unnatural (surrogate) daughter and therefore an unnatural woman, by Victorian standards, incapable of reproducing the compassionate generosity routinely ascribed to women; she also represents the cruelty that authors of slave narratives particularly ascribed to slave masters and overseers.

The text further characterizes the grandmother's ideal constancy and maternal love by recalling her difficult though successful struggle to buy some of her children out of slavery. Chapter XXVII entitled "Aunt Nancy" serves as the epilogue to that story. Aunt Nancy is Brent's dead mother's twin; thus she is Brent's ideal surrogate mother because she suggests an identical representation of Brent's deceased mother. Indeed, caring for Brent is the only way that Aunt Nancy experiences motherhood. Not only does Aunt Nancy attempt to care for her motherless niece in the Flint household, she also counters with steadfast encouragement her own mother's (and Brent's grandmother's) repeated expressions about the futility of trying to run away from slavery. Hence, Aunt Nancy faithfully strengthens Brent's resolve to risk escape for her children's sake by telling her time and time again, "I shan't mind being a slave all my life, if I can only see Linda and the children free" (p. 129).

At the end of *Incidents*, Jacobs depicted Brent securing freedom for herself and her children. Freedom here is both the dramatic conclusion to her story and its rhetorical strategy for closure. Jacobs wrote, "Reader, my story ends with freedom; not in the usual way, with marriage" (p. 210). This apostrophe acknowledges Jacobs's awareness that the appropriate conclusion for a domestic narrative is marriage, as Charlotte Brontë, for example, affirmed at the close of *Jane Eyre* (1844) with a similar apostrophe—"Reader, I married him." In effect, Jacobs had Brent marry freedom by explicitly asserting moral legitimacy and political autonomy for her maternity. Thus Jacobs feminized the act of heroic self-transformation by privatizing, indeed by domesticating the abolitionist discourse of racial justice for black people. Jacobs depicted freedom not simply as escape from the political condition of slavery but as the gaining of access to the social institutions of motherhood, family, and home.

Jacobs, then, specifically redefined the successful act of heroic self-transformation as a black woman's procurement of a home of her own for herself and her children, a home in which slavery has no domain. Because Jacobs doubly breached the social codes of feminine respectability by engaging in extramarital sex and by daring to write about it, she abandoned her claim to matrimony. Indeed slavery had already negated that claim at her birth. In Jacobs's historical moment and from her perspective as a female slave, matrimony and slavery could find no compatible place in the world of her text. Marriage and bondage, then, are not merely antithetical in *Incidents*; they are mutually exclusive. Marriage thus serves as an ideal, though unrealizable, sign of liberation for this text.

As we have seen, in *Incidents*, Jacobs appropriated and revised the conventional rhetoric of women's sentimental literature and the thematics of the slave narratives in order to frame the abolitionist poetics of her text. In fact, Jacobs's narrative subverts the dominant tenets of both literary traditions. First Jacobs exposed traditionally reticent stories of female sexuality and maternity in women's sentimental stories to express her moral outrage and advance her protest of slavery. Second, rather than center the presumably nongendered humanistic petition for black civil liberty found in Douglass's narrative, she gave that petition black *and* female specificity by presenting it as a domestic discourse about black female sexuality. And third, she refused to esteem literacy with the liberational imperatives that typify Douglass's narrative. *Incidents*'s resistance to the conventions of both literary traditions produces a disparate abolitionist discourse in domestic tropology.[26]

While abolitionist intentionality tightly circumscribes *Incidents*, producing a focus on Jacobs's sexual discourse, Wilson's *Our Nig*, published two years earlier in 1859, is a much more complex text for both its intended readers—Wilson's "colored brethren"—and those readers who live outside the historical exigencies of Wilson's epoch, namely ourselves. Set in New Hampshire during the first half of the nineteenth century, the story begins not with the events of the life of Frado (who is the novelized Wilson), the central character and alias "our nig," but with the circumstances surrounding her abandonment at the age of six, which are fictional. As I mentioned previously, the placement of young black children into indentured service was very common during the early nineteenth century; thus we late-twentieth-century readers must quench our eagerness to judge Frado's mother. Such placement, or abandonment, probably was not regarded as capricious parental neglect but as a necessary and understandable response to extreme economic hardship.

The novel's first two chapters reconstruct the life of Frado's mother, Mag Smith. Mag is a poor, white, working woman, who "*had* a loving, trusting heart" (p. 5, author's emphasis). A brief sexual relationship produces an unwelcomed offspring (who dies shortly after birth) and marks Mag as a ruined woman. She soon marries a hardworking free black man, Jim Adams, fully aware of the social prohibitions against interracial sexual unions. However, her economic needs far outweigh the dominant society's constructions of white female propriety, as Jim's proposal reminds her:

> "you's down low enough. 'Spousin' we marry! . . . You's had trial of white folks, any how . . . I's black outside, I know, but I's got a white heart inside. Which you rather have, a black heart in a white skin, or a white heart in a black one?" (p. 12)

His proposal so excessively appropriates polarized, racist color ideology of black and white that I question its motivation beyond securing the desired response. Has he merely internalized that ideology? Or does what seems to be his parodic exuberance signal an interrogation of the dominant ideology of white supremacy? For although exaggeration "is not essential to parody," as Gary Saul Morson explains, "exaggeration is, rather, simply one of several techniques parodists use . . . to inform readers that the text is a parody."[27]

Given the stringent prohibitions against miscegenation, Jim's desire to marry Mag legally seems more his exercise of racial protest than the moral prescription for cohabitation or the outcome of interracial ardor.[28] Thus his excessive reliance on the dominant society's racist constructions of white and black suggests a self-parody by which he censures that society's shallow moral judgments. By urging Mag to accept his proposal as a way of escaping her economic distress, he can possess the white body of this woman, which he regards as a forbidden "prize" (p. 11) or "treasure" (p. 14). By legally marrying her, he can also use civil law to affirm his free status, mounting an additional challenge to white hegemony.

Although Mag is well aware that by marrying Jim she is further severing her tie to white society, her economic needs are much more compelling. The text is emphatic on this point. To Jim's analysis of those needs the text adds, "foreigners cheapened toil and clamored for a livelihood, competed with her, and she could not thus sustain herself" (p. 8). The text employs an apostrophe to underscore that point further:

> You can philosophize, gentle reader, upon the impropriety of such unions, and preach dozens of sermons on the evils of amalgamation. Want is a more powerful philosopher and preacher. Poor Mag. She has sundered another bond which held her to her [white] fellows. She has descended another step down the ladder of infamy. (p. 13)

Despite the repeated references to Mag's poverty, the text is careful to construct her loving, trusting, and faithful nature. For although "[s]he cared for [Jim] only as a means to subserve her own comfort," the text insists that "she nursed him faithfully and true to marriage vows till [his] death released her" (p. 15). Failure to emphasize her emotional commitment to Jim would define her behavior as only financially expedient, and thus demean her character.[29]

When Frado's father dies, Mag returns to her prior condition of privation. Seth Shipley, her dead husband's business partner, tries to assist her, and she becomes his common-law wife without any remorse. By assuming the judgmental tone of white society to condemn Mag's repeated and willful transgressions of its moral, social, and religious laws, Wilson engaged the reader's sympathy. She juxtaposed Mag's presumably unforgivable social offenses to her extreme hardship:

> She [Mag] had no longings for a purer heart, a better life. Far easier to descend lower. She entered the darkness of perpetual infamy. She asked not the rite of civilization or Christianity. Her will made her the wife of Seth. (p. 16)

As if the mitigating circumstances of Mag's hopeless acceptance of her unworthiness were insufficient for supporting the reader's sympathy for Mag, Wilson presented two more events, also a part of the text's fictive maternal discourse, to construct Mag's motherly affection for Frado.

Mag does not simply abandon Frado at the first available place; rather, she carefully selects the Bellmont household as Frado's future place of service. Mag's decision is not based on conventional sentiments but on economics. She has worked for the Bellmonts and knows their circumstances and characters. Reasoning that Mrs. Bellmont "can't keep a girl in the house over a week; and Mr. Bellmont wants to hire a boy to work for him, but he can't find one that will live in the house with her" (p. 18), Mag locates reliable employment for Frado that will produce more sustenance than Mag is capable of providing. Despite both Mag and Seth's agreement that Mrs. Bellmont is a "she-devil" (p. 17), they conclude that Frado has traits that will ensure her survival. The text describes Frado as a "beautiful mulatto" who will be "a prize somewhere" (p. 17). Additionally, Frado possesses "an exuberance of spirit almost beyond restraint" (p. 17). "She's a hard one," said Seth, brushing his patched coat sleeve. "I'd risk her at Bellmont's" (p. 19). But before Mag can place Frado in the Bellmont household, Frado runs off, "giving a sudden jerk which destroyed Seth's equilibrium" (p. 19).

An irresponsible, callous mother would probably have accepted the fortuity

of this event as a means of avoiding the decisive action of abandoning Frado
and allowed her to remain lost. However, Mag and Seth, as the text reports,
"could not rest without making some effort to ascertain her retreat. Seth went
in pursuit, and returned without her. . . . All effort proved unavailing. Mag
felt sure her fears were realized, and that she might never see her again," a
somewhat ironic response given the plot of the story (pp. 19–20). When Frado
was found, "Mag was relieved to know her child was not driven to desperation
by their intentions to relieve themselves of her, and she was inclined to think
severe restraint would be healthful" (p. 20). In other words, Mag is consoled
to know that her decision to put Frado into indentured service did not cause
her to run away, and Mag subsequently takes precautions to prevent Frado
from departing again until she can surrender her to the Bellmonts. These are
somewhat peculiar responses. Frado's reaction suggests a capricious departure
and not a deliberate reaction to her pending abandonment. Mag's behavior
also does not foreclose the possibility that she felt maternal affection for
Frado, though in a manner disparate to sentimental constructions of embel-
lished motherly love. In fact, the dissimilarity undermines the reader's presumption of Mag's maternal irresponsibility and stresses instead the desolation
of Mag's maternity.

All of the events in the first two chapters must be presumed fictional inasmuch as their factual construction is beyond the competence of a young child's
memory and understanding. Therefore, these events are a part of this autobiographical novel's discourse of maternal desire, that is, Wilson's construction
of an inherently good mother and her motives for abandoning a child whom
she could not support. What is important for us to note is that all of these
fictive events are elaborately constructed mitigations of what Mag's white
culture regards as numerous transgressions of feminine virtue and maternal
responsibility. Wilson complemented these dramatic mitigations with repeated verbal characterizations of Mag as a poor, pitiful, fallen Christian;
"LONELY," "with . . . a heavy heart"; "unprotected, uncherished, uncared
for" (p. 5); overwhelmed by "a feeling of degradation oppressing her" (p. 7)
and a "feeling of cold desolation" (p. 15); "toil[ing] and suffer[ing]; yielding
to fits of desperation, bursts of anger" (p. 16). The emphatic delineation of
Mag's suffering seeks to allay her responsibility for abandoning her child and
ironically represents both Wilson's recovery of her mother's affection for her
and by implication Wilson's exoneration of the absent mother. With the sympathetic construction of the mother in place, the narrative focus shifts to
Frado, who for twelve years is overworked and abused in the Bellmonts'
household. This part of the story evolves much like a slave narrative, as the
title page implies.

Given Wilson's deliberate evocation of the discursive conventions of the
slave narrative and the extreme privation of Mag's and Frado's lives, we cannot avoid noticing a correspondence between their circumstances and those of
slaves. Like a female slave, the destitute Mag can neither define nor control
the conditions of her life. Also like a female slave, Mag is sexually vulnerable,
a theme I will return to when discussing the reticent sexual discourse in the

novel. Although Mag elects to leave Frado with the Bellmonts, the real agency of this decision is an economic determinism that is akin to slavery. Most important, like the heroic slave, Frado, the abandoned child, eventually reconstructs a liberated self in possession of self-esteem.

Social constructions of gender have historically designated the mother as the parent responsible for nurturing the child and consequently for initially engendering the child's positive esteem and self-worth. As psychotherapist Jessica Benjamin explains in *The Bonds of Love*,

> In our society it is usually the mother who is the bestower of recognition. She is the one who responds to our communications, our acts, our gestures, in such a way that we feel that they are meaningful. . . . This psychological or social nourishment, this giving of nurturance, is so evidently essential to mothering that we are tempted to make nurturance and mother synonymous.[30]

The mother's presence, then, enhances the likelihood of the child's formation of high self-esteem, while the mother's absence works to the child's detriment, suggesting that the child would probably experience an acute sense of personal worthlessness. Frado repeatedly demonstrates this dependency in her remarks about her condition of motherlessness:

> "I've got to stay out here and die. I ha'n't got no mother, no home. I wish I was dead." (p. 46)

> "Oh, I wish I had my mother back; then I should not be kicked and whipped so." (p. 51)

Frado regards her motherlessness and her oppression as mutually responsible for her condition. Because Frado is oppressed, she regards herself as unworthy of a mother's loving care; and because she is an abandoned child, she is oppressed. Quite remarkably, though, she does not hold her mother personally responsible for her plight, understanding rather that Mag had no choice. This is precisely the viewpoint that Wilson constructed in the first two chapters. Frado's feelings of unworthiness result in her passive acceptance of abuse from Mrs. Bellmont and her daughter Mary as if such treatment were her racial due:

> "Work as long as I can stand, and then fall down and lay there till I can get up. No mother, father, brother or sister to care for me, and then it is, You lazy nigger, lazy nigger—all because I am black! Oh, if I could die!" (p. 75)

The figurative terms in the last two quotations suggest that Frado has two options for escaping the oppression. She could die, or she could undergo an affirming self-transformation by recovering that which is lost—a maternal signifier for her absent mother. In other words, for Frado to mitigate her oppression and her resulting despair, she must positively reconstruct and re-possess the maternal signifier. This is precisely what the text accomplishes. As a complex maternal discourse, the novel provides Wilson with a double sym-bolic recovery of the lost mother. For not only does Frado reconstruct her own caring mother, but at the end of the novel Frado herself becomes another loving mother who assumes the place of the mother for whom she had longed as a child, an identity that is later corroborated in the novel's appendix.

Hence a complex maternal discourse of desire displaces Wilson's motherless-ness with discursively constructed maternal and filial affection. The appended section signed "Allida" records another act of maternal recovery, as Wilson found an adoptive mother in a Mrs. W. who "gave her a room joining her own chamber," indeed a home as the epigraph above reveals. In this section of the appendix, Allida corroborates the events depicted in the last chapter concerning Wilson's marriage and the birth of her son. Allida writes,

> . . . it seems she remained in this house until the birth of her babe; then her faithless husband returned . . . for a while he supported her and his little son decently well. But again he left her as before . . . and she saw him no more. . . . her struggles with poverty and sickness were severe. At length, a door of hope was opened. A kind gentleman and lady took her little boy in their own family and provided everything necessary for his good. (p. 136)

This summary repeats Wilson's own petition for aid initially proffered in the preface, presents circumstances that correspond to Mag's destitution at the beginning of the novel, and offers Wilson's maternal resolve as an alternative response to maternal destitution. Allida also inscribes her own partial biogra-phy of Wilson's life as yet another petition of aid for her:

> Reposing on God, she has thus far journeyed securely. Still an invalid, she asks for your sympathy, gentle reader. Refuse not, because some part of her history is unknown, save by the Omniscient God. Enough has been unrolled to demand your sympathy and aid. (p. 130)

While the first two chapters reconstruct Frado's mother in a reciprocating discourse of maternal and filial affection (that is, Mag's affection for Frado and Frado's affection for her mother), the last chapter "Winding Up the Mat-ter," the preface, and the appendix present another maternal discourse that merges with the initial ones. In the last chapter the mature Frado appears as a mother herself, who is struggling to fulfill her own maternal obligations to her son. Her plight repeats her mother's story of impoverished desperation, which is recounted in the preface and appendix as Wilson's own personal story of maternal desire. But rather than permanently abandon her child to indentured service, as her own mother had done, Wilson wrote of her struggle to reclaim that child. The novel itself, as Wilson recorded in the preface, is an "experiment [which she hopes] shall aid [her] in maintaining [her]self and child. . . . " The decision to write the novel, then, demonstrates Wilson's refusal to resign herself to the unalterability of the life of the abused, motherless, black girl who becomes an impoverished mother. The act of writing gives expression to Wilson's resolve to preserve the bond between herself and her child and transforms that resolve into an affirmation of her own autonomy as a black person who was a motherless child who became a woman, who became a mother, who was compelled to be a writer. Indeed, the very text *Our Nig* arises from the compatible resolution of what had to have been a difficult conflict arising from the coexistence of these multiple identities. By connecting the creation of the novel to the effort to recover her child, the text conflates the maternal obligation with authorial desire. Wilson's child and her novel become mutually dependent as signifier and referent.

In a very substantial way, then, Wilson used this novel to re-create herself in a novelized form. She displaced the motherless child (who was herself) with another child who possesses a loving mother (who is the adult Wilson). The partly fictive and autobiographical histories are symbolic discourses for re-engendering not only the self-worth of Wilson but others like her as well. Hence the text fulfills Frado's desire for both a mother and positive self-esteem by transforming her into a responsible mother. The text finds a way then to fulfill the adult Frado's frustrated maternal desire through the act of heroic maternal self-transformation. In so doing the text also has implications for her black contemporaries—free and enslaved, Northern as well as Southern—all of whom have been similarly oppressed. Her discourse of maternal desire suggests that it is possible to replace the social alienation inherent to racial oppression with symbolic mother love.

Wilson broke the chain of psychological oppression of race and motherlessness by transforming herself into a heroic, Christian mother with material independence, albeit symbolic rather than substantive. Hence the entire text is the symbolic embodiment of that transformation in which she invests the possibility of providing a home for herself and her child. Whereas the novel depicts Frado's awakened spiritual consciousness, the preface and appendix textualize Wilson's self-esteem as a black person, a woman, and a mother. Wilson embodied the virtuous construction of motherhood and substituted herself for her own missing mother. Her identity as mother, then, not only corrects a prior assumption of racial inferiority, but supplies the nurturing love of the missing mother, whose chronic absence finds repeated duplication in slavery as well. Wilson's genuine rather than self-professed Christian love and her maternal obligation, instead of enraged protest, dominate the transformative discourses of *Our Nig* and become the symbolic erasures of generations of black peoples' hopelessness, oppression, and self-hatred. However, as I shall discuss below, Wilson's depiction of Christianity does not arise without interrogation but as a faith subjected to her own experience, to her own parodic critique. In addition, the social requirement for female sexual reticence, the demand that Jacobs profusely subjugated herself for violating in

Incidents, becomes the very strategy that Wilson relied on to comment on the sexual vulnerability of poor women, her mother and herself in particular.

Wilson's effacement of Frado's sexuality, Wilson's invocation of Frado's Christian piety, and Wilson's allusion to the traditional signatory of the slave narrative all indicate that *Our Nig* is a complex variation on the intersection of the conventions of sentimental fiction and the slave narrative. However, the immediately evident circularity of identity of the title and signatory— *Our Nig* by "Our Nig"—expressed as pejorative diminution, points here to a self-parodic slave narrative. This text not only censures the social conditions of black Americans, free and enslaved, but also adopts and especially parodies the conventions of entitling and signing individual works of the genre. This granted Wilson authorial control at a time when black people had no socially sanctioned claim to literary professionalism. The authorial dimensions of the title as well as her request for patronage in the preface—"Deserted by kindred, disabled by failing health, I am forced to some experiment which shall aid me in maintaining myself and child without extinguishing this feeble life"—are particularly important to her various social critiques.

The full title of *Our Nig*—*Our Nig; or, Sketches from the Life of a Free Black, in a Two-Story White House, North. Showing that Slavery's Shadows Fall Even There. By "Our Nig"*—accommodates the author's conflicted ambitions for personal self-mastery and literary professionalism, on the one hand, and her society's ideology of racial inferiority on the other. In fact, that title announces an authorial desire independent of dominant ideology of white supremacy as an additional site of Wilson's discursive self-reconstruction. To free herself from the rhetoric of a racist culture, Wilson employed self-parody particularly in her selection of the title. Here she initially claimed self-authority and subsequently announced the retextualization of the title so as to insert a new semantic orientation to the racist arguments typically contested in the traditional slave narrative.[31] The title, the subtitles, and the pseudonymous authorial signatory, like the authorial posture, narrative tone, and perspective, vacillate between representing direct social criticism and self-reflexive derision, demanding that the audience consider the motivations behind such deliberately constructed double-voiced representations (Morson, pp. 71, 65).

The first subtitle—"Sketches from the Life of a Free Black, in A Two-Story White House, North" references direct social criticism about white people's hypocritical refusal to extend constitutional law to black people by evoking an incomplete analogy between Our Nig's place of residence—white house, North—and its absent referent—the idealized plantation mansion, South— and by parodying the popular idyllic plantation fiction of the day.[32] Indeed, this white house South is also reminiscent of the place of residence of the President of the United States, an allusion that sharpens the hypocrisy of professed republican zeal due to its racist customs. Possibly fearing that her audience might miss the rebuke of Northern racial oppression or perhaps deliberately resorting to exaggeration so as to alert the reader to parody,[33] Wilson added the additional subtitle: "Showing that Slavery's Shadows Fall Even There." This last subtitle implicates white abolitionists in the racial oppression of Northern black people and complicates what had to have been at least an indirect appeal to the very people who had the financial means to assist her by purchasing the book.

The lexical identity established between the novel's principal title—*Our Nig*—and its pseudonymous authorial signatory—"Our Nig"—inscribes a sophisticated mode of self-reflexive irony that extenuates direct public censure. The title and the signatory are locked in cyclic parody, like black people in tar face on the minstrel stage. As a result, the aspersion in the self-reflexive title circuitously and indirectly finds its real target—the very people whom Wilson claimed she wished not to offend in her preface—"our good anti-slavery friends at home." In this manner the text calls attention to the fact that they were largely responsible for the generally poor quality of life for those free black people who lived among them, a point that she made emphatically in the novel. In addition, by displacing the well-known slave narrative signatory—"Written by Him or Herself"—with the diminutive form of a racist epithet—"Our Nig"—the text shifts the Northern readers' predictable resentment of public censure to a deliberately constructed self-derisive humility. Hence the text exhorts the readers' verification of Frado's hardships and by implication those generally suffered by Northern, free, black people by viewing her from a privileged white perspective. After all, as Wilson insisted with her title, Frado was *their* "nig"; that identity was their construction and not Wilson's.

Inasmuch as national public opinion made black people, free or slave, subservient to white society, Wilson ironically capitalized on this viewpoint by borrowing the racist construction of a black person who is not dangerous. Thus, rather than a "big (and by implication, bad) nigger," Wilson presented Frado in double diminution, as a "little, sickly nigger," in short "a nig." By recreating her novelized self as chattel—"a nig"—to protest her plight, Wilson ironically appropriated the naming authority of the dominant society to subvert its influence and revise its pejorative designation. By denoting herself in terms of the odious epithet, she attempted to repudiate its aversion, projecting it onto those who so designate her. As *their* "nig," she told her own story of racial abuse from a third-person compassionate point of view so as to arouse the sympathy of her readers as well as demonstrate that her life was not substantially different from that of a slave. This authorial strategy also allowed her to abort much anticipated criticism from readers who might have regarded her story as atypical, exaggerated, or simply inappropriate because technically she was not a slave. However, like the speaking subject of the slave narrative, Wilson claimed first right of ownership in order to discard that disparaged name from her own identity.

Postmodern theorist Linda Hutcheon's succinct definition of parody has been particularly helpful to me in discerning the different types of parody, other than the rather obvious verbal word play of the title, operating throughout Wilson's novel as a way to censure forms of social oppression other than race. According to Hutcheon, parody is

> a form of imitation, but imitation characterized by ironic inversion, not always at the expense of the parodied text. . . . Parody is another formulation, repetition with critical distance, which marks difference rather than similarity.[34]

The title's evocation of the slave narrative calls immediate attention to "repetition with critical distance." Rather than seeking to invalidate the authenticity of legitimate slave narratives, *Our Nig* seeks to extenuate the moral authority of that genre to comment on the exploited lives of Northern free blacks.[35] However, the vile epithet "nig" is not diminished in the diminutive. Wilson's abolitionist and other social critiques (which I discuss below) notwithstanding, that term may have, in fact, alienated potential, sympathetic black readers who did not recognize the author's appropriation of it as an ironic mode of self-liberation as well as a subtle condemnation of the racist attitudes of Northern whites. The prominent use of so hated an epithet may have given black people cause to question the racial identity of the book's author; they may have erroneously concluded *Our Nig* to be a masked white-authored story about black inferiority. The inscription itself points to Wilson's (contested) presumption of authorial control, an issue I will address before discussing her various social critiques, which also rely on parodic expression.

The discourse of contested authorial presumption is embedded in Wilson's request for patronage, and concerns her assumption of professionalism at a time when asserting oneself as an author was problematic for white women and black people in general. Wilson's preface explains her motive for writing the novel—not as the fulfillment of an "erudite" ambition, but rather as "some experiment which shall aid [her] in maintaining [her]self and [her] child without extinguishing this feeble life." After explaining her motive, she makes a direct appeal to her "colored brethren universally for patronage." No doubt Wilson was well aware of the economic condition of the black people to whom she appealed. In fact, her own story suggests their common penury. Although the general economic condition of black people has continually improved, one-hundred years later black women writers were still often unable to support themselves (and their children) with their earnings from writing, even writing full-time. In fact, until the recent market success of writers like Toni Morrison, Alice Walker, and Gloria Naylor, that ambition was a delightful fantasy, as Zora Neale Hurston's life painfully illustrates. The question that arises, then, is could Wilson realistically expect to rescue her son from a foster home with income from writing? Does this ambition speak to her utter desperation? Or, does her so-called experiment to fulfill maternal love and obligation cloak yet another?

Feminist literary scholarship has directed considerable attention to examining "the anxiety of authorship" among eighteenth- and nineteenth-century white women writers.[36] White women wrote much of the popular literature of both periods, some at considerable financial reward. While several of these writers seem "comfortable with the idea of writing," others offered justifications for their occupations as writers.[37] They often claimed to be writers not for fame or fortune but because they had sick husbands, because they were widows supporting their small children, or because they were merely bored.[38] These writers also casually trivialized their own work, claiming to not be professionals who take writing seriously in deference especially to Victorian social conventions demanding female self-effacement. This too is Wilson's claim. For in the preface she explains, "Deserted by kindred, disabled by failing health, I am forced to some experiment which shall aid me in maintaining myself and child without extinguishing this feeble life." Given that the "colored brethren" to whom she appealed "universally for patronage" were not in an economic position or numerous enough in the Northeast to support her enterprise, the novel was probably meaningful to Wilson for other than economic reasons.

Our Nig is a symbolic narrative that recreates Wilson as an enduring historical subject, represented in the sanctioned role of the loving and dedicated mother. The novel and appended texts form a complex allegory about maternal desire. As the genre of "exiles, prisoners, captives, or others who have no room to act in their society," allegory accentuates Wilson's individual powerlessness while amplifying the discourses of desire that empower *Our Nig*.[39] If we read this novel in this way, Wilson's stated motive for writing, that is, her maternal obligation, and her expressions of literary humility achieve logical consistency. The self-interest of professional literary creation is cloaked in the selflessness of mother love, as the maternal and authorial discourses of desire become mutually expressive. Indeed, Wilson's expressed justification for the novel arises from her fulfilling the socially prescribed role of a mother. Her maternal commitment, a story that lies outside the text of the novel, inscribes a parallel story within the novel: the story of the mother-author's obligation to nurture a symbolic child—her text.

In the prefatory remarks, Wilson not only underscored her financial motivation for writing the novel, but effaced her erudition as well:

> In offering to the public the following pages, the writer confesses her inability to minister to the refined and cultivated, the pleasure supplied by abler pens. It is not for such these crude narrations appear. Deserted by kindred, disabled by failing health, I am forced to some experiment which shall aid me in maintaining myself and child without extinguishing this feeble life. . . . My humble position and frank confession of errors will, I hope, shield me from severe criticism. Indeed, defects are so apparent it requires no skilful [sic] hand to expose them.

Wilson's references to "errors," "abler pens," and "defects that are so apparent it requires no skilful hand to expose them" are inscriptions of conventional male models of prefatory effacement found in eighteenth-century sentimental texts, like Henry Fielding's *Tom Jones*, that both invite literary judgment and mask authorial ego. However, *Our Nig* deconventionalizes the male model of effacement by combining it with what contemporary feminist scholars have termed the female metaphor of writing as mothering the text.[40]

In addition to evoking the male mode of authorial modesty and the metaphor of literary maternity, *Our Nig* masks black authorial prerogative with the ironic assumption of presumed racial inferiority, again like a form of literary blackface minstrelsy.[41] Wilson doubly "blackened up" her novelized self Frado so as to satirize those who, like Mrs. Bellmont and Mary, perform hypocritical shows of piety, democratic principles, and good will. Given the frequent claims of impropriety routinely addressed to black men and white women writers who chose to criticize racial and sexual oppression, and given the charges of authorial inauthenticity leveled their way,[42] as a black woman Wilson may indeed have felt the need for an extenuated form of the authorial effacement usually found in the eighteenth- and nineteenth-century works of white male, black male, and white female writers. Wilson used all of their modes of effacement, emphatically fulfilling the dominant nineteenth-century society's respective prescriptives for black people and all women of subservience and maternal obligation.

In addition, Wilson's appropriation of maternal literary authority supports her self–re-creation in a semiotic of maternal love. She created a novelized self who not only condemns racism but fends off likely attacks from those who regarded black and female authorship as doubly unnatural. This reconstructed self also enables Wilson to express sympathy for her white mother who abandoned her, and possibly to retrieve her son from foster care. Moreover, complex narration, subtle reflexive irony, well-chosen epigrams from diverse English and American authors, and what Henry Louis Gates, Jr., calls "belabored erudition" (Gates, p. xl), all demonstrate her aptitude at a time when black people (and all women) were categorically presumed to be mentally inferior. To avert the charge of egoism, she expressed the hope that her "colored brethren" would not condemn her novel as an "attempt of their sister to be erudite." This indirect assertion of erudition also makes her story appear less personal by enhancing its literariness as a serious piece of writing.

Motherhood, then, both motivates and justifies Wilson's authorship. Motherhood also masks the author's intellectual and professional ego as well as plots the structure of the story. In addition, the maternal discourses throughout the novel and peripheral texts — about reclaiming the abandoning mother, condemning the unmotherly behavior of Mrs. Bellmont, depicting her own self as a heroic struggling mother, and proclaiming another Christian woman as her surrogate mother—provide the narrative context for Wilson's social commentary. Incidentally, Wilson's personal story of the struggle to support her son is historically factual. Ironically, the death notice of her child was the scholarly key for rescuing this particular allegory of black female desire from oblivion (Gates, pp. xii–xvii).

Our Nig clearly relies on the maternal discourses to present the text's dominant critique on the immorality of racist ideology, but embedded in those discourses are complementary social critiques on white Christian hypocrisy, presumed abolitionist beneficence, exploitative Northern labor practices, and the sexual vulnerability of women in a patriarchal culture. These critiques not only assume the discursive form of parodied questions but emerge as textual disruptions and unsettling narrative repetitions. They do not mount explicit condemnations of dominant social perspectives but subtly point "to the unexamined presuppositions and unstated interests" of the moral presumption of nineteenth-century Northeastern white society, so as to uncover "the divergence between [its] professed and unacknowledged intentions" (Morson, p. 73). Wilson's critique on the presumption of the moral beneficence of Christian piety and conversion in particular also rewrites the sentimental plot in which the heroine's virtue is qualified by her religious devotion. Because these critiques are embedded in the dominant maternal discourse as desire—that is, a child's desire for the absent mother, for the love that she represents, and for a home of her own—Wilson could rely on the uncontested strength of those desires to transform presumably innocent questions and observations into severe social censure. I use the phrase "presumably innocent" advisedly because the double-voiced nature of Frado's questions, disruptions, and discursive repetitions makes them appear both playfully naive and earnestly canny. Jacobs could ill afford a similar critique in *Incidents* due to the fact that she appealed to an audience that had not given much attention to examining its presumption of Christian beneficence. As a result, except in those instances in which she measured Mrs. Flint's religious professions against her grandmother's charity, Jacobs avoided the general subject of religious piety.

An important example of a disruptive signifier occurs early in *Our Nig*, when Wilson employed two words, "ravishing" and "ascend," for describing Mag Smith's sexual awakening that results in what the text terms her "ruin":

> She knew the voice of her charmer, so ravishing, sounded far above her. It seemed like an angel's, alluring her upward and onward. She thought she could ascend to him and become an equal. (p. 6)

We initially understand *ravishing* to mean something akin to pleasurably captivating; however, we cannot miss the presence and meaning of the interior word *ravish*. We also discern the secular meaning of the word *ascend* in the passage as Mag's desire to achieve a higher social class and "become an equal" "of her charmer." The secular reference for the term *ascend* confronts its spiritual counterpart on the same page: "Her [Mag Smith's] offspring came unwelcomed, and before its nativity numbered weeks, it passed from earth, ascending to a purer and better life" (p. 6). The association of the word *ascend* with illicit and exploitive sexual activity in the first passage becomes problematic when it later invokes a spiritual meaning in the second with the phrase "ascending to a purer and better life." The double entendre here interrogates the presumption of class superiority and impugns a religion that unrealistically disregards material circumstances as irrelevant to ideal spiritual aspirations.

Several scenes later, the text underscores this issue in Frado's presumption of the right to question Christian tenets by engaging in a seemingly guileless dialogue with James Bellmont, the friendly adult son, who has returned home for a visit. Frado is nine years old at the time, and the dialogue begins with James asking her,

> "Are you glad I've come home?" asked James.
> "Yes; if you won't let me be whipped tomorrow."
> "You won't be whipped. You must try to be a good girl," counselled James.
> "If I do, I get whipped," sobbed the child. "They won't believe what I say. Oh, I wish I had my mother back; then I should not be kicked and whipped so. Who made me so?"
> "God," answered James.
> "Did God make you?"
> "Yes."
> "Who made Aunt Abby?"
> "God."
> "Who made your mother?"
> "God."
> "Did the same God that made her make me?"
> "Yes."
> "Well, then, I don't like him."
> "Why not?"
> "Because he made her white, and me black. Why didn't he make us *both* white?" (p. 51, emphasis Wilson's)

Frado's exchange questions James's equation of goodness with what he assumes to be the certainty of heavenly reward. The text suggests that she discerns that his pat response is not only superficial but also reveals his refusal to address the material circumstances of her life. Her final question—"Why didn't he make us *both* white?"—points to the inherent hypocrisy of James's supplication and encourages the reader to sympathize with Frado's rejection of a deity who knowingly subjects her to pain. For her such a deity is fraudulent and does not deserve her devotion.

This verbal exchange is remarkably similar to one between the character Hester Prynne and her young daughter Pearl in Nathaniel Hawthorne's *The Scarlet Letter*, published in 1850,[43] and calls attention as well to the decided similarities between the characterizations of Frado and Pearl. Before I cite the corresponding dialogue between Hester and Pearl about the latter's origin, I want to set the stage for it by calling attention to the similarity in the descriptions of Pearl and Frado. Just prior to the referenced dialogue, Hester observes that "It was as if an evil spirit possessed the child," that Pearl is "like a little elf . . . danc[ing] up and down, with the humorsome gesticulation of a little imp" (Hawthorne, p. 72). The narrator forthwith describes "Pearl's rich and luxuriant beauty [as] a beauty that shone with deep and vivid tints; [she has] a bright complexion, eyes possessing intensity both of depth and glow, and hair already of a deep, glossy brown, and which, in after years, would be nearly akin to black" (Hawthorne, p. 75). Turning to the young Frado, the text describes her as "a beautiful mulatto, with long, curly black hair, and roguish eyes, sparking with an exuberance of spirit almost beyond restraint" (Wilson, p. 18). Mag additionally says, "'Frado is such a wild, frolicky thing, and means to do just as she's a mind to" (Wilson, p. 18). On arrival at the Bellmont household the Bellmonts observe "her wilful [sic], determined nature" (Wilson, p. 28). In school the text reports that "Nig's [Frado's] retorts were so mirthful" (Wilson, p. 38), and at the Bellmonts' the young child's "jollity was not to be quenched by whipping or scolding. . . . She was ever at some sly prank when unseen by her teacher, in school hours; not unfrequently [sic] some outburst of merriment, of which she was the original" (Wilson, p. 38).

The similarity in appearance and manner of Pearl and Frado emphasizes the corresponding similarity in their dialogues of origins. The dialogue in *The Scarlet Letter* begins with Hester imploring,

> "Child, what art thou?" cried the mother.
> "O, I am your little Pearl!" answered the child. . . .
> "Thou art not my child! Thou art no Pearl of mine! . . . Tell me, then, what thou art, and who sent thee hither?"
> "Tell me, mother!" said the child. . . .
> "Thy Heavenly Father sent thee!" answered Hester Prynne. . . .
> "He did not send me!" cried she, positively. "I have no Heavenly Father."
> (pp. 72–73)

Comparing this dialogue with that above between Frado and James, we see that both Pearl and Frado reject a religion whose deity willfully subjects innocent children to the cruelty of social convention. Although Hawthorne's enterprise is to bring a rebellious Pearl back to the laws of both her heavenly and earthly fathers, Wilson's objective seems to be to call both of these fathers into question, an interrogation further intensified by the fact of the Bellmont father's inability to assert paternal authority and prevent his wife from brutalizing the child.

Another dialogue that analogously interrogates Christianity occurs between Frado and the Bellmonts' Aunt Abby after Mary's death, when Frado is around fourteen years old. However, it is necessary to characterize Frado's anxiety over Christianity to present the context for that dialogue. Her anxiety arises from attending worship with Aunt Abby, diligently reading her bible, and entering into the following conversation with James who explains his impending death by saying,

> "I shall die pretty soon. My Heavenly Father is calling me home. Had it been his will to let me live I should take you to live with me; but, as it is, I shall go and leave you. But, Frado, if you will be a good girl, and love and serve God, it will be but a short time before we are in a *heavenly* home together. There will never be any sickness or sorrow there." (p. 95, emphasis Wilson's)

Frado offers no retort to him but is overcome with grief. When James dies and is buried, the text reports that Frado "did not love God; she did not serve him or know how to. She retired at night to mourn over her unfitness for heaven" (Wilson, p. 99). In addition, she "endeavored to make Christ, instead of James, the attraction of Heaven" (Wilson, p. 103). Like mother Mag before her, Frado accepts her extreme unworthiness as a sinner both to prompt a resolution to her spiritual crisis and to seek sympathy from the reader.

These excerpts present Frado's troubled spiritual condition, which later erupts as her own rational analysis of the similar state of the dead Mary's soul in the interrogating dialogue with Aunt Abby. Frado exclaims,

> "She [Mary] got into the *river* again, Aunt Abby, did n't she; the Jordan is a big one to tumble into any how. S'posen she goes to hell, she'll be as black as I am. Would n't mistress be mad to see her a nigger!" and others of a similar stamp, not at all acceptable to the pious, sympathetic dame, but she could not evade them. (Wilson, p. 107)

Frado's excessive appropriation of the racist Christian color ideology is similar to that found in her father's proposal to Mag, discussed above. Like that arrogation of racist assumptions, Frado's expression reinforces both his and her own prior parodic interrogations of Christianity. In this case the parody arises from Wilson's construction of Frado's naive spiritual depravity. Frado relies on her own logic for arriving at a moral tenet for dispensing heavenly reward and punishment. This logic can be paraphrased as follows: If being black means one is evil, being evil can also make one black. Interestingly, there is no powerful conversion scene in this novel[44]; rather, Frado prays as much for spiritual salvation as for mercy from Mrs. Bellmont's abuse, as the following scene demonstrates:

> "I'll beat the money out of her, if I ca n't get her worth any other way," retorted Mrs. B. sharply. While this scene was passing, Frado was trying to utter the prayer of the publican, "God be merciful to me a sinner." (Wilson, p. 90)

Frado also partly sustains her faith by initially projecting the face of James onto the image of the divine in the novel and subsequently that of Aunt J—onto God's countenance in the appendix. Although the appendix clearly characterizes Wilson as a pious Christian, unlike the faith of the typical sentimental heroine and her successors in the post-Reconstruction heroines, her faith is not without doubt and it mounts a sustained interrogation of the conventional practice of Christianity throughout the text.

The novel also calls our attention to its effaced sexual discourse by presenting an unsettling narrative repetition that characterizes the sexual maturation of both Mag Smith and her daughter Frado. On the opening page of the novel Wilson described Mag by writing, "As she merged into womanhood, unprotected, uncherished, uncared for, there fell on her ear the music of love, awakening an intensity of emotion long dormant" (p. 5). Near the end of the novel, Wilson employed the identical phrase—"merged into womanhood"— to describe the advent of Frado's adulthood: "Frado had merged into womanhood, and, retaining what she had learned, in spite of the few privileges enjoyed formerly, was striving to enrich her mind" (p. 115).

Whereas Mag's maturity immediately leads to sexual experience, Frado's maturation incites her desire to improve her mind. The appropriation of this revised version of a Platonic mind/body separation relegates all explicit reference to sexuality to Mag and distinctly disparate interest in the mental, intellectual, and spiritual to Frado. The text preserves this duality at the end of the novel, where sexual reticence surrounds Frado's initially nameless suitor. Interestingly, the text projects all ardor onto the suitor while Frado is decidedly passive. In describing his approach, the text reports,

> Such a one [a professed fugitive] appeared in the new home of Frado; and as people of color were rare there, was it strange she should attract her dark brother; that he should inquire her out; succeed in seeing her; feel a strange sensation in his heart towards her; that he should toy with her shining curls, feel proud to provoke her to smile and expose the ivory concealed by thin, ruby lips; that her sparkling eyes should fascinate; that he should propose; that they should marry? (Wilson, p. 126)

It is not strange that he should inquire about her. What is strange, though, is that there is no mention of how Frado felt about the new romantic experience in this autobiographical novel.

This is not the first marked absence of sexual ardor in the text; this one merely emphasizes the recurring effacement of Frado's sexuality. However, some readers have discerned intimations of covert seduction in the novel.[45] I am among them. The Bellmont sons' repeated references to Frado's beauty[46] and their frequent presence in her sleeping quarters as well as her presence in their own are particularly sexually suggestive. Then when we recall that the text initially employed the identical phrase—"merged into womanhood"—to present Mag and her resulting sexual misadventures as it used to address the onset of Frado's sexual maturity but displaced that awakening with intellectual concerns, all the reticence about sexuality surrounding Frado is underscored. The veiled presence of sexuality reemerges at the close of the novel, as the text petitions for the reader's compassion: "Still an invalid, she asks your sym[p]athy, gentle reader. Refuse not, because some part of her history is unknown, save by the Omniscient God. Enough has been unrolled to demand your sympathy and aid" (p. 130). Unwilling to extenuate her story with more misery and titillating sexual discourse, Wilson insists that she has revealed enough of her life story to merit sympathy from readers.

This petition accentuates Wilson's disparagement of the presumption of benevolence universally accorded to Northern abolitionists. The preface states, "I have purposely omitted what would most provoke shame in our good anti-slavery friends at home." At the conclusion of the novel, she proceeded to undercut that dubious tribute by explicitly censuring them in an enraged retort. For after completing her service to the Bellmonts, as the text explains, Frado finds herself stalked by another enemy:

> Watched by kidnappers, maltreated by professed abolitionists, who did n't want slaves at the South, nor niggers in their own houses, North. Faugh! to lodge one; to eat with one; to admit one through the front door; to sit next one; awful! (Wilson, p. 129)

Antebellum black authors, of course, were well aware of the racial hypocrisy of many abolitionists. But because black people were dependent on their collective aid, the authors tended not to express the duplicity of those abolitionists in their own polemical writing. As a Northern free black person, Wilson seems to have used her status to voice a protest otherwise muted, a protest about the Northern economic exploitation of the working poor—black and white, female and male. By referring to the conventional practices of racial discrimination in employment and housing in which many abolitionists were implicated, she associated those oppressive conventions with the abnormally low wages for all free laborers, a condition dramatized in Mag's story as well as her own. This particular exploitive practice incriminates many "professed abolitionists" (p. 129) in moral duplicity. In fact, Wilson's observation anticipates the violent competition for employment among blacks and whites, fostered by similar abusive wage-labor customs, that followed the Civil War in Northern cities.

Domestic ideation of political desire is pervasive in these two antebellum texts. Both *Incidents in the Life of a Slave Girl* and *Our Nig* represent freedom not simply as a desired political condition but as domestic ambitions—marriage, motherhood, and home—in which women have authority as well as men. Jacobs aligned freedom and marriage in her famous exhortation—"Reader, my story ends with freedom; not in the usual way, with marriage" (p. 201). However, she was quick to remind us that her freedom was less than ideal: "The dream of my life is not yet realized. I do not sit with my children in a home of my own" (p. 201). A home of her own for herself and her children would fulfill Jacobs's liberational ambitions, but these two domestic institutions—marriage and home—remain unrealized at the story's close, becoming ideal and elusive objects of the desire for freedom. *Our Nig* relies on Frado as the personification of Wilson's motherless childhood in order to construct both her own devotion for her absent mother and child as well as to reconstruct and repossess that mother's love. These mutually dependent maternal discourses, cast from the perspectives of mother and daughter, represent Wilson's desire for authority as a self-sustaining individual. As in *Incidents*, the construction of mother love in *Our Nig* as both subject and object of desire revises the identity of the narrative center, as the sincerity of motherly dedication is represented in the struggle to secure a home for the child. Indeed, that struggle assumes materiality in *Our Nig* as the very text of the novel, which Wilson explained as her experiment for maintaining herself and her child. Both *Incidents* and *Our Nig* are inscribed in and circumscribed by domestic, indeed maternal, tropes of inseparable personal and political desire. This inscription is the very process that black women writers of the post-Reconstruction era perfect in their domestic novels. While Jacobs and Wilson used autobiographical, maternal constructions to condemn social oppression and to express their desire for elusive freedom, the black women who wrote during the latter era exploited domestic fiction to sustain their faith in the conceivable satisfaction of that desire long deferred.

2
Legacies of Intersecting Cultural Conventions

Tall and fair, with hair of a golden cast, aquiline nose, rosebud mouth, soft brown eyes veiled by long, dark lashes . . . .
        PAULINE E. HOPKINS, *Contending Forces* (1900)

Jewel Bowen's beauty was of the Saxon Type, dazzling fair, with creamy roseate skin. Her hair was fair, with streaks of copper in it; her eyes, gray with thick short lashes, at times iridescent. Her nose superbly Grecian.
        PAULINE E. HOPKINS, *Hagar's Daughter* (1901)

—a white throat tinted by the firelight, a supple figure, a rapt young face, a head held with all a princess' grace, and dark, flashing eyes.
        PAULINE E. HOPKINS, *Winona* (1902)

he saw distinctly outlined a fair face framed in golden hair, with soft brown eyes . . . rose-tinged baby lips. . . .
        PAULINE E. HOPKINS, *Of One Blood* (1903)

Just as it was necessary to reconstruct the historical context for the antebellum reformist discourse of domesticity to appreciate the complex social criticism in Jacobs's *Incidents* and Wilson's *Our Nig*, so too is it essential to examine the impact of three intersecting legacies—antebellum black gender conventions, gentility as a bourgeois construction, and the latter's expression in literary sentimentality—to discern the emancipatory discourses of African Americans of the post-Reconstruction era. Reconstructing the social legacies of antebellum black gender roles and class mobility among postbellum (Reconstruction and post-Reconstruction) African Americans enables us to appreciate the post-Reconstruction domestic novel's depiction of bourgeois womanhood as a gendered discourse of citizenship.[1] Reconstituting the literary legacy of sentimentality also allows us to recover many of the cultural imperatives governing the authors' aesthetic choices as well as the expectations of their first readers. These reconstructions recuperate the racial discourses in the novels and reveal their close kinship to the contemporaneous novels written by black men.

51

Antebellum Gender Constructions of the Black Female

During the decade of the 1890s, just as during the antebellum era, the vast majority of black people resided in the South and worked as field laborers. After slavery they worked in a system of debt-peonage farming, commonly known as sharecropping. Economic dependence on farming was the standard for both black women and men during the postbellum period. Angela Davis has cited the 1890 Census Reports in her work *Women, Race, and Class* to underscore this fact. She writes that 2.7 million black females were wage laborers: 38.7 percent worked in agriculture; 30.8 percent were employed in household domestic services; 15.6 percent performed laundry work; and 2.8 percent worked in manufacturing.[2] Although sharecropping and laundry work were physically exhausting, they provided black women with the greatest possibility for self-regulated black family life. By contrast, domestic service in white households was the least preferred type of female wage labor, not only because of the psychological oppression and labor exploitation routinely associated with such work, but also because the worker was frequently in danger of sexual abuse.[3] Furthermore, domestic service severely limited the amount of time that black women could spend in their own homes, and thus restricted their ability to be the nurturing authorities in their households. It is important to emphasize here that black and white women's relationship to housekeeping, as an expression of personal meaningfulness and family solidarity, was decidedly different due to the fact that black women's housekeeping ambitions were severely limited by their domestic service in white homes and by exploitive black labor practices in general.[4]

The labor preferences of the vast majority of black people during the antebellum era were, of course, irrelevant, because slavery defined them as chattel. The consequences of chattel slavery for postbellum social constructions of gender and class formation, as represented in African-American literary culture, are seldom explored. Rather we, as Angela Davis has argued, tend to "assume that the typical female slave was a houseservant—either a cook, maid, or mammy for the children in the 'big house'" (p. 5). Television depictions of slavery in films like "Gone with the Wind" and "Roots" have especially contributed to this viewpoint. This assumption makes the line between the domestic bondwoman and the black domestic heroine seem short and direct. However, that assumption is erroneous.

Davis refers to the statistical evidence that Kenneth M. Stampp collected in his work *The Peculiar Institution: Slavery in the Antebellum South* (1956) to refute this assumption. She finds that a sexual division of labor did not primarily govern the distribution of labor to slaves. Referring to Stampp, Davis explains that "Around the middle of the nineteenth century, seven out of eight slaves, men and women alike, were field workers. Since women, no less than men, were viewed as profitable labor-units, they might as well have been genderless as far as the slaveholders were concerned" (p. 5). Stampp's work assists Davis additionally to explain that the bondwoman's life did not adhere to traditional (that is to say white) feminine gender roles, because "The slave woman was first a full-time worker for her owner, and incidentally a wife, mother and homemaker" (p. 5). "Judged by the evolving nineteenth-century ideology of femininity, which emphasized women's roles as nurturing mothers and gentle companions and housekeepers for their husbands," Davis argues that "black women were practically anomalies" (p. 5).

Although the plantation system usually designated labor on the basis of physical arduousness, slave women were not routinely exempt from heavy tasks. Neither were domestic tasks restricted to female slaves. Historian Jacqueline Jones explains that

> The dual status of a bondwoman—a slave and a female—afforded her master a certain degree of flexibility in formulating her work assignments. When he needed a field hand, her status as an able-bodied slave took precedence over gender considerations, and she was forced to toil alongside her menfolks.[5]

Historian Linda Perkins also corroborates the flexibility of sex roles in the slave-labor force by providing an explanation for the relative absence of male privilege in slave culture compared with the dominant white culture:

> The disenfranchisement and oppression of all blacks left little room for male chauvinism. Because the institution of slavery forced black women into work situations alongside the black male, having to endure the same punishments and hardships, sex role differentiation was minimized to a large extent within the slave community. . . . Although the traditional sex roles of cooking for females and hunting for men were prevalent, it was not uncommon to find slave narratives depicting men as sewing, caring for children, or cooking. By the same token, women were frequently found as preachers, doctors, conjurors, storytellers, champion cotton pickers and respected leaders within the slave community.[6]

Perkins refers to Thomas Webber's study of life in the slave quarters, *Deep Like the Rivers: Education in the Slave Quarter Community, 1831–1865* (1978), who writes that he found no evidence to support either male privilege or female dominance in the slave society (Perkins, p. 321).[7] Deborah Gray White, another historian of slavery, further corroborates this viewpoint in her study *Ar'n't I a Woman: Female Slaves in the Plantation South*. Referring to the plantation owners' failure to balance the female slave's required labor in the fields with her required reproduction of the labor force, Gray White substantiates the frequent absence of consistent sex-role divisions in the slave-labor force:

> The extent to which the slave owner consciously emphasized one or the other ultimately depended on his needs. In antebellum America, these were often determined by the region of the country in which he was settled. The lower black fertility rates in the lower and newer regions of the south (Alabama, Mississippi, Louisiana, and Texas) may be an indication that

female labor in the fields superseded childbearing in importance. In both the upper and lower South however, slave owners attended to the proverbial bottom line by striving to maximize profits.[8]

Despite the overwhelming evidence in support of sexual equality in slave culture, it is extremely important, according to sociologist Susan A. Mann, to be mindful that male privilege is relative: "The degrees of domination characterizing different patriarchies may vary by women's class, race, ethnicity, and sexual orientation" as well as with historical period.[9] By the dominant society's standard of white patriarchal privilege, black male dominance appeared absent in slave households. But as Mann has argued, "the slave households were in fact characterized by patriarchy" (p. 795). Thus she is careful to point out that what scholars have generally identified as sexual equality in slave households is "greater relative equality":

> It is possible that due to racist restrictions on the accumulation of wealth or power by Blacks, slaves and Black sharecroppers may have experienced relatively more sexual equality than middle- or upper-class whites. That is, these restrictions precluded Black husbands and wives from being separated by the more extreme gender-based differentials in economic rights and privileges that well-to-do whites experienced. However, this greater relative equality should neither be exaggerated nor romanticized given the fact that it was premised on the poverty and deprivation of both sexes. (p. 796)

Mann also calls our attention to the fact that "both slavery and sharecropping existed within the contexts of a larger capitalist mode of production predicated on private property" (p. 796), and this economic mode was fundamentally patriarchal, negotiated dialectically through relative positions of male social power.[10] Keeping in mind that when scholars refer to sexual equality in slave culture they actually mean relative sexual equality as measured against a presumed middle-class, patriarchal standard, I turn to a related factor—constructions of female self-reliance—that is integrally related to variable expressions of sexual equality.

In the context of her discussion on the relative absence of consistent sex-role divisions in the slave-labor force, Deborah Gray White specifically examines the capacity of self-reliance that slave women developed during slavery which repeatedly surfaces in the historiography of slavery. Gray White focuses on this particular trait as a counter argument to those by such noted historians of slavery as John Blassingame, Eugene Genovese, and Herbert Gutman, who have defined slavery as the status of the male slave (pp. 21–22). Their focus on the centrality of the male figure in the slave household, she contends, seems to be a deliberate rewriting, indeed refutation of E. Franklin Frazier's description of the early black family as matriarchal and disorganized when compared with the presumed nuclear standard.[11] Historian Evelyn Brooks-Higginbotham joins Gray White's interrogation of black male-centered historiography in her essay "The Problem of Race in Women's History,"[12] and together they clearly suggest that, although slave women regarded their male counterparts as very important to the sustenance of the slave household, they could not afford to be as dependent on black men as white women were dependent on white men. Moreover, we should extend these arguments so as not to interpret the high degree of self-sufficiency among black bondwomen as indicative of their transcendence of patriarchal economy or as a consequence of their personal desire (or lack of desire) to have the male figure present in the slave household, for their choice mattered little to those who regulated the peculiar institution.

All types of plantation slave labor — field, domestic, and ultimately the reproduction of the slave-labor force — were based on a racist exploitation of slaves that was as disruptive to the black woman's conception of female self-worth as it was to the black man's definition of his masculinity. What is especially significant about the development of self-reliance among slave women and the concentration of research in this area for my study is that this particular characteristic indicates just how polarized the antebellum gender constructions were in shaping the lives of black and white women. Brooks-Higginbotham acknowledges this extreme polarization by characterizing bondwomen as constituting their own unique social category, distinct from both black men and white women. "While part of this workforce," she maintains,

> black women experienced forms of sexual discrimination unknown to white women regardless of class. Race and sex discrimination, along with structural changes in the economy over time, combined to make the labor participation and domestic expectations of black women different from all other groups. (p. 127)

Sociologist Joyce A. Lander has further argued that

> It is clear that within the cultural context of the dominant society, slave women were forced to assume the basic duties and responsibilities toward their families men assumed in the white world. The impact this had on black men is immeasurable.[13]

The self-sufficiency of bondwomen was not a peculiar racial characteristic but an adaptation of slavery that passed into modern history, for "had there not been a continuing need for black women to continue to fulfill these functions their roles would have probably been little different from those of most white women" (Ladner, p. 282).

For nearly three-hundred years, antebellum black women and men were alienated from both West African gender constructs and white American ideologies of gender, both of which were patriarchal in design and practice.[14] Those held in slavery created their own intraracial relationships and social practices as adaptations to the brutality of this institution, relationships that maintained a veritable equality between the sexes. They reflected the mutual respect that grew out of domestic and field labor and sharing of their common fate of racial oppression. Gray White observes that "slave families were unusually egalitarian" (p. 158). She adds that such equality

> could not have been based on sameness because, while slave men and women often did the same kinds of work and provided similar services, many jobs and responsibilities still belonged by definition to one sex or the other. This suggests that equality within the slave family was founded on complementary roles, roles that were different yet so critical to slaves' survival that they were of equal necessity. (p. 158)

Nearly three centuries of slavery molded these adaptations into gender conventions of slave culture, into what I term *antebellum black gender constructions*. The legacy of the self-reliant bondwoman remains with us today, though frequently perverted into the myth of the black matriarch (promulgated by Daniel P. Moynihan,[15] among others), which stands as an alleged sign of gender aberration in the black community.

In referring to these historical studies on the labor of black bondwomen it is not my point to argue that they worked as hard and performed the same kinds of physical labor as did their male counterparts or that they were governed by patriarchal institutions. Those observations have been made and documented beyond contestation. Rather my point is to emphasize the consequences of self-defined black gender differentiation on the processes by which the newly emancipated adapted to sharecropping, wage labor, and bourgeois decorum and professionalism. Moreover, as I will elaborate below, this gender legacy also helps to explain why many among the black middle class of the post-Reconstruction era adopted very conservative attitudes about appropriate social roles for black women and asserted a direct relationship between those roles and racial advancement. For the highly noticeable exercise of conservative Victorian gender roles was a candid sign of the black middle-class' claim on respectable citizenship,[16] just as the appropriation of bourgeois gender conventions in general were fundamental to the emancipatory discourse of nineteenth-century African Americans.

After the Emancipation, black people believed they could realize their desire to be full citizens by freely adopting the values of the dominant society. Thus freedom drastically altered the ways in which the black individual constructed the self. According to historian Lawrence W. Levine, "Freedom ultimately weakened the cultural self-containment characteristic of slaves and placed increasing numbers of Negroes in culturally marginal situations."[17] With emancipation, African Americans marginalized slave culture with the adoption of dominant values, as schools and churches taught them that the survival codes of slavery and strategies for racial advancement often stood in mutual opposition. The newly freed black population assimilated the tenets of bourgeois individualism, as propounded by such white American writers as Ralph Waldo Emerson and Henry David Thoreau. Consequently, recently emancipated African Americans came to understand that the will of the individual regulated the quality of his or her life. This perspective was unmistakably different from the communal nature of antebellum black culture. In addition, black people acquired a wealth of social values from white civilization directly from textbooks, teachers, and preachers, as Levine explains:

> Young black children who were inducted into the mysteries of *McGuffey's Eclectic Readers* and similar textbooks were ushered into a world in which no one had to be poor, in which there was no need to fail, in which all could be successful if only all would follow a simple formula summed up in simple stories and poems:

> Once or twice though you should fail
>   Try, try Again;
> If you would, at last, prevail
>   Try, try Again; . . .
> All that other folks can do,
> Why with patience, should not you:
> Only keep this rule in view
>   Try, try Again. (p. 143)

Emersonian tenets of individual willful self-advancement were not only heavily inscribed in the pedagogy of dominant culture but soon became the dominant feature in postbellum black religion as well. For example, "Sinners could *choose* conversion and the Christian life; conversion and salvation were primarily *individual* experiences" (Levine, p. 144, emphasis in original). As a consequence of their wide-scale adoption of dominant cultural values, postbellum black people increasingly associated upward mobility with dominant values, while analogously associating those of slave culture with poverty and racial oppression (Brooks-Higginbotham, p. 128). Nevertheless, slave culture was most resilient. African Americans became bicultural; that is, they deliberately acquired dominant bourgeois constructions of individual and collective success, while retaining to various degrees the folk wisdom of slave culture.

For black people of the Reconstruction era, bourgeois gender constructions had tremendous impact on sex-role divisions in the black labor force. Historians Frazier, Genovese, Gutman, and Jones, among others, "interpret the withdrawal of black women from the workforce in the immediate post-Civil War South as the desire of freed people to replicate the gender roles prevalent in white families" (Brooks-Higginbotham, p. 129). "Black wives and daughters sharply reduced their labor in the fields and instead devoted more time to child care and housework," as social historians Steven Mintz and Susan Kellogg add.[18] "For the first time," they continue, "black families could divide their time between fieldwork and housework in accordance with their own family priorities" (p. 77). Hence the decided absence of black women in field labor after Emancipation indicates that "sharecropping families placed greater priority on women's roles in household labor, which further reinforced a traditional sexual division of labor" (Mann, p. 783). Although the wide-scale economic exploitation of black laborers soon forced these women to return to the fields and white people's kitchens, or put another way, to exchange "production for subsistence" for "production for exchange" (Mann, p. 777), "this reversal does not imply a rejection of their preference for domesticity" (Brooks-Higginbotham, p. 129).[19]

As the works of Brooks-Higginbotham, Frazier, and Jones, in particular, additionally reveal, Yankee missionary women at work in the South during Reconstruction also directly influenced the postbellum black church's sanctioning of the patriarchal family in which the father held authority and the mother was his complement in maintaining the home and family (Brooks-Higginbotham, p. 129).[20] Although "the structural conditions of poverty, discrimination, and segregation prevent[ed black] people from achieving many mainstream middle-class values and aspirations," as sociologist Charles Valentine's study on African-American biculturation demonstrates, black people generally gave their allegiance to middle-class gender roles and social values (Brooks-Higginbotham, p. 129), which they learned from the dominant culture.[21] Indeed, for black people, middle-class life-style became synonymous with their constructions of freedom, as attaining that standard of living became the measure of achieving social equality. Consequently, the desire to attain middle-class social status became an important goal on which racial protest would soon focus.

As African Americans gained more access to academic education (at such celebrated white and black institutions as Harvard, Oberlin, Michigan, and Pennsylvania and Howard, Hampton, and Tuskegee, respectively) and utilized that education for the enterprise of racial uplift, they also increasingly executed the ideologies of the dominant society, particularly those regarding male dominance and the supremacy of light skin color; for it was impossible to separate Western intellectual tradition from its heritage of male and white privilege. It is rather disheartening, although understandable, to observe that those who had been victimized by the racism of slavery and had survived it due partly to the equality of skin color and sexual equality would practice colorism and sexism among themselves in times of increasing relative prosperity. Yet these two prejudicial ideologies were heavily woven throughout the fabric of African-American postbellum social culture not as discourses of desire but as actual facts, because the dominant society sanctioned male privilege and those with light skin color generally had more access to opportunities of advancement in both the black and white cultures.

Many African Americans criticized both practices. For example, black educator Anna Julia Haywood Cooper did not direct her turn-of-the-century campaign for black women's access to academic education to white society; she directed it to the new black academic patriarchs.[22] In addition, the notorious "blue veins" that the writer Charles Chesnutt censured in his short story "The Wife of His Youth" was a product of the intraracial tyranny of light skin color that remains with us still.[23] The impact of Eurocentric enculturation on African Americans of both the Reconstruction and the post-Reconstruction eras, then, undermined their antebellum social constructions of relative sexual equality and advanced the intraracial privilege of light skin color. Insofar as the vast majority of late-nineteenth-century black Americans were concerned, enculturation meant access to U.S. citizenship. Thus, during this period, black literature, particularly the domestic novels, endorsed the bourgeois values of the dominant society.

Gentility, Color, and Social Mobility

White America's adoption of Victorian gentility as evidence of its presumed superior civilization, while grossly violating the human rights of black people, seems contradictory to contemporary readers. Yet white American Victorians held those two social customs in tight alignment. This was the society that the rising black middle class became intent on imitating after the Civil War, not because of pretentious social desire but because appropriation of gentility meant approximating racial equality. However, on ascent, upwardly mobile black people not only confronted the increasing opposition of white people but also the resistance of old, upper-class families of color who were free before the Civil War. "The free people of color, born and reared among the very class which had once held them slaves," as social historian Willard B. Gatewood has explained, comprised the "colored aristocracy."[24] This elite class of African Americans practiced Victorian genteel culture with as much or more rigor than their white counterparts in order to preserve the social purity and hopefully the social privilege of their ranks.

Their elite social status and that generally in the African-American population was inextricably associated with skin color, as "color . . . correlated closely with opportunity, hence with the acquisition of education, wealth, refinement, and other attributes of high status" (Gatewood, p. 83). This elite class of "colored" Americans, who could often be identified by their light skin color, claimed refined respectability as their rightful lot and erected rigid social requirements for admission to their class (which included family heritage, education, culture, and gentility), in order to distinguish themselves from "those considered vulgar and crude" (Gatewood, p. 209), namely those whom they designated as common Negroes. This elite class excluded other black people from its social stratum in a desperate attempt to elude the racist covenants that were becoming more pervasive.

Granted that for some among the colored aristocracy,

> genteel performance became an end in itself. Others, overwhelmed by the magnitude of the task of reforming the conduct of the masses and convinced that they themselves were the products of a natural selection process, simply abandoned the struggle and withdrew into their own private social world of people with similar tastes, values, and genteel qualities. (Gatewood, p. 209)

The upwardly mobile of the newly emancipated adopted many of the viewpoints of this elite class of African Americans (who were actively imitating white American Victorians), and

> pursued the elusive quality of gentility for the same reasons as other Americans: they assumed that proper conduct was indicative of character. . . . [M]any aristocrats of color believed, for a time at least, that blacks would be accepted or assimilated into society on a purely individual basis as each demonstrated merit and worthiness. (Gatewood, pp. 208–9)

However, these viewpoints not only clearly express prescriptive attitudes about polite decorum, the ethic of hard work, and the acquisition and display of wealth, to say nothing about the presumed bourgeois standard; they also encode problematic attitudes about color and class that work at cross-purposes with broad initiatives of collective racial advancement. These conflicting attitudes are especially important to keep in mind when examining the black literary culture of that epoch, due to the fact that black writers and their reading audience were for the most part members of the striving and elite classes. The characters in their works, therefore, resemble the exemplars of these classes.

One such model was Josephine Bruce, the wife of Blanche Bruce, who in 1874 became the black senator from Mississippi (Figure 3). I refer to her specifically because she bears a striking physical resemblance to the near-white or racially indefinite heroines of black women's post-Reconstruction novels, as the following public portraiture of Mrs. Bruce demonstrates. Although the white press extolled her "intelligence, refinement, and courtesy. . . . [Her] complexion received more detailed treatment . . . than any other of her notable attributes":

> The *Boston Journal* referred to her as "a great beauty of the Andallusian type," while another white daily asserted that she resembled "what we all imagine a beautiful Spanish lady to be." . . . A white journalist argued that fair appearance of the wife of the Mississippi senator was proof that all theories about the telltale "signs of African blood" were absolutely false. (Gatewood, p. 33)

Despite all the hoopla, Mrs. Bruce was a Negro, no matter now fair of skin or how much she embodied the attributes of the ideal Victorian lady. While the post-Reconstruction domestic novels repeatedly depicted heroines who resembled Josephine Bruce, it was her deportment that black authors and readers of the post-Reconstruction era explicitly claimed to be particularly important. Deportment could be acquired, whereas physical appearance was only an arbitrary genetic consequence. For example, in 1899 when Booker T. Washington appointed Josephine Bruce as the woman principal at Tuskegee Institute, a major part of her job "was to be a model of the genteel lady for the female students" (Gatewood, p. 208). For like her general constituency,

> she believed that instruction in proper conduct, no less than uplift activities of a purely economic nature, was a critically important part of "service to the race." To inculcate Negro youth with ideals that produced patterns of

Figure 3. This photograph of Josephine Willson Bruce (1852–1923) was taken at the time of her marriage to U.S. Senator Blanche K. Bruce. Courtesy of the Moorland-Spingarn Research Center, Howard University.

> behavior marked by dignity, decorum, and virtue was to strike a blow against the prejudice that whites showed against blacks in general. (Gatewood, p. 208)

We late-twentieth-century readers suspect that Bruce's physical appearance had great bearing on her value as a model of female deportment. Be that as it may, Josephine Bruce embodied as well as reflected the social values of the Victorian-conditioned U.S. society in which black writers of the post-

Reconstruction period emerged. Thus it is not surprising that she represented her constituency in its collective viewpoints about the social power of
appropriate decorum, which, as literary historian Dickson D. Bruce, Jr., explains, also characterized the mannerly tone of late-nineteenth-century black
writing:

> The substance of literary assimilationism was established not only in
> protest writing. It also presented a world that was fully in keeping with
> middle-class orientation of black writers. This was a world informed,
> above all, by ideas of gentility.
>   The Victorian world into which the black middle class emerged in the
> late nineteenth century gave a crucial place to gentility, understood as the
> development of inner virtue through the cultivation of proper thoughts
> and feelings, or proper "sentiments." These sentiments were to be fine and
> pure, noble and tender. . . . Thus, just as literary gentility remained a
> mainstay in much of American popular writing, no subversive elements
> appeared in the works of black writers of this period. For them, the ideals
> of gentility remained wholly positive; and their literature remained wholly
> faithful to its tenets.[25]

As a consequence, African-American writers of that era repeatedly used their
works explicitly to argue that professional attainment, social esteem, intellectual and cultural refinement—in short, class—were more important than an
individual's racial designation. While these writers declared that race was
inconsequential, they simultaneously and categorically depicted their cultivated heroes and heroines in shades of skin color ranging from light brown to
white. In other words, black writers, like their immediate constituency,
"tended to think of themselves in class, rather than racial, terms" for arguing
their social parity (Gatewood, p. 147), but those best able to mount this
argument tended to be light of skin. Class status was a fluid designation,
which according to the creeds of U.S. social culture of the late nineteenth
century was, at least in theory, governed by willful self-advancement. However, skin color in black society was often a very important index of class and
potential social mobility.

Problematic attitudes about class and color emerge in the portrayals of
heroes and heroines in post-Reconstruction black fiction. The novels of the
two most prolific black male writers of the period—Charles Chesnutt and
Sutton Griggs, for example—reveal a preponderance of light-skinned heroes
and heroines, while the comic and local-color character roles are reserved for
the folk who are literally black in hue.[26] In the works of their black female
counterparts, the heroines categorically seem to resemble Josephine Bruce (despite all of their talk about the absolute importance of social, educational,
and spiritual development), as the partial descriptions of Hopkins's four heroines given in the epigraphs that begin this chapter illustrate. In the eleven
domestic novels, ten of the heroines are either pale-skinned mulattas or racially
nonspecific, which implies white identity. Tillman's Caroline Waters of *Clancy
Street* is the only heroine described as having a brown face. This is not to say

that there are no brown or dark-skinned supporting heroines; there are a few. Lucille Delany of Harper's *Iola Leroy* is a highly educated version of true black womanhood, who is proud to claim the absence of white blood in her veins. Ruth Dean in Kelley-Hawkins's *Megda*, who lives in a poor neighborhood and is repeatedly described as having a dark face and hands, attains civility, compassion, and, like Lucille, more education than her light-skinned friends. Like Lucille, Ruth marries a fair-skinned suitor; nevertheless, she is clearly a marginal character.[27] Even in Hopkins's novels, all of which emphatically agitate for racial justice, the heroines embody Eurocentric beauty. Hopkins's one notable dark-skinned female character, Venus Johnson in *Hagar's Daughter*, pays lavish tribute to the inseparable whiteness and goodness of the fair heroine and her family: they "is *white* right through; mos' too good for this world."[28] The text reveals Venus's integrity, intelligence, and courage, but her presence does not disrupt or even challenge the viewpoint that she is not the material of which real heroines are made.[29] Without a doubt the ideology of Western beauty had conditioned readers—black and white alike— to expect fair heroines and to bestow sympathy on the basis of the purity of character, aligned to the purity of their Caucasoid comeliness. Perhaps it was simply too burdensome for these novelists to disturb that ideology while attempting to teach new social codes about moral development, social responsibility, and equal opportunity to black and white audiences. But by not attending to the implicit privilege of light skin color in their works, they set themselves up for serious censure by twentieth-century scholars.

Despite the implicit ideological conflict between their dramatizations of social reform for the benefit of racial equality and their privileging of conventions of Western beauty, post-Reconstruction black women writers still explicitly maintained that genteel class membership as a lady or gentleman was based more on individual virtue, dignity, and decorum than on constructions of noble black heritage arising from a racially mixed ancestry. While subscribing to the rigid standards of Victorian ladyhood, which social historian Barbara Welter has designated as "the cult of true womanhood,"[30] these writers enlarged its criteria, thereby granting their heroines access to Victorian ladyhood that served to counter the racist stereotype of black female wanton sexuality. Unfortunately, these writers found themselves locked not only within color codes but within Victorian codes of literary gentility as well.[31] Thus the codes that sanction the heroine's unquestioned social station not only prescribe her appearance but restrict topics for fictional treatment, restrict the manner of their presentation, and define the work's audience. To argue for social parity meant that these authors had to exalt bourgeois values *and* appropriate the social decorum designated for Victorian (white) ladies as the sign of their admirable character as women. Hence, to lay even tenuous claim on Victorian ladyhood as the means of asserting racial parity meant that black women writers had to follow stringent literary and social codes. These codes demanded, in particular, that they delete all references to "coarse language, coarse manners, and coarse ideas," which included not only allusions to sexual passions but anger as well (Bruce, p. 19).

With the advantage of hindsight we late-twentieth-century readers can see that these writers were working at cross-purposes on at least two fronts. To activate social reform, the women writers used the accepted "uplift" conventions—social and literary—and these conventions undercut the urgency of reform. To highlight their adoption of Victorian conduct, they implicitly relied on the viewpoint that near-white characters best espoused its tenets, a viewpoint that undercut comprehensive racial advancement. Because of their own aspirations as upwardly mobile, female black activists, black women writers of this period acquired a double dose of prescriptive genteel propriety that not only defined the nature of their writing but makes it appear excessively artificial and contradictory to contemporary readers.

We late-twentieth-century readers understand the motivation for censoring the expression of explicit sexuality in black writing of the post-Reconstruction era as a response to racist sexual constructions of black people. In fact, protesting the presumption of black licentiousness, a central tenet of the retrogressionist ideology, motivated the founding of national black women's clubs[32] and mobilized black authors, particularly black women writers, as well. While we understand the sexual exigencies of black writing of the period, we have difficulty appreciating why black women writers deleted anger from their works. Doing so ultimately meant that they could seldom mention race in a realistic context, and certainly they could not mention directly the "race problem." This restriction did not arise from choice but from convention. The only way that black "lady" writers could make their literary works address racial protest was "to demonstrate the extent to which black people were capable of expressing fine thoughts and feelings" (Bruce, p. 22). By appreciating the conventions of literary gentility or sentimentality for communicating the reformist agenda of black women writers, we come to understand the rationale for what initially seems to be wholesale "whitewashing" of the race problem. In this context, these authors' racially transcendent, sentimental domestic stories[33] become not only emphatic refutations of retrogressionism, a corruption that white people presumed permeated all aspects of black life, but also a pedagogical instrument among black people for disseminating lessons about exercising citizenship and for promoting social justice.

The Pedagogy of Sentimental Literature

Recent feminist literary scholarship has recovered cultural readings of white women's sentimental fiction during the nineteenth century, while also documenting how traditional twentieth-century scholarship has marginalized that fiction.[34] That discussion is also pertinent to black women's writing of the post-Reconstruction period, for it contends that sentimentality was a narrative strategy of female agency in social reform and suggests that gender shapes very different racial arguments in narratives of black female and male authority and that the manner of their presentation is likewise largely gender specific.

The pedagogy of sentimentality had considerable influence on white and black American literary culture. Black writers apparently appropriated many sentimental conventions to give expression to their social concerns and to demonstrate their intellectual competence in terms that the dominant culture respected. As Nina Baym has explained, popular white American literature from 1820 through 1870 was largely composed of novels written by (white) women, which she labels "woman's fiction" for two reasons. First, the label is a deliberate allusion to the volatile social issue of woman's suffrage, then known as the "woman's question." Second, Baym invokes the term because these novels fulfill three basic conditions: "They are written by women, are addressed to women, and tell one particular story about women" (Baym, p. 22). Joanne Dobson has enlarged Baym's argument by adding that aside from being merely entertaining, very popular works of women's fiction—like Susan Warner's *The Wide, Wide World* (1850), E.[mma] D. E. N. Southworth's *The Deserted Wife* (1850), Fanny Fern's *Ruth Hall* (1855)—are principally didactic.[35] Susan K. Harris has contributed to this discussion by identifying subversive lessons encoded in these novels, which she designates "exploratory novels": they "undermine cultural ideologies, expanding reader's horizons of acceptable female behavior as they posit alternatives to conventional female roles."[36] Harris's analysis is particularly helpful for discerning how late-nineteenth-century sentimental domestic fiction—white and black alike—disseminates new role models by inspiring ideal female ego formation in stories that evolve as the consequence of the heroine's pragmatic responses to her difficult situation. Rather than endorse the dominant, patriarchal feminine gender ideology (prescribing female innocence, reticence, selflessness, and helplessness), "woman's fiction" (to use Baym's term) or female "exploratory novels" (to use Harris's) rely on sentimentality to form the "overplot that valorizes marriage as the ultimate goal of a woman's life" (Harris, p. 200). The "overplot" makes a resistant text of female self-determination, intelligence, courage, and resourcefulness appear as an appropriate text of feminine virtues.

Janet Todd has also explained that the word *sentimental* alone has contributed to much of the critical disparagement that twentieth-century scholars have associated with women's domestic fiction.[37] She argues that over the years many scholars have not only conflated the terms *sentiment*, *sensibility*, *sentimentality*, and *sentimentalism*; they have also not preserved the changing historical meanings of the terms (Todd, pp. 6–9). In addition, these scholars have usually employed the word pejoratively to characterize standards for judging the general ambience of a work, rather than use it to describe the discursive conventions that qualify a particular period in literary history (Todd, p. 8). Thus these scholars have labeled "sentimental" those works of fiction that accentuate to various degrees the heroine's sensitivity, innocence, delicacy, tenderness, prettiness, diminution (and so the list could continue)—or "sentimental 'effusions'"[38]—for the purpose of inciting heightened reader responsiveness to the injustice of the heroine's plight. The resolution to the sentimental story usually involves morally distributive justice. But the degree of heart-rending accentuation of the heroine and the pervasiveness of the equitable distribution of justice required to trigger the reader's respective responses of moral outrage and affirmation, and thereby to designate a text as sentimental, is not fixed; rather, that degree of accentuation varies with time and in cultural context.

As Baym, Davidson, Dobson, Harris, and Todd, among others, have convincingly argued, the label *sentimental* is not merely a code word for describing domestic narratives that moralize about proper male and female spiritual, familial, and social conduct all in the conventions of hyperbolic emotionality. Neither is it a term for identifying "self-indulgent fantasies bearing little relationship to life. The sentimental novel spoke far more directly to the fears and expectations of its original readers than our retrospective readings generally acknowledge" (Davidson, p. 112). Rather the label *sentimental* designates a strategy for allowing a woman "to view her own life as largely the consequence of her own choices and not merely as the product of the power of others in her life" (Davidson, p. 123). "As an added bonus," Davidson explains,

> in not a few of these novels, women readers encountered women characters whose opinions mattered. Numerous sentimental novels . . . took time out from the main seduction plot to show women discussing politics, law, philosophy, and history—those same arenas of discourse from which the woman reader was often excluded. (p. 123)

These novels, then, offer a vision of female self-authority while relying on an effusion of sentimental rhetoric to mask the heroine's desire for and achievement of revised sexual attitudes, values, and roles that transcend the female sphere. By applying these cultural readings of sentimentality to black women's domestic novels of the post-Reconstruction era, we late-twentieth-century readers can discern their emancipatory protocol; for the novels inscribe not merely artificial discursive conventions for depicting an idealized courtship story but strategies for enlarging the social roles for black women and for defining as well as regulating their citizenship as gendered civil performance.

Although local color and modes of realism were moving into black and white literary production during the 1890s, the sentimental conventions that portrayed virtue and vice didactically seem to have had tremendous impact on black post-Reconstruction domestic novels, especially those written by black women.[39] In addition to the didacticism of sentimental domesticity, the material circumstances of black writers suggest that they would have had greater access to the older and widely popular women's sentimental works of the mid century (such as Warner's *The Wide, Wide World*, Fern's *Ruth Hall*, and Southworth's *The Deserted Wife*) to use as models. These novels initially appeared as inexpensive volumes and by the late nineteenth century were available as used books, which were cheaper than recently published novels. Given these material conditions along with the well-established "didactic aim of sentimental literature" (Todd, p. 9) and its pedagogic effectiveness in revising social values and performance, it is not surprising to find pronounced formal, thematic, and stylistic similarities between mid-nineteenth-century white "woman's fiction" and post-Reconstruction domestic novels, in general, and those of black female authorship in particular. For dramatized in the "woman's fiction[s]" were the tenets of the Victorian American society—moral piety, genteel decorum, sexual purity, bourgeois individualism, and the ethic of hard work—that black people increasingly embraced, initially to demonstrate that they too were U.S. citizens and ultimately to counter persistent allegations of their inferiority. Black women writers of this period used their works to disseminate these values among black people and particularly to define gender roles for themselves that would promote black women's access to professional and social activist opportunities.

Male and Female Generic Narratives of Racial Protest

While both female and male texts[40] inscribe racial distress and black people's desire to participate in what was then an emergent bourgeois-capitalistic society, the inscription of race in post-Reconstruction male texts, like Chesnutt's *The Marrow of Tradition* (1901), generally assumes the form of a polemical discourse of racial protest rather than one of domestic idealism. A typical plot line of the male text evolves as follows. In attempting to enact his prescribed roles as citizen, family patriarch, and participant in an emergent industrial-capitalistic economy, the hero confronts civil injustice because he is black. If he is married, the domestic story grants him social respectability, and the post as family head emphasizes his racially contested patriarchal position. However, racial bigotry causes him to fail at achieving a victory against civil injustice, and as a result he cannot exercise black male heroic agency. That agency is reduced to one of desire. In other words, because he cannot entirely fulfill the role of a patriarch, he can only desire that position; and the desire is not simple longing but chronic desire, indeed an ideal discourse of racialized patriarchal desire.

Black, heroic agency usually does not achieve dominance in the male text because that position is reserved for the discourse of racial protest. The primary discursive enterprise of black male texts, then, is to incite public disapprobation by dramatizing the frustrated moral claim of black patriarchal desire and to represent that dramatization in systems of value formation defined by male voice, experience, perspective, and prerogative. Moreover, the lofty language of sentimentality, the ideology of romantic love, and idealized character portraiture all emphasize the injustice of the hero's frustrated claim to patriarchal heroism and further underscore the tragedy of his defeat. The black male text, then, usually depicts explicit petitions for social justice through the agency of frustrated patriarchal desire, and social justice accordingly becomes the narrative's unrealizable object of racial desire.

By contrast, the inscription of race in female texts like Harper's *Iola Leroy* (1892), Hopkins's *Contending Forces* (1900), Kelley-Hawkins's *Four Girls at Cottage City* (1898), and Tillman's *Beryl Weston's Ambition* (1893), for example, assumes the form of a domestic discourse of ideal familial formation. These female texts repeatedly exchange gendered discourses for racial polemics; that is, they explicitly refer to gender and class while marginalizing or effacing interracial hostility. Whereas male-centered, post-Reconstruction texts generally create frustrated black male heroes, corresponding female texts usually succeed in creating optimistic black heroines who realize their domestic ambitions. The female texts enable the achievement of the heroine's ambitions by circumscribing the story within situations of family, school, and church and by inscribing a context of social justice as an embraced object of racial and sexual desire. If we measure the situations depicted in these texts against the actual social and material history of black people at the temporal moment of the texts' genesis (the 1890s), those situations seem decidedly artificial.

However, the contrived settings and plot lines of the sentimental courtship story in black women's post-Reconstruction domestic novels encode allegorical political desire in the form of fulfilled (rather than frustrated) liberational aspiration in the tropology of domesticity. The marriage story and resulting idealized domesticity assume discursive dominance in black female-centered narratives, whereas in male-centered narratives the position of discursive dominance is reserved for the story of racial protest. In the female texts the narrative is usually controlled by an explicitly feminized discourse with the resolution of conflict represented by harmonious family formation and productive domesticity; the racial plot is marginal or effaced. In corresponding male texts, the dominant discourse is a racial one among men. This discourse controls the unfolding story and focuses on white/black male hostility with no equitable resolution. While the dominant discourse in the male texts is also gendered, its civil imperatives are expressed in presumably standardized masculine signification that masks the texts' gendered attributes. As a result, the expression of what is actually black patriarchal desire in these texts takes on the appearance of general racial protest.

By the time that black women of the post-Reconstruction era used didactic sentimentality for their writing, it was already time-worn in the dominant literature. By the second decade of the twentieth century, readers would regard the excessive use of bourgeois sentimental comportment in these novels as a particularly artificial and ineffective way of subverting racialist culture. Aside from the gross unreality of these fictions, even if bourgeois ambitions were more widely available to black people at the turn of the century, after the turn of the century those ambitions were no longer unquestioningly accepted as indicative of a meaningful life. Moreover, while the dramatized domestic appeals, which were "committed . . . to the idea that black people should change to render themselves more acceptable to society,"[41] were probably effective in reforming the conduct and subsequently the social status of black individuals, those appeals were ultimately ineffective as interventionist strategies in racist hegemony. In addition, the aesthetics of the black nationalistic discourse of the 1960s further conditioned our late-twentieth-century reading expectations, displacing the prior bourgeois aesthetic with one centering the material culture of working-class black folk.

However, when we read black women's post-Reconstruction domestic novels from the theoretically reconstituted cultural expectations of that constituency, we can discern that the rhetorical conventions of sentimentality define black heroines not simply as prettified sexual objects in racial and class polemics but as agents of their own desire. The heroines of these works are not simply the recipients and practitioners of genteel social conventions, but individual characters who use the mantle of feminine bourgeois comportment to authorize the enactment of their own decisions about social advancement in an idealized, intraracial domestic sphere that impacts on their communities. By historicizing these novels, I seek to reduce our aesthetic distance to them, in order to simulate the reception of their first readers. This process enables us as late-twentieth-century readers to discern recurring plots of desire about racial justice, personal ambition, and the liberating possibilities of the community embedded in the sentimental courtship story. Historically informed readings, then, can assist us specifically in recovering racial plots that are often hidden behind opaque stories about what seems to be pretentious gentility. Such readings enable us to see the ways in which race, gender, and class have specifically shaped the symbolic political discourses in women's domestic novels of the post-Reconstruction era.

3

To Vote and to Marry:
Locating a Gendered and
Historicized Model
of Interpretation

*She was stretched on her back beneath a pear tree soaking in the alto chant
of the visiting bees, the gold of the sun and the panting breath of the breeze
when the inaudible voice of it all came to her. She saw a dust-bearing bee
sink into the sanctum of a bloom; the thousand sister-calyxes arch to meet
the love embrace and the ecstatic shiver of the tree from the root to tiniest
branch creaming in every blossom and frothing with delight. So this was
marriage! She had been summoned to behold a revelation.*

*"Tain't Logan Killicks Ah wants you to have, baby, it's protection. . . .
And Ah can't die easy thinkin' maybe de menfolks white or black is
makin' a spit cup outa you: Have some sympathy fuh me. Put me down
easy, Janie, Ah'm a cracked plate."*

    Zora Neale Hurston, *Their Eyes Were Watching God* (1937)

*"I worked twenty years and bought this house myself," she went on. "I'd
be happy when I died if I thought Bess had a husband like you."*

*Later, after I had grown to understand the peasant mentality of Bess and
her mother, I learned the full degree to which my life at home had cut me
off, not only from white people but from Negroes as well. To Bess and
her mother, money was important but they did not strive for it too hard.
They had no tensions, unappeasable longings, no desire to do something
to redeem themselves. The main value in their lives was simple, clean, good
living and when they thought they had found those same qualities in one of
their race, they instinctively embraced him, liked him and asked no questions. But such simply unaffected trust flabbergasted me. It was impossible.*

    Richard Wright, *Black Boy* (1945)

In this chapter I employ a somewhat startling postmodern vantage point to
locate my interpretative model for recovering the symbolic configurations of
political desire in the domestic novels of post-Reconstruction black women. I
rely on an historically nonsequential framework to generate my model by

70

interrogating gender constructions and discourses of racial and sexual desire in two modern black novels—Zora Neale Hurston's *Their Eyes Were Watching God* (1937) and Richard Wright's *Black Boy* (1945). Hence I look to the future, initially to compare two incidents in these novels that feature marriage and subsequently to examine the attitudes about matrimony and personal autonomy held by the respective female and male narrative centers. I have chosen these two novels because they are well known and because both depict marriage as antagonistic to the liberational ambitions of black individuals, whether female or male. This antagonism is a stark reversal of the abolitionist protocol in Jacobs's *Incidents in the Life of a Slave Girl*, discussed previously, in which marriage and bondage were mutually exclusive and thus marriage and freedom were equivalent signs in an emancipatory discourse. When gender and social class surface as fundamental categories of analysis for understanding the discourses of desire, as they do in these two modern black novels, we can begin to understand how gender and class qualify political ambitions and their social discourses.

This modern perspective on marriage prompts my interrogation of the change in esteem in the relationship between marriage and freedom that writers and scholars inscribe in African-American literary culture. My reading reveals that gender in particular is a significant social construction because it plays such an important role in determining how a population experiences and also represents dominant cultural values and institutions. Marriage is a good site to interrogate gender because, as a civil institution, a religious sacrament, and an intimate personal relationship, it is the intersection of complex gendered social exchanges. The site of marriage also highlights differences in black male and female desire; we can see that male and female discourses of desire vary not only with respect to the sexual identities of the author and the central characters but over time as well. Without an historicized and gender-sensitive problematic, the symbolic structures of racial desire in the post-Reconstruction domestic novels appear so opaque that twentieth-century readers are predisposed to regard them as nonpolitical. As I argue in subsequent chapters, these novels repeatedly present a correspondence between reformed gender roles of husbands and wives and ideal family formation, on the one hand, and the enhancement of that family's participation in the public sphere of civil interactions, on the other. Thus my interpretative model helps us to discern domestic tropology as the basis of a sustained allegorical discourse about political desire in black women's post-Reconstruction novels.

A Modern Paradigm: Antagonistic Discourses of Marriage and Freedom

The epigraphs at the beginning of this chapter reflect key incidents in two very prominent African-American novels—Zora Neale Hurston's *Their Eyes Were Watching God* (1937) and Richard Wright's *Black Boy* (1945)[1]—and both incidents critique marriage. The novels provide the basis for both my exploration of the symbolic representation of their central characters' motivating desire as gendered and my determination of an interpretative model for recovering this gendered desire from its symbolic representation.

The first incident is precipitated by the sixteen-year-old Janie's dreaming under the pear tree and her grandmother Nanny's witnessing Johnny Taylor kiss her. Janie associates the desire for emotional autonomy and perceptual awareness with the pear tree that blooms in her grandmother's yard:

> It [the pear tree] connected itself with other vaguely felt matters that had struck her outside observation and buried themselves in her flesh. Now they emerged and quested about her consciousness. (Hurston, p. 24)

The pear tree's connection to the "vaguely felt matters" and "the inaudible voice of it all" awakens Janie's self-consciousness to the possibility of pleasurable fulfillment in life. Hence the pear tree in bloom directs her attention to desire in its gratified and harmonious state, a condition that the text parallels to her awakening sexuality:

> Oh to be a pear tree—*any* tree in bloom! With kissing bees singing of the beginning of the world! She was sixteen. She had glossy leaves and bursting buds and she wanted to struggle with life but it seemed to elude her. Where were the singing bees for her? (Hurston, p. 25)

The duality of Janie's desires become sharper when we locate the sexual and existential referents for the pear tree in these passages. We see that her desire is not simply libidinal; sexual desire here is both metaphor and metonym for her growing awareness of the possibility of self-authority in life and her responsive desire to embrace such a life with active self-consciousness.

Janie conflates these parallel desires when she later says, "Ah wants things sweet wid mah marriage lak when you sit under a pear tree and think" (p. 43). Hence the text relies on the domestic sign of marriage and an allusion to pleasurable sexual intimacy in it to represent anticipated delight in a contemplative and self-critical life. Janie's leisured speculation under the inspirational pear tree, then, constitutes a passionate engagement with life, whose consummation Janie designates as marriage. The text defines her vague longings as an ontological quest for self-awareness, a supportive community, and harmony with the physical world. Because the text conflates that quest with her sexual desire (an appropriate symbolic representation inasmuch as both the quest, desire, and fictive discourse achieve fruition with climaxes), marriage and sexual pleasure mutually signify Janie's exploration of self, other, and world. The text depicts pleasurable satisfaction of the ontological quest in tropes of sexual desire and its socially endorsed consummation in marriage, thereby placing the search for self-knowledge within the "cover-plot" or "cover story"[2] of marriage (one of two generic closures of the domestic novel).

However, Nanny does not share Janie's text of desire for interpreting life and its possibilities but relies on another, a text that has evolved from her own experience of sexual exploitation in slavery. Her experience compels her to believe that male sexual privilege and female biological vulnerability doubly threaten her granddaughter. Thus she sees (indeed reads) Janie's innocent sexual curiosity, reflected in Johnny Taylor's kiss, as vulnerability and demands that Janie be "married right away" (p. 26). Whereas Janie desires "things sweet" with her marriage, Nanny wants what she understands to be the protection of a marriage contract for Janie. According to Nanny, love is not essential for black women: "Lawd have mussy! Dat's de very prong all us black women gits hung on. Dis Love" (p. 41)! With protection in mind, she arranges Janie's marriage to Logan Killicks, the proud owner of several acres and a mule (property ownership being associated with freedom during the Reconstruction era). Life has taught Nanny the necessity of postponing her "dreams of whut a woman oughta be and to do" (p. 31). Nanny disavows Janie's text of desire by insisting that she marry Killicks, but she nevertheless encourages her to retain its memory by saying, "Youse young yet. No tellin' whut mout happen befo' you die" (p. 43).

After the ceremony, Janie tries to love Killicks without success. She soon realizes that her loveless marriage has degenerated into a contract for her manual labor on Killicks's farm. But before Janie plows one field, she runs off with another man, Joe Starks. She subsequently marries him with no mention of a divorce. Under the genteel domestic tyranny of her second marriage, Janie's self-consciousness becomes split, into a respectably married, objectified woman who is silenced, on the one side, and an emerging, independent, and speaking female self, on the other. This duality makes her see that marriage is most often a form of socially sanctioned brokerage in which women serve as currency in masculine but not feminine fulfillment. She also realizes that marriage is the culmination of a socially regulated and reductive form of desire in which female identity is sacrificed to selflessness. Last, she recognizes that marriage, as her community defines it, is a deterrent to a woman's achieving self-authority. Female desire is short-changed by restrictions, rather than nourished to full maturity. To escape these restrictions Janie must redefine the terms of exchange in another marriage, which she eventually does in her conjugal relationship with Verigible Tea Cake Woods.

The second incident, in Wright's *Black Boy*, involves the protagonist Richard's stay at the Moss household in Memphis. Mrs. Moss is eager to have him marry her daughter, Bess, and settle down. Soon after meeting Richard, Mrs. Moss tells him, "I'd be happy when I died if I thought Bess had a husband like you" (p. 186). A day or so later Mrs. Moss renews her offer: "You and Bess could have this house for your home. . . . You-all could bring up your children here" (p. 197). Richard explains his desire to relocate in the North, an ambition that no doubt will be difficult to realize without the added burden of a wife and possibly children. He declines Mrs. Moss's offer as gracefully as he can, proposing to move. She, exasperated by his rejection of what she considers an exceptionally generous offer, angrily accepts his proposal to move out of her house. Although she later apologizes and begs him to stay, Richard sees that his freedom is in jeopardy and resolves to preserve it by avoiding what he regards as conjugal entrapment. Freedom here is not so much represented as individual choice as the preservation of the ambition to migrate to the North, the liberating goal for fugitive slaves. In addition, this episode presents a young black woman as emblematic of loss of freedom. She represents compromised masculine desire and the dissolution of male autonomy. The measure of a black man's autonomy, then, seems to be his steadfast desire for freedom, which is here portrayed not only as Richard's aspiration for flight northward but also his flight from female entanglement, the definitive example of which is marriage.

Black Boy and *Their Eyes Were Watching God* are my modern paradigmatic texts for exploring the gendered representations of personal desire as aspiration, ambition, and longing, which can be immediate, practical, and realizable or displaced, conflicted, and implausible. These two texts are also the basis for my model for discerning both how gender negotiates representations of desire and our understanding of it. *Black Boy* presents Richard's extremely self-conscious and personal ambition to experience "life's possibilities" (p. 227), which the text portrays both as living outside that "place" the South designated for those it termed "nigger[s]" (p. 227) and as "full flight—aboard a northward bound train" (p. 225). Hence the novel clearly defines Richard's flight as a full-fledged existential quest in the world at large where the most persistent and perilous challenge to his freedom is interracial hostility among men.

Whereas a pleasurable ontological engagement with self and other(s) characterizes Janie's quest, physical movement as well as psychological isolation, alienation, and anxiety characterizes Richard's quest. Unlike Richard, who begins a (linear) journey northward as a self-conscious individual, Janie achieves self-consciousness and self-authority at the end of a (circular) journey. Unlike Richard, who situates the realization of his desire in the external world, that is, out of doors, at *Black Boy*'s conclusion, *Their Eyes* closes with the memory of Janie's sexual desire reflected on the walls of her bedroom and the further awakening of her contemplative life, as she combs "road-dust out of her hair" (p. 286). Whereas Richard's primary heroic contest involves transcending interracial conflict, Janie's primary heroic contest is the more immediate intraracial struggle to free herself from black male authority as well as intraracial gender restrictions in order to achieve an awareness of her own desire and its centrality to her life. While Richard's entire quest—from the age of four to young adulthood—is directed by his highly self-conscious desire to define himself, Janie at age forty begins to achieve the self-consciousness intimated under the pear tree years before and becomes aware that she can voice and enact self-definition. *Black Boy* identifies racist hegemony and female entanglement as Richard's antagonists, whereas *Their Eyes* portrays the oppressive sexual attitudes of Janie's first two husbands and her community as Janie's antagonists. Although racism resides at the margins of *Their Eyes* and at the center of *Black Boy*, Janie's self-authority, like Richard's, demands equal protection of the law, which she does achieve in the parodied murder trial.

This parodic microdrama embodies much of the novel's interracial protest, while that protest subsumes virtually every dramatic event in *Black Boy*.

Their Eyes Were Watching God relies on different narrative strategies and figurative constructions for characterizing Janie's desire for engagement with "life's possibilities," to use Wright's phrase. Janie's engagement forms two heroic stories in the novel: one about personal sexual fulfillment and thus a folk version of the ideal bourgeois domesticity of the post-Reconstruction novels; and another about her existential possibilities. *Their Eyes* presents Janie's heroic aspiration as the journey to the horizon, the image for linking worldly exploration with self-discovery. However, Janie must free herself from the gender conventions that circumscribe a woman's life before she can gain access to that external quest. This is precisely what she has done by the end of the novel, as she explains to Pheoby the meaning of her three marriages and their relationship to her evolving self-consciousness in the trope of the mythic quest: "Ah done been tuh de horizon and back and Ah kin set heah in mah house and live by comparisons" (p. 284). After Pheoby's departure, Janie makes those comparisons: "Dis house ain't so absent of things lak it used tuh be befo' Tea Cake come along. It's full uh thoughts, 'specially dat bedroom" (p. 284). Once again Janie conflates self-critical contemplation of her life and what might be called her existential awareness with the allusion to sexual pleasure, a conflation that recalls her recurring ventures in self-discovery in the tropology of love. Despite her multiple efforts, Janie's "love game" (p. 171) with Tea Cake is her only narrated engagement with "life's possibilities." However, self-reflection at this moment in the story also presents intimations of another opportunity of existential possibility, another trip to the horizon that is external to romantic adventure. The beginning of this story is located at the novel's closure.

Before discussing this visionary and unnarrated journey, I take a moment to describe the attitudes of Janie's three husbands, to illustrate the changing historical viewpoints about gender in black culture and to demonstrate how they conditioned Janie's self-definition in terms of heterosexual love.[3] Her first husband, Logan Killicks, tells Janie, "You ain't got no particular place. It's wherever Ah needs yuh" (p. 52). Killicks portrays an antebellum slave gender construction in which black women had no prescribed sex-role division of labor. However, rather than assert relative gender equality, Killicks assumes the position of the plantation patriarch in his designation of Janie's place of labor without regard to sex-role divisions, claiming that it is as appropriate for Janie to plow the fields as to care for the home. By contrast, Janie affirms a postbellum gender construction for herself by claiming, "You don't need mah help out dere, Logan. Youse in yo' place and Ah'm in mine" (p. 52). Her second husband, Joe Starks, counters Killick's antebellum designation and Janie's postbellum construction by taking the latter to an extreme. He announces directly to the black community of Eatonville and indirectly to Janie that "She's uh woman and her place is in the home" (p. 69). Thus Janie's domestic role becomes oppressive, as Starks both assumes and imposes the patriarchal power that Killicks sought. It is her third husband, Verigible Tea Cake Woods, who offers Janie the greatest freedom from both places because he does not subscribe to either of these gender constructions, although he also is not free of sexist attitudes. He offers Janie a modern companionate marriage, which Hurston depicts as Janie's opportunity to "[find] herself glowing inside" (p. 146), to learn her "maiden language all over" (p. 173), and to see him as "a bee to a blossom" (p. 161). In short, Tea Cake enables Janie to reclaim her first girlhood dream, the desire for pleasurable ontological discovery, or, in Janie's words, "Ah wants things sweet wid mah marriage lak when you sit under a pear tree and think" (p. 43). However, we should notice that the full breadth of her life's possibilities, envisioned as contemplation under the symbolic pear tree, have been prematurely circumscribed by heterosexual romance.

Interestingly, at the end of both *Their Eyes* and *Black Boy*, cosmic imagery suggests the possibilities of quests beyond the social constraints of their respective protagonists. *Black Boy* characterizes Richard's effort to secure a life free of interracial strife as a struggle of galactic proportion in an amoral, impersonal context:

> I headed North, full of a hazy notion that life could be lived with dignity, that the personalities of others should not be violated, that men should be able to confront other men without fear or shame, and that if men were lucky in their living on earth they might win some redeeming meaning for their having struggled and suffered here beneath the stars. (p. 228)

A racially indifferent terrain sharpens the intensity of Richard's drive; his heroic quest for the "redeeming meaning" of living a life of dignity seems to have no boundaries. In Janie's story, too, while images of constriction abound — walls, rooms, draped shoulders — within the closure of the story is the genesis of another visionary journey, as Janie becomes aware once again of life's possibilities. The new story appears as Janie "sat down. Combing road-dust out of her hair. Thinking" (pp. 285–86). This scene repeats an earlier one that occurred just before Janie announced Joe's death: "She tore off the kerchief from her head and let down her plentiful hair. . . . She took careful stock of herself, then combed her hair and tied it back again" (p. 135). Soon after taking stock of herself, Janie begins her adventure with Tea Cake. This second scene of self-inventory points to another adventure, though it is not presented in the novel. "Though Hurston often denies this quest story in favor of the romantic plot," Mary Helen Washington has observed, "her interest in Janie's heroic potential is unmistakable."[4] No doubt the romance plot was easier to write, given its formulaic structure and social currency, while the female quest story, with a plot external to female sexual and domestic aspirations, was a suppressed discourse and therefore obviously difficult to write.

The difficulty of constructing the plot of such a story is clearly a problem in *Their Eyes*. Hurston seems to have attempted to resolve it at least partially by intimating the new story beyond the novel's ending. By contrast, the wide circulation of the masculine quest plot is so well established that it is not surprising that *Black Boy* closes with Richard still in quest, pursuing an elusive freedom, signified as a trip of a great distance (like that to the horizons, but in this case) to a nonspecific, even unearthly, region, a place where, as he says, "I was taking a part of the South with me to transplant in alien soil, to see if it could grow differently . . . respond to the warmth of other suns, and, perhaps, to bloom" (p. 228). While Wright had a tradition of male heroic quests on which to draw, Hurston confronted the stunning absence of a female heroic tradition in realist fiction.

These two incidents emplot modern black female and male desire; they also reflect modern attitudes about marriage that diverge from the Victorian viewpoint of the institution as the unquestioned basis of civilization and an important means of enhancing the quality of the individual life. By comparing these two incidents, we discern modern conflicting views of marriage, arising from a growing apprehension on the part of their respective protagonists that marriage does not enhance personal gratification or self-esteem. Each novel also reflects a reductive premodern construction of socially regulated desire that is represented as the conjugal ambitions of Nanny and Mrs. Moss for their female progeny and a modern (or post-Victorian) construction of individuated, personal desire that is represented by Janie's and Richard's desires for self-definition outside the marriage plot. What is missing in both works is the viewpoint of the post-Reconstruction domestic novels that marriage is a viable medium for developing the self, the other, and the community, a joint venture in which wives and husbands construct mutually fulfilling and productive futures while improving the quality of life in their community. Marriage in these novels serves the interest of racial uplift by constructing it as an aggregate of happy, enterprising conjugal units. For this society, "the household, not the individual, is the unit of the State."[5] By contrast, modern desire seems motivated by isolated self-interest rather than governed by group interests, social institutions, or attendant conduct codes.

The narrative perspective of each of the above incidents as well as the novels from which they were excerpted evolves from modern, individuated desire that is racially, generationally, and gender specific. The specificity of these discourses undoubtedly contributed to the two novels' initial critical reception, a reception that is now legendary. For instance, Richard Wright contended that Hurston was perpetuating minstrel stereotyping.[6] Ralph Ellison has called *Their Eyes* a "bright calculated burlesque."[7] Arthur P. Davis has written that "the telling of the story reminds one a little of the film *Green Pastures*."[8] Comparing the largely positive commentary that Wright's *Black Boy* has received with the largely negative commentary given to *Their Eyes*, the critical difference in the reception of the two novels suggests that traditional scholars and critics, namely those writing largely in the 1960s from a black patriarchal viewpoint, generally identified with the representation of racial, sexual, and generational ambitions and attitudes associated with the autobiographical character Richard.[9] They generally regarded *Their Eyes*, if they encountered it, as reactionary and nonpolitical, contending that it contributed little to the sanctioned racial discourse of social protest.[10]

This reading protocol strongly suggests that traditional scholars have recognized the political worthiness of *Black Boy* because the critical imperatives of black protest writing and the Black Aesthetic (of the Black Arts movement), which I summarize below, had already conditioned their reading expectations. Hence they have acknowledged as protest the conventional, black, male-centered discourses of racial desire inscribed in that novel, or what I might generally term "black male narratology," to modify Susan Winnett's term.[11] When, however, traditional scholars encountered the unfamiliar domestic discourse of racial desire of the black female narrative center, or "black female narratology," in *Their Eyes*, they were unable to discern similar political content; thus their generally negative response. That scholarly mode arises from presuming that the confrontational male-constructed protest is universally applicable to all African-American texts instead of appreciating that other orientations, such as racialized domestic affirmation, also give voice to racial protest.

Twentieth-Century Critical Imperatives

To understand why traditional African-Americanist scholarship has accepted the confrontational orientation as a revered racial perspective, it is necessary to survey its development. The critical imperatives of this scholarly tradition evolved largely during two particular moments of literary history. The first was during the politically charged period following the Great Depression, when racial protest works by Richard Wright (like *Native Son* [1940] and *Black Boy* [1945]) were big sellers. The second was during the Black Arts (or Black Aesthetic) movement of the late 1960s and the early 1970s. This movement celebrated the inscription of black protest and cultural nationalism in African-American writing. Insofar as the Black Arts movement was concerned, a text achieved aesthetic significance to the degree that it raised the social consciousness of its readers. In the words of Black Arts proponent Ron Karenga, "The real function of art is to make revolution, using its own medium."[12] Black Arts criteria for identifying literary texts worthy of its attention became not merely explicit but prescriptive, as the prefatory remarks of scholar Addison Gayle, Jr., who edited the critical manifesto *The Black Aesthetic*, reveal:

> The question for the black critic today is not how beautiful is a melody, a play, a poem, or a novel, but how much more beautiful has the poem, melody, play, or novel made the life of a single black man? How far has the work gone in transforming an American Negro into an African-American or black man? The Black Aesthetic, then, as conceived by this writer, is a corrective — a means of helping black people out of the polluted mainstream of Americanism.[13]

The domestic novels of post-Reconstruction black women do not so much chart a course apart from the "polluted mainstream of Americanism" as they affirm the belief that bourgeois aspirations are realized by the meritorious irrespective of color. (Of course, that mainstream seemed more polluted in the second half of the twentieth century than during the last decade of the nineteenth century for reasons not necessary to elaborate on here.) In sharp contrast, the Black Arts movement engaged an ideological survey of that route and an interrogation of its destination. Like the proverbial slave who read self-interest as a negation of the master's consideration, the Black Aesthetic eagerly and willfully discarded all values associated with white society and the black middle class, seeing the latter as a pretentious exaggeration of the former. The Black Aesthetic does not sanction a bourgeois life-style as the exemplar for black social desire, but rather consolidates class distinction in a racial protocol. Hoyt Fuller, another contributor to *The Black Aesthetic*, explains that protocol by conflating class and race: "The black artist must construct models which correspond to his own reality. The models must be non-white" (Gayle, p. 329).

Their Eyes does not dramatize these tenets. To say that black women's post-Reconstruction domestic novels do not subscribe to the doctrines of either protest literature or the black cultural nationalism of the Black Arts movement is an understatement. They seem precisely among those works that Richard Wright had in mind when he censured early black literature in his famous essay "Blueprint for Negro Writing"[14]:

> Generally speaking, Negro writing in the past has been confined to humble novels, poems, and plays, prim and decorous ambassadors who went a-begging to white America. They entered the Court of American Public Opinion dressed in the knee-pants of servility, curtsying to show that the Negro was not inferior, that he was human, and that he had a life comparable to that of other people. (Gayle, p. 315)

Wright dominated the literary protest era, probably instigating a series of literary manifestoes that appeared during the 1940s, 1950s and 1960s, among them Ralph Ellison's "Richard Wright's Blues," "Twentieth-Century Fiction and the Black Mask of Humanity," and "The World and the Jug" and James Baldwin's "Everybody's Protest Novel" and "Many Thousands Gone."[15] Wright was also the principal precursor of the Black Arts movement. From the perspective of this movement, the absence of visible interracial hostility and explicit racial protest makes the domestic novels appear as collaborators with the enemy, thus their extreme obscurity. Similarly from that perspective, these novels' recurring focus on genteel marriage, bourgeois propriety, and elite material consumption makes a bad situation worse, further alienating Black Arts scholars who were/are likely to view the individual bourgeois pursuits depicted in these fictions as detrimental to the collective advancement of black people. (We should recall here that bourgeois material pursuits were denigrated during the period of the Black Arts movement.) To exacerbate things further, the domestic novels' civility, rigors of courtship, and white- or light-skinned heroines appear to undercut racial affirmation, working-class solidarity, and black cultural nationalism, all of which the Black Arts movement deemed important. The sharp divergence of the post-Reconstruction domestic novels from the typical working-class ethos of racial protest literature and the tenets of the Black Arts movement meant that these works were buried under the ideological weight of both movements. As a result of this critical history, we contemporary readers have largely applauded the representation of freedom found in masculine black protest critiques or an unconsciously male rendition of black cultural nationalism, while we have disparaged domestic stories as narratives of confinement, as narratives of status quo.

Neither the Black Arts movement nor its predecessor questioned its own reading strategies. Neither asked whether, for example, the preponderance of light-skinned characters in the late-nineteenth-century domestic novels signaled a meaning other than racial ambivalence and/or intraracial privilege of light skin color. However, the mulatto characters seem to have produced different meanings at the turn of the century, as Hopkins's Mrs. Willis explains in *Contending Forces*:

> "I would not worry about the fate of the mulatto, for the fate of the mulatto will be the fate of the entire race. Did you never think that today the black race on this continent has developed into a race of mulattoes. . . . It is an incontrovertible truth that there is no such thing as an unmixed black on the American continent. . . . I will venture to say that out of a hundred apparently pure black men not one will be able to trace an unmixed flow of African blood since landing upon these shores."[16]

Mrs. Willis regards all black people who are not one-hundred percent pure African as mulattoes irrespective of skin color.[17] She reflects what seems to be Hopkins's disinterest in discerning degrees of racial mixture for designating social difference in that population, a concern that her contemporary Charles Chesnutt depicted in much of his writing. Several of his stories are about fair-skinned black characters who cross the color line. By contrast, Hopkins's stories are about similar characters entangled in it, and her sister writers who gave expression to racial arguments appeared not to have written passing stories. Insofar as Hopkins and these women writers were concerned, dark- and white-skinned mulattoes were inclusive parts of the African-American population. Unlike these female authors, twentieth-century readers generally use the term *mulatto* as one of exclusion rather than inclusion; that is, to designate black people who claim or appear to claim privilege as a consequence of light skin color. Thus what the black protest writers and the proponents of the Black Arts movement have disparaged as racial ambivalence or denial in the mulatto characters of early black literature, their post-Reconstruction counterparts probably saw as evidence of the altered genetic stock of African Americans, a change that made them distinctly different from their enslaved African predecessors. This difference in meaning is just one instance of the importance of reading the domestic novels from value constructions of their own era rather than from ours. In addition, these novels seem not to have questioned their adoption of bourgeois tenets of individuation, the nuclear family, and material consumption as the modes of racial progress, all of which distance these novels' ambitions from those of black nationalism.

However, the representation of the quest for freedom from racial oppression is also gender, class, and historically specific. The antebellum works are inscribed in a slave-gender construction that does not privilege either bondmen or bondwomen, that is inherently sexually nonhegemonic. Thus, as far as the slaves are concerned, these works are stories about the collective desire for civil liberty among African Americans. As a result the sexual discourses in these works seem less antagonistic to their liberational intentions.

For example, Douglass represented himself in *The Narrative of the Life of Frederick Douglass* as an heroic individual, and he also deliberately argued that his condition as a slave was representative; he claimed to be a generic slave. However, when mid-twentieth-century historians and literary scholars whom I label "traditional" (who are largely men, and who have been shaped by modern patriarchal gender constructions) have viewed Douglass's narrative as the prototypical slave narrative, they have routinely (and perhaps unconsciously) inscribed a masculine identification for the slave experiences.[18] For such readers, Douglass's identity as a black man assumes, on the one hand, gender specificity in a male narratology in which two "master narratives"[19] — the black liberational and the Western patriarchal discourses — condition his heroism and, on the other hand, categorical racial representation in which Douglass's sexual identity is conflated into a standardized, generic racial discourse. The centrality of these two master narratives in African- and Anglo-American cultures, in which traditional African-American scholarship is grounded, transforms *The Narrative* into *the* prototypical black master text. In other words, its gender specificity, implicit and explicit, inscribes the act of black heroic self-definition, or what Robert B. Stepto has called "heroic self-transformation" as a masculine discursive event.[20]

A key event in that transformation is Douglass's physical confrontation with Covey:

> from whence came the spirit I don't know — I resolved to fight. . . . This battle with Mr. Covey was the turning-point in my career as a slave. It rekindled the few expiring embers of freedom, and revived within me a sense of my own manhood. . . . It . . . inspired me again with a determination to be free. . . . It was a glorious resurrection from the tomb of slavery, to the heaven of freedom . . . and I now resolved that, however long I might remain a slave in form, the day had passed forever when I could be a slave in fact. I did not hesitate to let it be known of me, that the white man who expected to succeed in whipping, must also succeed in killing me. . . . From this time I was never again what might be called fairly whipped, though I remained a slave four years afterwards. I had several fights, but was never whipped. (pp. 112–13)

It is important to understand that this event defines heroic self-transformation as violent and aggressive, that is, as a traditionally masculinized confrontation with conflict. Thus physical violence enhances the possibility of freedom of choice in Douglass's life. As a consequence, he becomes increasingly more self-confident of his determination to free himself from enslavement. We unconditionally and emphatically have regarded such violent confrontations with oppression as heroic and political.[21] As a result, we have categorically precluded female heroism and implicitly understood the heroic transcendence of slavery not as the experiences of slaves—female and male—but predominantly as the confrontational experience of the male slave, cast from a masculine perspective wherein the activity of protesting slavery is seen as masculine, violent performance.

While Wilson's *Our Nig* and Jacobs's *Incidents in the Life of a Slave Girl* dramatize the acts of liberational self-affirmation, passive resistance rather than violent, physical confrontation is the strategy of resistance in these works. The narrative centers of both female texts revise their status as objects of the white people's desire, though their political condition remains essentially unchanged. In *Incidents* Brent negates her status as her master's object of sexual desire by achieving a sexual exchange. She transforms herself into a subject of desire by willfully engaging in a sexual association with another white man, one of her own choice. In *Our Nig* Frado's psychological liberation occurs when she claims that her Christian conversion gives her the authority to refuse to accept her mistress Mrs. Bellmont's repeated physical abuse. In other words, Frado's self-assertion undermines Mrs. Bellmont's total authority over her. However, Frado does not attempt to escape from servitude but serves out her term.

Each text, then, records the rise of black female agency as a resistant force to racial oppression. But because neither Brent nor Frado substantively alters the material conditions of her life, the claim to a feminized version of full or uncompromised heroic stature is unobtainable. To compound this reading problem, slave stories about the sexual oppression of female slaves generally became a dominant mode of constructing racial protest in female antebellum texts, like *Incidents*. This type of racial oppression is seldom if ever associated with male slaves in slave narratives. Indeed, female slave narratives often concentrate on the subject of sexuality, the area that the corresponding male texts marginalize or efface.

Inasmuch as an antebellum reading of female slave narratives would share the author's construction of gender, such a reading would maintain that protesting the master's sexual abuse was equivalent to protesting slavery in general. However, late-nineteenth- and twentieth-century readings of female slave narratives would not presume an antebellum gender code of relative sexual equality, as evident from the traditional readings of *Incidents*.[22] Such readings see difference instead of correspondence, with the presumption that a sexualized discourse of protestation is a personal, private, indeed a female-gendered complaint and thus not a full-fledged, public expression of racial protest. Under these circumstances, the critical power accorded to Douglass's *Narra-*

tive of the Life to become a dominant text in African-American canons becomes obvious. *Narrative of the Life* defines the black liberational discourse as a male discursive event by making a violent enactment of racial protest the dominant strategy for achieving heroic self-transformation.

Traditional readings of the post-Reconstruction domestic novels frequently become problematic due to their failure to sympathize with the novels' focus on constructing a successful bourgeois family while omitting overt interracial hostility. Such readings thus tend to be preoccupied with the idealized domestic settings without realizing that for the novels' first readers these settings were inherent subversions of racist ideology. What traditional readings tend to regard as racially displaced or reticent domestic fantasies in these novels, a post-Reconstruction protocol of reading would designate as race literature.

The Aesthetic of Race Literature

In an address entitled "The Value of Race Literature," delivered at the First Congress of Colored Women of the United States in Boston, Massachusetts on July 30, 1895, the well-known, black social activist and writer Victoria Earle Matthews defined and discussed the social significance of race literature.[23] "By Race Literature," Matthews wrote,

> we mean ordinarily all the writings emanating from a distinct class—not necessarily race matter; but a general collection of what has been written by the men and women of that Race: History, Biographies, Scientific Treatises, Sermons, Addresses, Novels, Poems, Books of Travel, miscellaneous essays and the contributions to magazines and newspapers. (p. 3)

According to Matthews, not only does race literature provide black people with role models that would advance their real life social ambitions; such literature also engenders a people's "true fame" (p. 12), which, as she contended, is readily recognizable to open-minded white people. Race literature also serves as an important index of black people's "intrinsic worth . . . breadth of mind . . . boundless humanity" (p. 12). Matthews further insisted that any individual who would know black people can accomplish that feat by reading race literature, adding that

> Though Race Literature be founded upon the traditionary [sic] history of a people, yet its fullest and largest development ought not be circumscribed by the narrow limits of race or creed, for the simple reason that literature in its loftiest development reaches out to the utmost limits of soul enlargement and outstrips all earthly limitations. (p. 7)

Race literature, she continued, "will be a revelation to our people, and it will enlarge our scope, make us better known wherever real lasting culture exists" (pp. 7–8). Race literature, then, would instruct black people in all areas of social development and inform white people about that pursuit.

Several of Matthews's contemporaries gave explicit expression to the cultural consensus among black intellectuals of the post-Reconstruction era about the necessity of didacticism in African-American literature. Gertrude Bustill Mossell outlined an arduous path for race literature in her 1898 essay "Life and Literature," published in *The A.M.E. Church Review*.[24] In this work Mossell insisted that serious literature is a product of "painstaking research, accurate knowledge, originality, both of thought and of style, terseness, clearness, beauty, and that spark that men call genius" (p. 323). Literature, she continued, "interprets for each individual his own inmost thoughts and gives to them expression" (p. 322). Hopkins's prefatory remarks to her 1900 novel *Contending Forces* reveal similar faith in the didactic value of race literature. "In giving this little romance expression in print," she wrote, "I am not actuated by a desire for notoriety or for profit, but to do all that I can in a humble way to raise the stigma of degradation from my race." She added,

> The colored race has historians, lecturers, ministers, poets, judges and lawyers, — men of brilliant intellects who have arrested the favorable attention of this busy, energetic nation. But, after all, it is the simple, homely tale, unassumingly told, which cements the bond of brotherhood among all classes and all complexions. (p.13)

According to Hopkins, "it is the simple, homely tale" that has the greatest chance of reforming social codes of interracial and intraracial conduct. Hopkins went on to fortify her "simple tale" with historical authenticity, insisting that her "daring venture within the wide field of romantic literature" (p. 13) was more fact than fiction:

> The incidents portrayed in the early chapters of the book actually occurred. Ample proof of this may be found in the archives of the courthouse at Newberne, N.C., and at the national seat of government, Washington, D.C. (p. 14)

Charles W. Chesnutt recorded similar motivations nearly two decades prior to their realization in *The House Behind the Cedars*, in his journal entry of May 29, 1880:

> I think I must write a book. . . . If I do write, I shall write for a purpose, a high, holy purpose. . . . I consider the unjust spirit of caste which is so insidious as to pervade a whole nation, and so powerful as to subject a whole race and all connected with it to scorn and social ostracism — I consider this a barrier to the moral progress of the American people; and I would be one of the first to head a determined, organized crusade against it. . . . The Negro's part is to prepare himself for recognition and equality, and it is the province of literature to open the way for him to get it — to accustom the public mind to the idea.[25]

Harper as well expressed similar authorial intentions for *Iola Leroy*, grounding them in the story's historical veracity and stating them explicitly at the end of that novel:

> From the threads of fact and fiction I have woven a story whose mission
> will not be in vain if it awaken in the hearts of our countrymen a stronger
> sense of justice and a more Christlike humanity in behalf of those whom
> the fortunes of war threw, homeless, ignorant and poor, upon the thresh-
> old of a new era.[26]

For late-nineteenth-century black readers, Harper's *Iola Leroy* and the other
post-Reconstruction domestic fictions of her black female contemporaries
were categorically race literature. Like the other domestic novels, *Iola Leroy*
embodies the pedagogic intentionality of race literature to refute, in addition
to the retrogressionist idology, the racist presumptions of the eighteenth-
century Enlightenment.

Prominent proponents of the Enlightenment, like David Hume, Georg Wil-
helm Friedrich Hegel, and Thomas Jefferson, constructed the inferiority of
black people partly around "the widespread doubt about the African's inherent
incapacity to create the arts and letters."[27] Refuting that inherently racist viewpoint evolved into a preoccupation for virtually all nineteenth-century black
writers, as Henry Louis Gates, Jr., explains:

> What seems clear upon reading the texts created by black writers in English
> or the critical texts that responded to these black writings is that the
> production of literature was taken to be the central arena in which persons
> of African descent could, or could not, establish and redefine their status
> within the human community. Black people, the evidence suggests, had to
> represent themselves as "speaking subjects" before they could even begin
> to destroy their status as objects, as commodities, within Western culture.
> (p. 129)

Gates's analysis results from discerning the defensive nature of much of the
literature and literary commentary written by African Americans during the
post-Reconstruction period.

To characterize this defensive posture further I refer to the work of the
black bibliophile Daniel Murray of the Library of Congress, who wrote at the
turn of the century. In "Bibliography of Negro Literature," Murray identified
"nearly fourteen hundred books and pamphlets by Negro authors" in order to
affirm that "literature is the highest form of culture and the real test of standing
of a people in the ranks of civilization."[28] Murray contended that "this showing must undoubtedly raise the Negro to a plane previously denied him, but
which, in spite of every drawback he has honestly won" (pp. 25–26). In a
later essay, "Bibliographia-Africania," Murray reiterated this viewpoint, insisting that "The true test of the progress of a people is to be found in their
literature."[29] The aforementioned tenet of the Enlightenment probably directed the course of Murray's scholarly ambition, prompting him to dedicate
himself to compiling bibliographies of books and pamphlets of African-
American authorship as proof of black intellectual parity.

Race literature, then, had a very specific charge during the post-Reconstruction era, and this gave rise to black literary production with a very definite

pedagogic intent. Because black women's post-Reconstruction domestic novels are categorically a part of the polemical tradition of race literature for refuting retrogressionism and because they also appropriate the pedagogy of nineteenth-century sentimentality, these novels got a double dose of didactic, political intentionality that contemporary readers no longer recognize. Severe racial segregation conditioned the expectations of black authors and readers of the post-Reconstruction era; they understood the need to invest intraracial institutions—particularly the church, school, and home—with political meaning. Unlike our nineteenth-century black counterparts, we twentieth-century readers have primarily invested public desire in the infrastructures of politics of state—civic, commercial, transport, and legislative policies.[30] In addition, traditional protocols of reading have not readily recognized black domestic fiction as race literature, that is, as writing that subverts racist ideologies and affirms black solidarity. Rather, those readings have tended to regard these novels' highly individuated domestic quests as exaggerated, even perverted middle-class pretensions and not as expressions of racialized political desire. But that is precisely what these texts are.

I refer to Harper's *Iola Leroy* again to illustrate the issue of solidarity in the novel's discourse of racial inclusion because this work is probably the most widely read of the post-Reconstruction domestic novels discussed here. The novel focuses on the lives and eventual marriages of two light-skinned African Americans, Iola and her brother Harry Leroy, who had unknowingly passed for white until young adulthood. Given their education and genteel social rearing, they could easily continue to pass for upper-class white people. However, they refuse to do so and instead celebrate their black slave heritage and dedicate their labor to the advancement of the race. Their behavior encodes a pattern of desire that is immediately instructive for those black people who can also pass for white. The novel instructs them to view pride in African-American heritage as the object of their racial desire and to regard that newly engendered racial pride as the source of their self-esteem. However, these racial issues are not independent polemical features of the text. They arise within the stories of courtship, marriage, and family formation, stories of individual desire that have too frequently side-tracked traditional readings of the novel. For instance, Iola's refusal to marry a white doctor and pass for white arises not from the problems associated with passing but from refusal to forsake her heritage as an African American. Thus constructions of identity and community solidarity arise from the politics of family formation and not from platform politics.

The black women's post-Reconstruction domestic narratives, like their antebellum counterparts, rely heavily on domestic tropes for expressing racial desire. But, unlike the antebellum narratives, the post-Reconstruction works are products of early modern character development arising from a particular bourgeois orientation that accompanied the rise of the middle class during the latter part of the nineteenth century. By the turn of the century the black heroic character no longer appears as one of many, engaged in a representative, collective, or communal struggle for meaning, value, and direction. The character's motivating desire no longer arises from group ambition but from individual longing to emulate an exemplary model. The post-Reconstruction characters, then, are fundamentally different from their antebellum counterparts in that their quests, while implicitly racial, also evolve from decidedly self-conscious, individuated, bourgeois desire.

The silencing of the racial discourse in the novels of Johnson and Kelley-Hawkins, which produces racial ambiguity and nonspecificity, enhances the individuation of character formation. For example, the ambiguous racial identity of Meg Randal in Kelley-Hawkins's *Megda* (1891) appears within a highly insular context. The racial ambiguity of characters like Meg, who wants to be a professional elocutionist and actress, further underscores ego individuation and ironically supports the novel's liberational discourse due to the fact that Meg's ambition does not subscribe to racial stereotypes. Such ego individuation also appears in the black heroines. For instance, Tillman's Beryl Weston is an "Afro-American girl" whose desire to graduate from college cannot be construed as a racially representative one. Rather it arises from a set of personal goals that she sets for herself. Hence the ideality of female models, like Meg and Beryl, does not reside in their representational status but in their singleness of purpose and fundamental belief in willful self-definition. These attributes underpin the novel's liberational discourses.

Interpretative Model: Domestic Desire as Political Discourse

While characters of the post-Reconstruction novels evolve as a consequence of individuated ego formation in a climate of social optimism among African Americans, black modern characters, like Janie and Richard, similarly evolve but as a consequence of their respective encounters with increased domestic frustration as well as chronic racial alienation. Establishing meaningful lives and positive personal relationships is more problematic for them. For example, not only is Richard cut off from white society; he is so alienated from the goals of home ownership and family formation, which have traditionally formed the bedrock of social prosperity in the black community, that he expresses little understanding of or sympathy for these goals, as the beginning epigraphs from *Black Boy* suggest. Janie similarly finds herself out of touch with Granny's antebellum gender values, even after she escapes the physical distastefulness of marriage to Killicks to establish the materially advantageous marriage to Starks. In addition to marriage, both Janie and Richard also seem particularly cut off from the social institutions of religion and education, which were the centerpieces of the black, post-Reconstruction social system. These institutions had provided unquestioned, collective meaning for premodern African Americans. But as modern characters, Janie and Richard stand apart from their post-Reconstruction counterparts. They typify the new character who celebrates a wholly individual quest for self-definition or existential desire as the site of personal meaning, rather than any Western social institution.

These modern female and male versions of that quest seem somewhat mutually antagonistic. Janie's desire to define her own life, indeed her existential desire, is represented as the achievement of an alienated self-consciousness: she becomes emotionally and psychologically aware of herself as an individual who stands apart in her community. Two of her three husbands seek to block the development of her self-awareness, as they advance their own desire. The third, Tea Cake, seems not to have formulated a self-conscious viewpoint of his desire, and thus he can encourage the early stages of Janie's quest. Whether he would have continued to nurture Janie's growing self-awareness and her desire for self-definition is difficult to ascertain, though the text suggests that he might not have been so accommodating by its creation of circumstances that cause Janie to kill Tea Cake in self-defense.

Male desire seems antagonistic to female desire throughout *Their Eyes* and *Black Boy*. In *Black Boy* in particular, domestic enterprise appears not as a trope of personal or racial liberational desire but as sexual entrapment. Similarly, marriage in *Their Eyes* mediates, though only temporarily, Janie's desire for female subjectivity with promises of matrimonial bliss and social respectability. Both novels depict marriage and individual freedom as oppositional, indeed antithetical. We are familiar with this form of domestic antagonism because contemporary U.S. culture abounds with cliches associating marriage with male bondage and female kitchen-bound blues. As a result we readily apply this antagonistic context to African-American novels that depict marriage.

In addition, traditional scholarship's discussion of the genesis of black literature and its general preoccupation with freedom affirms *Black Boy* as a legitimate black text, while contesting *Their Eyes*'s claim to this status. As Stepto has notably argued, to write and to be free were dual historical imperatives for literary representations of black Americans in bondage (Stepto, pp. 3–31). These imperatives, however, arise from male models; for when we discern the relationship between literacy and liberation in black female antebellum texts, that historical imperative does not seem to be so firmly in place.[31] Traditional African-Americanist critical practice has nevertheless celebrated this relationship and made it an expectation. Thus when we read texts that not only fail to endorse that model but focus on marriage and privilege that institution as well, while also heeding tenets of traditional black (male) narratology, as do black women's post-Reconstruction domestic novels, we are likely to find ourselves casting this large body of writing into the margins of literary history because it seems not to address racial liberation and intellectual freedom but racial denial and bourgeois pretension.

Just as there is an historicized way to read the mulatto character in these domestic texts, historicized readings of bourgeois materialism, family formation, and economic self-interest also surface when we recall that late-nineteenth-century American society regarded material comfort and family security as signs of the virtuous life. Rather than simply petitioning for white approval, these texts propose strategies for black economic prosperity by making the black family a cooperative unit for self-improvement. By calling attention to the fact that African Americans were not categorically poor, these texts also disrupt the general conflation of black people with poverty and endorse the viability of self-advancement in the world as well as in the story. Hence these novels argue for increased black participation in the not yet tarnished American dream of middle-class economic prosperity and for the social elevation of black people in general. In this context, then, what seems to be post-Reconstruction black women writers' general preoccupation with elegant clothing and refined household articles becomes a semiotic of an emergent bourgeois capitalism in which black people are envisioned as full and virtuous participants. As participants in what Gillian Brown terms "the liberal tradition of possessive individualism, in which individual rights are grounded in the principle of self-ownership," sentimental formulations of commodity consumption reflect a stable and autonomous individualism.[32] The characters' participation in costly commodity consumption reflects their self-ownership. But when read transparently, that is, without the late-nineteenth-century cultural codes in place, the novels' preoccupation with expensive commodification seems grossly out of touch with the actual material conditions of the majority of black people; thus the repeated allegations of scholars of the protest and the Black Aesthetic eras that this writing is unrealistic, pretentious, and nonpolitical. But, of course, twentieth-century codes of ideal value formation were not consensus during the late nineteenth century. While the proponents of the Black Aesthetic saw in the ethic of hard work a repeatedly failed strategy for achieving racial advancement, the post-Reconstruction black women who wrote domestic fiction evidently believed that willful self-advancement would hold sway against the racist backlash of that era.

When gender becomes a significant factor in the analysis of African-American literature, the disparate sites and plots of desire in texts of male and female authority prompt the following two questions: What happens to the discourse of political desire when the discursive authority is a black woman? And to what extent is such a discourse self-consciously complex, unique, black *and* female, requiring what I might call a black female narrative logic or narratology for interpretation?

My comparative analysis of the domestic discourses of desire in *Their Eyes Were Watching God* and *Black Boy* yields my problematic. By yoking together the discourses of liberation and matrimony in the two incidents from these modern novels, I discern an antagonism on the part of the principal characters, who find that their notions about marriage and freedom do not peaceably coexist. Traditional African-American literary scholarship also reflects an antagonism toward marriage, which categorically prejudices its view of black women's domestic novels. The domestic novels center marriage; traditional scholarship valorizes freedom. The resulting antagonism demands interrogation: What are the temporal limitations of this antagonistic viewpoint of marriage and freedom? What historical factors induced and later disrupted the representation of racial desire as domestic tropes in the post-Reconstruction novels? In other words, how do the cultural values of black people of the post-Reconstruction era and their twentieth-century counterparts influence the textual meaning of these novels? These questions indicate the necessity of constructing an historicized reading model that is both gender *and* race sensitive for viewing black women's post-Reconstruction domestic novels as race literature and for restoring them to contemporary scholarly prominence.

The post-Reconstruction era was one historical period when a black readership would have been conditioned to read the black marriage story not as a discourse of domestic incarceration but as a liberational discourse. Therefore a crucial enterprise in my discussion about black women's domestic novels of that era is, first, theoretically reconstructing, from a late-twentieth-century black feminist perspective, a community of assumptions held by late-nineteenth-century black people regarding the institution of marriage and, second, hypothesizing the modes in which black women writers of that epoch represented their political as well as personal desires for the individual and racial self. Coming to these issues hermeneutically prompts me to ask whether late-nineteenth-century black people were generally apt to regard marriage in the same way as do a large portion of twentieth-century black male characters, like Richard does in the epigraph, that is, as a negation of personal autonomy, a negation of freedom? Or might post-Reconstruction black people have seen marriage as an opportunity for moving to a new institutional terrain on which struggle for political hegemony was to be played out in privatized terms? Might a representative black man of the post-Reconstruction era have referred to his wife, even in jest, as "the ball and chain"?[33] Or did access to civil marriage afford black people of this era an opportunity to define that institution as a means for achieving racial liberty and equality?

In an effort to construct answers to these questions, I direct my attention to reconstructing a theoretical consensus among postbellum black people about the centrality of marriage to social advancement. In this discussion I consider marriage primarily as a civil institution rather than a social one, thus more appropriate for discussion here than in the context of the legacy of antebellum, black female gender constructions. I begin the reconstruction by referring to the judicial and statutory definitions of the dominant society to which black people generally subscribed. Subsequently I refer to historical evidence of their collective domestic conduct, which I contend characterized their viewpoints of marriage and freedom. It is necessary to reconstruct these historicized viewpoints so that when we read the post-Reconstruction domestic novels written by black women we can read them as their first readers would have, that is, as race literature. From this perspective these novels appear political, indeed liberational.

John Bouvier's *A Law Dictionary Adapted to the Constitution and the Laws of the U.S.A.* and *Judicial and Statutory Definitions of Words and Phrases*, collected, edited and compiled by members of the editorial staff of the National Reporter System[34] provide the following composite of judicial and statutory definitions for marriage that are instructive for understanding how the dominant culture of nineteenth-century America regarded this institution. Marriage is defined as civil status, condition, and relation, created by a contract, which is regulated by law, that involves the mutual agreement of a man and a woman, competent to contract, to live together as husband and wife for the purpose of civilized society (*Judicial*, pp. 4390–93; Bouvier: 1883, p. 156; 1848, p. 116). "Unlike other contracts, [marriage] is the one instituted by God himself, and has its foundation in the law of nature" (*Judicial*, p. 4390). Thus marriage is the foundation of the family and indeed the very foundation of society, without which there would be neither civilization nor progress. Civilized society, then, is that management of human relationships and resources, serving to multiply, preserve, and improve the species through the procreation and education of children (*Judicial*, pp. 4390–93).

During the antebellum era, slaves could not enter into legal marriage because they had no civil status (Bouvier: 1848, p. 116). Although slaves might participate in slave marriages by "jump[ing] the broom" or "marry[ing] in blankets,"[35] a ceremony easily imagined, these extralegal marriages were not sanctioned by law, but were regulated by the caprice of slave owners. The history of slavery as well as its literary representations records the practice of slaves marrying and practicing monogamy to the best of their ability. However, such marriages were routinely dissolved at the auction block, where families were torn apart with bills of sale. In addition, because slave marriages existed outside of Western concepts of civil law, these unions also existed outside of Western concepts of morality, civilization, and human progress.

President Lincoln's Emancipation Proclamation of 1863 freed Negro slaves in the Confederate States still in rebellion. The Thirteenth Amendment to the Constitution completed the abolition of slavery throughout the United States in 1865. But it was the Fourteenth Amendment that granted citizenship to all black people who were born or naturalized in the United States, and citizenship conveyed gender-specific rights and responsibilities, especially prior to universal suffrage. Thus with its ratification in 1866, black people secured political status as civil entities. Black men secured enfranchisement, and black women secured political representation through male mediation. As citizens, black people became competent to enter into civil contractual obligations, of which marriage was clearly the most popular.

In his *The Black Family in Slavery and Freedom*, Gutman provides statistical evidence for the rates by which newly freed black people registered their slave marriages, and I suggest, affirmed their new civil status. He compares 1860 population figures for adult slaves throughout several Southern states, county by county, with the actual number of ex-slave marriages in the same regions in 1866. He finds that an unusually high number of ex-slaves legally reaffirmed their "common-law" marriages by purchasing "Negro Cohabitation Certificates" or securing marriage certificates by repeating their marriage vows, despite the fact that most former slave states had passed legislation automatically legalizing existing slave marriages (Gutman, pp. 411–13).

Such evidence supports the viewpoint that late-nineteenth-century black as well as white people were well aware of the social value invested in marriage as a sign of meritorious citizenship. Both groups staunchly sanctioned civil marriage as the vehicle for promoting family stability, social progress, and respectability; indeed, marriage was the sanctioned sign of civilization. Black people in particular regarded marriage as an important index of their propensity for civilization and as incontestable evidence for their moral commitment to social progress. In fact, many advocates for racial justice referred to the high marriage statistics for ex-slaves to counter popular retrogressionist arguments about the decline in morality among the newly freed blacks (Gutman, p. 429).[36] In this context, then, marriage has tremendous social value and utility as well as cultural interpretative significance. Exercising the civil right to marry, I am arguing, was as important to the recently freed black population as exercising another civil right, inscribed into the Constitution as the Fifteenth Amendment in 1879 — Negro suffrage. For black people, the importance of marrying in the private sphere of domestic affairs may have paralleled that of voting in the public sphere. For voting and marrying were signs of the race's ascent to high civilization. To vote and to marry, then, were two civil responsibilities that nineteenth-century black people elected to perform, twin indices for measuring how black people collectively valued their civil liberties.

The political discourse of citizenship is gender specific. To participate in the agency and rhetoric of that discourse, black people had to formulate gendered standards of civil performance. This is precisely the task that the domestic novels of black post-Reconstruction women embrace. These novels define for late-nineteenth-century black men and women ideal civility, morality, and piety in the contexts of individual and collective aspirations.

The aesthetic distance between late-nineteenth-century African Americans and us is considerable. While the expectations of race literature conditioned the first audience of post-Reconstruction domestic novels to regard them as defenses against racism, the expectations of black protest writing and the Black Arts movement have conditioned us to esteem as such only that literature that realistically depicts the material conditions of the majority of black people. This is precisely what black women's post-Reconstruction domestic novels do *not* do, for there is little representative social realism in these works. There are no familiar battles of interracial hostility here; neither is there any verbal play that we could associate with fighting words. As a consequence, when we read these texts transparently we see what appear to be simple stories about unquestioned faith in the American work ethic and the reward of Christian virtue, fashioned as genteel narratives of idealized, bourgeois domesticity. Whereas the very popular black literature of the twentieth century has taught us to expect racial conflict, not intraracial harmony, social realism, not domestic idealism, the first audience of the post-Reconstruction domestic novels expected heuristic and didactic meaning in fiction, an expectation that was affirmed in pleasurable, repetitive stories. For them, bourgeois domesticity, an assimilationist discourse for inspiring racial integration, was a politically liberal objective. For them, bourgeois domesticity was a part of a progressive enterprise of racial inclusion and was not a conservative conduct code or rhetoric for maintaining white male privilege under the mantle of preserving "family values," the family being implicitly understood as white and patriarchal.[37] Thus domestic tropology was a fundamental cultural feature of the nineteenth-century emancipatory discourse.

Like the domestic heroine in nineteenth-century British women's novels that

Nancy Armstrong identifies in *Desire and Domestic Fiction*,[38] the heroines of the post-Reconstruction novels accept marriage as central to their personal advancement, as central to the prosperity of their families and communities, indeed as central to the progress of civilization itself. Armstrong argues that the domestic heroine represents a sexual contract "for the enactment of a mutually beneficial exchange" of love, nurturance, and moral guidance for influence in public matters of the economy, society, and polity (pp. 31–42). I draw on her argument to reveal how the heroine of each post-Reconstruction novel relies on her position as an esteemed member of her community to regulate its social ambitions. Thus with the domestic responsibility of this heroine comes not quiet, isolated housebound duty but an obligation to provide moral, maternal, and material sustenance for the community within the text and in the world besieged by racial assault. In addition to revealing the social power of the exemplary heroine, "stories of courtship and marriage offered their readers a way of indulging, with a kind of impunity, in fantasies of political power that were the more acceptable because they were played out within a domestic framework" that did not threaten the patriarchal and, I add, racist order (Armstrong, p. 29). However, rather than simply indulging a fanciful desire for political power, I argue that the post-Reconstruction domestic novels provide their readers with practical lessons on how to effect their own personal success as well as civil reform under the cover of domesticity. For in "rewrit[ing] political history as personal histories that elaborate on the courtship procedures ensuring a happy domestic life," the domestic novels designate the admirable couple and the household respectively as the agents and the site of social reform (Armstrong, p. 38). This placement is a very important strategy of empowerment for African Americans of the "nadir" who possessed virtually no civil authority due to their categorical disenfranchisement and subjection to extensive segregation in addition to the racial terrorism of lynching and rape. Hence by expressing civil agency as a domestic rite, those otherwise powerless to confront the formidable and often impersonal domain of patriarchal racism achieve symbolic as well as actual power to resist its oppression.

Jane Tompkins's discussion of mid-nineteenth-century white American women's sentimental fiction in *Sensational Designs*[39] also assists me in discerning cultural agency in the post-Reconstruction domestic novels of black women. According to Tompkins, works like Susan Warner's *The Wide, Wide World* and Stowe's *Uncle Tom's Cabin* "do not attempt to transcribe in detail a parabola of events as they 'actually happen' in society; rather they provide a basis for remaking the social and political order in which events take place" (p. xvii). A similar intentionality seems reflected in the black post-Reconstruction novels. For their first readers this writing was by definition race literature; it was inspirational, indeed transformative, due to the fact that it was implicitly engaged in social warfare to fight retrogressionism, repudiate Jim Crow legislation, and promote the economic, educational, and moral advancement of black people. Thus by using Tompkins's reading strategy, which I quote at length below, the reader finds that the presumably artless idealized characters and formulaic plots in the black domestic texts become literary agents of cultural transformation:

> When literary texts are conceived as agents of cultural formation rather than as objects of interpretation and appraisal, what counts as a "good" character or a logical sequence of events changes accordingly. When one sets aside modernist demands—for psychological complexity, moral ambiguity, epistemological sophistication, stylistic density, formal economy— and attends to the way a text offers a blueprint for survival under a specific set of political, economic, social, or religious conditions, an entirely new story begins to unfold, and one's sense of the formal exigencies of narrative alters accordingly, producing a different conception of what constitutes successful characters and plots. (pp. xvii–xviii)

Tompkins's strategy tempers our "modernist demands" for artistic complexity and transparent political complaint. But when we late-twentieth-century readers rely on traditional protocols of reading, we are likely "to equate popularity with debasement, emotionality with ineffectiveness, religiosity with fakery, domesticity with triviality, and all of these, implicitly, with womanly inferiority" (Tompkins, p. 123). In addition, for us the wholesale adoption of the dominant society's bourgeois values is self-delusive. Moreover, we generally understand the central heroine's fulfillment of individuated desire not as a model to be replicated throughout the black population but as pretentious bourgeois egocentrism and romantic indulgence. Without suspending that traditional protocol, we are predisposed to condemn the extremely romanticized heroine and trivialize her text of social reform. We seem to have an affinity to those fictions that reflect our modern frustrations, chronic social alienation, and failures of faith—social and spiritual—rather than to those that extend tenuous assumptions about the rewards of willful self-advancement. However, for the first audience of these novels, the ideal heroine stood both within and above the group; she embodied their ambitions. As a representation of their personal and political desires, she reflected their conviction in the perfectibility of the black individual.

Theoretically recovering the cultural meaning that African Americans of the post-Reconstruction era invested in the marriage plot points to the urgency of historicizing other social practices and value constructions. This exercise in recovering temporally obscured cultural meaning also demonstrates the importance of interrogating the ideological assumptions embedded in social performances of our own epoch as well, for insinuated in them are arbitrary values that hegemonic systems have represented as natural, authentic, universal, unchanging. Projects in historicism are complicated largely because they seek to answer the silenced questions, questions that structures of dominance have represented as having indisputable answers or a priori assumptions. However, formulating critical reading models for recovering historically obscured cultural meaning greatly facilitates the process.

Hazel V. Carby's *Reconstructing Womanhood* provides a significant model, especially for reading the novels of post-Reconstruction black women writers, and I am particularly indebted to that study. It examines the early novels of Harper and Hopkins against late-nineteenth-century African-American history of political activism of black women who pressed for antilynching and anti-rape legislation as well as worked for women's suffrage and temperance. By carefully analyzing these novels in the context of self-authorized discourses of black womanhood that arise from "political lecturing" and "the politics of fiction" and other polemical works (p. 7), Carby convincingly argues the importance of historicizing these novels in order to gain access to the political meaning encoded in their plots.[40] *Reconstructing Womanhood*, then, "is a cultural history and critique of the forms in which black women intellectuals made political as well as literary interventions in the social formations in which they lived" (p. 7). Her study evolves "within the theoretical premises of societies 'structured in dominance' by class, by race, and by gender and is a materialist account of the cultural production of black women intellectuals within the social relations that inscribed them" (p. 17). Carby makes us critically aware that cultural scholarship cannot presume to analyze racism and sexism ahistorically. She also directs scholars to identify "historically specific forms of racism" and "gender oppression" so as to discern changing features in the dialectic between racial and sexual ideologies over time in the maintenance of white patriarchal power (p. 18).

My study—*Domestic Allegories of Political Desire*—builds on Carby's cultural critique as well as extends the critical models of Tompkins and Armstrong in order to highlight a particular aspect of the post-Reconstruction heroine's authority—her desire. By reading these novels as interventions in late-nineteenth-century social and literary ideologies, I regard black women's domestic novels as symbolic expressions of their own racial, sexual, and personal desires. I theoretically reconstitute those desires by juxtaposing the narrative features of their novels—plots, settings, character portraits, dialogue, for example—to the material, social, and cultural histories of black people at this time. By foregrounding desire in this way, my model features the disparate elements of desire: desire as wistful longing, reflective dream, emotional displacement, sanctioned aspiration, and practical ambition, conscious and unconscious, rational and irrational, potentially real or exclusively imaginary. By regarding the domestic novel's repetitive, female-centered story of ideal family formation within an equitable social context as the symbolic representation of desire, I read these novels as allegories of racial and sexual liberation, as plots of self-definition, self-individuation, indeed as quests that privilege an exploration of the black-female desiring subject of the post-Reconstruction era. These novels inscribe a uniquely female-gendered, racial proprietary authority in which the consummated marriage and resulting family represent realized social justice and personal aspirations. Hence I argue that the stories in these novels are domestic allegories of uniquely black *and* female political desire. The ideal domestic discourses in these novels form the plotting strategies of black female agency that were gratifying to their first readers precisely because of their commonplace experience with racial hostility. The popularity of these novels among those readers, which we can adjudge by their recurrence, arises from their ability to gratify vicariously that readership's desire for racial equality and female agency in the creation and maintenance of happy, productive families.

My model, then, foregrounds discourses of desire in literary culture, and arises out of an awareness that expressions of desire, like racial and sexual discourses, are historically conditioned. Desire, often disparate in form, compels authors to write, motivates their characters' actions, prompts readers to read, and even generates scholarly criticism. In fact, the works of author and scholar alike are textualized desire.[41] My interpretative model historicizes the racial, sexual, and personal desires of post-Reconstruction heroines so as to locate the major cultural forces that motivate the plotting of those desires in fiction. By reading the resulting plots as surface stories or domestic allegories, I seek to recover black female-centered expressions of political desire for a fully functional citizenship that have become obscured over time. In this context, the idealized civility of black women and men in the private realm as wives and husbands becomes a gendered paradigm for responsible citizens in the public realm.

4

Allegories of Gender and Class as Discourses of Political Desire

Kindred hopes and tastes had knit their hearts; grand and noble purposes were lighting up their lives; and they esteemed it a blessed privilege to stand on the threshold of a new era and labor for those who had passed from the old oligarchy of slavery into the new commonwealth of freedom.
FRANCES HARPER, *Iola Leroy* (1892)

United by love, chastened by sorrow and self-sacrifice, he and she planned to work together to bring joy to hearts crushed by despair.
PAULINE E. HOPKINS, *Contending Forces* (1900)

. . . when I saw what a good housekeeper she made for her aunt, I thought: 'Lottie is the girl to help a fellow get on in the world.'
AMELIA E. JOHNSON, *The Hazeley Family* (1894)

Black women's post-Reconstruction domestic novels used bourgeois gender conventions as an emancipatory text. The novels mediated the changing constructions of femininity at the turn of the century to define woman as exemplary citizen. At one extreme were authors who used their heroines to celebrate the roles of domestic nurturer, spiritual counselor, moral advocate, social activist, and academic teacher—feminine roles that Barbara Welter might have designated as extenuated aspects of "the cult of true womanhood" of the mid-nineteenth century. For this reason I term this ideal the "true black woman." At the other extreme were authors who celebrated the ideal "woman as the housewife, as the charming and resourceful superintendent of a blissful and attractive home."[1] For the purpose of distinction I term the latter the "charming lady."

In dramatizing "the image of [true] woman as 'the domestic educator,' the Christianizer and civilizer of the home" and "the woman of social compassion" (Wills, p. 3), the novels of Harper and Tillman in particular relied on heroines, to use Harper's words, "to do something of lasting service for the race" as writers, thinkers, and teachers.[2] Near the close of *Iola Leroy*, Harper depicted Iola "preparing to teach [and spending her] leisure time in study" (p. 270). After her marriage, though, Iola's teaching seems restricted to Sunday School. However, Lucille Delany, the novel's supporting heroine, more than fulfills Iola's initial desire. After marrying Iola's brother, "Harry and Lucille are at the head of a large and flourishing school" (p. 280). Tillman was more vigilant in preserving her heroine's professional resolve and commitment to public service; she had the heroine Beryl of *Beryl Weston's Ambition* achieve a career as college educator after her marriage and the birth of two children. These differences in female heroic ambition notwithstanding, both Harper and Tillman depicted female characters who quietly refuse to accommodate their society's increasingly conservative gender roles for women. Despite the fact that Harper (born in 1825) and Tillman (born in 1870) were of different generations, these two novels suggest that they were fervent believers in the mid-nineteenth-century ideology of love as duty.

By contrast, the ambitions of the new charming lady were directed toward the home, not the community, and she was not an equal partner in a mutually defined mission of social uplift for those less fortunate. Rather she was a sweet consoler, a competent household manager, and an obedient helpmate. Johnson dramatized this model in her novels *Clarence and Corinne* and *The Hazeley Family*.[3] To elaborate I refer to the heroine Corinne of the former novel. She "secure[s] a position as teacher" at the local school and "devote[s] herself to the [care of her foster parents]. . . . And Corinne was glad that she could prove her affection and gratitude . . . by lovingly and faithfully administering to them" (pp. 180–81). The novel provides no explanation for Corinne's decision to become a schoolteacher, other than implying that teaching facilitates caring for her foster parents. In fact there is no discussion of this aspect of her life, only the pronouncement. Neither is there any discussion about whether public service or self-willed ambition is appropriate for the heroine. Johnson's heroine Flora Hazeley enhances Corinne's characterization by extending the role of homemaker to become what Barbara Christian terms "a social housekeeper."[4] Flora embodies "the capacity to create a nurturing and beneficial space within which the family might flourish" (Christian, p. xxx). While Harper and Tillman closed their novels with heroines assuming authority for their lives and dedicating themselves to family nurturance and public service, Johnson's Corinne learns to relinquish self-authority, as evident by her repetition of the New Testament scripture of "Casting all your care upon him; he careth for you" (p. 135). This novel does not insinuate a heroine's text beyond the novel's ending. Rather it so centers the marriage portal of happy domesticity that marriage seems like the threshold of heaven, indeed a realm where personal volition is irrelevant. The text nevertheless incites the reader's sympathy for the downtrodden who seek to improve their circumstances, though there is virtually no interventionary discourse of direct feminine agency or female self-improvement.

Granted that this novel and others like it reiterate the conservative female gender prescriptions of white culture; nevertheless, the charming-lady heroine marks a radical change in antebellum black female gender constructions of relative sexual equality. Moreover, the charming lady in black society also seems an inversion of the "new [white] woman" who attended college, aspired to a professional career, and outwardly displayed her challenge to gender codes in what were then termed outrageous dress and manner.[5] The endorsement of the charming lady in black fiction was probably as much a product of the aspirations of many among the black middle class to gain social acceptance in the dominant culture by affirming its orthodox gender codes as that group's attending to the anxieties of white culture by masking assertive advocacy for broadly based social uplift behind the cover of genteel domesticity. Gender, then, became another terrain on which the battle for social equality and prosperity was fought.

As viewpoints about what constituted the ideal heroine became more problematic, the domestic novels of post-Reconstruction black women provided sites for mediating differences. What is particularly significant about these novels is that despite their different strategies for promoting racial progress and the enlargement of women's roles, these strategies all rely on ideologies of romantic and sentimental love and domesticity. By *ideology* I mean "an ordered system of cultural symbols" and "symbolic actions" that represent "a coherent, comprehensive set of beliefs."[6] Late-nineteenth-century black cultural beliefs are emplotted in these novels as social performances specifically about heterosexual love, courtship, matrimony, and domesticity.[7]

For example, in those domestic novels that explicitly protest racism, there is usually a symbolic contest between amorous desires of noble and corrupt intentions that reflect two conflicting political perspectives. Referring to the novels of Harper and Hopkins for illustration, we find that they dramatize the battle between racial oppression and social equality as the contest between honorable and dishonorable love for the self-identified heroine. In Harper's *Iola Leroy*, Iola's choice of the black Dr. Frank Latimer instead of the white Dr. Gresham dramatizes the novelist's refusal to discredit African-American identity, solidarity, and racial equality. In Hopkins's *Contending Forces*, the racially instigated rape of Sappho, qualifying her as a compromised woman, is displaced by Will Smith's proposal and enactment of marriage. In *Hagar's Daughter*, the battle between racism and racial equality is depicted twice as the contests of three white men—Enson Ellis, his brother St. Clair Ellis, and Cuthbert Sumner—for the mulatta heroine Jewel Bowen. The contests involve the strength of true love versus conviction in racist covenants. *Winona* plots the violent struggle between a white Englishman, Warren Maxwell, who genuinely comes to love the mulatta heroine Winona, and the Southern Colonel Titus, who regards her as a high-priced slave to be sold for his profit. Last, *Of One Blood* evolves as a contest between two men presumed white—Reuel Briggs and Aubrey Livingston (the former honorable, the latter not)—for the mulatta Dianthe Lusk. The conflict between oppression and liberation or equality, then, is plotted in Hopkins's novels in the ideology of true love. Hence the civil conflict of social equality is narrated symbolically as a private, sexual dispute among characters. By depicting their ideal heroines in marriage stories, Hopkins, Harper, and also Tillman not only revised the abolitionist equation between civil polity and household management. These writers also celebrated the institutions of domesticity—matrimony, home, and family—as important mediums for enhancing individual ego formation and promoting social progress through reform, whether through discrete domestic and community activity or through broadly based public activism.

In those domestic novels in which the racial discourses are reticent, particularly the works of Johnson and Kelley-Hawkins, the sexual contest becomes a much more abstract conflict between good and evil. Goodness is represented as justice, piety, or moral commitment, and evil is depicted as ill-treatment, unjust accusation, or social class prejudice. In Johnson's *Clarence and Corinne*, the impoverished Corinne, who is victimized much like Harriet Wilson's Frado, relieves her distress by trusting in God's will. In *The Hazeley Family*, Flora's devotion to improving the quality of other's lives, regardless of their station, is the perfect practice of Christian duty. Meg's resolve to remedy the unfair school dismissal of a poor student in Kelley-Hawkins's *Megda* is a metonym for protest against more explicit forms of institutional prejudice. The girls in *Four Girls* remedy the poverty of Charlotte Hood and find the means to restore the health of her son Robin, while Charlotte teaches the girls about the power of Christian faith, piety, and conviction. What is key in these novels is that one form of social oppression implies others, and its rectification is depicted as the Christian's spiritual and moral obligation. Like the domestic novels that are set in a black social context, reform in these racially reticent works is also plotted as courtship stories in which resolution of social conflict is confirmed by the novel's ending in marriage.

Perhaps even more interesting than the mediation of social conflict in the eleven domestic novels is that each responds to the conservative and liberal female-gender formations. For example, the heroes of all these novels desire wives in possession of different types of self-authority, ambition, and compassion, whether they are women with professional or only domestic ambitions. Some of these authors, as we shall see, go so far as to critique the encroachment of patriarchal privilege in their culture by allowing their heroines to have greater social freedom in the work than in the world. What is important for us to remember is that the system of domestic symbols for encoding an ideology of personal and general social advancement, like all such systems, changes over time; this is to say, that time eventually obscures the linkage between the symbolic network and the attitudes, beliefs, and conventions that constitute the symbols' original referents. With time, new and competing cultural symbols dislodge the old figurative patterns from their former ideological meanings. This is precisely what has happened to the ideological connection between ideal domesticity and civil liberty in black women's post-Reconstruction domestic novels, indeed, domestic novels in general. The figurative structures of these novels do not communicate their social significance to late-twentieth-century readers, due to the fact that more unreserved references to civil liberty have supplanted the old symbols. If readers can recover, at least in part, the dominant ideological codes of the post-Reconstruction period, these domestic novels can once again become politically readable. My study attempts to re-cover those codes by reconstructing the social desire of the novels' first read-ers. This reconstruction allows us to see the plots of desire in these novels as black woman-centered strategies of "emancipatory resocialization"[8] for late-nineteenth-century African Americans.

As descriptions of middle-class decorum, professionalism, family economy, and tasteful consumer consumption, all framed in courtship stories, these novels are allegories of desire—specifically domestic allegories of black politi-cal desire, public and private. They depict an ideal black family formation in which the realization of the heroine's conjugal happiness and personal fulfill-ment parallels community prosperity in the context of an equitable society. Several features call our attention to the allegorical nature of these novels: the repetition of the ideal marriage story, the striking disparity between the fictive context of social justice and the extreme racial oppression occurring in the real world during the actual period of the novels' production, and the perva-siveness of the Victorian viewpoint of corresponding male and female spheres of social influence, a duality that readily lends itself to the double-voiced discourse of allegory.

This repetitive story of extreme textual and contextual difference points to a deeper level of meaning for the story—its allegorical meaning. As cultural anthropologist James Clifford has explained, allegory calls our attention to "a practice in which a narrative fiction continuously refers to another pattern of ideas or events" and this practice has a specific pedagogic intent (p. 99). This is precisely my hypothesis—that post-Reconstruction domestic novels of black women are allegorical literary performances of political desire that (re)tell a surface story about an exemplary marriage and a deeper story about the social climate that would promote such a marriage. Hence the story about ideal family formation refers implicitly to another—a public discourse about an equitable political system that distributes rewards on the basis of personal integrity, commitment, and hard work. This external, largely unnarrated con-text makes the domestic story with its compatible and compassionate conjugal relationship possible by assuaging racial and/or other forms of social discrimi-nation. Hence these novels rely on domestic ideology to present "a whole new mythic narrative" specifically about racial and sexual desire for their readers to embrace.[9]

An allegorical reading of these novels draws our attention to features of cultural description as symbolic representation, not transparent presentation. These features entail self-authorized black womanhood in the context of civil justice, racial equality, relative sexual impartiality, and self-willed prosperity in a fluid class structure. A "recognition of allegory emphasizes the fact that realistic portraits [in the work], to the extent that they are 'convincing' or 'rich,' are extended metaphors, patterns of associations that point to coherent (theoretical, esthetic, moral) additional meanings" (Clifford, p. 100). By view-ing these novels as allegorical discourses of specifically black women's racial and sexual political desires, we can discern many of the ways in which their authors utilized a uniquely gendered narrative strategy to negotiate the re-entrenchment of racist oppression and rise of female gender conservatism within the black population during the post-Reconstruction period. The novels not only represent the desire for social equality but that for female agency, whether in the home or the community, in domestic tropes as well. In fact, the consummation of the domestic ideal of marriage, prescribed by the literary genre of domestic fiction, simultaneously signals the realization of both the liberational desires of the social protest and the sexual discourses in the story. Hence the racial and sexual discourses of desire in these fictions are mutually signifying.

The Intended Readers of Black Women's Post-Reconstruction Domestic Novels

Given these constructions of desire, the domestic stories incite a particular type of reader, one who readily shares an affinity for the dual discourses of racial and sexual desire, a reader whom Wolfgang Iser has called the "intended reader." The "intended reader" or "implied reader," as Iser explains, is conceived as an "heuristic construct."[10] My interpretation of the cultural significance of the domestic novels of post-Reconstruction black women throughout this study relies on precisely such a theoretically reconstructed reader.

While Iser conceives of his implied reader as strictly a theoretical construction, I supplement his theory with Hans Robert Jauss's work on aesthetic reception to recover an actual readership.[11] Together their works designate theoretical readers as well as two specific real-life first audiences for the post-Reconstruction domestic novels of black women: one real and ideally suited and the other real and sympathetic. Although the extreme racial segregation and prejudice at the turn of the century as well as the generic expectations of the pedagogy of sentimentality make it likely that the first readers of these novels were black and female, an actual sympathetic first reader could have been female or male, black or white. What all of these readers share is an affinity for the heroine's ambitions and a longing for the exemplary distribution of justice. What separates the sympathetic real reader from the ideal one is the latter reader's ability to cross the racial divide so as either to desire to emulate the personal development of the heroine (who may or may not be identified as black) or to desire a woman like that heroine as the object of affection.

I illustrate the reception of these two types of first readers—one ideal, the other sympathetic—by referring to Johnson's *Clarence and Corinne* (1890) and to the commentary about it written by the black educator I[rwin]. Garland Penn in his book *The Afro-American Press, and Its Editors*.[12] Here Penn, an ideal first reader, explained that this novel was published by the American Baptist Publication Society, a white publishing company. He insisted that "[t]he book was written from affection for the race, and loyalty to it, the author desiring to help demonstrate the fact that the colored people have thoughts of their own, and only need suitable opportunities to give them utterance" (pp. 425–26). The fact that Johnson placed the novel with a white publishing concern probably accounts for her deliberate employment of racially indefinite characters—or what Hortense J. Spillers has termed "ethnic neutrality"[13]—which, in turn, foregrounds a generic discourse about class equality and equal opportunity rather than one specifically about racial justice. Spillers goes on to explain (and I paraphrase) that while late-twentieth-century readers do not recognize the efficacy of Johnson's narrative strategy of racial and ethnic neutrality, her own contemporaneous black readers emphatically regarded the novel as an instrument of racial protest.[14] Spillers supports her observation by referring to Penn's discussion of Johnson's motivation for writing the novel. Spillers writes,

> [I]t is only through the black religious press that we understand more precisely why the perspective from which this work was produced appears (to contemporary readers) somewhat odd. Baltimore's *Baptist Messenger* decided that Johnson's narrative "is one of the silent, yet powerful agents at work to break down unreasonable prejudice, which is a hindrance to both races" (Penn, p. 426). From this angle, it is unimportant exactly *what* and *how* Mrs. Johnson wrote, but altogether significant *that* she did. Her contemporaries apparently saw the testimonial, exemplary force of her work as an instance of sociopolitical weaponry. (Spillers, p. xxviii, emphasis in original)

Such weaponry and racially indefinite characters did not work at cross purposes for Johnson's first readers. Apparently she conceded to the viewpoint that Alice Walker so aptly summarizes in her characterization of racially sympathetic nineteenth-century white readers. Walker contends that such readers

> more often than not . . . could identify human feeling, humanness, only if it came in a white or near white body. . . . the black-skinned woman, being dark and female, must perforce be whitened, since "fairness" was and is the standard of Euro-American femininity.[15]

Because black novelists of the post-Reconstruction era—female and male—had to appeal to a supportive white readership out of market demand and political necessity, those writers often shaped their works in ways to court the sympathy of that readership. By not designating the racial or ethnic identities of her characters, Johnson undoubtedly wanted her white readers to see them in the same light in which they saw themselves so as to foster their compassion for remedying the class prejudice that causes the characters' predicaments.

Penn's commentary also provides a portrait of the first sympathetic white reader and an excellent illustration of how the discourses of gender and social class status subvert through displacement the prejudice of the dominant society. Penn, who was a member of the novel's first audience, venerated Johnson in the words of the white periodical *The American Baptist* of Louisville, Kentucky: "'Mrs. Johnson has the deserved distinction of being the *first lady author* whose manuscript has been accepted by this society'" (p. 424, emphasis mine). By citing passages from *The Indianapolis Daily Journal*, *The Baltimore Baptist*, and *The Baptist Teacher*, three other white newspapers, he illustrated the wide public notice that her novel had received from members of the targeted, generally sympathetic white audience. However, unlike *The American Baptist*, each of the sympathetic entries in the latter papers respectively identifies Johnson as "the first colored woman to be thus honored," "a colored author," and "a colored writer" (Penn, p. 425). Hence these commentaries racialize their tributes and replace the class word "lady" with "woman," "author," or "writer." By contrast the ideal reader of *The American Baptist* erases the racial designation and refers, instead, to the dominant gender discourse, yielding the description of "lady author."[16] This is precisely the tactic that Johnson used throughout her novel; she shaped her work specifically in terms of class and gender. What was important for Penn and *The American Baptist* was that Johnson's character, training, and integrity designated her as a lady, irrespective of race.

This pattern of gender and social-class value formation recurs repeatedly in the domestic novels of post-Reconstruction black women. Gender and social-class designations displace discourses of prejudicial racial difference. By relying on a bourgeois construction of the merit of the individual, the ideal reader emphasizes class fluidity and deemphasizes race. Such a displacement would be ineffective as a strategy of social intervention if Johnson's readers had not already been conditioned to regard this form of displacement as a mode of racial affirmation (and by implication of racial protest) as well. What is essential to remember is that while we contemporary readers do not generally recognize this mode of protest as an unreserved and forceful disruption of racial prejudice, Johnson's intended readership regarded the novel as "a powerful [agent] . . . to break down unreasonable prejudice, which is a hindrance to both races" (Penn, p. 426). Penn's commentary further recovers that racial meaning for us by expressing Johnson's strong commitment to racial uplift. He wrote,

> The author of "Clarence and Corinne" feels confident that there are those among the race who needed only to know that there is a way where there is a will, to follow her example, and no doubt far surpass this, her first experience in book-making; and she is happy in knowing that come what may, she has helped her people. (p. 426)

What we should also remember is that in publishing the novel as a self-identified African-American author, "the wife of a noted and successful Baltimore pastor" (Penn, p. 425), Johnson made the act of writing in itself politically and racially charged, irrespective of the silenced racial discourse in her novels.

The Politics of Desire

The racial plot of desire in the domestic novels of post-Reconstruction black women arises from frustrated civil ambitions but evolves from envisioning the enforcement of constitutional law. Its complementary sexual plots of personal and professional desire are gendered extensions of civil aspirations inside and outside of the sanctity of the family domain. For without political justice black families as well as personal and professional enterprises face both economic and psychological devastation. This duality of public and private desire is represented in the novels as domestic tropes, whose consummation signals their mutual satisfaction. These discourses of desire can also be characterized as "intentional structures [because they are] goal-oriented and forward-moving," to use the words of Peter Brooks.[17] Brooks sees "[d]esire as a narrative thematic, desire as a narrative motor, desire as the very intention of narrative language and the act of telling all [of which] seem to stand in close interrelation" (p. 54). While Brooks sees desire as both the force and the substance of narrative, poet and essayist Audre Lorde contends that the source of power for desire lies in the erotic. The erotic is "an assertion of the life force," a "creative energy empowered," which is "self-affirming in the face of a racist, patriarchal, and anti-erotic society."[18] She adds that

> The erotic is a measure between the beginnings of our sense of self and the chaos of our strongest feelings. It is an internal sense of satisfaction to which, once we have experienced it, we know we can aspire. For having experienced the fullness of this depth of feeling and recognizing its power, in honor and self-respect we can require no less of ourselves. (p. 54)

Desire here exceeds sexual pleasure to become consummate self-affirmation, a confirming life force charged with transformative power. A focus on the erotic, then, in the post-Reconstruction domestic novels, to draw on Lorde's words and to extenuate her theory, reveals them as celebrations of "the deepest feelings [of their authors and first readers, who] . . . beg[a]n to give up . . . being satisfied with suffering and self-negation and with the numbness which so often seems like their only alternative" (p. 58). "In touch with the erotic, [they were] less willing to accept powerlessness" (Lorde, p. 58), and the authors used their writings as expressions of politicized erotic power. As a result their heroines seek an ideally compatible spouse who is simultaneously a reflection of the self and the loving "other." Together they affirm themselves as ideal African-American citizens who nurture the community as their family. The politicized erotic power of the extended exemplary family is a sign of black bourgeois prosperity.

I refer to a contemporary facsimile to illustrate this point—"The Cosby Show." Although these novels, like the television show, repeatedly depict happy domesticity, both have other social intentions. Both are deliberately "plotted" strategies, as Brooks might explain, to unsettle many of our negative racial assumptions about black family life. I take a moment here to elaborate, for the familiar "Cosby Show" provides a basis for demonstrating how ideal bourgeois domesticity in a black social context influences the social attitudes of viewers.

In episode after episode, romance not only is sustained after more than two decades of marriage, but more important, is characterized by tenderness, humor, compassion, and creativity. These qualities in turn are represented in the semiotic of bourgeois consumerism—gift giving and celebratory consumption of food and entertainment—made possible by an equitable distribution of goods, services, opportunity, and rewards. This is a bourgeois construction of Lorde's "uses of the erotic."[19] Marginal in "The Cosby Show" are the exhibitions of flamboyant sexuality, "super stud" verbal bravado, and flashy consumer extravagance that were so prevalent during the 1970s in media productions like "Shaft" that this version of black (folk or working-class) sexuality became standardized. In the "super stud" shows there was little display of ardent titillation between the lovers (who were seldom married) due to the "let's get it on" objective, represented by sexually enticing clothing and explicitly seductive verbal playfulness.

My point is not to celebrate bourgeois domesticity but to point out that its performance in "The Cosby Show" promotes another form of black desire—a middle-class eroticism—that falls outside racist stereotypes of oversexed black people, and that eroticism is fundamentally political. Claire and Cliff Huxtable characterize spousal romance, foster a compassionate family, participate in the bourgeois economy, and regulate a gender exchange of virtual equality at home and at work; all are characteristics *not* routinely associated with black families because retrogressionism has survived the Civil Rights and Black Power movements as well as the Rainbow Coalition. Hence "The Cosby Show" repudiates the hundred-year-old retrogressionism by affirming social desires about black middle-class values and seeks to erase a broad spectrum of racist attitudes from its white viewers who have been conditioned to define themselves in opposition to the black deficient Other.

But in so doing the show marginalizes the masses of people of color who cannot or choose not to participate in a bourgeois economy, as well as those who demand that this economy be self-critical. The Huxtables are hardworking achievers, but their personal success should not suggest "that blacks are solely responsible for their social conditions, with no acknowledgement of the severely constricted life opportunities that most black people face."[20] In many episodes the Huxtables are cut off from the material circumstances of the black working class as well as from the real-life conditions of the black middle class. For example, the Huxtables evidently have no trouble attracting the attention of New York City taxicab drivers; neither are they victims of routine discrimination, as when white salesclerks ignore them to attend to the needs of white customers. Their children have no problems with "red lining." Crack cocaine dealers sell outside their urban neighborhood. And although they live in New York City, they have never been burglarized, robbed, or assaulted. The Huxtables live in a pleasant racially diverse urban community with no dramatized history of its origins. Indeed, the world of the Huxtables is a visionary world much like the world of the post-Reconstruction domestic novels. No doubt the new role of Cousin Pam is a vehicle for tying these ideal Huxtables to the real world with a long string.[21] For Pam's job is to sustain a black working-class critique of those pretty people in their beautiful brownstone and to emphasize the work ethic as the viable means of class mobility for the black population. "The Cosby Show" situates the desire of the racial-ized Other—whether black and privileged or black and poor—as agent in a plot of expectations associated with the dominant bourgeois culture—a plot of equitable, capitalistic opportunity—rather than maintains an exclusive im-perial discourse of opposition in which Others of color are inherently deficient and therefore unalterably external to opportunity, reward, and resulting do-mestic harmony.

Like "The Cosby Show," the post-Reconstruction domestic novels are delib-erately plotted strategies for playing out their authors' bourgeois racial and sexual desires and for sharing the satisfaction of the play with first readers through the act of reading. To invoke Roland Barthes's terminology, the nov-els are *figurations* of black women's desire for an ideal black polity inside and outside of the home.[22] By figuration I mean that these novels present that desire in their fictive worlds rather than represent the already existing social order that exists external to the text. Thus the domestic novels of post-Reconstruction black women are not interested in representing the racial and sexual restrictions that oppress them. To the contrary, they envision, create, figure social realms of their own desire in print. The playing out (or figuration) of fictive racial and sexual desires—the latter specifically for requited female love, an enlarged female sphere of professional activity (albeit in some in-stances, the professionalization of housewifery that came into currency at the turn of the century), and equal opportunity in a bourgeois capitalistic econ-omy—is not merely gratuitous. The play is most importantly the author's method for indirectly reproaching the prejudicial social climate and motivating first readers to emulate the heroine's personal, domestic, and public interests. By so doing these readers became agents in the enterprise of racial justice and uplift, even if only at the level of the individual family.

Embedded in these post-Reconstruction domestic novels of black female authorship, then, is a deep structural plot of gendered racial desire that moves to fruition as the narrative moves to closure with marriage. In work after work, as we shall see, the heroine's commitment to her individual achievement shapes a parallel story about courtship and marriage, transforming the text into a complex narrative of female development. When the heroine also em-braces racial (or reformist) desire, the plots of courtship and female profes-sional development engage an enlarged object of desire, the prosperity of the community as well as the family. By uncovering the racial and gendered plot-ting structures of desire in these allegorical fictions, we can see that these are not merely fanciful narratives about escaping the politics of racial oppression, as traditional scholarship has contended,[23] but stories about racial justice and female autonomy.

The desire for social equality, which these novels represent in domestic figuration, reflects black people's chronic quest for civil liberty, a quest that has been and continues to be fundamental to virtually all aspects of their lives. Thus, what I am arguing here is that these works portray not just the desire for racial justice but for enlarged female opportunity as well. Most important, in the novels these discourses of desire are satisfied, not deferred. Thus the plotting of desire in the black female texts is substantially different from that in corresponding male texts, in which the hero's desire for public respect is repeatedly frustrated. As mentioned above, the gender designation here does not refer to the sexual identity of the author or the central character but rather to feminine or masculine gender conventions associated with the work's discursive authority.

Black female narrative desire in the domestic novels is decidedly plural, that is to say, dialogic, due to its mediating both black male and female domestic and civil desires, on the one hand, and the racialist codes of the post-Reconstruction period as well as the social constructions of bourgeois esteem on the other. These dialogic discourses make the female generic narratives of racial desire seem more opaque, thus more symbolic, because they rely on what Susan Winnett has called "situational-thematics" that fall outside the traditional masculine framework with which twentieth-century readers have become familiar.[24] Under these circumstances, these female plots of desire require more interpretation to uncover their meanings. By contrast, the plots of desire in the corresponding generic male texts of racial protest seem much more transparent due to their celebration of a familiar story about the struggle for male power—the patriarchal plot or "Freud's masterplot" (Brooks, pp. 90–91). In a racialized context, this master plot of male desire for political power seems clearly mimetic rather than symbolic (or formulaic) because it represents instead of transcends the then current social order. As a result we know well the interpretative code for its representation and employ it automatically. Not only do we readily recognize black patriarchal desire, we also readily recognize its frustration due to the fact that white hegemony repeatedly defeats the realization of that desire in both the real and fictive realms. Despite their differences, though, the plots of desire in both the male and female texts share a common basis of narrative drive; the desire for racial justice propels each story forward.

In the female text the three mutually signifying plots about racial, professional, and conjugal ambitions advance together as the heroine realizes that each is mutually interconnected. As the narrator uses the heroine to incite corresponding desire in the reader, the narrator, and reader collaborate in reading and advance the heroine to the ideal culmination of the dominant domestic discourse of the text—marriage. The emphatic culmination of one plot line with the heroine's marriage, then, signals the climax of the other two plots as well. Matrimonial "desire as narrative thematic, [matrimonial] desire as narrative motor, and [matrimonial] desire as the very intention of narrative language and the act of telling all seem to stand in close relations" in these racialized domestic novels (Brooks, p. 54).[25] As the heroine embraces the object of her desire in the compassionate husband at the text's close, the reader vicariously shares the heroine's satisfaction. The reader's pleasure is short-lived, however, not simply because it is an imaginary construction but also because the heroine's fictive world critiques the reader's real world. The text's projection of fulfilled racial desire onto an imaginary fictive topography thus incites the reader to work for a nurturing, liberated household and community in the real world (and to read another domestic fiction for more vicarious pleasure and fortification of worldly resolve).

Domestic Narrative as Racial Discourse

By referring to the commonplace abolitionist equation of the nineteenth century between domestic ideology and reformist discourse, we are empowered to recognize these domestic novels' opposition to institutional forms of social injustice. Harper called our attention to this relationship in the epilogue to her 1892 novel *Iola Leroy*, which is representative particularly of those domestic novels with explicit racial content. Contending that her story is a symbolic expression of racialized desire, she wrote,

> From the threads of fact and fiction I have woven a story whose mission will not be in vain if it awaken in the hearts of our countrymen a stronger sense of justice and a more Christlike humanity in behalf of those whom the fortunes of war threw, homeless, ignorant and poor, upon the threshold of a new era. Nor will it be in vain if it inspire the children of those upon whose brows God has poured the chrism of that new era to determine that they will embrace every opportunity, develop every faculty, and use every power God has given them to rise in the scale of character and condition, and to add their quota of good citizenship to the best welfare of the nation. (p. 282)

When we late-twentieth-century readers cast black women's post-Reconstruction domestic narratives of ideal black family life against both the hostile interracial climate and the pervasive poverty of black people of that period, these narratives may seem like fantastic stories of wish fulfillment. However, I must reiterate that they are not altogether mimetic. They assert a new "epistemology of representation" that refuses to assume that art duplicates reality and "re-presents something both external and prior to the work of fiction."[26] To make the authenticity of black literary culture dependent on external social reality fundamentally reinscribes the authority of white patriarchal hegemony, which is precisely what has occurred in the critically acclaimed works of so-called "black social realism." Rather than challenge that hegemony by envisioning emancipatory possibilities, such works basically reify the power that they protest, making it obvious why the dominant literary culture has celebrated discourses of realism. As Wahneema Lubiano astutely has observed, realism and liberational discourses are inherently problematic: "Realism poses a fundamental, long-standing challenge for counter-hegemonic discourses, since realism, as a narrative form, enforces an authoritative perspective."[27] The authors of the post-Reconstruction domestic novels abandoned the oppressive racial reality of their collective experience to effect in fiction their political desires for racial equality and an enlarged domesticity. Their works are allegorical (and formulaic) representations of the consequences of the daily implementation of constitutional ideals and Christian tenets that were to permeate U.S. national character, cast from the vantage point of black female citizenry.

Allegorical depictions of the desire for racial equality and social prosperity repeatedly recur in black women's post-Reconstruction domestic novels as discourses of "Negro Improvement." While the corresponding male texts typically rely on polemics that evolve as explicit arguments about the immorality of racial injustice, the female texts tend not to do so, but rather rely on settings, tone, and "situational thematics" that call attention to an affirmed, ideal black domesticity as the site of improvement. These texts are habitually set within small, cozy, domestic-like spaces (in households, especially in kitchens, parlors, and girls' bedrooms, or in girls' schools). Although the situational thematics of ideal family formation displace the external site of interracial conflict, the first readers of the domestic novels no doubt regarded the home setting as racially affirming, comparable to public racial protest about thwarted black male ambition because they were very familiar with the politics of uplift of their day. "From Booker T. Washington to Marcus Garvey," historian Wilson J. Moses has rightly contended,

> the proponents of "Negro Improvement" argued that the proper way for black people to secure their fortune was by changing themselves rather than by attempting to change their environment. Under slavery, the Negro Improvement tradition had not addressed itself directly to the cause of immediate abolitionism. Rather it sought to demonstrate the Afro-American's fitness for emancipation by proving the fitness of black people for freedom. Schemes for black uplift were associated with the trade school movement in the Northern states, and with the back to Africa movement. The Negro Improvement advocates believed that if black culture could be developed both at home and in Africa, whites would be inclined to believe in the black man's worthiness for inclusion in American life. There was only one thing wrong with such programs. They did not take into account that prejudice is irrational. No matter how much the Afro-American people achieved, they would still be victims of prejudice. Racism is blind to achievement.[28]

I refer once again to the conduct manual *Golden Thoughts*,[29] specifically to an illustration from that work to characterize the "Negro Improvement" agenda of willful self-reformation (Figure 4). The lesson depicted here makes personal conduct the qualifier of the condition of an individual life. Thus if the black boy in the picture avoids "cigarettes and self-abuse, impurity and dissipation, vice and degeneracy," in favor of "study and cleanliness" as well as "purity and economy," he will achieve "honorable success" and "venerable old age." Unlike the first readers of *Golden Thoughts* and the domestic novels, though, we late-twentieth-century readers find that the ideology of willful self-advancement and domestic displacement of political desire are problematic, probably because the former was always compromised to hege-

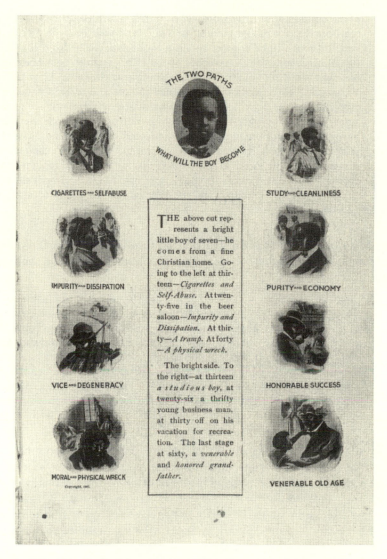

Figure 4. "The Two Paths," from *Golden Thoughts*, 1903. Courtesy of the Afro-American Studies Resource Center, Howard University.

monic forces and the latter was largely a failed strategy. Consequently we tend not to discern the ideal domestic setting of these novels as a site of political desire among black people but as one primarily concerned with evading racial subjugation.

While we find the optimism of these novels troublesome, their first readers shared that optimism. Dickson D. Bruce, Jr., has provided a particularly perceptive analysis of their optimism. Thus I quote him at length:

> [T]he combination of gentility with protest was especially well suited to the post-Reconstruction period. In 1877, and well into the 1880s, there was still much to be hopeful about in race relations. If, from the perspective of hindsight, the catastrophes of the 1890s seem to have been inevitable, they were not so clearly comprehensible at the time. After all, in the 1870s and 1880s, black men continued to vote and to hold public office, especially in the South. Public accommodations were still integrated in some places. The fight for equality was not by any means viewed as a losing battle; worsening conditions appeared to be nothing more than a temporary setback. The early black historian William Alexander caught something of this mood in 1887; in reviewing recent difficulties, he suggested that such problems should simply inspire black Americans to "renewed exertion," arguing that "the possibilities for them, as a race, are boundless."[30]

Bruce goes on to explain that the genteel tradition in early African-American literature was an expression of black peoples' social optimism, and not a discourse of self-delusion:

> The genteel literature produced by post-Reconstruction black writers was a measure of their optimism about the possibilities for the future. There was nothing evasive about observing genteel themes and conventions. Racial barriers were not seen as impregnable. Given this point of view, genteel literature conveyed the fully assimilationist message at the heart of black middle-class racial ideas during the post-Reconstruction era, as black writers claimed their right to and their desire for recognition as Americans. (p. 32)

With the advantage of hindsight we contemporary readers know that their optimism was ill-fated. This mistaken judgment among the black women writers of the post-Reconstruction period does not disavow the political intentionality that they invested in their domestic discourses. For as Wilson Moses adds in his discussion of the "Negro Improvement" agenda, not only did turn-of-the-century black people not anticipate the irrationality of racism; they also did not expect Victorian social values to change:

> What was to guarantee that when black people had accomplished certain achievements, the achievements would still be considered important? If black people were to achieve a genteel standard of [V]ictorian sexual conduct, for example, could it be guaranteed that Victorian morality would always be important to Americans? (Moses, p. 964)

Bruce's and Moses's discussions of the racial attitudes, motivations, and ambitions of post-Reconstruction African Americans are particularly instructive for late-twentieth-century readings of the domestic novels under examination here, for those discussions allow us to understand the pervasive optimistic tone, characters, settings, and incidents of the domestic novels as both symbolic representations and strategies (ill-fated and myopic though they were) for attaining black political power during and after the 1890s. The focus on domestic settings and family formation in these works then becomes an index of late-nineteenth-century black people's middle-class ambitions, whose acquisition was in turn the political goal of racial protest. Without this theoretical black feminist reconstruction of political intentionality, these stories would appear to have no connection to the social reality of black people's lives at that historical moment and would instead seem like isolated fantasies of romantic and sentimental love in which the latter exalts sexual difference and the former requires frustration to sustain ideal desire.[31]

Bruce's first passage is remarkably similar to the following excerpted from the 1924 novel *There Is Confusion* by Jessie Fauset.[32] Together both passages suggest how pervasive and enduring the discourse of racial optimism was during and the decade after the era of post-Reconstruction. Fauset's passage refers to an incident in Philadelphia around 1899 in which Joel Marshall, the father of the heroine Joanna, explains that she must not let racial prejudice restrict her ambitions:

> Joel believed that all things were possible. "Nothing in reason," he used to tell Joanna, "is impossible. Forty years ago I was almost a pauper in Richmond. Look at me to-day. I spend more on you in a month, Joanna, than my mother and I ever saw in a five-year stretch. One hundred years ago and nearly all of us were slaves. See what we are now. Ten years ago people would have laughed at the thought of colored people on the stage. Look at the bill-boards on Broadway."

Although Joel measures his success here solely in terms of money, and thus appears as a somewhat naive proponent of bourgeois aspirations, money provides a very practical racial service for those in the middle class. Having money reduces middle-class black people's exposure to the more flagrant forms of racial discrimination. Therefore domestic fictions that celebrate black professionalism as the means of acquiring money for purchasing homes also promote strategies for avoiding the more extreme indignities of racism. As Fauset went on to explain in the novel, black homes accommodate social performances normally associated with public facilities:

> Like many of the better class of colored people, the Marshalls did not meet with the grosser forms of color prejudice, because they kept away from the places where it might be shown. This was bad from the standpoint of the development of civil pride and interest. But it had its good results along another line. The children took most of their pleasures in their house or in those of their friends and devoted their wits and young originality to indoor pastimes. (p. 49)

The domestic site in *There Is Confusion*, as well as those in the precursory post-Reconstruction domestic novels, promotes strategies for swelling the ranks of the black middle class and middle-class aspirants. Both groups use the privilege of that social class to assault and to withstand racial prejudice and discrimination in order to assert and preserve what Fauset called "the spirit of life, of ambition and hopefulness" (p. 51) among African Americans.

An excerpt from Chapter III — "Meg an Home" — of Emma Dunham Kelley-Hawkins's *Megda* (1891)[33] illustrates the typical domestic setting of the post-Reconstruction novels. This setting inscribes middle-class desire as the sign of social justice:

> Meg's appearance in the small, cozy kitchen was welcomed in the usual way. The mother had a fond, loving smile for her; Elsie [Meg's older sister] a kiss and soft little pat for each cheek; Hal [her older brother] a boyish hug and pinch of the pretty ear; and Meg received the welcome in her usual way. To the mother an answering smile; to Elsie a loving but careless kiss; to Hal a playful box on the ear and a laughing— (p. 27)

Evident here is no social anxiety, only familial playfulness. The story's conflicts are set within a context of domestic stability; while conflict may momentarily agitate individuals, it does not disrupt this stability.

With this setting I compare one found in a typical black male text of the same period. This passage from Charles Chesnutt's *The Marrow of Tradition*[34] depicts the familiar consequences of segregated rail travel for a black person at the turn of the century. Here Dr. Miller is traveling with a white colleague:

> When the train conductor made his round after leaving the station, he paused at the seat occupied by the two doctors, glanced interrogatively at Miller, and then spoke to Dr. Burns, who sat in the end of the seat nearest the aisle.
>
> "This man is with you?" he asked, indicating Miller with a slight side movement of his head, and a keen glance in his direction.
>
> "Certainly," replied Dr. Burns curtly, and with some surprise. "Don't you see that he is?"
>
> [The conductor walks away, and after several minutes returns.]
>
> "Excuse me, sir," said the conductor, addressing Dr. Burns, "but did I understand you to say this man was your servant?"
>
> "No, indeed!" replied Dr. Burns indignantly. "The gentleman is not my servant, nor anybody's servant, but is my friend. But, by the way, since we are on the subject, may I ask what affair it is of yours?"
>
> "It's very much my affair," returned the conductor. . . . "I'm sorry to part friends, but the law of Virginia does not permit colored passengers to ride in white cars. . . . The law gives me the right to remove him by force. I can call on the train crew to assist me, or on the other passengers. If I should choose to put him off the train entirely, in the middle of a swamp, he would have no redress—the law so provides. If I did not wish to use force, I could simply switch this car off at the next siding, transfer the white passengers to another, and leave you and your friend in possession until you were arrested and fined or imprisoned." (pp. 52–55)

Domestic scenes, like the previous excerpt from *Megda*, are stock events in the domestic novels, while the scene depicting interracial conflict, as in the excerpt from *The Marrow of Tradition*, represents the site of interracial contest typically found in corresponding male texts. These are symmetrical events. However, the heroine's domestic displacement of civil politics here is a tactic for inscribing racial affirmation in the security of domestic resilience, a tactic illustrated as well in Tillman's 1893 domestic serial novel, *Beryl Weston's Ambition: The Story of an Afro-American Girl.*[35]

In an early scene in this novel we find a pretty, young, identifiably black heroine, Beryl Weston, taking the train to Tennessee, presumably from a Northern city, without any mention of the Jim Crow car. Railway segregation was an undeniable reality of Tillman's day due to the facts that in 1884 the U.S. Supreme Court overturned the Civil Rights Act of 1875 and shortly thereafter the Supreme Court of Tennessee ruled that segregated transportation was constitutional.[36] Unlike *Megda*, in which there are no scenes in public places, in *Beryl Weston's Ambition* Tillman presented a public transportation scene comparable to that in Chesnutt's *Marrow of Tradition* (published a few years later). But unlike Chesnutt, she used her authorial power to transform the typical racial episode in the passenger car into what seems like an intimate tea party for the initial encounter of her heroine and her future husband, Dr. Norman Warren:

> While Beryl was speaking, the train came steaming into the depot, and the good-byes were hastily exchanged. The good-natured porter found Beryl a pleasant seat and she soon became so absorbed in thought as to be utterly oblivious to her surroundings. . . . Presently the train stopped, and the gentleman who had been watching Beryl so closely, got up and left the couch, and Beryl noticed him for the first time.
>
> He was a splendid type of Afro-American manhood. . . . To Beryl's surprise, upon the stranger's return (for the train stopped about a quarter of an hour), he brought her some fresh rolls and a cup of tea. (pp. 209–11)

At first look it is difficult to determine whether Tillman assumed that her intended readers were already much too familiar with railway segregation to require an explicit reference to the Jim Crow car (for the scene fails to mention public accommodation), or whether the expressed deletion may have represented her calculated refusal to accept the legitimacy of railway segregation. A close reading of this scene, however, reveals that neither is the case. We note that the porter (who would have undoubtedly been black) and not the conductor (who would have undoubtedly been white) finds a comfortable seat for Beryl in a (possibly) segregated car. In addition, the parenthetical remark about the train being stopped, presumably at a railway station in a town, is not merely a narrative detail but a probable sign of the public accommodations on the train being prohibited for black people. This incident (marked by parentheses and thereby accorded meager discursive status) plausibly provides the "splendid" black gentleman, seated across from Beryl, an opportunity to leave the train to purchase refreshments for her, thus advancing the courtship scenario.

Near the close of the scene the reader discerns that what has appeared to be a romantic effacement of racism is not an erasure of Jim Crow transportation legislation but actually a subtle interplay of historical chronology that sets the train incident in the mid 1880s, before compulsory segregation became rampant, and not in the 1890s, when the novel was published.

By delaying the explicit reference to chronology, that is, by allowing temporal markers to emerge only after Beryl is seated, after the handsome stranger has brought her refreshments, and also after he has returned to reading his newspaper, Tillman elicited two temporal settings. She did so probably because contemporaneous readers, like us, were likely to assume a setting nearly concurrent with the novel's publication date. The polite conversation between the heroine and the stranger about their destinations provides the story's actual temporal setting:

> "I am on my way to Westland, Tennessee," replied Beryl.
> "Can it be possible? That is my own destination." . . . [He shows Beryl a photograph of his mother, explaining,] . . . "I haven't seen her for twenty years. I was born under slavery's cursed ban, and sold from my mother at the age of seven." (p. 212)[37]

A few pages later we learn that Beryl's mother "had been a lady's maid in the days of slavery" (p. 213); thus, if Beryl is in her late teens, not too many decades can have transpired. The same is true for the handsome stranger, who was born in slavery but who is at the time of the story in the prime of masculine vigor. In addition, half-way into the narrative the stranger, Norman Warren, purchases the recently published race books—George Washington Williams's *History of the Negro Race* and William J. Simmons's *Men of Mark*—which appeared in 1883 and 1887, respectively. Hence Tillman's railway scene presents a series of realistic, carefully constructed events that marginalize explicit encounters with the racist transportation laws of her day as well as recall what railway travel was like during a less restrictive period of post-Reconstruction. These indirect and discreet narrative features allow Tillman to manipulate the temporal setting and the circumstances of the characters' journey so as to preserve the dignity of black passengers as well as imply the racist conditions of rail travel at the time of the story's production.

At first glance the scene suggests a romantically indulgent author. However, Tillman was not engaged in a flight of romantic fantasy away from the racial realities of her day. While she presented a series of events that were credible, given the social climate of the 1890s as well as the mid 1880s, she also fashioned exemplary black characters who are not frustrated by racism. Thus Tillman presented her scene so as to, on the one hand, adhere to the racist limitations of the late nineteenth century and, on the other, promote black civil liberty and suggest the possibility of realizing individual aspirations despite racist conventions.

Difference in narrative focus and its resulting plot of desire surfaces by comparing the railway scene in Tillman's novel with the one excerpted above from Chesnutt's corresponding black male text, *The Marrow of Tradition*. Instead of using the railway setting as a site of racial protest, as Chesnutt did, Tillman did not allow racial issues to dominate her story. Instead she shifted the narrative focus to a romantic encounter between a handsome stranger and her heroine Beryl Weston. Rather than dramatize Beryl's confrontation with racism, the text switches the racial code of protest to the gendered code of courtship; it displaces the interracial discourse of civil political protest with an intraracial domestic discourse of desire. Hence Tillman's story converts racial protest into racial affirmation and renders political desire as a black woman-centered domestic allegory. This code switching is the single most important discursive strategy that drives the domestic allegory of political desire in this particular work and in the ten other domestic novels in this study.

The eleven domestic novels feminize and privatize (or neutralize) the racial discourse by placing it into an intraracial context of social harmony that initiates the heroine's courtship. The novels, then, become allegorical, micro depictions of realized racial desire or racial affirmation, cast specifically as female-centered stories of black, idealized, bourgeois domesticity. Corresponding male texts of frustrated civil liberty depict racial protest as the familiar, polemical social discourse. Despite these differences, the deep structural plots of desire or the motivating agencies for both male and female stories are their authors' shared dedication to advancing the social equality of African Americans. As we can see, this embedded discourse of desire surfaces differently in the texts advancing male and female narratologies, assuming what appear to be gender-specific strategies of representation.

We late-twentieth-century readers readily recognize the racial discourse in texts like Chesnutt's *The Marrow of Tradition* largely because our reading history has been shaped by black male writers—Frederick Douglass, Charles Chesnutt, James Weldon Johnson, Langston Hughes, Jean Toomer, Richard Wright, Ralph Ellison, and James Baldwin,[38] for example—who were commonly included in the undergraduate curriculum after 1968. These writers fulfilled the critical expectations of traditional scholarship largely because they responded to the black protest tradition by inscribing discourses of black male desire that evolve from black male experiences, perspectives, ambitions, and patriarchal prerogatives (though all are usually contested).[39] Such texts make racial protest appear as the desire for black–white patriarchal parity. Hence the measure of racial equality here seems an extension of white patriarchy to the black male protagonist so that he may share its privileges, specifically what Valerie Smith designates "its definitions of manhood and power" and which, according to Deborah McDowell, include "the rights [of] ownership of wives and children."[40] Racial rage transforms black male texts into emphatically explicit racial protest. However, while producing favorable critical commentary and in turn high marketability, the expression of such rage has become highly repetitive in black literature. The rage and the commentary are ironically preservers rather than disrupters of the status quo. But when we encounter the nonconfrontational, masked representation, indeed transformation and disruption, of racial rage in black female texts like Tillman's *Beryl Weston's Ambition*, the story becomes one about ideal black family formation, partly because nineteenth-century gender constructions of the lady author prohibited the display of anger and also because the plots of racial and sexual desire in these novels seek gratification.

Another important narrative tactic associated with the idealized domestic setting is the extreme silencing of racial thematics, or what Barbara Christian has called a "race-free" polity (Christian, p. xxxvii), particularly in Johnson's *Clarence and Corinne* and *The Hazeley Family* and Kelley-Hawkins's *Megda* and *Four Girls at Cottage City*, whose authors were largely known to be black at their publication.[41] (This tactic of character portrayal separates these novels from those written by Harper, Hopkins, and Tillman and indeed from what would become an African-American novelistic tradition requiring a dominant black cultural milieu.[42]) With the exception of *Four Girls*, the other three novels present characters whose racial identities seem either nonspecific or contradictory. No doubt confident that her readers would presume her characters to be white, Johnson in particular relied on "ethnic neutrality" to enhance her novels' appeal to the white American Baptist Publishing Society (Spillers, p. xxvii). Although this presumption enlarged the novels' first white readership, it undoubtedly contributed to the novels' obscurity in traditional African-American literary scholarship, which routinely judged all literature of black authorship against the discursive standard of masculinized racial protest.[43]

At first glance the four novels appear to be set in a white milieu because readers have generally come to equate an absence of racial and ethnic designations with the dominant Anglo-American culture and identity. Bell Hooks cites white supremacy as the force suppressing the linguistic marker "white" in dominant discourse:

> In a racially imperialist nation such as ours, it is the dominant race that reserves for itself the luxury of dismissing racial identity while the oppressed race is made daily aware of their racial identity. It is the dominant race that can make it seem that their experience is representative.[44]

However, in each of these racially neutral novels there are what seem to be black signifiers—characteristics that first readers would probably have associated with black culture. Although some might contend that my so-called signifiers are the product of over-determined reading (especially in the cases of Johnson's novels), I present them nonetheless.

In Johnson's *Clarence and Corinne*, the young heroine Corinne encounters the character Jack who seems much like a personified version of the once-popular, minstrel-stage, black buffoon—Jim Crow. The text describes Jack "pulling off his piece of hat, and rubbing his bushy hair vigorously" (p. 126), both of which constitute familiar stances of Jim Crow minstrel stage buffoonery.[45] In addition, Jack "turn[ed] a somersault" (p. 126), and generally created such "a rueful countenance that Corinne could not help laughing" (p. 127). Later, Corinne's best friend, Bebe Stone, emphatically corrects the error of her brother's prejudicial attitude about Corinne:

> "Charley," said his sister, gravely, "you know very well that you are saying naughty, ugly things, and you ought to be ashamed of yourself. Can she help being what she is? I wouldn't let *that* hinder me from being a friend to any one." (p. 154, emphasis in original)

The "that" of the quotation refers to the facts that Corinne is a pauper and the daughter of a drunkard. Bebe's ideal response to what seems to be class prejudice would serve equally well as a condemnation of racial prejudice when placed in a racialized context. Because class prejudice here is subject to immediate correction, the implication is that similar instruction—attending to "God's way"—in a racial domain eradicates racial prejudice as well. Thus class here may be read as a metonym of race due to the fact that black people of this era almost categorically belonged to the social class of working poor.

In Johnson's *The Hazeley Family*, the heroine Flora Hazeley mistakes a little girl named Jem as a boy, given her appearance and name. However, the name Jem, we are soon told, is a shortened version of "Jemima," a name that is the distinctly frequent appellation of black women.[46] Moreover, the text describes Jem as an "odd-looking little creature" (p. 24) with a "pair of inquisitive brown eyes" (p. 23). She also speaks an exaggerated prattle reminiscent of black plantation English:

> "I'm Jem . . . and I didn't mean nuffin . . . don't you see I've gut a napron on wif pockets in? . . . Tain't none. . . There ain't anythin' else's I can see. . . . Don't see anythin' to remire." (pp. 24–25)

In addition, Jem's description invokes the impish, nongender-specific name and appearance of the character Topsy in Stowe's *Uncle Tom's Cabin*, who was also a well-known literary and black stage personality of Johnson's era. Jack and Jem, then, not only elicit comic relief, but more important, their Jim Crow and Topsy character types suggest racial valences.

In Kelley-Hawkins's *Megda*, the racial designations are often contradictory. The novel presents numerous references to Megda's white slender hands and pretty white face in addition to references to the pretty to beautiful, pure, white, innocent, delicate, girlish women who comprise Megda's circle of friends. As Molly Hite accurately notes in the introduction, *Megda* is full of racist color iconography (pp. xxvii–xxx). In the midst of this white-skinned adolescent society are Megda's brother, Hal, who has "strong brown hand[s]" (p. 32) and Ruth Dean, who is plain, poor, virtuous, and dark (pp. 75, 177, 256) and who also lives on the other side of town. These rather contradictory racial characteristics mark what seems to be a racial schizophrenia that distinguishes the entire novel. But the key to racial identity is the resort town of Cottage City where Meg vacations (p. 285). This town is modeled on the real-life black resort town of Cottage City on Martha's Vineyard, now known as Oak Bluffs.[47] Black readers of the author's epoch were likely to have recognized this setting and thus the African-American cultural milieu of this novel. With this key in place, I suggest that although the characters, with the exception of Hal and Ruth, may look white, they are legally African Americans by the then current codes of racial purity, dictating that if one has one-sixteenth part black blood, one is black.

To place *Clarence and Corinne*, *The Hazeley Family*, and *Megda* categorically in a white social milieu would mitigate the significance of their subtle but revolutionary arguments, given the time frame, on human perfectibility and racial equality. By adopting what from our late-twentieth-century vantage point are conservative bourgeois values, these novels ironically offer a radical repudiation of race and class origins as the absolute determinants for qualifying the characters' personal esteem, access to virtue, and success. Therefore the erasure of the routine social designations of race and class is not only political, but radically political indeed, especially during the post-Reconstruction period. Although some may contend that my racial reading of these two novels is based on circumstantial evidence, the fact that Kelley-Hawkins and Johnson were black, that the novels widely circulated in black culture, and that the racial identity of many of the characters is indefinite, self-contradictory, or subtly encoded make my interpretation more than mere guesswork. Like the domestic novels of the black female contemporaries of Kelley-Hawkins and Johnson, these three works emphatically eliminate color and class prescriptives as requirements for social advancement. What is important to heed in these novels, then, is the direct relationship between talent, virtue, love, and hard work, on the one hand, and human perfectibility on the other. This new equation seeks to displace prejudicial views that privilege white and light skin color and wealth by having the poor and dark-skinned characters receive just rewards for their meritorious behavior. This argument, like the erasures, is not apolitical; to the contrary, it is radical, racial politics.

Kelley-Hawkins's second novel—*Four Girls at Cottage City* (1898)—again focuses on a group of adolescent girls and boys. However, unlike *Megda*, *Four Girls* does not rely on racial indeterminacy. Two of the girls are characterized as white mulattas, like most of the characters in *Megda*, while two others—sisters—have more distinct African-American racial traits that make them subject to restricted seating in "nigger heaven" (p. 81) of some theaters. Garnet and Jessie Dare, the two sisters, have rich complexions and bewitching dark eyes (pp. 35, 52, respectively). Furthermore, Jessie has "hair . . . so thick it seems impossible for a pin to go through it" (p. 50).[48] These characteristics reference African-American identity. In addition, the setting of *Four Girls* is even more tightly circumscribed than that of *Megda*. The story evolves around a domestic setting—a cottage room—in the same black resort town of Cottage City that was mentioned in *Megda*.

The powerful presence of the restricted domestic setting in these novels silences the texts' social outrage as well as masks their political content. However, the idealized domestic mask is not a denial or erasure of black people's political desire but what I call a metonymic cryptograph for their acquisition and full exercise of that desire. This is to say that the exemplary black home life can only arise in a setting where the racial politics have been amicably resolved.

The Heroine as Agent of Racial Desire

As agents of racial desire, the heroines of the post-Reconstruction novels affirm civil rights as their rightful claim to middle-class domestic rewards, rewards resulting from industry, frugality, and piety. The heroines do not emphasize racial prejudice or argue for racial parity like their male counterparts, who routinely confront interracial hostility. The domestic texts usually focus on depicting feminine ideals. Their characters live in fictive domestic spheres where racial identity does not automatically preclude social mobility. Hence these novels present the discourse of racial protest as a story about virtuous female and male character development, and the characters are engaged in productive middle-class family enterprise. In this way these female texts maintain reticence about racism while appropriating gender prescripts to demonstrate the high moral fiber and disciplined productivity of the characters as well as their eagerness to endorse middle-class values. The novels repudiate racial prejudice and discrimination by marginalizing or erasing their presence in a recontextualized domestic setting where racial obstacles are often recast as improvident behavior such as vanity, avarice, indolence, stealing, lying, and intemperance.

Just as the traditional protocol of reading has not recognized the discourse of racial affirmation in these novels, that protocol also has seldom recognized the portrayals of the enlarged feminine domain and the absence of female deference to masculine authority as expressions of relative sexual equality and female agency. Such portrayals at best seem only weak approximations of equality between the sexes. However, we late-twentieth-century readers must be ever mindful that our notions of sexual equality differ greatly from those of the late-nineteenth-century writers. We must be vigilant to place the assertion of female agency in these works in the context of the gender codes of their epoch.

For example, these texts repeatedly give us female characters (like Dora Smith in Hopkins's *Contending Forces* and Meg Randal in Kelley-Hawkins's *Megda*) who live in households headed by widowed mothers. Although the texts make no explicit remark about the managerial competence of these mothers, the material conditions of the heroines' lives makes such competence self-explicit. Even in households where the father is present, like Johnson's *The Hazeley Family* (1894), the daughter-heroine serves as its organizing force, contributes significantly to its maintenance, and mentors the development of family members. In short, these domestic heroines do not serve the patriarchy as simple complementary objects of masculine ambition, prerogative, or esteem. To borrow literary theorist Paul Smith's terminology, as subjects these heroines "are construed as . . . unified and coherent bearer[s] of consciousness" that are here governed by specifically domestic "systems of knowledge, power, and ideology."[49] Each heroine then is an "agent of conscious action and meaning which is consistent with [that action]" (Smith, pp. xxxiii–xxxiv), and represents not only resistance to racialism and/or class restrictions but the assertion of self-willed success in a semiotic of domestic materialism.

To promote the heroine's agency of political contestation in the rhetoric of domesticity, these texts repeatedly provide her with a brother and/or suitor with whom she establishes a near egalitarian relationship. The sibling relationship provides the heroine an initial opportunity to practice self-definition through self-assertion with someone whose affection is assured, and this mode of behavior ultimately becomes the basis for asserting self-authority in the conjugal relationship. I am not suggesting that the heroine as wife asserts herself independently of the gender prescriptives of her day. To the contrary, the verbal playfulness of gender decorum that frequently mitigates prescriptions for female deference to patriarchal authority in these texts calls attention to the fact that the heroine is subject to patriarchal ideologies, but she assumes the power of mediation.

To illustrate my point, I cite a small sample of the dialogue from Kelley-Hawkins's *Megda* between the heroine Meg and her husband Arthur:

> "Shall I go, Arthur?"
> "How do you feel about it?" he asked gently.
> "I would like to go very much."
> He kissed her lips. "We will go," was all he said; but Meg knew he was greatly pleased. (p. 383)

It is not important to know where Meg wants to go or why to appreciate the meaning of this exchange, for immediately apparent is the mediation of female desire in the context of nineteenth-century male authority. We notice Arthur's pleasure in his encouraging response to Meg's desire. However, neither Meg's self-asserted question nor his response signals female autonomy for late-twentieth-century readers. But by placing Meg's behavior within the gender codes of her period, the author lets the careful reader know that she is not the silenced heroine who allows her husband to make the decision for her. She does not respond with the proverbial non-answer, "What do you think?" She has her own opinion and gives it expression, albeit in carefully postured deference to masculine authority. As significant as her behavior is for revising the imposition of female silence and selflessness, what is crucial here as well is that the husband's behavior is also considerably reformed. He does not simply expect his wife to reflect his viewpoints or have none; he asks her opinion, rather than dictate. Moreover, he takes great pleasure in doing so, indeed assisting his wife to realize her own desire. I agree with late-twentieth-century readers who may contend that there is no real sexual assertion here but only

Meg's servility due to the fact that she must appeal to her husband. But the point is that Meg becomes a mediating agent of her own desire in this dialogue, and marriage here becomes the site of that mediation. Thus the episode's resolution is a negotiated one between Meg, whose pragmatic agency engages a female-based rhetoric of pleasant, demure arbitration, and her husband, who has been conditioned to respect female autonomy of this type.[50] Indeed his telltale kiss confirms his pleasure. Meg then is a bona fide agent in the marriage and a mediating subject. She is not a selfless object to whom her husband dictates his desire. Contextualized against the gender codes of Meg's era, her response becomes an arbitration of conservative and liberal gender rites.

Similar contextualization is essential as well for reading the liberational discourses in the other post-Reconstruction domestic novels. We thus observe black women and men enact their civil responsibilities by becoming exemplary wives and husbands. But before we examine the ways in which these novels revise the social texts of exemplary spouses, it is necessary to discuss, first, nineteenth-century politicized discourses of black manhood and womanhood as gendered discourses of citizenship and, second, black women writers' use of those and other liberational discourses in literary culture to effect social intervention.

5

Sexual Discourses of Political Reform of the Post-Reconstruction Era

A race is but a total of families. The nation is the aggregate of its homes.
    ANNA JULIA COOPER, *A Voice From the South* (1892)

Home is undoubtedly the cornerstone of our beloved Republic . . . and marriage constitutes the basis for the home.
    MRS. N. F. [GERTRUDE B.] MOSSELL, *The Work of the Afro-American Woman* (1894)

"I am particularly anxious that you should think upon this matter seriously, because of its intrinsic value to all of us as race women. I am not less anxious because you represent the coming factors of our race. Shortly, you must fill the positions now occupied by your mothers, and it will rest with you and your children to refute the charges brought against us as to our moral irresponsibility, and the low moral standard maintained by us in comparison with other races."
    PAULINE E. HOPKINS, *Contending Forces* (1900)

In the 1890s black writers—female and male—depicted marriage emphatically as a valuable civil institution, for like their white counterparts, as discussed especially in Chapter 3, they viewed marriage as the basis of civilization. Implicit in their endorsement of marriage was a counterargument to their alleged "low moral standard," to which Hopkins refers in the epigraph. In this passage Hopkins, in the voice of her character Mrs. Willis, is passing on the mantle of the advocacy of race to the next generation of black women. However, rather than committing this generation of "race women" to the promotion of platform politics, as we late-twentieth-century readers might expect, Hopkins has Mrs. Willis charge them with repudiating the very basis of racist ideology—retrogressionism—by maintaining high moral conduct within the black family. Hopkins's *Contending Forces*, like the other domestic novels in this study, attacked that tenet of racist ideology with persistent, impassioned

124

portrayals of exemplary black families. These works taught black people that by preserving, indeed celebrating, the moral fiber of the family they could strike out at virtually all forms of racism. Together with numerous surveys of notable black Americans, published in the last years of the nineteenth century, these real and fictitious black exemplars helped to undermine the retrogressionist viewpoint.[1]

The central plot of marriage in black women's domestic novels of the post-Reconstruction era tended to yield not a story of passionate romance but one of duty, regardless of whether that story relied on liberal or conservative female gender roles. Love constructed as duty was the ideal mode of courtship and marriage during the mid-nineteenth century, in contrast to the late-century insurgency of arduous romantic love, which largely shapes contemporary romantic aspirations.[2] These stories draw on three prominent mid-nineteenth-century African-American constructions of exemplary behavior. The first two are the polemical discourses of manhood and womanhood that literally and symbolically wed one another to express the third—conjugal ardor constructed as mutual respect, admiration, dedication to working together as responsible citizens for a noble purpose. Thus social (indeed civil) duty and not passion prompts the heroine's sentimentalized romantic exuberance, while esteem kindles affection, and mutual commitment to advancing the race both engenders and sustains conjugal love. For example, in Harper's 1892 novel *Iola Leroy*

> Her [Iola's] noblest sentiments found a response in his [Frank Latimer's] heart. In their desire to help the race their hearts beat in loving unison. One grand and noble purpose was giving tone and color to their lives and strengthening the bonds of affection between them.[3]

In this context matrimony is the very sign of social progress and is the site for women to carry out the convictions of exemplary black citizenship. The couple's "loving unison" of domestic and civil enterprise is an important black *and* female signifier for political engagement that repeatedly occurs in the domestic novels. It affirms black people's desire to be full participants in the ethic of hard work for racial prosperity. The political intentionality of "their desire to help the race" becomes the symbolic equivalent of sexual desire in an idealized discourse of marital love, and both ambitions are mutually unified, fortified, and signified. As a consequence, the marriage story in the domestic novels not only inscribes the sanctity of the institution of marriage, but the consummation of that story becomes an allegorical discourse about the fulfillment of enlightened black self- and group interest.

These novels instruct readers not to regard the wedding ceremony as an elaborately planned church ritual, as the presumably culminating moment of a woman's life, but as the incorporation of an industrious partnership between exemplary spouses who project their ambitions beyond the ceremony. For example, we do not observe Iola in lace and satin, walking down the proverbial aisle, for as one of Harper's characters insists, "there is a great deal of misplaced sentiment at weddings" (p. 277). In the chapter entitled "Wooing and Wedding," Iola's wedding is presented as "a pleasant gathering of friends" (p. 274). The matrimonial effacement is precisely the heroine's contention in Johnson's *The Hazeley Family*, framed as an innocent question: "Suppose we did have all the fine things, you named ['white satin, and orange blossoms, and lots of presents, and a great big wedding cake'], how much happier would that make us?"[4] By contrast, Tillman in *Beryl Weston's Ambition* presented what we have come to recognize as the traditional bride:

> Beryl never looked fairer than upon her wedding-day. She wore a costume of rich white satin, with a cluster of magnificent roses fastened to her corsage, and a beautiful diamond cross, the gift of Norman's English friends to his bride. . . . Upon her hand shone a costly ring set with pearls and sapphires, Norman's gift to his bride, and from her ears swung two glittering diamond pendants, the gift from [Norman's mother]. A deed to the New Queen Anne house, which had just been completed, was Jim Weston's gift to his daughter, and a handsome writing desk came from Miss Hand [Beryl's teacher].[5]

"Indeed," the story continues, "Beryl was the recipient of many useful gifts, for she had many friends" (p. 245). This portrait of Beryl dressed in matrimonial splendor is not the culminating point of Beryl's life, to be frozen in memory. Rather this display of wealth is a semiotic of sound character and the just rewards of hard work. One generation removed from slavery, Beryl and her husband Norman Warren as well as their community have successfully risen from the poverty of slavery to middle class. From this position they do not merely reign over the social life of their community; to the contrary, as self-conscious citizens they lead useful lives by working in and contributing their resources to "every movement for the advancement of their own oppressed race" (p. 246). In Kelley-Hawkins's *Megda* and *Four Girls at Cottage City*, in which there are repeated depictions of brides dressed in white silk and lace, the finery is more the affirmation of the characters' attainment of middle-class status, values, and economic security than a gratuitous display of wealth. Given these material portraits of matrimony, we cannot deny that the court-ships embrace bourgeois gentility and expectations of the nuclear family. However, these bourgeois prescriptions ought not distract our attention from the fact that these fictions ultimately define social advancement in domestic terms.

The marriages in these post-Reconstruction domestic novels are compassionate unions whose unifying strength lies in their mutual commitment to the development of the self and the race. These values, as we shall see, define social advancement in terms of domestic enterprise and grant the individual control over his or her fate. These novels characterize racial progress as the product of individuated aspirations centered around the life of the family. No doubt the black heroine's placement in a self-contained, fictive sphere of late-nineteenth-century intraracial domesticity of family and friends reflects the desire of the authors to eschew the increasingly segregated pattern of

American life. For unlike the hero of corresponding male texts, this heroine does not directly encounter the racist limitations of the dominant society. Artificially freed from racial prejudice and discrimination, she devotes her talent to self- and group improvement and earns rewards on the basis of her personal merit.

Unlike the domestic novels by post-Reconstruction African-American women, contemporaneous male texts tend to make the marriage story marginal to the hero's effort to preserve his personal integrity as a black man in a racist social milieu. As a result, the black male text largely recounts the traditional patriarchal story about the struggle for power among men in a specifically interracial context, thus becoming what we might call a racialized Oedipal discourse. We late-twentieth-century readers know well how to read that text, for we have been conditioned to engage a "homoaesthetic erotics of reading"[6]; that is to say, we have traditionally been taught to universalize masculine voice, desire, prerogative, and expectations, in short, masculine reading pleasure. It is precisely the sharing of black male (dis)pleasure in the frustrated desire of patriarchal privilege between author and reader that characterizes traditional African-American literary scholarship and produces an implicitly "[black] male narratology" as the critical standard (Winnett, p. 508).

By contrast, as we shall see, the post-Reconstruction novels of black female authority seek distinctly black and female pleasure and thus engage a black female narratology. These novels center an exemplary heroine whose agency in the formation of the ideal marital union reaches fruition as the courtship story unwinds in marriage. The heroine and hero mutually admire and desire the other's characteristics, a process that sets the courtship story into motion. Hence, as the heroine achieves increasing awareness of herself as an ambitious individual and a responsible citizen, she simultaneously attracts and becomes attracted to a like-minded man who assists her development and shares her ambitions. Marriage fulfills their mutual sexual desires (a reticent discourse in these fictions), and their union forms an enterprising unit for the satisfaction of their other ambitions — personal advancement, family and community prosperity. In short, the generic demand that domestic fiction culminate in marriage serves as an empathic sign for the mutual fulfillment of the personal and political desires of the heroine and her hero husband.

While corresponding black male texts repeatedly depict the hero's contest with a racist white society to assert his civil rights, seldom is there a story of the struggle for public male power in the female domestic fictions. Due to the frequent absence of that expected, highly readable story of social reality and given the interracial climate at the turn of the century, we late-twentieth-century readers have usually been at a loss about how to interpret the fairy-tale endings of these texts. Their unquestioned endorsements of the bourgeois ambition of individual willful self-advancement sever the heroines and their mates from the material circumstances of the large majority of black people. As a result, the domestic novels initially seem delusory rather than realistic strategies for teaching social reform.

But despite their differences, it is the polemical discourses of black manhood and womanhood that sustain the liberational agenda of citizenship in the disparate post-Reconstruction works of male and female African Americans. The writings of the well-known race men—Booker T. Washington and William E. B. Du Bois, for example—and their not so well-known female counterparts Anna Julia Haywood Cooper and Gertrude Bustill Mossell—provide striking illustrations of these discourses as well as the political context for the domestic heroine in which she emerges as a sign of ideal feminine citizenship. What is also important to remember is that Cooper and Mossell were probably real-life models for many of the exemplary heroines of black women's domestic novels.

(Black) Manhood and Womanhood as Racial and Political Signifiers of Citizenship

Despite the political differences in the arguments of Washington and Du Bois,[7] the terms of contestation center the conception of black manhood in a civil rhetoric that had been in place since the abolition era, namely a rhetoric representing freedom as a discourse of manhood. Thus to struggle for freedom was tantamount to achieving (black) manhood, which after the Emancipation would be equivalent to securing citizenship. Frederick Douglass, for example, revealed this abolitionist code in his *Narrative of the Life of Frederick Douglass*, when he resolved to escape from slavery. He wrote,

> I began, with the commencement of the year, to prepare myself for a final struggle, which should decide my fate one way or the other. . . . I was fast approaching *manhood*, and year after year had passed, and I was still a slave. I therefore resolved . . . to secure my liberty. But I was not willing to cherish this determination alone. My fellow-slaves were dear to me. . . . I talked to them of our want of *manhood*, if we submitted to our enslavement without at least one noble effort to be free.[8] (emphasis added)

Douglass initially represented manhood as the attainment of adult maturity; but more important, he subsequently employed manhood to signal the personal and social integrity of the free black male. During the post-Reconstruction era, Booker T. Washington relied on a similar masculine authority, but rather than emphasizing its signifier, "manhood," he seemed deliberately to efface that term throughout his autobiography *Up from Slavery*,[9] (1901), no doubt because the term had become synonymous not only with black male enfranchisement but also with black male agency at a time when both provoked white hostility. Thus throughout *Up from Slavery* Washington deliberately characterized black people without reference to their political assertiveness in an attempt to mediate the extremely hostile interracial climate that violently prohibited black political activity. For instance, in Washington's famous "Atlanta Exposition Address" of 1895 that is transcribed in its entirety in the autobiography, the trope of toiling hands, disconnected from the mental capacities of heads and the comprehensive intentionality of bodies, is the forceful image empowering his depoliticized discourse of black labor:

> In all things that are purely social we can be as separate as the fingers, yet one as the hand in all things essential to mutual progress. . . . Nearly sixteen millions of hands will aid you in pulling the load upward, or they will pull against you the load downward. (p. 148)

Washington effaced the black bodies and displaced agency onto toiling hands. Gillian Brown's discussion of the function of the hand as a synecdoche of self-sovereignty is particularly helpful for recovering the agency of the black working (if not speaking) self. She explains that "[t]he faculties of hands, which dictionary definitions list as those of grasping, producing, possessing, controlling, and authorizing, recapitulate the proprietary character of individualism."[10] By referring to proprietary influence implicitly associated with hands, we can discern that Washington's laboring hands constitute a metonymy of black authority as working subject rather than laboring object.

While masking collective black agency in *Up from Slavery*, Washington also referred indirectly to himself in the role of the speaking male subject in repeated scenarios about his reception by white men of state. In other words, Washington repeatedly assumed the prohibited politicized agency of black manhood and became its exemplar by using the trope of hand. An example of this tactic occurs in his description of the events following the delivery of his Address. He wrote, "At the request of myself and others, he [President Grover Cleveland] consented to spend an hour in the Negro Building, for the purpose of inspecting the Negro exhibit and of giving the coloured people in attendance an opportunity *to shake hands with him*" (p. 151; emphasis added). Washington was the only identified individual who extended the invitation to Cleveland and his was the only identified hand that grasped Cleveland's in the sign of mutual recognition among (states)men — the handshake.

However, Washington did not maintain a textual posture of self-appointed agency long before taking cover in the role of servility. He cloaked his assertion of the emancipatory discourse of manhood in this Address and in the enterprise of Tuskegee Institute by relying on domestic rhetoric to efface but nevertheless communicate issues of political concern to the black population of that era. Immediately apparent in probably the two most famous lines of Washington's "Atlanta Exposition Address" — "Cast down your bucket where you are" and "In all things that are purely social, we can be as separate as the fingers, yet one as the hand in all things essential to mutual progress" (pp. 147–48) — is a striking display of the modified trope of hands for veiling black self-appointed agency. Both passages use the rhetoric of domestic labor to petition the dominant society for support of black industry: the industry is configured as manual and service oriented rather than intellectual or political. By reconfiguring what is essentially political power as domestic labor, thereby invoking the cultural subordination of woman's sphere, domestic tropes mask political assertiveness in the semblance of conciliation. As a consequence the

Address switches discursive codes; it feminizes the rhetoric of political power, transforming politics of state into a female sign of domestic labor—washing laundry and household scrubbing. In doing so Washington's Address, like black women's domestic novels of the period, reconceptualizes black society as a well-organized, industrious household, separated from white public enterprise. By evoking the rhetoric of domesticity, then, Washington effaced the desire of African Americans for interracial equality and appeared as well to depoliticize the conventional political rhetoric of civil rights. Rather than foreground black political aspiration, he foregrounded the desire for intraracial self-sufficiency, like the independent and prosperous household(s) in the black women's domestic novels. The economically and emotionally stable home then becomes the symbolic paradigm for black political institutions and their aspirations, a reconfiguration that also averts the offensiveness of segregation in the public domain.[11] In this context idealized black husbands and wives are relatively equivalent as gendered discursive *signs* as well as real-life proponents of exemplary citizenship.

At the turn-of-the-century, Tuskegee Institute was a highly visible sign and institution of intraracial (e.g., segregated) self-sufficiency. The political image that Washington deliberately constructed for the Institute with slogans like "the gospel of the toothbrush" (p. 122) masks its own willful political self-authority in inconsequential, domestic activity and imagery. As in the Address and Up from Slavery, the discourse surrounding the Institute also relies heavily on domestic configuration to efface black political self-assertiveness and to erase the implication of inferiority arising from racial segregation. However, implicit in both the agency implied in the Address, as mentioned, and the activities of the Institute is an economic and social authority dependent on the civil polity of due process. The posture of the Address and the institution mediates civil power from covert and apparently inferior privatized and feminized positions. Domestic configuration throughout his enterprise, then, enabled Washington to represent emergent black economic power as nonthreatening to the dominant culture.

Although Washington claimed that he cared little for fiction, favoring biography instead (p. 173), his strategies of political self-effacement seem very similar to those in the post-Reconstruction domestic novels of black women. His effectiveness also suggests the high readability of domestic ideation for representing political desire among his black constituency. Virtually all black people of this era were familiar with Washington's program, whether or not they were proponents, and they no doubt realized that its symbolic sign was domestic labor but its referent was civil polity. Thus, when a subset of that population read the black domestic novels in which similar political ideation appeared, it is very likely that this readership was already familiar with the domestic code for expressing civil ambition.

While Washington effaced the discourse on (black) manhood and enfranchised citizenship, that discourse became a more self-evident mode of political petition at the turn of the century as black male and female writers alike explicitly referred to the authority of manhood to empower their civil protests.

My analysis of Washington's use of domestic tropology is not meant to suggest that the patriarchal conventions of his age conditioned his attitudes about gender any less than those of other "race men," or that he was more or less sympathetic than they to black women's desire to share the leadership of racial uplift. Neither is the case. Rather my point is that he used domestic tropes both to construct the conciliatory appearance of his program and to conceal its political assertiveness.

By contrast, Du Bois, another turn-of-the-century "race man," accentuated the domestic discourse in his *The Souls of Black Folk* (1903) to depict the resignation of political ambition. In the chapter entitled "Of Our Spiritual Strivings," Du Bois insisted that when black men succumb to racial prejudice and accept the subordinate positions of cook and servant, they become "half-men":

> But the facing of so vast a prejudice could not but bring the inevitable self-questioning, self-disparagement and lowering of ideas which ever accompany repression. . . . *[W]e cannot write, our voting is vain*; what need of education, since *we must always cook and serve*? And the Nation echoed and enforced this self-criticism, saying: *Be content to be servants*, and nothing more; what need of higher culture for *half-men*?[12] (emphasis added)

Unlike Washington, who made domesticity a metaphor for civil political agency, Du Bois set up a rhetorical relationship between domesticity and civil polity that was mutually exclusive, binary. Literacy and citizenship in this passage are for Du Bois metonyms of political agency, which here are understood as specifically the activities of men due to his invocation of enfranchisement, which at the turn of the century was explicitly a masculine privilege. The passage displaces writing and voting with cooking and serving, which we understand as culturally subordinate because in a white patriarchal culture these activities are designated to serving-class white women or people of color. Being female activities they are also understood as inherently inferior to activities of men. The discursive logic of the passage sets up a binary relationship between politics and gender: Men become "half-men" when they become depoliticized.[13] Thus when patriarchs are disavowed by emasculation or feminization (or domestication), they become surrogate women. And as women they are external to political agency.

· In the quoted passage Du Bois clearly broke the female abolitionist equation between home and state, between ideal domesticity and moral civil polity. Indeed his discourse of manhood provides a striking example of the disempowerment of domestic tropes and the erasure of the sign of womanhood for expressing political ambition, a dismantling of the politicized discourse of womanhood that would become increasingly more pronounced with the advance of the twentieth century. Du Bois articulated a modern understanding of domesticity as a depoliticized institution, which is quite distinct from its Victorian understanding as half of the mutually complementary public/male and private/female spheres of social, moral, and political influence.

However, during the decade of the 1890s the domestic discourse of political desire still retained its expressive potency in black women's writings. These authors and their first readers seem to have understood that the domestic discourse encoded political desire to achieve racial justice and equality. Moreover, these writers embraced the rhetoric of manhood as an emancipatory discourse to be mediated by both men and women. Harper's *Iola Leroy*, for instance, asserts that conception of manhood when a minor character insists that black people cannot "begin too early to teach our boys to be *manly* and self-respecting . . . " (p. 253, emphasis added). Hopkins's *Contending Forces* provides a particularly explicit illustration of this form of ideation that sustains an equation between enfranchisement and manhood. In the chapter "The American Colored League," the League's president exclaims, "This new birth of the black race is a mighty agony. God help us in our struggle for liberty and *manhood*!" (emphasis added). Harper's and Hopkins's use of the trope of manhood seems an expression of the collective political ambition of black people—male and female—as citizens rather than a trope specifically referring to the patriarchal aspirations of enfranchised men, as in the passage from Du Bois's *The Souls of Black Folk*. Nevertheless, the masculine-specific configuration of manhood, like the one Du Bois presented in that passage, would become dominant in the twentieth century, as the black Victorian configuration of gender complementation receded. With the rise of masculine exclusivity in the polemical symmetry between black manhood and racial protest, it is not surprising that we late-twentieth-century readers regard the dramatizations of black male desire in African-American literature as synonymous with the discourse of racial protest.

By relying on black Victorian gender complementation, Cooper and Mossell defined the liberated black American not in the conceptual framework of black manhood but of black womanhood instead, focusing on the responsibilities of feminine citizenship to represent the black body politic.[15] The titles of the first chapters in their respective works—*A Voice From the South* and *The Work of the Afro-American Woman*—illustrate the centrality of black womanhood for representing collective black advancement: "Womanhood a Vital Element in the Regeneration and Progress of a Race" and "The Work of the Afro-American Woman."[16] In these chapters as well as throughout their works, we find the construction of black womanhood in an enlarged intraracial domesticity as the signifier for enlightened, politicized black self-authority, self-interest, and self-development. Mossell and Cooper constructed this signifier by drawing on the currency of the reformist discourse, equating domestic efficiency with political, economic, and moral vitality of a people. As discussed above, Booker T. Washington also relied on tropes of domestic labor but for effacing black political agency in an interracial context, further strengthening the equation between domesticity and polity among post-Reconstruction black people. It is precisely this distinctly black *and* female construction that repeatedly appears as the heroine of black women's post-Reconstruction domestic novels. That cultural coding was already readable and thus available for black women writers like Cooper and Mossell to employ.

On examining the title page of Mossell's *The Work*, we find that she invoked the equation immediately. She expressed her desire for public ambition by subtly effacing the agency of her authorial person behind patriarchal approbation for the domestic wife and mother. She referred to herself as Mrs. N. F. Mossell rather than Gertrude B[ustill]. Mossell, while simultaneously assuming the public role of spokeswoman under the guise of designating the work of social and moral nurturance for black women. As Joanne M. Braxton has rightly asserted,

> By this strategy of public modesty [writing under the initials of her husband], the author signaled her intention to defend and celebrate black womanhood without disrupting the delicate balance of black male-female relations or challenging masculine authority. . . . Thus she invited and received the enthusiastic support of influential black men and spread her mission further than if she had taken a different track.[17]

To provide additional sanction for the alignment of wife, mother, and social reformer, Mossell also represented herself in the frontispiece of the book in a photograph flagged on each side by a daughter to whom she dedicated the volume (Figure 5). On the opposite page she inscribed the dedication: "To my

Figure 5. Gertrude Mossell and her daughters, Mary Campbell and Florence Alma Mossell. From Mossell, *The Work of the Afro-American Woman* (Oxford University Press, 1988 [1894]).

two little daughters, Mary Campbell and Florence Alma Mossell, praying that they may grow into a pure and noble womanhood, this little volume is lovingly dedicated" (p. 4). The signs — Mrs., the picture, and the text of the dedication with its expressed diminution of the book's significance — all reference proper feminine posture for a middle-class woman, while the text appropriates the world of African-American public and private affairs for her domain. Carefully ensconced in the book's frontispiece, then, is the conflation of the home and the state, the private and the public, that together represent the complementation of black manhood and womanhood in the liberational racial discourse. Hence we find a black female discourse of desire for full social participation as citizen, mediated on the one hand by the political institutionalization of black womanhood, black motherhood, and the professionalization of the domestic sphere all in the name of intraracial progress and, on the other by carefully voiced female expressions of patriarchal civility. This conflation and mediation form a principal discursive strategy of black women's post-Reconstruction literary culture for intervening in the reformation of black society.

Literary Interventionism

From the position of the humble mother who dedicated herself to improving the quality of life for her children, indeed, for all black people, Mossell began "A Sketch of Afro-American Literature" by asserting the primacy of intellectual development for a people — male and female — and making African-American literary culture fundamental to the racial uplift agenda of social reform. In what we might term a review essay that surveys the literary production of African Americans, Mossell argued that language is the conveyor of knowledge and discourse is its principal mode of representation and dissemination:

> The intellectual history of a people or nation constitute to a great degree the very heart of its life. To find this history, we search the fountain-head of its language, its customs, its religion, and its politics expressed by tongue or pen, its folklore and its songs. (p. 48)

Mossell designated herself an interpreter and proprietor of black history. In addition she specified that history was the basis for a sustained critique of African-American social culture. In so doing, she explicitly united African-American literary culture to its political agency.

Mossell divided her survey into three periods — slave importation, two-hundred and fifty years of bondage, and twenty years of freedom. Her exercise in periodization claims interpretative authority over the collective experience of black Americans as well as provides an epistemic framework for the dominant themes that appeared in the race literature of her day. Mossell appraised the works of Phillis Wheatley, Gustavas Vassa, Frances Harper, and David Walker, underscoring the significance of literary culture for "giv[ing] inspiration to the youth of the age" (pp. 59–60). Referring specifically to the novella

Aunt Lindy by Victoria Earle Matthews,[18] Mossell insisted that race writing "shows most conclusively the need of the race to produce its own delineators of Negro life" (p. 61) in order to foster a sympathetic understanding of black people. For "he who would know the Afro-American of this present day must read the books written by this people to know what message they bear to the race and to the nation" (p. 60).

Mossell's arguments about the intellectual and discursive bases of literary culture foreshadow many aspects of contemporary literary theory. For example, Mossell contended that the institution made black people into objects of racist desire, thus prohibiting their access to the authority of written language:

> As a rule, a race writes its history in its laws and in its records. Not so the Afro-American: he could make no law; deprived of the opportunity to write, he could leave no written record; he could only protest against the injustice of his oppressors in his heart, in his song, and in his whispered consolations to the suffering and dying. (p. 49)

Mossell was also one of the earliest scholars to discuss spirituals as the collective effort of slaves to secure authorial subjectivity initially over their psychological (spiritual) and subsequently over their material and social lives. Throughout her work she demonstrated an understanding that literacy is a principal medium of socialization. By reading race literature, she explained that black people could assimilate information about their own culture and learn to be agents of their own liberation. The influence of black literary culture would not only enhance black self-definition but also serve as a repository of American culture. "With all its drawbacks," she wrote, "the race has built up a literature of its own that must be studied by the future historian of the life of the American nation" (pp. 50–51). She concluded this essay by presenting a list, her canon as it were, of African-American literature, beginning with "Phyllis Wheatley's Poems, 1773" and concluding with "The Negro in the Christian Pulpit, Bishop J. W. Hood" (p. 66). Acknowledging that her inventory of black expressive culture[19] was probably incomplete, Mossell solicited additional entries for "a possible future edition" (p. 66).

The writer who, in Mossell's words, made "one of the strongest pleas for the race and the [female] sex" was Anna Cooper (p. 61).[20] In *A Voice From the South* (1892) Cooper also emphatically linked the literary culture of African Americans to their assertion of political agency. In the chapter "The Negro as Presented in American Literature," she explained that

> our writers have succeeded in becoming national and representative in proportion as they have from year to year entered more and more fully, and more and more sympathetically, into the distinctive life of their nation, and endeavored to reflect and picture its homeliest pulsations and its elemental components. (p. 176)

This contention countered the charges that race writing inherently lacks depth and originality by relating such deficiencies to the oppressive conditions under which black Americans have struggled. Despite their origin in oppression, these early efforts at black self-expression are valuable, for she contended,

> No man can prophesy with another's parable. For each of us truth means merely the re-presentation of the sensations and experiences of our personal environment, colored and vivified—fused into consistency and crystallized into individuality in the crucible of our own feelings and imagination. (pp. 176–177)

Cooper concluded by exhorting that race literature is fundamentally important because it truthfully embodies the unique experiences, reflections, and inspirations, indeed the true character of the African American.

This chapter has additional objectives. First, by dividing literary expression into two distinct categories, which she termed "singing literature" and "preaching literature," and by insisting that the "writing of the first class will . . . withstand the ravages of time" (p. 183), Cooper prescribed a course for future race writing. Second, by analyzing many "[white] writers who have hitherto attempted a portrayal of life and customs among the darker race" (p. 185), Cooper exposed the racist polemics in operation in their works. For example, she argued that

> we should not quarrel with *An Imperative Duty* [by William Dean Howells] because it lacks the earnestness and bias of a special pleader. Mr. Howells merely meant to press the button and give one picture from American life involving racial complications. . . . it is an insult to humanity and a sin against God to publish any such sweeping generalizations of a race on such meager and superficial information. . . . Were I not afraid of falling myself into the same error that I am condemning, I would say it seems an *Anglo Saxon characteristic* to have such overweening confidence in his own power of induction that there is no equation which he would acknowledge to be indeterminate, however many unknown quantities it may possess. (pp. 201–4)

Third, by calling into question white writers' prejudicial depictions of black life and culture, Cooper launched a discussion of the so-called "race problem," couched as a critical discussion of literature. Good writing about black people, whether preaching or singing, written by black and white authors alike, she explained, would be

> at once aesthetic and true to life, presenting the black man as a free American citizen, not the humble slave of *Uncle Tom's Cabin*—but a *man*, divinely struggling and aspiring yet tragically warped and distorted by the adverse winds of circumstance. (p. 223)

Cooper closed this chapter by stating that such a man "has not yet been painted," and in her opinion "that canvas awaits the brush of the colored man himself" (p. 223).[21] "In literature," she explained, "we have no artists for art's sake" (p. 223). The absence of "singing literature" does not originate in a lack of originality or inherent talent but in oppression. "The fact is," she added, "a sense of freedom in mind as well as in body is necessary to the appreciative and inspiring pursuit of the beautiful" (p. 224). In the absence of that freedom, African-American artists have produced "the eloquence and fire of oratory rather than the genial warmth and cheery glow of either poetry or romance":

> A race that has produced for America the only folk-lore and folk songs of native growth, a race which has grown the most original and unique assemblage of fable and myth to be found on the continent, a race which has suggested and inspired almost the only distinctive American note which could chain the attention and charm the ear of the outside world—has as yet found no mouthpiece of its own to unify and perpetuate its wondrous whisperings—no painter-poet to distill the alembic of his own imagination the gorgeous dyes, the luxuriant juices of this rich and tropical vegetation. (p. 224)

Given this history of African-American artistic accomplishment, Cooper argued that black scholars need not resort to racial defensiveness and become overly zealous in their estimation of their literature. She called for them to become engaged in genuine criticism that has clarity of vision and exact scales to measure the literary culture of African Americans. She concluded the chapter by giving this mission divine approbation:

> With this platform to stand on we can with clear eye weigh what is written and estimate what is done and ourselves paint what is true with the calm spirit of those who know their cause is right and who believe there is a God who judgeth the nations. (pp. 226–27)

Roughly two decades before white American literature achieved canonical status, Cooper and Mossell canonized African-American literature and identified specific characteristics as ennobling of black novelistic ventures. Both writers discouraged polemics, viewing lasting art as "singing" (Cooper, p. 183), as "vivid and truthful" (Mossell, p. 61). Cooper designated Chaucer as a model for black writers because he understood the significance of vernacular culture to a people and its artistic creations in the shaping of their national identity: "it was the glory of Chaucer that he justified the English language to itself—that he took the homely and hitherto despised Saxon elements and ideas, and lovingly wove them into an artistic product . . . " (p. 224). Cooper and Mossell also characterized a self-authorizing criticism of "calm clear judgment of ourselves" (p. 225). "What I hope to see before I die," Cooper wrote, "is a black man [or woman][22] honestly and appreciatively portraying . . . the Negro as he is" (p. 225).

When we observe the heroines of the domestic novels of the black female contemporaries of Cooper and Mossell, we view fictive versions of women like them. Like Mossell and Cooper, these heroines possess rational intelligence, personal discipline, compassion, and high moral character. In the more liberal works, formal academic training enhances these attributes. Most significantly, these heroines are agents of cultural transformation and political intervention in the cultural traditions that shaped the lives of their first black readers.[23] Like the white domestic heroine that cultural critic Nancy Armstrong identifies in *Desire and Domestic Fiction* (1987), the heroine of the black domestic texts accepts marriage as central to her personal advancement, central to the prosperity of her family and community, indeed central to the progress of civilization itself.

While many late-nineteenth-century black women writers might have been sympathetic to the so-called "new (white) woman's" rejection of traditional domestic roles and attendant radically revised gender constructions, their black heroines are not so extreme.[24] After all, such heroines could hardly reject what had not been broadly within their domain to embrace. As discussed above, their real-life black female predecessors—antebellum black women, slave and free—were not traditionally viewed as gendered, domestic servants but as general laborers.[25] As we shall see, black women authors of post-Reconstruction domestic novels became important agents for institutionalizing stable gender roles that were both similar and dissimilar to those of white bourgeois society.

Through the agency of an exemplary domestic heroine, these authors helped to revise the black antebellum gender constructions for their first audience, significantly retaining the antebellum practice of relative sexual equality, though not without contestation. As a self-possessed, rational, and yet compassionate model for individual and group desire, black womanhood as ideal heroine dominates their domestic stories. This heroine forms the nexus of moral, economic, social, and political codes for improving the living conditions of black individuals, families as well as the entire race. As the object of social desire for upwardly mobile black people, this heroine of the liberal domestic novels prescribes a progressive socialization for a new generation of freed people in which women are the equals of men. In the more conservative works, this heroine asserts the fundamental importance of her nurturing role by concentrating on preserving and perfecting the power of the domestic sphere. Both models embody ideals for black women to aspire to embrace and for black men to select as those most fitting the desirable wife. Just as important, the attributes of both types of heroines also designate a set of complementary characteristics for her mate, indeed for all black men. But most important, as a wife this heroine becomes a citizen with electoral influence mediated by her husband. In this context the heroine becomes a major political sign in black women's post-Reconstruction discourses of racial advancement, a uniquely black *and* female construction of emancipatory desire.

The Domestic Heroine and Black Bourgeois Individuation

The doctrines of the eighteenth-century Enlightenment and of nineteenth-century Emersonian willful self-advancement also contribute to the formation of contemporary black cultural values. Unlike our black counterparts of the post-Reconstruction era, though, our faith in Western intellectual discourse and in its doctrines of individuation are conflicted. When they read late-eighteenth-century and nineteenth-century British literary texts that redefined relationships among white people in society and culture by discarding the limitations of birth and allowing class mobility, they saw characters with whom they probably identified. The rise of interest in autobiography and in the novel as crytobiography, indicated by the names of fictive individuals as titles of early works, as in *Tom Jones, Pamela,* and *Emma,* reflects the new focus on bourgeois individualism in white literature. For such characters to appear in British fiction, the social construction of the individual had to have undergone a revisionary process such as Armstrong outlines in *Desire and Domestic Fiction.*[26]

Armstrong's argument lends support to my hypothesis that a similar cultural revisionary process occurred during the last decades of the nineteenth century, transforming antebellum collective representations of black people into postbellum constructions of African-American individuation. While nineteenth-century white domestic fiction reflects and fosters the rise of bourgeois individualism, early black fiction similarly instructs postbellum black people that reward is a direct product of moral superiority, practical intelligence, and hard work and is not a consequence of kinship, Caucasoid physical features, and inherited wealth. Hence postbellum African Americans came to realize that they have as much right to upward mobility as their white counterparts. Before this perspective could achieve consensus, though, it had to displace the field of value formation that originated in the codes of racial prejudice, discrimination, and segregation that were the legacies of slavery. These prior social codes of privilege were based on white racial purity, leisure-class membership, and inherited wealth. Insofar as the dominant plantation society was concerned, self-willed improvement pertained only to white people, due to their viewpoint that black people did not possess the necessary acumen.

As late-twentieth-century readers, we accept the values of assertive self-definition and the merit of individual virtue as if they were the timeless dictates of both divine and natural laws. Since this is so, the social consciousness of postbellum black (and white) people had to have been resocialized in this new value system. Late-nineteenth-century black autobiographies—Douglass's *The Life and Times of Frederick Douglass* (1881) and Booker T. Washington's *Up from Slavery* (1901)—for example, depict this pattern of resocialization. Turn-of-the-century black fiction followed suit.

For instance, Chesnutt wrote about the highly individual social desire of characters like John Walden in *The House Behind the Cedars* (1900), who decides to pass for white so that he can become a lawyer, and Dr. William Miller in *The Marrow of Tradition* (1901), who proudly endeavors to fulfill his grandfather's desire to have his heirs "be gentlemen in the town where their ancestors had once been slaves."[27] While the black heroes of such male texts almost always meet frustration due to racial prejudice, this is not the case for the heroines of the domestic novels of post-Reconstruction black women. Not only were these latter works instrumental in characterizing black bourgeois individuation and ambition; they also repeatedly characterize that process as fulfilled, as the heroine rightfully attains the rewards of virtue. In addition, these heroines mark the sites of individuated ambitions, as the personalized titles of the following representative novels suggest—*Iola Leroy*, *Megda*, and *Clarence and Corinne*; and become exemplars for individuals within their communities as well.

The pedagogic codes of resocialization in black women's post-Reconstruction novels rely on a domestic rhetoric of gendered, enlightened subjectivity for defining the modern black woman and by implication her complement, the modern black man. These texts were important agents for teaching the black population of the post-Reconstruction era revised truths about the social, oral, and physical perfectibility of the black male and female as gendered subjects. What is essential for us to understand when we read black women's post-Reconstruction novels from a late-twentieth-century perspective, then, is that this writing helped to extend the tenets of willful self-advancement to black Americans. The personal ambitions of the central figures in these novels contributed significantly to our understanding of modern black individualism as a gendered and politicized cultural construction.

I refer to the respective heroines in Jacobs's *Incidents in the Life of a Slave Girl* and Wilson's *Our Nig*—Linda Brent and Frado—to illustrate stages in the cultural transformation from antebellum collective to postbellum individuated constructions of identity. In an episode near the end of *Incidents*, Jacobs employed the language of commerce to condemn slavery's authority over her life:

> Reader, if you have never been a slave, you cannot imagine the acute sensation of suffering at my heart, when I read the names of Mr. and Mrs. [Emily Flint] Dodge, at a hotel in Courtland Street. It was a third-rate hotel, and that circumstance convinced me of the truth of what I had heard, that they were short of funds and had need of my value, as *they* valued me; and that was by dollars and cents. . . . Dr. Flint had left him [Mr. Dodge] no property, and his own means had become circumscribed. . . . Under these circumstances, it was very natural that he should make an effort to put me into his pocket.[28] (emphasis in original)

To defeat Mr. Dodge's purpose, Jacobs's white benefactor Mrs. Bruce purchased her and set her free. Mrs. Bruce, then, was compelled to participate unwillingly in the economy of slavery to secure Jacobs's freedom. Hence the attainment of freedom here was actually a reinscription rather than an erasure of slave codes. Moreover, Jacobs's description of this episode provides an important illustration of the failure of abolitionism to subvert the legal and economic authority of slavery. Her inability to redefine the contingencies of her identity external to the economy of slavery sustains the antebellum construction of black collective identity.

Her powerlessness to undermine that authority is reflected in her parodying of it with variations of the word "value." Shortly thereafter Jacobs emphasized her objection to participating in the economy of slavery to secure her freedom. She wrote,

> So I was *sold* at last. . . . I am deeply grateful to the generous friend who procured it [my freedom], but I despise the miscreant who demanded payment for what never rightfully belonged to him or his. I had objected to having my freedom bought. . . . (p. 200)

As Jacobs continued her explanation, she further stressed the displacement of slave codes for gendered domestic ones, though incomplete:

> the dream of my life is not yet realized. . . . I do not sit with my children in a home of my own. . . . But God so orders circumstances as to keep me with my friend Mrs. Bruce. . . . It is a privilege to serve her who . . . has bestowed the inestimable boon of freedom on me and my children. (p. 201)

Although Jacobs ran away from slavery, she did not ultimately escape the tyranny of its authority to define her life. Self-definition outside the rhetoric of slavery is beyond her grasp, and the "boon of freedom" must be bestowed on her (p. 201).

Unlike Jacobs, the technically free Wilson relied on her work's discourse of authorial desire to reconstruct her novelized self, Frado, as a worthy mother. In this way the text sustains a complex tension between dominant social constructions of racist definitions for Frado and her own effort at individuated self-definition, ultimately privileging the latter. Not only does the fulfillment of Frado's domestic ambition become the dominant motivating principle of *Our Nig*, eventually subordinating Wilson's protest of racial oppression, but the text's focus on maternal desire serves as the basis for constructing Frado's self-authority as well. Thus this text draws on Frado's externality to slavery to condition and sustain both its domestic and racial discourses by maintaining an alignment between protesting racist oppression and affirming maternity, indeed maintaining the feminist-abolitionist rhetorical equation between racial and domestic codes.

The domestic novels of post-Reconstruction black women rely on this rhetorical equation to inscribe a new pedagogy specifically for educating young black women of the period about bourgeois individuation. Whether assuming the conservative role of "the domestic educator" or the more liberal one of "the woman of social compassion"[29] the new domestic pedagogy identifies the black heroine as the authority of her own ego reformation as well as the instigator of similar reform in her community. The heroine uses both reason and compassion to select the proper mate to assist her in achieving her personal and communal ambitions. And finally, the heroine defines as well as manages an ideal household for an upwardly mobile family, mediating prosperity between the individual self and the collective black community.

In Johnson's *The Hazeley Family*, a conservative domestic novel, for instance, the heroine's education focuses on what seem to be general and rather abstract household responsibilities:

> "You are responsible for your conduct toward your parents. It is your duty to be a good daughter. There's your home, it is your duty to make it pleasant and comfortable." (p. 29)

Johnson goes on to explain that the maintenance of a comfortable home is a much more complicated skill than proficient cleaning and cooking. In the words of Mrs. Hazeley,

> "I used to be very unhappy . . . and it was because I expected life to form itself for me—either for pleasure or unhappiness. Then Flora [her daughter] came . . . ; I watched her closely, and I soon discovered that she had determined to make this house a home, and a delightful one." (p. 93)

"House-work," the text explains, "as all knew, was sweeping, dusting, cooking, and the other duties connected with caring for the house; but home-work was the making and the keeping of a home; helping those in it to be contented and happy; brightening and making it cheery by both word and deed, shedding a healthful and inspiring influence, so that those around us may be the better for our presence" (Johnson, p. 41). Thus "home-work" has at its base an epistemology of domesticity whose tenets embrace moral, practical, and compassionate labor; it has tremendous influence beyond the demands for a clean and orderly house. The knowledge is acquired, disseminated, and institutionalized across class lines by such commonplace real-life practices as family dinners, outings, and vacations, indeed even honeymoons,[30] the official launch point of family life, all of which become stock dramatic features of the post-Reconstruction domestic novels.

Granted, these duties and associated practices seem so general as to be insubstantial, as the former quotations illustrate. However, what is required to satisfy these domestic responsibilities, as Armstrong has further argued, is a revolutionary centralization of social and cultural power into a domain over which the woman as mother reigns—the home (Armstrong, p. 3). To protect the sanctity of the home, it is imperative that the woman as nurturer assume influence beyond its boundaries. One such effort engaged the Victorian male and female sphere complementation in which women utilized domesticity to empower reformist strategies. In this arrangement the domestic woman stands ready to reform/domesticate her society. This is precisely the viewpoint articulated in the essays of Cooper and Mossell, discussed above, as well as that dramatized in the domestic novels of Harper, Hopkins, and their black sister-writers.

The female domestic model of individuated desire became a decidedly visible gendered symbol of social progress for black Americans during the decade of the 1890s.[31] The fictive version of this model constructs a new understanding of personal worth for African Americans, grounded in individual achievement, piety, moral integrity, and self-sufficiency rather than in the antebellum communal values of group identity, originating in kinship. Armstrong's analysis is especially helpful for suggesting how the individual development of the domestic heroine changes community attitudes and ambition, as well as mobilizes subsequent action of social reform. According to her, "narratives which seem to be concerned solely with matters of courtship and marriage in fact seized the authority to say what was female, and . . . they did so in order to contest the reigning notion of kinship [and race] relations that attached most power and privilege to certain family [and color] lines" (Armstrong, p. 5). Thus the task of revising the black individual and the intraracial social hegemony was not exclusively played out in the civil discourse of black men like Washington or Du Bois or in the public discourse of feminized citizenship articulated in the clubs movement of late-nineteenth-century black women. The reconstruction of black identity was also played out in black women's post-Reconstruction domestic novels. The exemplary heroines of these works attempted to redefine and broadly disseminate the ideal sexual, racial, and personal characteristics for black women and men of an emergent bourgeois, capitalistic culture. The heroine's decorum and social values endeavored to produce new authoritative relationships with family members and friends; to modify the expectations of courtship, marriage, and family formation; ultimately to revise the mediation of social values and political representation both inside and outside of the household, indeed both inside and outside of the text.

Nancy Armstrong and Leonard Tennenhouse's *The Ideology of Conduct* is also particularly helpful to my analysis of the subtle political dynamics of black social transformation, particularly during the era of post-Reconstruction.[32] They argue that

> If it is true that in other cultures the rules that govern kinship relations also regulate the political economy, and that kinship relations are in this respect one and the same as political relations, then we must also assume that whatever it is that makes certain objects of sexual exchange more valuable than others also provides the basis of political authority. (pp. 1–2)

The culture of the United States, these authors hypothesize, "yield[s] to the same logic we identify in others" and it "reproduces a specific political order," as "sexual relations . . . uphold specific forms of political authority" (p. 2). Thus "the terms and dynamics of sexual desire must be a political language" and when the rhetoric of sexual desire is revised, so too is the political language (p. 2). "Because redefinitions of desire often revise the basis of political power, or human nature itself," Armstrong and Tennenhouse further contend, "one might say that changes in the understanding of desire, the practice of courtship, and the organization of the family are culturally antecedent to changes in the official institutions of state" (p. 2). I draw on their arguments to support my contention that the post-Reconstruction domestic novels of black women endeavored to reform their readers' sexual, economic, social, and religious desires. At the beginning of each novel, as we shall see in detail below, the heroine has an ambition that represents an oppressive viewpoint. By the novel's end she reforms her ambition and viewpoint by recasting them in an emancipatory context. Thus these works repeatedly recount a process for revising the heroine and make that process available to readers to duplicate in the real world so as to produce discrete and/or wide-scale social reformation.

Centering the Heroine's Virtue

The domestic fictions also negotiate sexual and social desires external to domesticity. One fact immediately evident when reading these novels is their preoccupation with light and white skin color, a preoccupation that no doubt is easily (mis)read as racial ambivalence. Such a reading suggests that these fictions endorse the social mobility of black people in direct relationship to their possession of white ancestry. However, that viewpoint, a legacy of plantation aristocracy, is precisely what this writing seeks to revise. Although there is a preponderance of characters with light skin color and straight hair, these physical characteristics do not reflect social privilege in an intraracial milieu. Rather, the compassion and dedication of the heroine and her husband to self and group development transform the old racist ideological imperatives into new stories of African-American success. Thus virtuous behavior and accomplishment, rather than physical appearance, are rewarded.

A similar shift in the construction of female value had already appeared in mid-nineteenth-century British and American women's novels. The white feminine ideal of early-nineteenth-century British and American fiction emphasizes female piety, discretion, modesty, and sympathy, all exemplified by the white heroine's fragile, fair beauty; by the mid-nineteenth century, however, that ideal centers moral and physical well-being independent of appearance. Self-possession rather than selflessness engenders this new female model, and a pleasing appearance becomes relatively unimportant, as the bright, virtuous, and compassionate but decidedly plain Jane Eyre of Charlotte Brontë's very popular novel *Jane Eyre* (1848) attests. This shift in gendered value construction, dramatized also in white American women's novels, probably influenced late-nineteenth-century black women authors' revision of the unquestioned privilege of light skin color. As a result, the social value of the heroine of post-Reconstruction black women's domestic novels resides not in her white appearance but in her virtue, comportment, and ability to enhance the virtuous prosperity of her family, as *Iola Leroy* poignantly illustrates.

Early in the novel the old contraband slave Tom uses Iola's white appearance as justification for his desire to rescue Iola from the villainy of his master Tom:

". . . but dere's a mighty putty young gal dere at Marse Tom's. I wish I
could get her away. . . . Oh, Marse bought her ob de trader to keep house
for him. But ef you seed dem putty white han's ob hern you'd never tink
she kept her own house, let 'lone anybody else's. . . . My! but she's putty.
Beautiful long hair comes way down her back; putty blue eyes, an' jis' ez
white ez anybody's in this place." (Harper, p. 38)

Tom's description is cast from the vantage point of a slave conditioned by
plantation aristocracy in which Negroid characteristics are presumed inferior.
For Tom, Iola's whiteness defines her beauty, which in turn signals her virtue.
In fact Tom and the white Yankee general, who orders Iola's release from
slavery, share the ultimately racist viewpoint that her Eurocentric beauty and
refinement make her more worthy of rescue than another woman of darker
hue and less social grace. This is precisely the viewpoint that the novel seeks
to revise, as another contraband slave, Robby (who is Iola's lost uncle), chas-
tises Tom for what we might call his "Tomish" ways, for believing that white
is right:

"Now, Tom, I thought you had cut your eye-teeth long enough not to let
them Anderson boys fool you. Tom, you must now think because a white
man says a thing, it must be so, and that a colored man's word is no
account 'longside of his. Tom, if ever we get our freedom, we've got
to learn to trust each other and stick together if we would be a people."
(p. 34)

Despite Robby's effort, Tom cannot reformulate his value structure so as
to eliminate decades of racist conditioning. That he soon dies is as much a
consequence of his inability to abandon the tenets of slavocracy as the bullet
that strikes him in battle.

As if to underscore this emancipatory discourse, the character portrayal of
Lucille Delany virtually erases Tom's racist judgment from the text. More
significant, Lucille's portrait marginalizes the intraracial social value of Iola's
white skin color and physical beauty as the ideal traits for feminine admiration. Granted that Harper characterized Iola as a classically beautiful, near-
white mulatta; the dark-skinned and college-educated Lucille Delany was the
fair Iola's "ideal woman" (p. 242). According to Iola, Lucille "is grand, brave,
intellectual and religious" (p. 242). A few pages later Iola insists that Lucille is
"one of the grandest women in America" (p. 244). From Iola's perspective,
Lucille Delany is an even truer version of feminine nobility and citizenry than
Iola herself. As Iola's ideal woman, Lucille is actually a heroine of a higher
degree than Iola. However, Iola serves a function that Lucille cannot. As a
free racial agent in that she can freely pass the color line, Iola is the arbiter
of ideal womanhood without restrictive racial qualification. Moreover, the
likelihood that Harper's contemporaries would know that Iola was the pen
name of Ida B. Wells-Barnett also associates racialized, militant political zeal
with the heroine of that name.[33]

Iola's white-skinned brother Harry further corroborates the marginality of skin color and Eurocentric beauty in the emancipatory cultural context. When mentioning that he would like to introduce Lucille to Iola, Harry emphatically remarks that, "She is one of the most remarkable women I have ever met" (p. 198). Iola responds by asking, "Is she young and handsome, brilliant and witty?" (p. 198), to which Harry replies, "She . . . is more than handsome, she is lovely; more than witty, she is wise; more than brilliant, she is excellent" (p. 198). Harper had Harry withhold Lucille's physical description, which would have been recalled at this point had he relied on Tom's value system. Finally, Iola prods him to add,

> "Well, she is of medium height, somewhat slender and well formed, with dark, expressive eyes, full of thought and feeling. Neither hair nor complexion show the least hint of blood admixture." (p. 199)

To which Iola comments, "I am glad of it" (p. 199). Not only is skin color the last rather than the first characteristic to be described in Harry's litany of his adoration of Lucille, Iola and her mother express their pleasure that Lucille is "a living argument for the capability which is in the race" (p. 199).

As if Lucille's admirable qualities were insufficiently emphasized, Harper further rewrote black female desirability by having Harry extend what was then considered the highest compliment that an eligible and exemplary man could bestow on a woman of that epoch—a proposal of marriage. Lucille's response to Harry's proposal extenuates the novel's critique on the intraracial privileging of light skin color that the text seeks to revise: "But," replied Lucille, "your mother may not prefer me for a daughter. You know, Harry, complexional prejudices are not confined to white people. . . . And Iola, would she be satisfied?" (Harper, p. 278). Harry emphatically depreciates light skin color by reporting that his mother is "too noble to indulge in such sentiments" (p. 278). As for Iola, he insists that "She is not one who can't be white and won't be black" (p. 278).

These are subtle condemnations of skin-color privilege that the traditional reading protocol either failed to notice or disregarded as unimportant. That protocol disparages Iola's light skin color and bourgeois background, because these characteristics counter the imperatives for a twentieth-century black nationalistic, Afrocentric, protest-based aesthetic. That protocol's definition of mulatto was also substantively different from the definition late-nineteenth-century writers, as Hopkins revealed in *Contending Forces*. Briefly to summarize her viewpoint, Hopkins spoke through her character Mrs. Willis to point out "that out of a hundred apparently pure black men not one will be able to trace an unmixed flow of African blood since landing upon these shores" (p. 151). Rather than regard *mulatto* as a generic term for designating the emancipated population and their heirs, indeed a race of new Negroes, as did Hopkins and her black contemporaries, we twentieth-century readers have generally viewed mulattoes as racially ambivalent African Americans who rely on their light skin color to bolster their self-esteem and bourgeois ambitions. Whereas Hopkins saw mulattoes as the racial stock of a new people, we have viewed this group not as representative of but antagonistic to the black population. By historicizing the racial construction of mulatto, we can not only discern a fundamentally different meaning of the designation but clarify what seems to have been at least one of Harper's purposes in characterizing Iola as a mulatta as well. *Iola Leroy* does not validate the presumed social privilege associated with mulattoes that contemporary readers have come to expect; rather the novel uses the mulatto's inherent transitional racial and class status to construct emancipatory resocialization, grounded in virtue, education, and hard work.

This perspective becomes particularly clear when we recall that the novel emphatically valorizes the dark-skinned Lucille Delany for being an exemplar of moral conduct, intellectual ability, academic achievement, and pious devotion to racial advancement. Like the other black women writers of this study, Harper made social mobility a product of practical and spiritual attributes rather than of light skin color and straight hair. Lucille is a lady not because of wealth or social station, which are deemed irrelevant, but due to her decorum, training, noble ideals, and meritorious performance. Thus it is essential for us to see that Harper and her sister writers, as well as their male counterparts like the editor I. Garland Penn discussed above, used fiction to reform the white supremacist attitudes of their black contemporaries with the celebration of a new model of ideal black womanhood, indeed a revised field of intraracial desire constructed as the desirable dark-skinned black woman as lady. Unfortunately, as black people increasingly adopted the dominant ideologies of beauty and male privilege, which I shall discuss below, they undermined the emancipatory constructions of the desirable dark woman and relative sexual equality.

Also during the post-Reconstruction era, evangelicalism continued to be increasingly popular among black people as a vehicle for enhancing personal authority, as evidenced by the growth in membership in the African Methodist Episcopal Church (as well as other black Christian sects) and by the repeated depictions of conversion scenes in black women's writing. Evangelicalism also provides an important liberational discourse for black women's writing; hence its celebration of piety is a means of encouraging characters and readers alike to imitate pious female characters who translate spiritual well-being into self-authority.[34] The heroine's conversion, evocation, and articulation of Christian doctrine provide both her and the readers of the novel with moral direction, fortitude, and conviction for making sound judgment within a socially sanctioned context. From Frado in Wilson's *Our Nig*, who relies on the authority of Christian conversion to cast moral censure on the Bellmonts so as to escape their physical and psychological abuse, to Meg in Kelley-Hawkins's *Megda*, who transforms personal vanity into will power that she lovingly surrenders to her Savior, the evangelical heroine uses moral and spiritual piety to gain control over her own life and to enrich the lives of others. In a racist and sexist society the concept of a black woman empowered by God is doubly radical.

Harper's *Iola Leroy* and Hopkins's *Contending Forces*, like the other post-

Reconstruction domestic novels examined in this study, envision (or figure) the new, gendered African American, both female and male, as she and he were in actuality in minute proportion and could be in larger numbers if black readers duplicated their exemplary lives. An important aspect of this resocialization concerns the selection of a mate. For example, Harper's first readers observe Iola's selection of Dr. Frank Latimer as her spouse partly because his notions about male and female ambition are not rigidly fixed by convention. Nevertheless, the text reports that Dr. Latimer "is a leader in every reform movement for the benefit of the community" (p. 279), while Iola "quietly [takes] her place in the Sunday-School as a teacher, and in the church as a helper" (p. 278). Dr. Latimer assumes the traditionally male-designated role as leader, and Iola assumes the complementary female role of helpmate. It is Iola's personal heroine Lucille Delany who revises this conventional gender role by assuming the nontraditional position of woman-as-leader. At the novel's close Lucille and Iola's brother Harry marry and "are at the head of a large and flourishing school. Lucille gives her ripening experience to her chosen work, to which she was too devoted to resign" (p. 280). Devotion and experience here efface Lucille's desire to fulfill personal, indeed professional, ambition outside the traditionally sanctioned female sphere. Moreover, this effacement seeks to cancel school board regulations that required female teachers to retire upon marriage.[35] Harper (and later Tillman) circumvented that regulation in her fictive realm by cloaking it with references to Lucille's extraordinary dedication and professional competence, as if these attributes were sufficient to override prevailing school-board directives. Not only does Lucille continue to work, thereby disavowing the code that middle-class women do not work outside the home, she also shares a position of leadership with her husband.

While Harper had the fair-skinned Iola remanded to slavery in the beginning of *Iola Leroy* and escape the racist sexual oppression of that institution with her virginity presumably intact,[36] Sappho Clark of Hopkins's *Contending Forces* is not so fortunate. Sappho does not fall victim to slavery but instead to the racist villainy of its aftermath. Her father's white half-brother kidnaps, rapes, and abandons her at a house of ill repute. She survives this encounter with racism, but she bears its scars. However, it is precisely her scarred womanhood that motivates her heroic self-transformation and thereby revises notions of female virtue beyond the scope of *Iola Leroy*.

Sappho is the vehicle through which Hopkins liberated conventionally restricting codes of feminine respectability and rewrote the patriarchal demand for premarital virginity. The text transforms Sappho from a passive and impure heroine—the sexually experienced object of perverse male desire—into an active female-hero, the subject of her own desire.[37] The text then asserts her virtue "on complex moral grounds," to use Jean Fagan Yellin's term,[38] rather than on the single issue of sexual purity. Hopkins signaled this act of heroic self-transformation with Sappho's change of name from Mabelle Beaubean to Sappho Clark. The latter name references the famous classical poet Sappho, who wrote gynocentric verse.[39] The revisionism is further affirmed at the close of the novel with the hero's interrogation of Sappho, in which he insists that loving devotion supersedes restrictive patriarchal gender conventions. He implores,

> "Why did you leave me, Sappho? Had you no confidence in my love for you? How meanly you must have judged me if you thought me capable of holding you responsible for the monstrous wrong committed against you." (Hopkins, pp. 395–96)

It is not necessary to recall the answers to these questions, for we already know the discourse on true love. What is important to notice, though, is that this text characterizes a woman who refuses to accept the guilt of sexual victimization as her fate. In addition, the novel ends by depicting a man whose courage to resist convention helps to revise her identity as a virtuous woman despite her past. Although the intensity of the representation of love in the last pages of *Contending Forces* seems to efface the racial discourse that dominates *Iola Leroy*, Hopkins merged the racial and sexual discourses throughout the text in an explicit summary about duty on the novel's final pages. She wrote, "United by love, chastened by sorrow and self-sacrifice, he and she planned to work together to bring joy to hearts crushed by despair" (p. 401). The sweeping reference to despair in this passage expands racial oppression routinely associated with slavery, and makes those generally in need of aid the object of reformist dedication.

The heroines—Iola Leroy and Lucille Delany in Harper's *Iola Leroy* and Sappho Clark in Hopkins's *Contending Forces*—satisfy their desire for individual and collective advancement by achieving in their marriages what Harper regarded as signs of "prosperity and progress" (p. 280). In fact the heroines' marriages to the right men instigate their continued personal growth. Although the idealized domesticity depicted in these and the other domestic novels of post-Reconstruction black women no doubt reflected the desire of turn-of-the-century black people to escape racism, a desire that African Americans still undoubtedly share, these texts exceed that desire. Rather than make civil protest their principal topic, *Iola Leroy* and *Contending Forces* make the affirmation of a racially validated and enlarged domesticity that topic. Hence the mutual "prosperity and progress" of black womanhood and the black family are these domestic novels' ultimate goals.

Rather than adopt the dominant society's stringent ideology of male superiority, the idealized family discourse in the domestic novels of post-Reconstruction black women emphasizes a compassionate companionship among spouses and what we late-twentieth-century readers would probably regard as relative spousal equality. Regardless of whether they support conservative or liberal gender conventions, the eleven domestic novels present the idealized domestic story in ways, as we shall see in the next two chapters, that revise the patriarchal roles of husbands and wives, granting both more educational opportunity and social freedom to invigorate the ongoing reform of black (and white) Americans. It is precisely this enlarged and idealized domesticity that empowers these novels' racial and sexual liberational discourses, making them reciprocal signifiers.

6

Revising the Patriarchal Texts
of Husband and Wife
in Real and Fictive Worlds

Education has not caused these women to shirk the cares and responsibilities of private life; rather, we believe, each feels the blessing which her example must be to the entire race. Education, with us, does not encourage celibacy but is developing pleasant homes and beautiful families. . . . No true man can object to thus developing the higher nature of women; we all have the happiness of knowing a far greater number of examples of women, intelligent and cultivated, active in good work, interested in all that is worthy of interest, who by the development of their faculties have added grace and luster to their natural attractions.

PAULINE E. HOPKINS, "Famous Women of the Negro Race"
(1902)

"A thing of beauty is a joy forever."
 This is equally true of woman. . . . The really beautiful woman is estimated by her genuine goodness of heart, the greatness of her soul, the purity and sweetness of her character, the amiable disposition, the intrinsic value she places upon morals and virtue (of which the latter adjunct is her crowning glory); if she be the possessor of these absolutely necessary qualifications she is both lovely and attractive; be her face ever so homely and her figure ever so plain, she it is who will make the truest wife, and heaven's best gift to the world.

ELLA WRIGHT-PLEASANT, The Women's Department,
The A.M.E. Church Review (1900)

The true woman takes her place by the side of man as his companion, his co-worker, his helpmate, his equal, but she never forgets that she is a woman and not a man. Whether in the home as wife and mother, or struggling in the ranks of business or professional life, she retains her womanly dignity and sweetness, which is at once her strength and her shield.

MRS. JOSEPHINE TURPIN WASHINGTON, Introduction to
Lewis A. Scruggs, *Women of Distinction* (1893)

Gender Rites and the Higher Education
of Black Women

In 1902 Pauline E. Hopkins wrote a series of articles for *The Colored American* magazine, entitled "Famous Women of the Negro Race." In the articles she surveyed the successful lives of several black women who had graduated from institutions of higher learning. She held up these women as models of accomplishment, proclaiming that their achievements "[did] not encourage celibacy" but in every instance led to the production of "pleasant homes and beautiful families."[1] The series was principally directed to the small, black middle class ("the Talented Tenth" in Du Bois's words), who, at the turn of the century, generally endorsed the model of the black Victorian family, characterized by historian Willard B. Gatewood as follows:

> Fathers and husbands . . . were the authority figures . . . [and] were clearly dominant in the marriage partnerships. . . . [They] provided the principal source of income for their family. Most were employed in white-collar and managerial occupations. Many [among the older generation] were likely to be found in service trades—such as catering, barbering, and tailoring—or in government positions and small businesses. While some were attorneys, physicians, and teachers, a greater number of their children were more likely to be found in these professions. Mothers and wives of upper-class black families were mainly "parlor ladies" who usually did not work outside the home. If they did, they were teachers,[2] lecturers, or writers. Even though many upper-class women had servants to assist with housekeeping, they spent much of their time and energy in managing their households and on child-rearing and home-related activities. . . . Outside the home they participated in ladies' guilds, church societies, and cultural organizations whose memberships were limited to women of their own social class. They figured prominently in the formation of the National Association of Colored Women. Like white women, they were viewed as the guardians of culture upon whom rested "the greatest privilege and responsibility."[3]

While only a very small segment of the post-Reconstruction black population had the educational and economic means to support the Victorian family structure, it became the ideal to which most working-class black people subscribed not only during the post-Reconstruction era but during the twentieth century as well. Consequently, like white Americans, black Americans increasingly associated social prosperity with the Victorian family model of male assertiveness and female reticence and leisure. Hence, defining intraracial values and providing direction for the institutions of home, church, and school were largely male prerogatives. Even though the black Victorian model permitted professional activity outside the home for the wife and other females of the household, modesty and reserve were essential. Those middle-class women (like Mary Church Terrell and Ida B. Wells-Barnett) who asserted positions of leadership, thus resisting that decorum, were often regarded as aggressive and immodest. They frequently became the objects of social criticism (Gatewood, p. 188).[4]

The adoption of gender values associated with the Victorian family and its "true" women among African Americans precipitated an intraracial controversy over the higher education of black women that somewhat duplicated a similar controversy simultaneously occurring in white society. Like their white counterparts, young black women increasingly applied to institutions of higher education and met opposition from their own constituency, as the excerpts from Hopkins's article reveal. Hopkins's emphatic disclaimers — "No true man can object to thus developing the higher nature of women" in the epigraph and "Even men who look only for agreeable companions, acknowledge that they are to be found rather among the educated than the uneducated" in that article — are cautious refutations of anticipated allegations of feminine impropriety arising specifically from this controversy. Hopkins attempted to mediate and perhaps intervene in the growing entrenchment of conservative black gender rites by constructing an attitude of masculine best self-interest to intimate what we late-twentieth-century readers would term "sexist attitudes" inherent in the positions of those African Americans who were reluctant to view the education of black women as an asset for racial advancement.

Several years prior to the publication of Hopkins's series, Gertrude Mossell, Anna Cooper, and Josephine Turpin Washington (among many others[5]) had also publicly promoted educated black womanhood in language that feminized the discourse of African-American citizenship. While all three women frequently ascended the lecture platform, they also used the pen to advance this cause. Among their numerous publications, Mossell and Cooper each wrote an important book, to which I again refer, now in terms of their promotion of higher education for black women. Turpin Washington used her introduction to the 1893 publication of *Women of Distinction* by Lewis A. Scruggs to align "the progressive woman" to the "true woman." She conceded that the woman who was "caricatured and held up as a horror and a warning to that portion of the feminine world who might be tempted into like forbidden paths" was present in society in "individual cases."[6] But this was not "the true type of the 'progressive woman' of to-day." To the contrary, this new "true woman"

> is modest and womanly, with a reverence for the high and holy duties of wife and mother. . . . She would not have women neglect home and husband and children to enter professional life, or to further any public cause, however worthy. . . . For [some of] them the prince may come, he may not. They are content to wait, not idly, not with folded hands and the feeling that if he come not all hope is lost and life not worth living, but working sturdily and blithely, developing the energies of mind and body, proving themselves worthy of their womanhood and fit mates for strong and manly men. (pp. xi, xiii)

With this progressive exemplar in place, Turpin Washington shifted her focus to revere the majority of black women, those self-sacrificing black wives and sisters who spend their days "bending over the wash-tub or the sewing machine, striving by their industry to add to the comforts or to the advantages of the idolized brother in school . . . or the husband pursu[ing] the course in school from which he was debarred in earlier life" (p. xvi). By appreciating these women, Turpin Washington not only grounded her discussion on the material reality of most black people but also paid tribute to patriarchal privilege in an effort no doubt to demonstrate that she was a "true woman" and not a "new" one. She extended her affirmation of the "widening of woman's sphere of thought and action" (p. xii) by looking to the future, hoping that "those who come after may be inspirited by the record of what has been wrought to make the most of their more liberal opportunities, and so hasten the time when our work may be criticized as that of human beings, and neither as that of colored women nor as that of women" (p. xvii).

In all probability such arguments would have been unnecessary prior to the Emancipation or during the period of Reconstruction (1863–77), for during those years practically all black people regarded education as a site of desire, beneficial to everyone without excessive gender stipulation. For example, historian Linda M. Perkins illustrates the eagerness of Northern antebellum black people to secure an education by citing an 1837 article:

> "To the Females of Colour" in the New York black newspaper, *The Weekly Advocate*, (Jan. 7, 1837) urged black women to obtain an education. The article stated, "in any enterprise for the improvement of our people, either moral or mental, our hands would be palsied without woman's influence." . . . In other words, [Perkins concludes] black females and males would demonstrate the race's intelligence, morality, and ingenuity.[7]

Indeed the joint desire of black men and women for education became an index of their exercise of freedom, as "[a]cess to education for themselves and their children was . . . central to the meaning of freedom," in the words of historian Eric Foner.[8]

During post-Reconstruction, though, as African Americans adapted the dominant society's patriarchal gender codes and gained control over their own educational institutions as well, their academic aspirations adhered to the pattern of male dominance; black men were designated as educational and spiritual leaders—in short, as race leaders—and black women as their wives.[9] According to Perkins, "As black men sought to obtain education and positions similar to that of white men in society, many adopted the prevailing notion of white society, of the natural subordination of women" (p. 24). By contrast, prior to the Civil War, Perkins adds, "public schools for blacks were overwhelmingly coeducational, and girls received primarily the same instruction as boys"; but after the war, black men outnumbered black women in higher education.[10] Needless to say, black women, like black men, were not unified in their acceptance of female educational subordination; many subtly resisted it and others openly challenged it. The type of education deemed appropriate for women was a topic widely debated in black intellectual circles, especially in literary culture, to which black women had greater access than to the pulpit or the public rostrum.

While my discussion of Cooper's and Mossell's respective books—A Voice From the South (1892) and The Work of the Afro-American Woman (1894)—in the preceding chapter focused on the emancipatory discourse of manhood and womanhood in addition to the centrality of black literary culture to the social advancement of African Americans, my discussion here concentrates specifically on their support of higher education for black women and the enlargement of the woman's sphere. By referring to the stultifying effects of narrowly interpreted feminine decorum, these women argue that black women's access to higher education is a most effective means for enhancing the accomplishment of the race.

I begin this discussion with Mossell's work because she (like Hopkins and Turpin Washington above) placed black female intellectual advancement into the discourse of the patriarchal family. In so doing she carefully situated her argument to mitigate male dissention. She effaced self-authority behind the approbations of maternity, much like the white Republican mothers whom I discussed previously. She then aligned the educational advancement of black women with the Emancipation:

> The emancipation of the Negro race came about at the entrance to that which has been aptly termed the Woman's Century; co-education, higher education for women, had each gained a foothold. The "Woman's Suffrage" movement had passed the era of ridicule and entered upon that of critical study. The Woman's Christian Temperance Union had become a strong factor in the reform of the nation. These facts made the uplifting of the womanhood of this race a more hopeful task than might otherwise have been . . . possible under a more unfavorable aspect of the woman question. . . . The men of the race, in most instances, have been generous, doing all in their power to allow the women of the race to rise with them.[11]

By relating the enlargement of the female sphere through education to the emancipation of slaves, Mossell avoided a direct conflict with those who support restrictive feminine gender codes by deflecting opposition with their indirect comparison to those who opposed emancipation. By couching her discussion within the context of black liberation instead of producing a polemic exclusively about sexual equality, Mossell used the power of the Emancipation and the desire of African Americans for social advancement to endorse the educational ambitions of black women. She also referred to the beneficial precedent of white women's activism to reassure her skeptical black readers about the favorable disposition of the dominant society on this issue. What is important to note here, then, is that rather than addressing the sexual politics of racial advancement (the problematic topic that she insinuated with the expression "in most instances"), Mossell extolled the generosity of black men who share widened opportunity with their female counterparts. With the tactics of effacement, deflection, and flattery in place, she directed the remainder of the introductory chapter as well as most of those subsequent to surveying the accomplishments of black women in a variety of professional fields. In this way she could celebrate the accomplishments of these women as a part of the discourse of racial progress, rather than argue exclusively for higher education of black women.

In the short chapter "The Opposite Point of View," Mossell directly addressed the problematic subject of sexual politics; however, here again she employed diplomacy. Ever careful to consider male perspective in fashioning her argument, Mossell did not address the gender prohibitions restricting black women from the intraracial public domain. Instead she employed the domestic paradigm of harmonious home life to characterize how narrow interpretations of femininity jeopardize the development of the black family, diminish the compatibility between the spouses, and ultimately decrease masculine pleasure. Thus as Hopkins did in "Famous Women of the Negro Race," Mossell constructed her argument around masculine self-interest to make her point while specifically admonishing women about the unproductive results of excessive feminine deference to masculine authority:

> For several years, every paper or magazine that has fallen into our hands gave some such teaching as this: "The wife must always meet her husband with a smile." She must continue in the present and future married life to do a host of things for his comfort and convenience; the sure fate awaiting her failure to follow this advice being the loss of the husband's affection and the mortification of seeing it transferred to the keeping of a rival. She must stay at home, keep the house clean, prepare food properly and care for her children, or he will frequent the saloon, go out at night and spend his time unwisely at the least. (pp. 118–19)

Announcing her "differ[ing] . . . view of the subject," Mossell stated, "I have come to the conclusion that women need these teachings least."

> The wife may fill the house with sweet singing, have the children dressed and ready to give a joyful greeting to the father, the breakfast might be fit to tempt an epicure, and yet the whole be greeted surlily by one who considers wife and home but his rightful convenience. (p. 119)

According to Mossell, female subscription to obsequious comportment would not ensure domestic happiness. Character and not manners dictates behavior. Moreover, unless husbands as well as wives are responsible for mutual domestic gratification, it will vanish. Mossell openly argued that an interesting and educated wife is more likely to create a productive, stimulating home life than an obsequious one. "I believe," she wrote, "that a woman who has a mind and a will of her own will become monotonous to a less extent than one so continuously sweet and self-effacing; and I believe history proves it" (p. 123). By contending that narrow interpretations of femininity impeded domestic harmony and racial progress, she did not have to mount a frontal argument about the inequity of restricting education to black women. Such a carefully framed presentation also averts black patriarchal retort.

By contrast, Anna Cooper was much less diplomatic in her criticism of stringent feminine gender conventions in *A Voice From the South*. Here she launched a veritable feminist polemic. Relying on reformist female gender constructions of the mid-nineteenth century, Cooper mounted her argument for the higher education of black women on the contention that they possess an inherently sympathetic and virtuous nature that makes them exceptionally suitable for effecting social reform. By surveying the expansive reach of women's domestic influence throughout society, she asserted in the chapter "Womanhood a Vital Element in the Regeneration and Progress of a Race" that the social advancement of a race is largely dependent on the condition of its women (a thesis that predates by more than two decades a similar argument in William E. B. Du Bois's "Damnation of Women," published in *Darkwater: Voices from Within the Veil* in 1920). "[T]he position of woman in society," she insisted, "determines the vital elements of its regeneration and progress" (Cooper, p. 21). "In this period," she added in another chapter ("The Status of Women in America"),

> when material prosperity and well earned ease and luxury are assured facts from a national standpoint, woman's work and woman's influence are needed as never before; needed to bring a heart power to this money getting, dollar-worshipping civilization; needed to bring a moral force to the utilitarian motives and interests of the time; needed to stand for God and Home and Native Land *versus gain and greed and grasping selfishness*. (p. 131, emphasis in original)

"In her hands," Cooper continued, "must be molded the strength, the wit, the statesmanship, the morality, all the psychic force, the social and economic intercourse of that era" (p. 143). In the white female reformist tradition, in which activist women saw themselves as "universal reformers,"[12] Cooper avowed that it is essential for women—black and white—to achieve full equality of opportunity to ensure the continued moral advancement of the whole nation. This position she practiced as well as preached; for during her career as teacher and principal of the famous "M" Street High School in Washington, D.C., she was a staunch advocate for the academic education of black people, especially black women.[13]

In the chapter "The Higher Education of Women," Cooper endorsed the viewpoint of the inherent moral superiority of women that was current, especially during the mid-nineteenth century, to support the Victorian complementation of the separate male and female spheres. She explained that there was "a feminine as well as a masculine side to truth; that these are related not as inferior and superior, not as better and worse, not as weaker and stronger, but as complements—complements in one symmetric whole" (p. 60). She insisted that women have a responsibility to promote the feminine side of truth and to "add [their] modicum to the riches of the world's thought" (p. 61). She also maintained that "intellectual development, with the self-reliance and capacity for earning a livelihood which it gives, renders a woman less dependent on the marriage relation for physical support" (p. 68) and thereby gives emotional integrity to a woman's motives for marriage rather than making marriage financially expedient. Like Mossell, Cooper moreover contended that education in no way "unfits [women] for the duty of wifehood and maternity or primarily renders these conditions any less attractive to them than to the domestic type of woman" (p. 71). To the contrary, "Knowledge of physiology makes [women] better mothers and housekeepers . . . while their training in other natural sciences and in mathematics . . . [helps them] obtain an accuracy and fair-mindedness which is of great value to them in dealing with their children or employees" (pp. 71–72). In this way Cooper emphatically disputed the patriarchal presumption of the intellectual inferiority of women, insisting that education for women was not a waste of time, effort, and money. Education, she wrote, did not diminish feminine appeal. Despite her explicit social criticism, Cooper shared the optimism of her constituency. She regarded the rapidly approaching twentieth century as a "new era" of opportunity for everyone, especially for women and black people. "To be alive at such an epoch," she later exhorted, "is a privilege, to be a woman then is sublime" (p. 143).

Cooper concluded this chapter by recounting the difficulty she personally encountered when she expressed her desire to study Greek "in a class *for the candidates for the ministry*" at the preparatory school of St. Augustine College (p. 77, emphasis in original).[14] However, rather than present her experience as an autobiographical narrative, she novelized that experience, inviting the voice of parody to censure the prohibitions that women routinely faced when they sought higher education:

> A boy, however meager his equipment and shallow his pretensions had only to declare a floating intention to study theology and he could get all the support, encouragement and stimulus he needed, be absolved from work and invested beforehand with all the dignity of his far away office. While a self-supporting girl had to struggle on by teaching in the summer and working after school hours to keep up with her board bills, and actually to fight her way against positive discouragements to the higher education; til one such girl one day flared out and told the principal "the only mission opening before a girl in his school was to marry one of these candidates." He said he didn't know but it was. And when at last that same girl announced her desire and intention to go to college it was received with about the same incredulity and dismay as if a brass button on one of those candidate's coats had propounded a new method for squaring the circle or trisecting the arc. (pp. 77–78)

In this scenario Cooper severely censured the inequality of opportunity facing black men and women in higher education. Not only did she give the voice of outrage to the female student in the anecdote; she pronounced the absurdity of such practices by parodying the incapacity of some black men to grant their female cohorts intellectual dignity.

While Cooper exhorted her readers to "expect something more of [our girls] than that they merely look pretty and appear well in society" (p. 78), her contemporary Mrs. Julia Ringwood Coston,[15] editor of *Ringwood's Journal of Fashion* (no longer extant), reiterated the viewpoint of Ella Wright-Pleasant in the epigraph given at the beginning of this chapter.[16] Coston heartily embraced the more conservative Victorian gender codes for black women, reflected in the description of her own character by "her dearest friends":

> There is nothing masculine or egotistic in the character of Mrs. Coston. She is a lovable woman, whose actuating desire is to serve the highest interests of the women of to-day, that their lives may be made more helpful by giving them modest publicity, and thus present them as worthy models for the emulation of our growing womanhood. (Scruggs, p. 143)

She celebrated those gender codes in her editorial, entitled "The Women Who Are Loved . . . ," published in *Ringwood's Journal of Fashion*, which Monroe A. Majors reprinted in *Noted Negro Women* and which I quote here in its entirety:

THE WOMEN WHO ARE LOVED ARE THOSE WHO ARE WOMEN

They have a place in all our hearts; the men adore them, and the women love them, yet they are essentially feminine. They know naught of woman's rights and universal suffrage; they are not troubled with the affairs of State, nor are they agents of reform. They are women, adorable women, into whose minds has crept no vicious longing for publicity and no hunger to usurp the sphere of men.

Would it not be well to make such women models for our girls? Would it not be well to consider a little what are the deepest, truest, highest rights of womankind? Would it not be well to look ahead a bit and ponder, what sort of a world will it be when femininity shall be extinct?

Women have so many rights that are truly theirs, so many opportunities for influence upon the great world, that they may stop and consider, not how to obtain more, but how to make the best use of what already is theirs.

There pertains to true womanhood a sanctity and a purity without which the world must suffer. Politicians, lawyers and financiers can all be recruited from the ranks of men, but where are we to find the softening, refining influences of life if our women cease to be such?

No one who comes in contact with homes that are happy and attractive can doubt the influence of her who is their inspiration. A truly feminine woman, one who is thoroughly in sympathy with great and noble thoughts, has a power so penetrating that our girls have need of careful training if they are to learn to wield it well.

Every true man has stored away in his heart an ideal woman such as would require all the strength and power of the real individual to realize. Surely the sphere can not be low or limited that possesses such possibilities, and surely the highest, most inalienable right must be that of realizing them.

Not for one moment is it meant to speak a light or disparaging word of that noble army of women who, finding themselves thrown on their own resources, have bravely taken up the burden and borne it through the thick of the fight. To these be all honor accorded.

It is not the silent army of workers who do harm, but the ostentatious seekers after notoriety. There is no good reason why a woman should cease to be feminine because she is compelled to work, but it too often happens that the girls who are forced to earn their own living become imbued with a spirit of bravado.

Gallantry belongs to all strong, vigorous men; their natural impulse is to protect and help the struggling woman? But what is to be done with an unsexed creature, a thing neither man nor woman? In every situation in life, at home surrounded by luxury, or in the world struggling for preference, a woman's womanhood is her surest, strongest shield.

Recently there has appeared in the world of letters a certain class of women writers who have thrown off the veil of modesty, and who, in the name of reform, pose as martyrs, sacrificing themselves to a great work. To all such would-be missionaries it may be admissable to hint that the loss of one chaste womanly woman does more harm than any number of novels can ever do good. Also, it might be suggested that, inasmuch as books are read, not by a limited class only, but by a large public, there is danger that more minds become polluted than purified by their influence.

Only an utter lack of femininity could make it possible for a woman to stand before the world and proclaim its vice. The harm her example may do to the young and ignorant aspirants for literary honors is only paralleled by the cause she has given mankind to hold her womanhood in light esteem. (Majors, pp. 253–55)

Despite Coston's conservative gender posture, reminiscent of Dickson D. Bruce, Jr.'s description of the demands of genteel deportment on writing,[17] Coston nevertheless argued that femininity and employment were not incompatible. No doubt she accepted the economic realities of her day that demanded gainful employment for most black women, but she rejected the increased personal independence and self-assertiveness that usually resulted from such labor, labeling that autonomy as the "spirit of bravado." Insofar as Coston was concerned, these characteristics are inappropriate for black women because they undermine their claim to femininity. Consistent with her zeal for Victorian femininity, she was reticent on the higher education of black women, which was intricately linked to their gainful employment. Confirming Bruce's observations on the demands of feminine gentility, Coston adamantly maintained that social agitation in word or deed is categorically inappropriate for black ladies.

Coston's viewpoint about a black woman's proper place is diametrically opposed to the viewpoints held by Hopkins, Mossell, and Cooper, all of whom contested male hegemony. Coston's appropriation of femininity in terms that Cooper identified as "stand[ing] on pedestals or liv[ing] in doll houses" (p. 75) is undoubtedly symptomatic of the categorical desire of black women to be granted the social courtesy routinely accorded to white ladies. Coston affirmed Victorian gender codes probably in the hope that their adoption would help to shield black women from both verbal and physical sexual assaults. Such a position is certainly understandable, though untenable. Ironically, Coston's insistence that the home was a woman's proper realm and her own entry into the public sphere, albeit on the margins as a business woman in order to promote her fashion journal, seem somewhat contradictory. Trying to secure a place in both realms, that is, affirming the dominant conventions of feminine civility while simultaneously realizing their practical limitations, might have been responsible for the inconsistencies in her viewpoint. Indeed her conservative position might also have served as a personal mask for her own venture into the public sphere as a journalist.

For comparison, I refer to Cooper's concluding remarks in the chapter "The Higher Education of Women" in *A Voice From the South*:

> It seems hardly a gracious thing to say, but it strikes me as true, that while our men seem thoroughly abreast of the times on almost every other subject, when they strike the woman question they drop back into six-teenth-century logic. . . . I fear the majority of colored men do not yet think it worth while that women aspire to higher education. . . . The three R's, a little music and a good deal of dancing, a first rate dressmaker and a bottle of magnolia balm, are quite enough generally to render charming any woman possessed of tact and the capacity for worshipping masculinity. (p. 75)

Cooper contended that advancing excessive feminization of black womanhood and advancing the race operated at cross-purposes. Rather than subscribe to the conservative Victorian attitudes on female educational restriction, she argued for equal access to education for black women as the most basic strategy for elevating themselves, their families, their communities, and ultimately their race. Rather than regard black women as dainty ladies or an underclass, circumscribed by genteel gender or racist prohibitions, Cooper considered black women as citizens with clearly defined social rights, expectations, and obligations. Although Coston supported black women's need to find gainful employment, unlike Cooper she approached work abstractly, and she made no comment on the economic conditions that required their employment and the types of work that routinely exploited them. Presumably it was her expectation that feminine black women would marry and devote themselves to their families.

However, even if black male family heads had received wages for their labor comparable to those of white men and therefore were able to support their families without the assistance of working wives, sisters, and daughters, the demography did not apportion a husband for all eligible black women.[18] This indisputable factor strongly influenced Cooper, Mossell, and Hopkins (among other black educators) to encourage black people to see the advantage of educating their daughters. Not only was an educated daughter a way out of poverty and therefore a persistent assault against the economic underpinnings of racism, but education provided unmarried or widowed black women a way to support themselves with dignity.

Gender Rites and Fictive Texts

Without a doubt Hopkins was a staunch supporter of higher education for African-American women; however, that outlook is not a dominant theme in her novels. Given the racial strife of the 1890s as well as the increasing gender conservatism among African Americans, no doubt Hopkins found herself unable to exude the optimism about educated motherhood and racial prosperity that the elderly Harper so readily expressed in *Iola Leroy*. In fact, *Contending Forces* seems to rewrite that novel by tempering its optimism on both fronts.[19] For instance, Hopkins did not permit the novel's near-white heroine Sappho Clark, who possesses more than a normal-school education, to proclaim the virtues of this education. The effects of education are stamped on her for us to observe; she is rational, self-reliant, and quite articulate. As Hazel Carby has rightly argued, "Sappho was the independent women who in . . . intimate moments . . . talked of the need for suffrage and the political activity of women" and the force that "disrupted [her friend] Dora's complacency with her existence that led her to 'generally accept whatever the men tell [her] as right' and made her reassess the importance of friendships with women."[20] However, Hopkins restricted Sappho's voice to private space, preventing her penetration into the public sphere of influence. Moreover, while Iola in *Iola Leroy* delivers her address on the education of mothers at a public meeting in the presence of men and women, gender restrictions in *Contending Forces* consign the topics of "the advancement of the colored woman" (p. 147) and sexual politics to the chapter entitled "The Sewing-Circle." For Harper the discourses of black womanhood were a part of those of race, but for Hopkins, who was evidently more constrained by the growing conservatism of gender rites among African Americans, Victorian gender codes separated the discourses of racial and sexual politics. Rather than promote the higher education of women, Hopkins uses Sappho as a vehicle for mounting an argument about employment segregation. For despite Sappho's training as a stenographer and *typewriter* (nineteenth-century term for a typist) and her highly respectable decorum, she is ostracized from the professional white world even in Boston because she refuses to pass for white.[21] She must take her assignments home for completion.

What is particularly important about Sappho's history is that it rewrites the antebellum sexual discourse designating black women as powerless sexual prey. While Iola's mission is to liberate black women from the sexual abuses routinely associated with slavery and to dramatize their ascent to the status of full-fledged Victorian heroines, Sappho revises the prerequisite that the heroine must be sexually innocent. This becomes clear when one compares Sappho Clark (alias Mabelle Beaubean) with another character in *Contending Forces*, Grace Montfort. Each has a history that evolves as the realistic consequences of rape. The antebellum discourse binds Grace to the conventional fate of the sexually violated heroine—death. By contrast, the postbellum discourse allows Mabelle to choose her own life as Sappho Clark. This novel presents a heroine whose virtue is not simply the product of sexual innocence; she qualifies herself as a virtuous person through the strength of her character.

Whereas female ambition is a part of the discourse of racial politics in *Iola Leroy*, that discussion in *Contending Forces* is largely a masculine discourse.[22] As a result, in the sequential chapters in this latter novel—"The American Colored League," "Luke Sawyer Speaks to the League," and "Will Smith's

Defense of His Race" — several black men speak, but the women are silent.[23] Although the membership in the League is restricted to "leading colored men all over New England" (p. 224), we know that women are present at the meeting due to the fact that Hopkins constructed their presence with the opening remarks of the president of the League: "'Fellow-citizens and men and women of my race'" (p. 244). Our late-twentieth-century perspective makes it very easy for us to claim that public silencing of black women presents an apparent inconsistency between Hopkins's editorial viewpoint and fictional practice, but would this inconsistency appear from the perspective of Hopkins's own era?

"The Sewing-Circle" chapter provides an excellent opportunity for us to observe some of the cultural implications of Victorian gender constructions especially for women of the emergent black middle class. As she did in her series "Famous Women of the Negro Race," Hopkins diverted attention from polemics with a display of exemplary personifications of her position. Thus, rather than give her argument explicit presentation, she presented the demonstrable talents of two widows. The first is the matron Ma Smith, mother of Will Smith, Sappho's future hero-husband. Ma Smith organizes the sewing circle in the parlor of her home to raise money to offset her church's mortgage. But this meeting has another purpose just as serious — to provide an intellectual social activity for the benefit of the girls of the congregation. The novel reports that "after the sewing had been given out the first business of the meeting was to go over events of interest to the Negro race which had transpired during the week throughout the country" (p. 143). The second widow is Mrs. Willis. That both women are widows is significant because they are the principal means for inscribing the absence of patriarchal desire in the text.[24] Indeed, widows are so numerous in black female post-Reconstruction fictions that they constitute not only a standard character type but also a popular tactic for transforming patricentric authority into matricentric influence.

Mrs. Smith is the uncontested exemplary widow of the novel, a fact underscored repeatedly by the maternal referral "Ma Smith." Her reticence, efficient domestic managerial skills, and genuine display of loving affection to her children underscore her idealized maternal characterization by late-nineteenth-century Victorian standards. By contrast, Mrs. Willis's widowhood is problematic. The text describes her initially in the context of her deceased husband. He was "a bright Negro politician" whom she had "loved . . . with a love ambitious for his advancement" (p. 145). The text further recalls, from her perspective as a loving wife, that

> His foot on the stairs mounting to the two-room tenement which constituted their home in the early years of married life, had sent a thrill to her very heart as she sat sewing baby clothes for the always expected addition to the family. But twenty years make a difference in all our lives. It brought many changes to the colored people of New England — social and business changes. Politics had become the open sesame for the ambitious Negro. A seat in the Legislature then was not a dream to this man, urged by the

loving woman behind him. . . . He grasped his opportunity; grew richer, more polished, less social, and the family broadened out and overflowed from old familiar "West End" environments across the River Charles into the aristocratic suburbs of Cambridge. Death comes to us all. (pp. 145–46)

Mrs. Willis is the proverbial ambitious woman behind the successful man. However, at his death there are no funds to meet her financial needs, and she has to find a way to maintain the standard of living to which she has become accustomed. The text reports that "she was forced to begin a weary pilgrimage—a hunt for the means to help her breast the social tide" (p. 146). For her, then, the question becomes what line of work can fulfill both her financial needs *and* personal ambitions. No longer able to represent her ambition as desire for her husband's advancement, Mrs. Willis finds that

> The best opening . . . after looking carefully about her, was in the great cause of the evolution of true womanhood in the work of the "Woman Question" as embodied in marriage and suffrage. . . . The advancement of the colored woman should be the new problem in the woman question that should float her upon its tide into the prosperity she desired. (pp. 146–47)

Hence Mrs. Willis comes to the woman's question not out of a passionate and self-sacrificing dedication to foster women's rights but out of the practical desire to gain economic support for herself and to advance herself, black women, and the race in that order. In short, she uses the "Woman Question" to meet her financial needs and to satisfy her professional ambitions. As she herself says, she is "a practical woman of the world" (p. 156), who has "succeeded well in her plans" (p. 147), which the text describes as "conceived in selfishness, they yet bore glorious fruit in the formation of clubs of colored women banded together . . . [to] better the condition of mankind" (p. 147). She then is the consummate politician. To her audience she is a "brilliant widow" (p. 143) who "could talk dashingly on many themes" . . . (p. 146).[25]

Observing how each woman provides for her children focuses the gender dissimilarities between Mrs. Willis and Ma Smith. Ma Smith fulfills social sanctions for feminine humility by remaining reticent about her ambition to give her children sound preparation for productive futures: "Deep in her heart was the cherished hope that when the mortgage was paid Willie [her son] would be free to choose a profession; but they [the mother, daughter, and son] never mentioned among themselves the hope which was cherished in each breast" (p. 85). Due to their careful financial management, Will eventually "receive[s] his degree from Harvard" (p. 359).[26] However, there is no family bravado with this accomplishment, for as the text reports, "the eager zest and joy of pursuit and accomplishment were gone; duty alone remained" (p. 359). By contrast "It was her [Mrs. Willis's] boast that she had made the fortunes of her family and settled her children well in life" (p. 147). Her character eschews reticence and modesty[27]; she is

> the pivot about which all the social and intellectual life of the colored people of her section revolved. No one had yet found the temerity to contest her position. . . . It was thought that she might be eclipsed by the younger and more brilliant women students on the strength of their alma mater, but she still held her own by sheer force of will-power and indomitable pluck. (p. 148)

The title of Mrs. Willis's address at the Sewing Circle—"The place which the virtuous woman occupies in upbuilding a race"—is indicative of her self-assertion of authority (p. 148). After a brief expression of her desire to see the young women before her mature into "race women," Mrs. Willis addresses questions about the inherent virtue of the "native African women," as a counterargument to the dominant society's charge of sexual promiscuity—retrogressionism—among black American women (pp. 148, 149).[28] In spite of Mrs. Willis's obvious superior ability, she incites "a wave of repulsion" in the heroine Sappho, who senses "her effusiveness, so forced and insincere" (p. 155). Sappho retreats from her "as from an abyss suddenly beheld stretching before her"; yet she is also "impressed in spite of herself, by the woman's words" (pp. 155, 157).

Mrs. Willis is a successful but problematic professional woman (or, in Josephine Turpin Washington's words, a poor model of "a progressive woman") who has stepped far into the public realm to work for racial uplift. She revises the traditional role of the retiring, reticent, widowed matron to become an outspoken race woman who attracts ambivalence precisely because she seeks self-authority rather than selflessness. Despite her beneficence in general and sound advice in particular to Sappho "to be happy and bright for the good of those about you" (p. 157), which seems a cliched expression, it addresses what Carby has provocatively termed Sappho's "desire for a pure black womanhood, an uncolonized black female body" (Carby, p. 144). This point becomes particularly clear when we recall that a major portion of Mrs. Willis's address concerns the "impregnable" virtue of "the native African woman" in which she defines virtue in a larger context than "animal passions" (p. 149).[29] While the text suggests that Sappho is agitated by her detection of Mrs. Willis's self-conscious desire to grasp power outside her sphere, feelings that Hopkins's contemporaries no doubt also shared, Sappho's agitation may be partly a product of her own ambivalence about confronting her sexual history as well.

Although Hopkins could not resolve the discomfort of her contemporaries about female will to power, she could mitigate its effect by deploying what Fredric Jameson has called "strategies of containment,"[30] which is to say that she allows Sappho to voice and control the likely expression of her contemporaries' objections. Hence by characterizing an effective but not idealized professional black woman, who constructs a social cover of feminine civility to mask her political ego, the text provides its first readers with a ready target for anticipated allegations of feminine impropriety, while simultaneously challenging them to decide whether gender prescriptions should silence the expression of wisdom and inhibit ability. By having her rational heroine reflect the resistance of her contemporaries, Hopkins avoided casting it from masculine perspective and also mitigated the likelihood of such resistance from her first audience. Moreover, by asserting a higher law than patriarchal authority, Hopkins indirectly invited that audience to grant women more latitude in the execution of their social responsibility without mentioning the problematic subject of sexual politics. Last, by having Mrs. Willis allude to but not specifically address either women's rights or intraracial sexual equality, Hopkins implicitly accommodated both controversial issues by their implication in a noncontroversial discussion on "uplifting . . . the race and womanhood" (p. 156).[31]

While constructing a discursive field that heeds patriarchal gender conventions, Hopkins mediated those conventions with liberational discourses of female sexuality and professionalism. For example, following "The Sewing-Circle," masculine retort to prejudicial racial politics becomes the subject of the chapters about the American Colored League, prompting the observation that self-defined political ambition in a man is not automatically met with ambivalence as in the case of a woman. Given Mrs. Willis's stunning performance in "The Sewing-Circle" and her absence in the subsequent chapters, the reader is compelled to wonder about what she might have said about the "race problem" at the League meeting if social convention had not mandated female reticence and if the text had not demanded her absence. Indeed, the similarity between the names of Will Smith and Mrs. Willis, the fact that both are persuasive speakers, and the presentation of parallel meetings prompt this question, but the text offers no explicit comment. Moreover, Sappho endorses perhaps unwittingly the ideology of female reticence; for although she makes no public disclosure on racism and sexism, she shares a critique on both practices with her friend Dora. Within the privacy of her room she protests to her friend, "But you can see, can't you, that if our men are deprived of the franchise, we become aliens in the very land of our birth? . . . Temporizing will not benefit us; rather it will leave us branded as cowards, not worthy of freeman's respect" (p. 125). And when she learns of the chauvinism of an influential black man, she bluntly refers to him as an "insufferable prig" (p. 126). These scenes suggest that Sappho is designed to do more than carry the bulk of the sentimental weight of the novel. Hopkins also used her heroine as an important though subtle political mouthpiece (Yarborough, p. xli). As Richard Yarborough has observed, "Sappho . . . comes most alive during the sewing group's discussion and in her conversations about men, work, and politics" (p. xli). These strategies allow Hopkins to respect the Victorian patriarchal gender conventions of her epoch and to construct situations that seem to demand that the reader ponder the rewarding possibilities of an enlarged social sphere for women. In so doing this novel can be said to draw on what Bakhtin called the "plasticity" of the novel's "dialogized" social discourses here specifically of the late nineteenth century both to assert and subvert the dominant gender conventions of that day.[32]

To late-twentieth-century readers, the gender codes and attendant portrayals of ideal family formation in black women's domestic novels of the post-Reconstruction era seem excessively preoccupied with bourgeois gentility. Yet these novels do not simply appropriate dominant gender codes; they also reform them. As we shall see, with the exception of Amelia Johnson's novels, two important social revisions recur in all the others. Those revisions depict professional ambitions for married women by placing their ambitions in an intraracial social context of increasing prosperity.[33] In addition, the novels depict sexual desire in ways that mitigate male superiority and spiritualize passionate love. These depictions constitute subtle means for characterizing as well as disseminating what were at the turn of the century liberal ideas about female agency, romantic love, self-construction, and the black family that censure dominant racist ideology. By adapting and revising the dominant culture's values that define the aspirations of the individual within the middle-class family, these writers portray the measure of success of the personal ambitions of women and men as well as racial progress in general on scales of domestic happiness and prosperity.

Love as a Strategy for Revising Spousal Roles

Idealized expressions of courtship in the dominant society ranged from a combination of social commitment, dutiful sympathy, mutual compassion, and spiritualized love at mid-nineteenth century to center erotic passion at the century's close. As historian Ellen K. Rothman explains in *Hands and Hearts: A History of Courtship in America*, suitors in the dominant culture at mid-century believed that

> Marriage . . . must be based not on transient passions but on sympathy and shared interests. The vision of romantic love that prevailed in the mid-1800s stressed mutuality, commonality, and sympathy between man and woman—precisely those qualities most likely to bridge the widening gap between home and world.[34]

By the last third of that century, however, "romance was fast losing its negative connotations and emerging as the only acceptable basis for intimacy between men and women. . . . Romance was redefined as the key to domestic harmony rather than as a threat to it" (Rothman, p. 103). This viewpoint about sexualized romantic love gained approval, so that by the end of the nineteenth century the dominant society accepted masculine displays of passion that would have been censured in earlier decades. Rothman characterizes this transition, explaining that while

> the safety and security of the social order . . . depended on the modesty and virtue of the female sex . . . , [young white men] were taught that the vigor of their 'animal instincts' was what made them powerful. . . . (Rothman, p. 187)

Like their predecessors, late-nineteenth-century white women desired male friendship, but white men offered something more—romantic passion. These suitors considered it "a generally accepted fact . . . [that] it is the addition of passion . . . which constitutes the difference between Friendship and Love" (Rothman, p. 195).

At the end of the nineteenth-century, when white men were "both condemned and celebrated for the power of their 'animal instincts,' young white women cast their ideals in the anachronistic tradition of medieval chivalry" (Rothman, p. 198). As a result of this new definition of love, white women found themselves in a balancing act as they attempted to control male ardor. "A man who was less than ardent in his wooing of a woman [at the end of the nineteenth century] risked appearing weak and unmanly, but one who was too passionate might seem to lack control over his baser instincts" (Rothman, p. 199). The ideal white man stood somewhere between being "aggressive, masterful, and sure of himself," on the one hand, and being "deferential, gentle, and pure," on the other (Rothman, p. 200). Modern romantic love, however, not only gave expression to ardor; "Romantic love was a process of individual development that involved emotional expression, the reciprocal demands of personal disclosure, and the self-enhancing exchange of reassurance and praise."[35]

White upper- and middle-class Victorian courtship practices may seem somewhat extraneous to a discussion of the literary culture of African-American women of the post-Reconstruction period. Nevertheless, it is precisely this group of white Americans who traditionally have defined the dominant gender codes to which black people largely subscribed and which were repeatedly inscribed to varying degrees in black women's post-Reconstruction domestic novels. While white women found themselves both criticizing and celebrating what we might call manly ardor, their black counterparts faced a very different collective sexual history that made them much more reticent on matters of sexuality.

For more than two-hundred years racist ideology had characterized black men and women as the possessors of overactive libidos; thus the dominant society held the viewpoint that black women were wanton and black men had insatiable sexual appetites. The racist ideology of retrogressionism intensified these allegations, prompting Hopkins's refutation in *Contending Forces*, discussed above.[36] Given such allegations, the black domestic novels generally avoided all expression of male erotic ardor as the source of masculine authority. In its place stood the heroine who modeled the prosperous family.

The eleven domestic novels also provide windows for viewing how romance was ideally viewed by turn-of-the-century black society. There is love in these novels; however, it is not passionate ardor but rather compassionate duty, spiritualized affection, and sentimental attachment. By resorting to the mid-nineteenth-century ideology of love, the authors of the post-Reconstruction domestic novels could have their proverbial cake and eat it too. This ideology allowed them to wed sentimental love to racial uplift, producing a marriage of mutual harmonious satisfaction in which the fictive spouses dedicate themselves to the progress of self, family, community, and race. In the racist climate of retrogressionism it is not surprising to find that the domestic novels of post-Reconstruction black women were reticent about romantic passion as the most important criterion for marriage; rather, mutual respect, admiration, and dedicated labor produced the ideal marriage in these stories as declarations of the heroic couple's commitment to working for a common goal—social progress—abound.

A few excerpts from the domestic novels in which the heroine discovers that she is in love illustrate the reticence of romantic ardor. For example, Iola's "admiration for Dr. Latimer was not a one-sided affair. Day after day she was filling a larger place in his heart. The touch of her hand thrilled him with emotion. Her lightest words were an entrancing melody to his ear." Lest we get too far astray in relishing romantic love, the next two lines draw us back to duty: "Her noblest sentiments found a response in his heart. In their desire to help the race their hearts beat in loving unison."[37] At the close of Kelley-Hawkins's *Megda*, Meg Randal marries the Reverend Arthur Stanley, but she does not express her fondness for him during the courtship until he opens the subject:

> Something in his voice made Meg's heart beat quickly for a moment, then almost stand still. She gave one fleeting glance into his face and dropped her eyes. He smiled and drew her gently to the open window. Then he stood and looked down into her face for a moment. . . . Then he spoke.
> I shall not tell what he said, but half an hour later . . . [Meg's brother Hal announces that] they must be brought back to earth before long. . . . [38]

Kelley-Hawkins assigned their personal expressions of mutual love to the private realm and thus the unreported part of the text.

In the case of Beryl Weston in *Beryl Weston's Ambition* (which I shall discuss in more detail below), Beryl's awareness of her love for Dr. Norman Warren initially resides in her subconscious: "the brave girl hid her secret so deep in the recesses of her heart that only God knew."[39] While Johnson's *Clarence and Corinne* omits the entire courtship of Corinne Burton, the heroine Flora Hazeley of her second novel *The Hazeley Family* is not even the subject of courtship; that discourse is displaced onto her best friend Lottie in several reserved sentences that indicate that Lottie is the object rather than the subject of matrimonial desire:

> "This is a delightful surprise. What next?" exclaimed Flora.
> "Shall I tell you?" asked Alec, coming forward and offering Lottie his arm, who evidently understood the whole situation; "it is simply this"—and the two fine-looking young people walked toward the window where Harry was standing, and paused before him,—"I love Lottie, and I think she loves me." Lottie's bright eyes dropped to the floor, her face suffused with blushes, with a bright little smile trembling around her mouth. "I love Lottie; and Harry, I want you to pronounce us husband and wife."[40]

The definition of love as duty is the central strategy for dramatizing the conjugal roles of the heroine and her hero-husband in these representative domestic novels. While they imply that love also incites more impassioned pronouncements, that discourse is silenced and placed in the unnarrated private realm; it is only suggested with smiles, blushes, fleeting glances, and faint trembling.

Such demure romantic beginnings evolve into tactics for revising patriarchal roles for the husband and wife of these novels. First, the ideal conjugal relationship resembles one between a loving brother and sister. The sibling affinity has two significant revisionist consequences: it eliminates romantic passion from the courtship and it fosters an approximate egalitarian relationship between the spouses.[41] A second stratagem adopts another mid-century courting pattern, namely, celebrating candor and confidence rather than control and power (Rothman, pp. 107–112). Lystra adds that "Self-revelation became the primary symbol of intimacy, closeness, and sometimes even truth in nineteenth-century middle-class American culture" (p. 33). This strategy blurs the distinctions between male and female comportment, encouraging men and women to reveal their thoughts, feelings, and behavior in ways that would otherwise have been sexually restricted. Lystra further explains that "The Victorian belief in romantic love demanded that men and women cross gender boundaries by disclosing and sharing, what, from the romantic view, was their essence" (p. 9). A third strategy adopts a standard feature of eighteenth- and nineteenth-century British novels and plays, namely, the inscription of the father's absence and the subsequent mitigation of patriarchal influence. Texts that rely on this tactic also frequently empower what I call the "mother's law" in order to establish matricentric authority. A fourth and last tactic, directly related to the preceding one, accords the role of competent domestic manager to the woman of the house.

Each of these four strategies revises the prior viewpoint of the patriarchal husband/father's sovereign right to rule his household. "No longer did the social definition of fatherhood emphasize the father's disciplinary role as 'governor' and 'moral force.'"[42] This new man as father is not so much characterized as the paternal force of the family as his wife's compassionate and companionate partner.[43] Their marriage is based on sympathy, respect, and commitment to their mutual happiness as well as to social progress. However, by the first decades of the twentieth century, black domestic stories began to inscribe erotic passion, as we shall see in the works of Angelina Weld Grimké.

Harper's *Iola Leroy*, for example, illustrates many of these strategies for redefining marriage as a sympathetic and resourceful union. Love and companionship form the basis of the conjugal bond, while preserving, as we would expect, the mid-nineteenth-century definition of ideal love as mutually shared duty rather than passionate ardor.[44] In this novel Iola's respect and admiration for her future husband Dr. Frank Latimer, to whom she refers when she says he "comes up to my ideal of a high, heroic manhood" (p. 265), ignites a compassionate and companionate relationship between them. In the chapter entitled "Wooing and Wedding," Iola candidly shares her ambition to become a teacher with Frank, and he responds by making his matrimonial intentions clear: he prescribes a "change of air, change of scene, and change of name" (p. 270) for her. "Seating himself near her," the novel continues, "he poured into her ears words eloquent with love and tenderness" (p. 270). A facility in the language of courtly love does not characterize Frank's proposal; to the contrary, Harper had him declare himself as "a plain man, who believes in love and truth" (p. 271), traits implied by his given name. But these ordinary words, as Harper explained, "were more than a tender strain wooing [Iola] to love and happiness, they were a clarion call to a life of high and holy worth, a call which found a response in her heart" (p. 271). Iola and Frank share a love woven of "[k]indred hopes and tastes" (p. 271), as "grand and noble purposes were lighting up their lives" (p. 271). Moreover, "they esteemed it a blessed privilege to stand on the threshold of a new era and labor for those who had passed from the old oligarchy of slavery into the new commonwealth of freedom" (p. 271). These excerpts reveal that their love is not characterized as impassioned pronouncements about their own mutual happiness; rather, their love draws on the reciprocal demands of personal disclosure and is buttressed against "the threshold of a new era and labor" (p. 271) for the advancement of black people.

We late-twentieth-century readers associate the honeymoon period of a marriage with purely gratuitous pleasure and emotional fulfillment for the new husband and wife. We certainly do not associate the honeymoon with an occasion for public service. However, this is precisely the commitment that *Iola Leroy* prescribes. Iola's and Frank's honeymoon gives them the opportunity to envision how they will commit themselves in marriage to working for racial uplift. In this way the novel conflates the ideological discourses of racial protest and companionate sentimental love, producing domestic idealism as a distinctly politicized sexual discourse of perfect intraracial affirmation and heterosexual affinity.

Near the novel's conclusion is a particularly significant verbal exchange between Iola and Frank that modifies the formerly prescribed separate realms of sexual experience, namely the Victorian male and female spheres. Under the auspices of true love, this verbal exchange reveals their mutual discursive competence on subjects conventionally seen as gender restricted. Iola prefaces this conversation with her expressed belief "that no other woman of [her] race will suffer as [she] has done" (p. 273). As a result of this declaration, Iola abandons the familiar antebellum racial discourse of female sexual outrage, found in the first part of the novel, and embraces a new communicative mode of sexual equality with her husband. Harry, Iola's brother, points out this new discursive form by insisting that she and her husband Frank have begun a peculiar form of referencing one another in their daily discussions. Harry contends that "I don't believe that there is a subject I could name to him from spinning a top to circumnavigating the globe, that he [Frank] wouldn't somehow contrive to bring Iola in. And I don't believe you could talk ten minutes to Iola on any subject, from dressing a doll to the latest discovery in science, that she wouldn't manage to lug in Frank" (p. 277). Iola's and Frank's manner of talking obscures the presumed distinctions between male and female discourse and between gendered constructions of public and private spheres of social influence. Although the novel does not explore the possibilities of these blurred gender distinctions in the public world, its inscription of them in the private sphere is suggestive of their future public enactment beyond the text's ending.

Frank's awareness of his civic role enables him immediately to become "a leader in every reform movement for the benefit of the community" (p. 279). Prior to their marriage, he suggests a corresponding role for Iola. He advises her to "write a good, strong book which would be helpful to them [black people]" (p. 262). However, she does not realize its fruition within the duration of the story. This is the ambition that Harper herself fulfilled late in her life by writing *Iola Leroy*. Hence Harper performs Iola's charge, using her novel to nurture the racial and sexual consciousness of her intended readership. Harper becomes the heroine of her novel by nurturing new instruments of African-American socialization — ideal womanhood and fiction.

When Harper inscribed Iola's desire to write "a good, strong book" and subsequently placed her "in the Sunday-school as a teacher, and in the church as a helper" (p. 278), neither Harper, her fictive heroine, nor her first audience were likely to view such roles as constituting genteel social work for a middle-class married lady, as we late-twentieth-century readers very well may. In addition, we probably view Iola's pious activism as circumscribed by feminine sentimentality. However, by nineteenth-century standards marriage and evangelicalism were politically charged traditions, and the latter avocation was the site of "the first agitation of the woman question" in the words of the social activist and abolitionist Lydia Maria Child.[45] Because Iola's story closes with marriage, we center marriage as the heroine's principal ambition. Thus for us Iola's entire enterprise probably appears as a part of the sentimental discourse of romantic love and a rather unrealistic discourse at that. But from Harper's historical perspective, the domestic did not exist apart from the political. Furthermore, her authorial note (following the final chapter) is a reminder that the novel is not a reflection of reality but of a visionary world, one that she challenged her readers initially to envision and ultimately to realize. In Harper's words, the novel's mission is to "awaken in the hearts of our countrymen a stronger sense of justice. . . . and thus add to the solution of our unsolved American problem" (p. 282). Hence the novel ends with the same political zeal that reverberates throughout the text and most emphatically in Lucille Delany's desire to "have our people . . . more interested in politics" (p. 250).

The significance of Harper's doubly signed authorial enterprise in the figuration of a heroine who desires to write a helpful book and a black woman writer who indeed satisfied this desire by ascribing that ambition to her heroine stands out particularly in the context of the changing social value of fiction reading in the nineteenth century. Lydia Maria Child (mentioned above), a major proponent for the social value of virtuous reading, advises writers in her work *The Mother's Book* that "it [was] better to paint virtue to be imitated, than vice to be shunned."[46] "Familiarity with evil," she continued, "is a disadvantage, even when pointed out as an object of disgust" (p. 91). Child's viewpoint represents the consensus among mid-nineteenth-century social reformers who increasingly used fiction to resocialize their readership. Given Child's history of abolitionism and racial benevolence as well as the pervasiveness of this viewpoint, it is probably no coincidence that *Iola Leroy* and most of the other black women's post-Reconstruction domestic novels also sanction such a position and revert to the literary tactics of the mid-century that recount the story of heroic virtue, rather than the tragic consequences of excessive passion, a story that was growing more popular with the rise of literary realism at the end of the nineteenth century. The domestic fictions usually attempt to fortify heroic virtue with the discursive repetition of a valiant story rather than to condemn the craving for excitement and what Child called "intellectual intemperance" (p. 91) by portraying their unfortunate results. She (and others like her) seemed to have believed that castigation of intemperate behavior would incite curiosity and entice the youthful reader into making poor judgments. As a result, all forms of intemperance were to be deleted from the writing of those who shared the conviction that an emphasis on virtue would reproduce itself among the literate.

With the rising literacy rates among the newly freed black population and the increasing availability of inexpensive books and serials, reading morally sound materials became an important method for reforming behavior and regulating social change.[47] Didactic fiction, in general, became a principal medium for disseminating new notions among African Americans about what constituted the laudable black self, family, and community. Inculcating new ambitions through inventive role models for African-American women and men as well as revising understandings about individual and group perfectibility are precisely the tasks to which black women authors of post-Reconstruction domestic novels directed their works. To realize those ends, much of this writing targets a youthful reading audience because adolescents, in search of entertaining leisure activities, were especially susceptible to the growing influence of reading for behavioral modification and because social change was effectively sustained by influencing the future generation of adults. Thus as we would expect, many authors in this study wrote for the adolescent market.

The moral demands of addressing this particular audience, combined with the fiction's heuristic and utilitarian functions, produced less artistic subtlety and more direct moralizing than we late-twentieth-century readers have come to expect or admire. Whether directed to an adolescent or adult audience, the domestic novels repeat the moral and social lessons that have been in our domain of common sense for decades. Consequently, these texts do not appear particularly novel or enlightening to us. But this was not the case for the black readership of the post-Reconstruction era due to the fact that dramatizations of idealized black domesticity, its attendant pursuit of economic advancement, and the transformative social value of reading were not tiresome repetitions.

For example, Tillman's novel *Clancy Street* (1898) and Kelley-Hawkins's *Four Girls at Cottage City* (1898) affirm the corrective value of reading appropriate fiction. In the opening pages of *Clancy Street* we meet the heroine—ten-year-old Caroline Waters—with a book in hand and her mother mildly scolding: "You've always got a book in your hand! I thought I told you to watch that meat that I put on to boil for your father's supper?"[48] No doubt Caroline learned her reading habit from her mother, whom the text describes as "an omnivorous reader, who maintains a small home library with a Bible, a copy of 'Poop O' Day,' 'Arabian Nights,' and a translation of 'William Tell,' and a miscellaneous assortment of 'St. Nicholases,' 'Wide-Awakes,' and 'Family Story Papers'" (p. 255) specifically for family entertainment.[49] In fact, Caroline's conscientious character is partly a reproduction of her mother's habit of reading morally inspiring works. To emphasize further the importance of reading such works, the text cites *Uncle Tom's Cabin* as the book that has distracted the young heroine from her chores, the book that Caroline's mother tells her "helped to free us" (p. 257).

Kelley-Hawkins's *Four Girls* is even more emphatic in arguing for the power of fiction to transform the quality of women's, and therefore men's, lives. While on vacation, the four girls assess the moral value of the literature of the day. They compare the works of Charles Dickens to entertaining sermons, but they criticize Alfred Lord Tennyson for making his women morally weak, and illustrate their point by summarizing the story of Queen Guinevere in his *Idylls of the King*. The girls contrast her moral laxity with Lady Elaine's strength of character, idealizing Elaine by reading large sections of her story to one another. By aligning love and morality, the girls use this text to set the stage for the story of the spiritual conversion of the character Charlotte Hood, which the novel recalls with the discursive cohesion of Tennyson's epic. This internal narrative has great impact on the lives of the four girls. Evoking the tradition of well-known "literary Evangelists," like Elizabeth Stuart Phelps,[50] Hood's story of the intervention that reading a woman's novel makes in her own salvation instigates the girls' spiritual conversion.[51] Thus one female narrative initiates reform in a series of women's lives.

Tillman and Kelly-Hawkins, like the other black women novelists in this study, repeatedly dramatized the home, school, and church as proponents of literacy. The activity of appropriate reading accordingly became a sanctioned vehicle for controlling the population's leisure time, social and spiritual values, and ultimately their general behavior. Over the decades since then, however, the power of fiction reading to shape public consciousness has diminished considerably. When we measure fiction against the more potent forms of print media, video journalism, and film, we are not likely to share our nineteenth-century counterparts' faith that fiction could effect a high degree of social change. Nor are we likely to view writing and literacy as fundamentally related to ideals of citizenship, as did our nineteenth-century black counterparts.[52]

That our cultural values and reading expectations differ greatly from those of late-nineteenth-century black people is the motivation for this study. The post-Reconstruction novels of African-American women endeavored to provide new bases for social value formation for their intended first readers; we contemporary readers already know these values but no longer regard reading

as an important source for them. These fictions taught their intended readership about individual esteem, self-definition, and willful self-advancement.
That audience learned that reward was a product of rational reflection, commitment, and meritorious performance and not a result of one's racial, class,
and sexual identity. Information for resocialization was emphatically inscribed
in these novels; this was revolutionary news for their first readers but not for
us. These fictions seem particularly empty of content due to the fact that we
do not need to read them to acquire stories of personal, domestic or professional success. We are already familiar with the characters, the plot, and the
message. But for their first readers, the idealized domestic stories were effective
mediums for enculturating new social truths about black individuation, personal and group social perfectibility. By erasing antebellum racial constructions of inferiority from the black identity and mounting new plots of ambitions fulfilled rather than frustrated, these stories offered their first readers
innovative possibilities about positive self-definition.

The remaining three tactics of revising patriarchal privilege — inscribing the
father's absence, designating women as domestic managers, and characterizing
the heroine's husband with the attributes of a loving brother — often function
in concert in the post-Reconstruction domestic novels. All three strategies
revise the patriarch's role, defined by Puritan tradition, by divesting that role
of unquestioned authority over household management and by decentering
the preeminence of the father in the nuclear family. Together these tactics
revise the family discourse and shift discursive dominance from male-centered
expressions of racial protest to female-centered expectations of domestic idealism.

While I refer to Hopkins's *Contending Forces* for an extenuated presentation
of this shifting dominance, a similar discussion could be mounted for all of
the 1890s novels in this study. Although *Contending Forces* sustains both
racial and domestic (or sexual) discourses, the former becomes increasingly
reticent throughout the story, while the latter, which inscribes the "mother's
law," becomes dominant. The mother's law centers a black matricentric morality; it metes out reward and punishment in direct proportion to the moral
character of one's deeds, privileges a female-centered ethical context, and
serves as a broader basis for redefining a virtuous woman other than on
grounds of sexual chastity. Last, the characters turn to the mother's law for
instruction, finding that the father's law is increasingly inappropriate for guid-
ing their moral and ethical decisions.

Two of the novel's minor characters, Luke Sawyer and John Langley, give
expression to the "father's law." In the chapter entitled "Sawyer Speaks to the
League," Sawyer recalls the kidnapping of Mabelle Beaubean (alias Sappho
Clark) by her father's white half-brother. Luke describes how he and Mabelle's
father recover her: "After *three weeks* of incessant searching we found her a
prisoner in a house of the vilest character . . . a poor, ruined, half-crazed
creature in whom it was almost impossible to trace a resemblance to the
beautiful pet of our household" (p. 260). Just in case there is any doubt in the
reader's mind about what the word "ruined" means, Sawyer goes on to say

that he left her at a convent, *"there she died when her child was born"* (p. 261, emphasis in original). Sawyer represents the father's law of patriarchal judgment, and it designates Mabelle as a "ruined" woman. The father's law concludes that she is better off dead than alive. But Mabelle does not die, rather she grants herself social rebirth by changing her name to Sappho Clark and asserting a self-authorized life.[53] John Langley defeats her intentions and corroborates patriarchal judgment when he uses his knowledge of Sappho's history to try to force her into becoming his *fille de joie* (p. 338). Although Sappho has struggled to deter such designations, Langley's action makes her conclude that the father's law is unavoidable and that she is indeed unworthy of becoming Will's wife, which prompts her to run away. Before departing, Sappho leaves a note for Will in which she writes, "[Langley] has made me realize how much such a marriage with me would injure you. Disgrace shall never touch you or yours through me" (p. 329). Not having the means to nullify the father's law, Sappho accepts her prior condemnation to social death.

Mrs. Willis is the principal proponent of the law of the mother. In "The Sewing-Circle" chapter (introduced above), Sappho shares a depersonalized version of her history, in which she pays credence to the patriarchal code and condemns the female victim for lack of virtue. She recounts that

> I once knew a woman who had sinned. . . . She married a man who would have despised her had he known her story; but as it is, she is looked upon as a pattern of virtue for all women. . . . Ought she not to have told her husband before marriage? Was it not her duty to have thrown herself upon his clemency? (p. 156)

After listening to Sappho's story, Mrs. Willis gives Sappho her advice:

> "I am a practical woman of the world and I think your young woman builded wiser than she knew. I am of the opinion that most men are like the lower animals in many things—they don't always know what is for their best good." (p. 156)

Mrs. Willis's advice does not sanction the father's law; instead, she insists that man's view is finite, while God's judgment is infinite (p. 157). She interprets God's infinity as "[Sappho's] duty . . . to be happy and bright for the good of those about [her]" (p. 157).

The widow Ma Smith also asserts woman-centered authority in directing the lives of the story's hero, Will Smith, and his sister, Dora. For them their father is a sacred memory, connecting them to a history of racial strength as well as oppression. However, his absence also diminishes the strength of patriarchal values on their immediate lives and permits their mother to become the authority figure who not only nurtures them but initially manages the household affairs as well. Although the text makes no explicit mention of the quality of their mother's managerial skills, it does inform us that she supported her children and educated them by converting her home to a rooming house. We also know that she taught her managerial skills to her daughter Dora. These details represent Dora's and Mrs. Smith's proficiency in domestic and financial management and encourage the characters (and us) to regard women not as masculine complements but self-sufficient individuals in their own right, deserving respect. The decentering of the father's law in the Smith household also permits the hero Will to follow his own desire in selecting his wife and to disregard the patriarchal code for premarital virginity. As a result he is free to marry the so-called "ruined woman" and care for her child outside of patriarchal codes. "Instead of representing a black manhood that was an equivalent to white patriarchy," as Carby has explained in *Reconstructing Womanhood*, "Hopkins grasped for the utopian possibility that Will could be a husband/partner to Mabelle/Sappho, when he accepted her sexual history, without having to occupy the space of father to her child" (p. 144).

In addition, the domestic novels almost categorically assert the sibling model of ideal love, thus further deconventionalizing the patriarchal roles of husbands and wives.[54] By reverting to the mid-century convention of portraying the heroine's choice of husband as a man who has been like her brother, the novels not only silence the expression of sexual ardor and engender romantic idealism but also give rise to greater equality between the spouses by eliminating the codes for the patriarchal head of household. The sibling-model husband enhances sexual equality. As a result, the couple can achieve an intimate relationship that displays spontaneous expressions of honesty, loyalty, geniality, and sympathetic criticism.

Clarence and Corinne and *Megda*, in particular, provide poignant illustrations of this strategy in operation. In *Clarence and Corinne*, the title characters Clarence and Corinne Burton endure the typical childhood hardship that sets most sentimental fiction in motion.[55] Faith, virtue, and hard work enable them to revise their early misfortune into prosperity as Corinne becomes a teacher and Clarence becomes a doctor. Together they maintain the household of their adoptive parents and eventually establish another for themselves based on sibling equality. This latter home is the idealized revision of their childhood hovel. What is particularly significant about their new home is that it becomes the domicile for two sets of male and female siblings: Clarence and Corinne Burton and their childhood best friends Bebe and Charlie Reade. The story closes with the text insisting that

> The sequel could be read without the book. But there was a marriage speedily, and the bride was Bebe Reade, while the groom was Dr. Burton. There was another, also, soon after. This time Corinne Burton and Charley Reade took the principal parts. (pp. 186–87)

The hero and heroine literally marry their surrogate siblings, and the two sets of cross-sibling spouses set up an ideal household in which they are not merely husbands and wives; they form a collective of helpmates and mutual friends. Described as "our friends" (p. 187), they become exemplary models, available for their intended readers' immediate emulation. Together the two couples emphatically revise conventional notions about the nuclear household and the preeminence of the patriarchal head of the family. This and the other domestic novels are afforded the opportunity to subvert patriarchal law because the heroines' fathers are absent, whether due to the demands of work or death.[56]

Not only do these sibling-like marital unions arise from long-term friendships, mutual respect, and piety, but a good sense of humor frequently sustains these companionate relationships as well. For example, in addition to employing the sibling-based marriage to revise the conjugal relationship, *Megda* links piety and humor together to subvert gender conventions. Near the beginning of that novel, a hilarious scene occurs during a rainstorm, involving Meg and her future husband, the young Reverend Arthur Stanley, as he ties his wind-blown out-of-shape derby to his head with Meg's neck ribbon, much like a bonnet. This bit of symbolic cross-dressing is not merely indicative of good humor. Like the honeymoon discourse between Frank and Iola in *Iola Leroy*, this scene in *Megda* transposes gender traits and deconstructs traditional notions about masculine and feminine decorum, thus liberating men as well as women from artificial standards of behavior. It is particularly significant to note that gender flexibility enhances the good nature of this compassionate man, who is, interestingly enough, a minister. These traits, as the text insists, make him an especially effective spiritual leader, in contrast to the boring patriarchal preacher that Kelley-Hawkins mentions in *Four Girls*, where three of the "four girls" also marry sibling-like men.[57]

Four Girls also subverts the presumption of male privilege. For example, the girls frequently remark that the two young men, who show up at Cottage City and serve the socially sanctioned role of escort, are unwelcomed guests, thus indirectly criticizing the prescriptive that respectable women must have escorts to protect their virtue when they venture outside the home and the popular viewpoint that young women are always anxious for the attention of young men. In addition, the character of "Grandpa" Althernon, one of the owners of the guest cottage, is the submissive domestic partner whom his wife, called "Mother," repeatedly bars from entering the girls' room. Mother, then, is clearly the force of obedience in this household. Female gender specificity here further reinforces matricentric value formation, reminiscent of what I earlier termed the mother's law. In fact the repeated references to Mother's husband as "Grandpa" rather than Father further negate the possibility of his claiming the dominant patriarchal role by weakening his claim with the assumption of old age. The text also affirms his subordination by having one of the girls say, "Those who look as though they were born to rule are generally the ones who are ruled" (p. 43).

Indeed, *Four Girls* seems self-conscious in its marginalization of men, and this marginalia is especially important to its evangelical mission. It is especially grounded in spiritual feminism and is, therefore, committed to showing that the way to Christ is mediated by women, as Deborah McDowell notably argues.[58] Not only does the evangelical mission here marginalize the traditional ecclesiastical patriarch, the minister, but men in general no longer presume patriarchal prerogatives. The novel portrays traditional ministers as ineffective and boring and a patriarchal god as callous and unsympathetic. The novel also censures superficially demonstrative conversion signs, associating them "with a lot of shouting Methodists" (p. 49). Instead of the traditional minister, the girls rely on the sermonic power of a woman's (Charlotte Brooks's) quiet and sobering story of her personal salvation (McDowell, p. xxxii), which she renders with the narrative cohesion of a novel. This process of inspiriting the spiritual conversion of the four girls and their two escorts somewhat duplicates Brooks's own conversion experience that resulted from reading a woman's novel. In this manner evangelical women and their novelized spiritual stories mediate the salvation of other women and their male companions, displacing ineffective traditional ministers. (This is precisely the function of Kelley-Hawkins's two novels.)

Four Girls also revises the divine trinity by deifying a symbolic mother and child—Charlotte Hood and her paralyzed young son Robin—and by placing them into the context of transcendent spirituality, while eliminating the father altogether. Hood becomes the "mother-savior,"[59] and the youthful converts demonstrate newly engendered spiritual dedication by committing themselves to securing medical attention for Robin and restoring his corporeal body to healthy vigor. *Four Girls*, then, insists that the spiritually saved are entitled to a rewarding earthly life as well as a heavenly one, thereby rewriting the typical other worldliness of spiritual reward.

Black women's post-Reconstruction novels frequently dramatize spiritual resolve or conversion in which the heroine learns to place her fate into God's hands.[60] For like Beryl Weston, each heroine of the domestic novels must learn "to give up [her] own rebellious will and . . . [follow] the will of [her] Heavenly Father . . . " (p. 237). Just as Corinne repeats the biblical text "Casting all your care upon him; for he careth for you" (p. 109), Beryl reads again and again in her well-worn Bible the lines "Cast thy burden upon the Lord, and He shall sustain thee" (p. 237). Lessons in piety also form the dominant story of *Megda*, in which the heroine Meg learns to mediate her highly individuated willfulness into exemplary spirituality. That mediation occurs as Meg transforms her excessive independence, vanity, and personal ambition into the basis of a new feminine ideal that is characterized by moral pride, tenacity, *and* pious devotion. Thus in the midst of that novel's excessive display of sentimentality, diminution, and gentility, Meg forsakes her ambition to be a famous elocutionist while negating the presumed obsequiousness of the Victorian wife. The novel attributes Meg's positive transformation to the "five years of constant companionship with such a man as Mr. Stanley" (p. 376). Though she is not a perfect wife and the text asserts no desire of making her so, she is also not bound by patriarchal notions of the reticent wife. Meg is free to display her "little fault[s] . . . the little flashes of temper, the spirit of pride that shows itself now and then, the natural willfulness of her disposition" (p. 376) without fear that her husband will withhold or redirect his affection. As the text insists, he "loves every little fault in her . . . for, as he once laughingly said . . . 'Meg would not be Meg without them'" (p. 376).

Like *Four Girls'* Jessie Dare (a name whose literalness bears obvious relationship to Meg's "natural willfulness"), Meg identifies a new model of feminine character for the heroine that becomes prominent in the late nineteenth century — the independent, spunky girl. Reminiscent of Louisa May Alcott's Jo in *Little Women* (1869) and of Henry James's Isabel Archer in *The Portrait of a Lady* (1881), Meg proudly exclaims that she sees "no reason why a woman should not possess character as well as a man" (p. 60). The poetic justice of sentimentality tangibly rewards Meg's revised text of wifely character by supplying her with a companionate, sibling-like husband, the Reverend Mr. Arthur Stanley, who greatly appreciates his wife's vitality. Although Meg still seeks her husband's love and approval, his approbation is not the only source of her pleasure. Meg voices her own opinions and relies on Christian piety to grant her the authority to become the agent of her own decisions. Dedicated to "noble work — in her home and in the world outside" (p. 394), the text mentions but does not explore Meg's life of public service. Her commitment is replicated in the lives of Iola Leroy (Latimer), Lucille Delany (Leroy), Beryl Weston (Warren), and Sappho Clark (Smith).

7

From Domestic Happiness
to Racial Despair

*The day of Beryl's wedding dawned fair and clear. The little village was
alive with excitement, for Beryl Weston's wedding was a grand affair.
. . . The path that led to the Afro-American Church was strewn with flowers, and the church was beautifully decorated with pond-lilies, roses and
other flowers.*

      KATHERINE D. TILLMAN, *Beryl Weston's Ambition* (1893)

*Little Eva now a young woman of eighteen, Caroline's exact counterpart
so everyone says, has just finished the high school, those who are intimate
friends of the family say that Otto Lewis has been waiting for her and that
there will be a wedding soon.*

      KATHERINE D. TILLMAN, *Clancy Street* (1898)

*Cuthbert Sumner views life and eternity with different eyes and thoughts
from what he did before he knew that he had wedded Hagar's daughter.*

      PAULINE E. HOPKINS, *Hagar's Daughter* (1901)

*They knew what the future would be. They loved each other; they would
marry sooner or later, after they reached England, with the sanction of
her grandfather, old Lord George; that was certain. American caste prejudice could not touch them in their home beyond the sea.*

      PAULINE E. HOPKINS, *Winona* (1902)

*Caste prejudice, race pride, boundless wealth, scintillating intellects re-
fined by all the arts of the intellectual world, are but puppets in His hand,
for His promises stand, and He will prove His words, "Of one blood have
I made all races of men."*

      PAULINE E. HOPKINS, *Of One Blood* (1903)

The Heroine's Work

The domestic novels of post-Reconstruction black women generally rely on effusive sentiment to describe the heroine's emerging subjectivity. However, another group of black women writers—Katherine Davis Chapman Tillman, Victoria Earle Matthews (the author of "The Value of Race Literature," discussed previously), and Octavia Albert,[1] for example—fleshed out their heroines' lives in ways that more closely duplicated the tangible realities of the lives of contemporaneous black women. No doubt influenced by the advent of realism in the works of writers like Samuel Clemens, Sarah Orne Jewett, Bret Hart, and George Washington Cable, as well as by the oral histories of black Americans finding their way into print in newspapers, serials, and books, these black women writers slowly abandoned the assumption that art was meant to represent human ideals in favor of its recording the daily struggle to live a moral and ethical life. They believed that art ought not be overtly didactic, moralistic, or sentimental. Observing the daily details of ordinary people's lives, recording and interpreting them rather than celebrating physical or spiritual beauty, and heroic admiration were the subjects for this new art form. Unable to abandon explicit didacticism, this new generation of writers aligned their daily observations with pragmatic rather than exemplary moralizing. And like their predecessors, they found ways to inscribe in their works discourses of racial and sexual desire. While Tillman subscribed to the mid-nineteenth-century model of love as duty, her two novels reveal the shifting aesthetic terrain between sentimental and realistic fiction as well as the expansion of spiritual piety to embrace a secular gospel of social progress.

Early in *Beryl Weston's Ambition* Tillman described the title character, Beryl Weston, as "a very pleasant picture" (p. 210), dressed for mourning, a conventional event in sentimental fiction. She is "[r]obed in a black gown, that fitted her slender form perfectly, her long, black hair coiled in a classical knot at the back of her head, her great black eyes . . . were somewhat red, and her pale face swollen from weeping" (pp. 209–10). Unlike the case with the typical heroine of this genre, Beryl's dilemma does not arise from financial hardship inasmuch as she is "the eldest child . . . of a successful farmer, who had a snug bank account and many acres of rich land which he had accumulated by sheer force of pluck and thrift since the day of his emancipation" (p. 213).[2] Beryl's dilemma arises from her dear mother's request that Beryl abandon her personal ambition to become "an instructress in the modern languages and higher mathematics" (p. 217) and accept what seems to be the rather ordinary responsibility of managing her family-household: "Beryl must take her mother's place as far as possible. See that the meals were served promptly; look after the dairy and garden produce; patch, darn, have the entire charge of the children" (p. 226). Thus Beryl's desire to be a professional woman must be exchanged for a modest life of domestic self-sacrifice. By demanding what at first seems to be an unfair exchange, the text ultimately seeks to teach its readers that ambitious self-interest in the public realm and personal self-sacrifice in the domestic are ironically interconnected and that self-sacrifice is often the prerequisite for professional success.

What is particularly provocative about Tillman's depiction of her heroine is the realistic manner in which Beryl speaks and the detailed delineation of her daily chores. Undoubtedly, heroines like Iola Leroy would have had similar domestic responsibilities, given their time frames; however, Harper chose not to represent them in the text. Instead she focused on Iola as a spokeswoman for what Harper believed to be a central ambition for the late-nineteenth-century black woman—education. In contrast to Iola's lofty declamations about black people's ambitions for prosperity, rendered in hyperbolic abstraction, such as, "My heart . . . is full of hope for the future. Pain and suffering are the crucibles out of which come gold more fine than the pavements of heaven, and gems more precious than the foundations of the Holy City,"[3] Beryl simply says, "I like churchwork. I am so glad there is a prospect of a new church for Westland" (p. 240)! At the conclusion of Iola's address entitled the "Education of Mother," exuberance abounds: "there was a ring of triumph in her voice, as if she were reviewing a path she had trodden with bleeding feet, and seen it change to lines of living light" (p. 257). Indeed Harper characterized Iola as a veritable angel: "Her soul seemed to be flashing through the rare loveliness of her face and etherealizing its beauty" (p. 257). Although Tillman characterized Beryl as "one of the noblest young women. . . . [who] exerts [great influence] over the young women in her Sunday-school class, married and single" (p. 238), Beryl is a heroine of flesh and blood, and her influence is the product of her labor. In addition, Beryl's beauty is not ethereal like Iola's, whose angelic radiance transcends, for example, mention of clothing. Throughout the work, the text makes us aware of Beryl's corporeal presence. Her face gets swollen from weeping, and the references throughout the text to her careful selection of clothing show both a realistic detail of her life and her good taste, which was at the time a very important index of social worthiness.

Beryl's long list of domestic responsibilities also makes us well aware that she is an historical subject, bound to the material circumstances of her day. It is precisely the realistic depiction of her household industry, combined with her dedicated desire to learn rigorous academic disciplines—geometry and Greek—that dramatizes not only what Tillman perceived as appropriate education for black women but also Tillman's refusal to polarize two distinct theories about Negro education. Like Pauline Hopkins, who wed Booker T. Washington's pedagogy of industrial education to William E. B. Du Bois's academic education by making their fictive proponents in-laws in *Contending Forces*, Tillman characterized Beryl's education as a combination of industrial training and academic scholarship, placing both in the context of religious piety. Beryl's ambition also embraces the arduous performance of domestic duties in the spirit of Christian devotion. The union of these skills and aptitudes produces a veritable litany of enterprise, a "daily routine of labor" for Beryl:

> She arose at 4 in the morning, exercised for a few moments with a pair of Indian clubs . . . assisted [a day worker] Binie in preparing an early breakfast for the farm hands, dressed [her brother] Joey, read a chapter in her Bible, and did the house work. In addition to all this, she heard the chil-

dren's lessons from 9 to 10 o'clock in the morning, and recited lessons in geometry and Greek to Norman Warren between the hours of 10 and 12. In the afternoons she ironed, sewed or read, as the occasion demanded. At night she read aloud from some interesting book, helped Binie with her English studies, and practiced her music. (p. 230)

As Tillman's first readers observed the methodological detail of Beryl's daily routine, they were urged to define domesticity, in part, not simply as tiresome repetition of household chores but as a practical application of industry, intellect, piety, and training to the management of the home, reminiscent of the heroine Flora Hazeley in Johnson's *The Hazeley Family*, as already discussed. In this manner the novel elevates domestic management to the rank of a skilled discipline, to be executed with professional competence.

Indeed Beryl is a product of the very educational program for black women that Iola Leroy referenced in her address, which is inscribed in exuberance and title alone. The "ring of triumph in [Iola's] voice. . . . her words a call to a higher service and nobler life" (Harper, p. 257) are personified in Beryl's life. "Bound up in her books, children [her siblings] and church," the daily content of Beryl's life makes her a nurturer of home and community and predicts "that God intends her to play an important part in the work of uplifting the race" (Tillman, p. 238). The alliance of virtue, labor, and accomplishment underscores a direct relationship between the pragmatic role-model that the novel offers its readers and the reproduction of that model in real life. By following Beryl's example, black women readers of Tillman's epoch learned that hard work, self-sacrifice, and mental discipline could advance their ambitions. Hence characters like Beryl no doubt had significant impact on the quality of real women's lives.

Fiction was not the only medium for depicting the benefits of education on the lives of exemplary women. Daily routines like Beryl's were frequently outlined in homilies, newspaper columns, pamphlets, and full-scale conduct manuals at the turn of the century. *Golden Thoughts* was one such handbook.[4] Directed specifically to African Americans, this 1903 guidebook of social virtue and sexual hygiene provided the following advice for young black women by referring to an excerpt from Julia Ward Howe's *Reminiscences*[5]:

> Learn to make a home, and learn this in the days in which learning is easy. Cultivate a habit of vigilance and forethought. With a reasonable amount of intelligence, a woman should be able to carry on the management of a household and should yet have time for art and literature of some sort. . . . If you have at your command three hours *per diem* you may study art, literature and philosophy, or learn foreign languages, living or dead. (p. 73)

This advice fosters an undertaking remarkably similar to Beryl's daily enterprise, advancing the viewpoint that a disciplined mind enhances a woman's domestic proficiency. A few pages later this manual gives emphatic maternal affirmation to the academic training that Beryl eventually secures:

a good mother must not only be capable of bearing and caring for her children during infancy, but must also be their intellectual companion and guide during the period of youth. . . . College does a great deal more for a woman than simply to give her a diploma at the conclusion of a prescribed course of instruction. It . . . gives her intelligent appreciation of the best in art and life. (*Golden Thoughts*, pp. 79, 81)

Like *Beryl Weston's Ambition* (and virtually all black women's post-Reconstruction domestic novels), the manual fosters higher education for women. Both works—one fiction, the other not—intervene in the controversy over the appropriate education for black men and women, promoting the viewpoint that men and women must be similarly educated and that the ideal education for African Americans in general is not Du Boisian academics or Washingtonian industry but various combinations of both.

The novel also explores another topic that was particularly important at the time of its publication—expatriation of black people in general and especially their repatriation to Africa. At the beginning of the novel, Dr. Norman Warren, who has been reared in England, "was inclined to the opinion that the Afro-American should emigrate to places where prejudice does not exist" (Tillman, p. 233). However, by the end of the story he has changed his mind and settled down with his wife Beryl in the fictive Westland; the two to work for racial advancement as U.S. citizens. By contrast, the Reverend Harold Griswold, who initially exhorts, "I know that we have fearful odds against which to contend, and that the race between the two races is an unequal one, but I believe that we ought to remain in America, and 'push the battle to the gates'" (p. 234), at the close of the novel leaves Westland for "far-away Africa, laboring for the redemption of those who sit in great darkness" (p. 246). Although the reader can easily surmise by the heroine's position which side of each issue Tillman favored, Tillman did not categorically dismiss other viewpoints. To the contrary, like her sister authors, she seldom polarized ideological opposition as a polemical battle (in this case about appropriate education for black people or their expatriation); both viewpoints not only tend to coexist in their novels but are often symbolically inscribed as outlooks held by close relatives in the domain of the extended fictive family. This method of allaying opposition stresses that there is not simply one way to produce social prosperity among African Americans; as a result time and energy would be better spent pursuing objectives than attempting to erect a unified position.

Like the other domestic novels, *Beryl Weston's Ambition* sanctions the primacy of domestic nurturance as essential for the survival of the family, for the collective progress of black Americans, and indeed for the maintenance of civilization itself. However, that endorsement does not arise from gender prescriptions but from a pragmatic response to the real-life circumstances of African Americans. By Beryl's example the novel presents a convincing dramatization of the social importance of fulfilling a black woman's domestic ambition rather than simply gratifying her desire for success in the realm of professional accomplishment. However, what both Tillman and Harper shared is the outlook that fulfilling a black woman's domestic ambition(s) need not preclude professional accomplishment. This position is very important because, by recharacterizing Beryl as a college "instructress" of mathematics and foreign languages, especially after she admirably assumed her deceased mother's modest role as family caretaker, the text promotes a new feminine ideal, one that allows a woman to extend her sphere beyond the home to embrace ambitions routinely associated with upper-class men without arousing the social ambivalence that Hopkins's Mrs. Willis does.

In Tillman's fictive milieu, higher education is not the site of increased religious doubt, as in the dominant culture, but one where spiritual piety, academic training, and personal ambition are united. The text projects educational opportunity not as the exclusive result of individual, worldly desire but as divine intervention as well. Most important, personal ambition is not cast as human vanity but as the faculty on which God places His trust, as Beryl's teacher, Miss Hand, exclaims at a student assembly,

> "Do you know," continued the speaker, who was no other than Miss Hand, "that God is giving you these blessed opportunities of college life and good associations, that you may be better able to glorify His Name? . . . I see before me an army of young Afro-American men and women, filled with ambition, who are preparing to fill various positions in the world. Ah! let me entreat you not to start forth on your life-work with Christless lives." (pp. 216–17)

As a Christian and intellectual facilitator, Miss Hand inspires her students to dedicate their lives and educational training to fighting sin, ignorance and prejudice (p. 216). Thus the professionally ambitious student body becomes a Christian army to carry out God's purpose rather than egotistical individuals. It is most fitting that at this gathering Beryl "arose and asked for help to begin a life for Christ" (p. 217), which, as we shall see, is also a life of personal satisfaction. Thus this novel depicts spiritual dedication not simply as self-sacrifice and exuberant faith but as personal fulfillment as well. In addition, pious commitment finds admirable performance in both the secular and the spiritual realm. Indeed, personal success in noble secular enterprise here is a significant sign of divine veneration.

Given the enlargement of Beryl's spiritual realm, it is not surprising that the domestic domain is similarly enhanced. Consequently, it is not necessary for Beryl to eschew domesticity for a life that exceeded traditional sex roles, as did the so-called "new [white] woman" of the turn of the century, inasmuch as the revised domestic life here does not foreclose possibilities for equality among spouses and the professional development of women. To the contrary, the ideal state of the heroines of black women's post-Reconstruction novels is married to virtuous, ambitious, compassionate, and companionate men who encourage their personal growth, as marriage is central to the lives of black heroines and essential to their individual accomplishment.

Like the novels of Tillman's black female contemporaries, this work also reclaims the erotic ideal of the mid-nineteenth century. Tillman portrays love in terms of duty, respect, and admiration. The text recalls Beryl's growing love for Norman Warren, her future husband, as her growing respect for him. Their loving devotion for one another arises from their daily activity of reciting geometry theorems and declining Greek verbs as well as from an occasional, friendly game of croquet. As Tillman explains, Beryl held him in a "kind, brotherly regard" (p. 232) and he admired her "in the light of a sister" (p. 232), reminiscent of the sibling-like spouses discussed previously. So far removed from romantic passion is Beryl's admiration for Norman that she is unconscious of her affection for him, which the text describes as a "secret so deep in the recesses of her heart that only God knew" (p. 232). Similarly, he only becomes aware of his "great tenderness for Beryl" over the course of "weary weeks of watching" her tend to her dying little brother (p. 241). The growing love between them is subject neither to display nor explicit expression:

> Like Jonah's gourd, in the night-time of sorrow and despair, his love grew and flourished. Neither by word nor look did he betray himself to the girl whom he had learned to love, but contested valiantly with the Death Angel from morning until eve. (p. 242)

Following her brother's death, Beryl and Norman become aware of their mutual feelings, and from that point forward their courtship resembles the pattern set by Iola and Frank in Harper's *Iola Leroy*. Beryl and Norman express their devotion to one another as tender pronouncements of their desire to work together for the advancement of the race.

In contrast to the evolving, understated mutual affection of Beryl and Norman are two ill-fated, budding romances that serve to illustrate the weak foundation of passionate love. During a visit, Beryl's friend Cora becomes infatuated with Norman, and the new minister Harold Griswold is similarly struck by Beryl. Despite the intensity of their respective passions—Cora's desire to have "this village Adonis at [her] feet" (p. 236) and Griswold's belief that Beryl is "the one woman in the whole wide world whom [he] desire[s] for a wife"—both are ill-conceived because they evolve from the gratification of superficial romantic sentiment and the frivolity of the moment and not from steadfast mutual respect, admiration, and compassion. By the end of the story, not only do their aspiring romances fail, but Cora and Reverend Griswold eventually forsake their illusions about love and marry one another.

What is significant about this novel is that it does not end on Beryl's wedding day or shortly thereafter. Rather the story continues explicitly to redefine a woman's ambition as larger than her husband, children, and home. For after Beryl embraces domestic selflessness, she retrieves her original ambition to become a teacher in the same institution that she had to forsake. Beryl must have returned to school after her marriage, although Tillman is reticent on exactly how Beryl achieves her career goal. This reticence nevertheless implies that as an ideal companionate husband, Norman Warren was instrumental in assisting his wife both to retain and to realize her long-term ambition. At the close of the story Beryl is not simply a happily married woman—wife and mother—but a professional woman as well. These realized ambitions are personally rewarding for Beryl, and they are also important to racial progress. In this respect *Beryl Weston's Ambition* seems to rewrite the conclusion of the earlier-published *Iola Leroy* (as well as *Megda* and *Clarence and Corinne*). Whereas at the close of *Iola Leroy* Frank Latimer is characterized as the "Good Doctor," as "a leader in every reform movement for the benefit of the community" (p. 279), *Beryl Weston's Ambition* closes several years after the wedding of Beryl and Warren Norman, insisting that "Dr. Warren *and his wife* are everywhere recognized as *leaders* in every movement for the advancement of their own oppressed race . . . and knowing that Beryl is useful, honored and happy, let us leave her for her highest ambition now is to serve her Lord" (p. 246, emphasis added). Beryl is not merely his helpmate; she is a leader in her own right.

At the turn of the century Tillman portrayed in Beryl Weston a more liberal heroine than those of her sister writers. Beryl is an exemplary woman, who even by late-twentieth-century standards possesses a rewarding career, a loving and successful husband, and two healthy children as a consequence of clear-sighted ambition, disciplined training, and hard work. In Tillman's milieu, to be useful, honored, and happy were the undisputable signs of having achieved one's "highest ambition"—"to serve the Lord" (p. 246). In serving the Lord, Beryl also attends to her own desire. While successful realization of noble ambitions usually marks the life of the sincerely devout, worldly honor and professional success exceed the conventional boundaries of the spiritual domain. In this regard it is important to observe that this text shifts its emphasis from religious to secular fulfillment, inasmuch as church work is no longer the only proper realm for realizing the ideal heroine's public ambition. Whereas Iola "quietly took her place in the Sunday-school as a teacher, and in the church as a helper" (Harper, p. 278) and Meg's "life [as a minister's wife] was filled up with work—noble work—in her home and in the world outside,"[6] the domestic, spiritual, academic, and professional aspects of Beryl's life mark her emphatic movement among the domains of home, church, school, and professionalism, and thereby reconfigure these as intersecting Christian social spheres instead of isolated, divergent ones.

Iola Leroy and *Beryl Weston's Ambition* are set during Reconstruction and the early years of post-Reconstruction, respectively. Despite the close proximity of their temporal settings and the one year separating their dates of publication, different feminine gender ideals shape their domestic heroines. As the product of an elderly author, Harper's Iola seems somewhat ambivalent on asserting her place in the public sphere. As a result, she works in the church and is her husband's helpmate. Tillman's Beryl is a younger black woman's more assured formulation of multiple exemplary feminine roles both in and out of the traditional female spheres. Hence Beryl is a new generational model for womanly ambition that evolves from ordinary, disciplined, daily labor; careful planning; and professional training rather than from a captivating physical presence, extraordinary personal experience, and effusive piety. Most significant, Beryl's ambitions are not subject to the patriarchal contention of feminine impropriety, as Tillman extended Harper's critique on the regulation that married women retire from teaching.[7]

Harper made Lucille Delany the violator of this regulation, keeping heroine Iola safely ensconced in female space. By contrast, Beryl's position in the public domain as a married college instructor expands the traditional dimensions of the woman's sphere to coincide with her competence and aspiration. Beryl's ambition clearly encroaches on a professionalism that, during the period of the story's production, was usually deemed appropriate only for men. Her ambition, then, further erases the arbitrary boundaries between the masculine and feminine domains and public and personal ambitions. The repetition of the word *ambition* throughout the story calls our attention to the term's redefinition outside egotistical limitations to include pious devotion to personal as well as racial advancement.

Tillman's second novel, *Clancy Street* (1898), a partly sentimental and partly realistic "conduct" story, was also serialized in *The A.M.E. Church Review*. Several features distinguish this novel from the more sentimental courtship stories of *Beryl Weston's Ambition* and the other domestic novels of the 1890s. First apparent is the novel's local color, its sociological analysis of multi-ethnic urban communities of the post-Reconstruction period, and the story's focus on dramatizing the daily economic consequences of emergent capitalism on ordinary, working-class black people. By the end of the story, another difference appears. The work relies on the other generic ending of domestic fiction—the death of the ideal heroine—to uphold and enhance genteel domesticity.

Set during the 1870s in a poor section of Louisville, Kentucky, *Clancy Street* dramatizes the life of a rather ordinary black girl, Caroline Waters, and a variety of black residents whose speech, appearance, and daily activities resonate with concrete ethnographic details that typify the urban, black, working poor.

> Clancy Street in Louisville, Kentucky's populous metropolis, some thirty years ago was held in great disrepute by the inhabitants of the adjoining streets—for this street for several blocks was the home of a large settlement of Negroes. . . . Just now they were intoxicated with their new possession [freedom], and too often acted like so many children in the face of the grave responsibilities that confronted them. . . . Clancy Street was narrow and ill paved, but fairly clean and fairly filled with rickety tenements and mouldy cottages. . . . High up in the first block and farthest removed from the smoke and smell of the factory, in the most inviting of the cottages . . . lived Anne Waters, the foreman's wife. . . .[8]

The realistic temporal and spatial detail of *Clancy Street* are a contrast to the "unlocatable places" and "undifferentiated" chronological time of Amelia Johnson's *Clarence and Corinne*.[9] Indeed, the material specificity of the first chapters of this novel foreshadows the opening scenes of mid-twentieth-century novels like Ann Petry's *The Street* (1940) and Paule Marshall's *Brown Girl, Brownstones* (1958). Through the hope and despair of the black residents of Clancy Street, Tillman presents the cultural reasons for their vices: stealing, infidelity, drinking, and wastefulness. In this way Tillman distinguishes their racially conditioned intemperance and capriciousness from bona fide criminal behavior. Concerning stealing, for example, Tillman writes,

> For two hundred and fifty years . . . [ex-slaves] had been deprived of the fruits of their toilsome labor. . . . A proverb was current among them, that a man who had belonged to a white man, could steal anything from white people—he only took what rightfully belonged to him. From this you will readily see that their ideas concerning the tenth commandment were badly warped. In regard to the sacredness of the marriage tie, matters were worse. Allowed by many masters to form this relation at will, well used to the separation of wives and husbands at the convenience of their owners, to say nothing of the constant amalgamation that went on during the whole dark period of bondage, now, that they were free men and women, [they] saw no good reason why they should burden themselves with the vows of the marriage contract, or having done so why they should not break them *ad libitum*. (p. 252)

The text explains that these and other vices were the "bad feature[s] of slavery's training school," thus calling into question Booker T. Washington's implication in his autobiography that slavery provided beneficial instruction for African Americans.[10] This story contradicts that viewpoint and asserts instead that, due to slavery, lessons in morality must be relearned and that fiction is a most appropriate instrument of instruction. By focusing on the virtuous life of the young Caroline, this story seeks to reproduce her moral character and personal ambition in the real world as the means of attacking these and other social ills. Like most of the other domestic novels written by black women of this period, *Clancy Street* also effaces interracial hostility, although the principal characters acknowledge that such hostility is routine and that "'Down South' was a very undesirable place for Negro men in those days" (p. 268).

Caroline's story is intertwined with discussions about black superstitions—"cunjerin', fixin', trickin', poisonin' and hoodooin'"—and is accented with the then-popular ethnic interjections referencing European immigrants, like "If that don't beat the Jews" (p. 260). Caroline is a virtuous Negro girl who becomes an emblem for the perseverance, generosity, and compassion of an oppressed people. But unlike the ideal characterizations of the other sentimental heroines, Caroline is a rather ordinary "colored" girl who is representative of the masses of urban black youth and subject to the realistic consequences of poverty: inadequate education, employment discrimination, and ravaging epidemics. The text introduces her as an eager barefoot child with a "sweet [brown], sensitive face" (p. 255), wearing a homemade shift, reminiscent of the clothing worn by slave children. The reader can taste and smell the extremes of her life by sharing a seat at the Waters's "pine table scrubbed to almost immaculate whiteness" (p. 256) and waiting for dinner of either a "choice bit of boiled shoulder, yellow corn-cakes, tea and a pitcher of Orleans molasses" (p. 256) in good times or "army coffee" (brown meal and water), "corn cakes and boiled potatoes" in bad times (p. 265). Unlike Beryl, Caroline does not live in a comfortable farmhouse; she and her family are crammed into three small rented rooms. Moreover, Caroline cannot expect to complete high school; matriculating at an African-American college, like the pretty Beryl, is far beyond her greatest hope. Repeatedly described as an ordinary, vulnerable, poor, and dark-faced girl, Caroline stands apart from prior African-American heroines whose fair-skinned comeliness has been the traditional sign of their virtue. In fact, Caroline's mother further reinforces her plight when she discards a principal tenet of the code of feminine gentility to initiate her daughter into "the facts of life" that prescribe the condition of many a poor girl: "You're only a colored girl, Ca'line, and poor; but I'd rather see you going barefoot in your little sunbonnet and calico slip, and know you're alright, than to see you in silks and satins and know you didn't come by them honest" (p. 273). Even the story's romantic element is marginalized and transformed into a lesson in academic discipline by its presentation as an adolescent crush. As a consequence, "when Caroline found out that Otto Lewis . . . attended school in the same building . . . , the news filled her with girlish excitement. . . . The girl thought Otto not unlike the heroes of whom she read in books and she worshipped him accordingly" (p. 279). However, the text reports that "the little brown-faced maiden just turning thirteen" impresses him by "resolv[ing] always to have her lessons so well that no evil report of her stupidity should ever reach her hero's ears" (p. 279).

Because *Clancy Street* departs from the dominant pattern of the novels in which courtship leads to ideal family formation, it is necessary to recall the story. Shortly after we meet Caroline, she secures a light domestic job in the Langdon home. On seeing the girl's sweet face, "[t]he Confederate colonel's daughter [Mrs. Langdon] thought of the Negro mammy who had cared for her through the first sixteen years of her motherless existence, and of the little Negro playfellow and maid, now a teacher in the far South, whom she had taught by stealth the rudiments of knowledge" (p. 274). She hires Caroline for the "munificent offer" of fifty cents a week, her board and schooling (p. 276). After faithfully serving Mrs. Langdon and her family for seven years, Caroline is ready to graduate as valedictorian of her high-school class. But while rehearsing her graduation oration, she learns that Mrs. Langdon is very ill with typhoid fever. Caroline goes to her mistress's aid, refusing to leave her side to attend the graduation ceremonies. As a result of her dedication, Mr. Langdon "no longer doubt[s] the capabilities of [her] race" (p. 285). Unfortunately, Caroline contracts the fever from Mrs. Langdon and dies. Drawing on the other stock closure for sentimental fiction, this novel reinforces the work's ethic and evangelical mission. Thus rather than marry the ideal suitor, Caroline in her noble labor becomes worthy of the bridegroom of heaven.

Just before Caroline dies, Tillman presents a scene that is remarkably similar to the famous death scene of Eva(ngeline) in Stowe's *Uncle Tom's Cabin*, in which death is domesticated by heaven being described as an ideal home.[11] In the chapter "The Little Evangelist" of Stowe's novel, Eva speaks to the slaves, whom she calls servants, about their souls:

> "You are thinking only about this world. I want you to remember that there is a beautiful world where Jesus is. I am going there, and you can go there. It is for you, as much as me. But, if you want to go there, you must not live idle, careless, thoughtless lives. You must be Christians." . . . A bright, a glorious smile passed over her [Eva's] face, and she said brokenly, — "Oh! love, — joy, — peace![12]

Tillman's death scene repeats its famous predecessor in *Uncle Tom's Cabin*, the novel which fascinated both Caroline and her mother years before:

> "Everything is so pleasant," [Caroline] said. I had a lovely dream just now. Mother, father, are you all here?" she asked faintly. . . .
> "Kiss me good-by," she said, and they tearfully complied. "Be good, Abe. Let not your heart be troubled," and with this she fell asleep. A careless observer might have thought the young life wasted because its ministry was so short, but it is true that "we live in deeds, not years." But not so one who followed the fortunes of the family and friends of the young girl. (p. 286)

While the death of Eva sets the stage for the spiritual conversion of Topsy and Miss Ophelia's assumption of motherly responsibility for her, Caroline's death incites spiritual beneficence in the lives of her family and friends. Caroline's former best friend Hettie repents her life of sin. Mr. Langdon and his wife make good their vow "to consecrate the bulk of their fortune to the education of Negro youth" (p. 286). Caroline's eldest brother Abe and her childhood suitor Otto are their first beneficiaries; they become "stalwart minister[s] of the gospel" (p. 287). As if to accentuate the relationship between Caroline and Stowe's Eva, Tillman closed her novel by reminding her reader that Caroline's youngest sister, named "Little Eva," is now eighteen: "Little Eva now a young woman, Caroline's exact counterpart so everyone says, has just finished high school . . . " (p. 287). Little Eva fulfills Caroline's academic expectation and domestic mission by marrying Otto just beyond the story's closure, granting the text's discourse of domestic desire an opportunity to come to fruition.

Clancy Street clearly breaks the Victorian code of silencing intemperate behavior by explicitly exposing female sexual vulnerability and subsequent exploitation, especially for poor women living in urban areas. Thus the novel departs from the convention of depicting virtue for imitation, for no doubt late-nineteenth-century writers found that repeatedly delineating a virtuous woman's life neither ensured virtue in other women nor increased the likelihood for their domestic happiness. Instead, *Clancy Street* explicitly addresses the financial lure of prostitution for poor "colored girls" by admonishing them to avoid the advances of white men, which according to Caroline, "almost always meant disgrace; and disgrace was worse than death" (p. 271).[13] The text initially couches this admonition in Mrs. Waters's explanation of how she got her "white face and straight hair and features like white folks" from a slave master-grandfather during slavery (pp. 272–73) and how Caroline's fair-skinned friend Hettie similarly acquired that feature (p. 155). "In slavery times," Anne says, "these things couldn't be helped, but they can be helped now, and every colored girl that wants the respect of black folks, and white folks as well must stay in her place and keep white men folks in theirs" (p. 273). Therefore, embedded in the admonition about prostitution is also the text's decided refusal to celebrate the attractiveness of light-skinned women, for in associating light skin color with white men's sexual exploitation of black women it repudiates Western standards of feminine beauty.

Although the word *prostitution* is never mentioned, the novel dramatizes that subject by referring to Hettie who succumbs to its lure. Adhering to strictures that forbade respectable women to mention this word, Tillman employed what have become traditional coded references—an "honest" woman (p. 272) and "life of sin" (p. 282). In the former case a woman's honesty had nothing to do with prevarication and everything to do with sexual purity, and in the latter "sin" referenced only one. This interpretation of honesty endorsed the reductive standard by which a woman's entire character was measured by her sexual continence, a standard both Jacobs and Hopkins had critiqued in their works. Tillman mitigated this stricture by placing prostitution into a religious context; therefore this sin, like others, reserves the possibility of repentance, which the text reinforces with reference to the redeemed Mary Magdalene (p. 282). Thus, rather than using spiritual conversion to enhance the general prosperity of the self and the community, as in *Beryl Weston's Ambition*, *Clancy Street* relies on spiritual conversion to reclaim those who have slipped into sinfulness:

> Caroline and Anne went after Hettie who had now embarked upon a life of sin. Through their pleadings and prayers, Hettie repented of her sins and, like Mary Magdaline [sic], with her face bathed in repentant tears, set her face resolutely toward the city Beautiful. (p. 282)

Redemption for the fallen woman is possible in the biblical context, but the patriarchal society of the nineteenth century did not widely promote this view, preferring to sanction premarital virginity for women. Sexual inconstancy, insofar as this society was concerned, was irretrievable. However, the moral framework of *Clancy Street* is a black woman-centered morality, which mitigates the potency of the father's law for premarital virginity. As a result, a woman's moral character is more important than a prior sexual transgression, and a contrite character is the only prerequisite for spiritual redemption. The ultimate sincerity of Hettie's character erases the sin of her former life and transforms her into "a worthy woman" (p. 286), made evident through her assumption of Caroline's place in the Langdon's household after Caroline's death. The evidence of Hettie's redemption is her assumption of morality and civility, whose standards are set by her white employer Mrs. Langdon as well as by Caroline. By rewriting the patriarchal code of the unalterable fallen woman, the novel foreshadows Hopkins's *Contending Forces* (published two years later in 1900) by setting up a correspondence on the one hand between the mother's law and on the other, social and spiritual salvation.

Black Heroines, the Racial Discourse, Formula Novels, and the Test of True Love

While Hopkins's *Contending Forces*, Kelley-Hawkins's *Megda* and *Four Girls at Cottage City*, and Johnson's *Clarence and Corinne* and *The Hazeley Family* appear to share the temporal setting of their 1890s production dates, Harper and Tillman placed their domestic fictions, also written in the 1890s, in a prior period. This factor of temporal displacement has little bearing on the interracial character of the four latter novels due to their closely circumscribed social settings and their silencing of the racial thematics, discussed above. Consequently, they effectively elude the interracial hostility and violence of the 1890s as well as preserve their racial optimism. By contrast, Hopkins's *Contending Forces* derives its title precisely from that violence and gives vigorous expression to racial protest. In the words of one character, Luke Sawyer,

> "Friends, I am thirty years old and look fifty. I want to tell you why this is so. . . . I want to tell the gentlemen who have spoken here tonight that conservatism, lack of brotherly affiliation, lack of energy for the right and the power of the almighty dollar which deadens men's hearts to the sufferings of their brothers, and makes them feel that if only *they* can rise to the top of the ladder may God help the hindmost man, are the forces which are ruining the Negro in this country. It is killing him off by the thousands, destroying his self-respect, and degrading him to the level of the brute. *These are the contending forces that are dooming this race to despair!*" (p. 256, Hopkins's emphasis)

Whereas Harper did not avoid depicting racial hostility in *Iola Leroy*, she confined it to the antebellum period, and subsequently placed most of the novel's action in the Reconstruction era, a period that ended almost two decades before the novel's publication date. In so doing Harper could draw upon the racial optimism of Reconstruction to intensify the desire for social advancement among African Americans of the post-Reconstruction era. Tillman's *Beryl Weston's Ambition* and *Clancy Street* share a similar charge. But, while the latter novel is set in the period of Reconstruction, like Harper's *Iola Leroy*, *Beryl Weston's Ambition* was set in the decade of the 1880s, a time when black people were still generally more optimistic about their collective future in the United States as African Americans than they would be in the next decade. Tillman's characters are thus shielded from the extreme resurgence of racism of the 1890s, enabling them to be optimistic about their social positions. This allows the author to rely on domestic idealism to symbolize their future prosperity. As her happy couple embrace young, healthy children at the close of *Beryl Weston's Ambition*, Tillman made the optimism of racial uplift resolute, insisting that her readers leave Beryl knowing that she is "useful, honored and happy . . . for her highest ambition now is to serve the Lord" (p. 246). Reporting that Meg has learned the blessedness of "returning good for evil," *Megda* by Kelley-Hawkins closes similarly:

> God surely rewarded her in the years that followed. Her life was filled up with work—noble work—in her home and in the world outside. Beloved by everyone, with a tender, loving husband to guide and protect her, Meg's heart was filled full of gratitude to her Heavenly Father, and with tender pity for all his suffering children. (p. 394)

Like *Beryl Weston's Ambition, Megda* emphasizes the heroine's utility, piety, and resulting happiness; however, rather than explicitly asserting racial optimism, this latter novel is set within a racially silenced milieu that critiques pride, intemperance, and other moral transgressions.

Idealized womanhood is an important symbol in black women's post-Reconstruction domestic novels not only for representing the virtuous lives of individuals and an exemplary feminized citizenry but also for preserving the confidence among African Americans that they would eventually secure their civil rights. Idealized domesticity, then, is a significant symbol for representing the consummation of racial justice. That black women repeatedly wrote during the 1890s about the happy family in a socially just milieu, a decade that was probably one of the most oppressive in interracial history, cannot be denied. Despite the severe racism that their authors encountered, these fictions are decidedly hopeful, because the authors retained, at least for a while, their post-Civil-War optimism, as Dickson D. Bruce, Jr., remarks:

> The genteel literature produced by post-Reconstruction black writers was a measure of their optimism, about possibilities for the future. There was nothing evasive about observing genteel themes and conventions. Racial barriers were not seen as impregnable. Given this point of view, genteel literature conveyed the fully assimilationist message at the heart of black middle-class racial ideals during the post-Reconstruction era, as black writers claimed their right to and their desire for recognition as Americans.[14]

Although we late-twentieth-century readers might contend that black idealized domesticity was not an effective response to the racism of the era, in all likelihood these domestic novels were very satisfying for their first readers, as evidenced by their popularity. By depicting personal and racial desires realized, these novels kept their readers' political goals before them like a pleasantly recurring dream rather than as the living nightmare that confronted them daily in the form of demeaning consumer images, violated civil rights, Jim Crow segregation, and racial violence. They hoped that "the nadir" was merely a temporary backlash and that racial oppression would abate during the rapidly approaching twentieth century. The happy endings of the domestic novels reflected and reinforced their optimism.

When the new century arrived, however, "the nadir" continued, producing increased, indeed chronic despair among African Americans. To continue writing optimistic domestic fictions was a feat evidently too great, for, as mentioned above, black women writers in the prime of life, like Kelley-Hawkins, Johnson, and Tillman, apparently stopped publishing them. Like depictions of marriage and slavery in the abolitionist domestic texts, those of domestic idealism and chronic racism in the post-Reconstruction ones seem to have been incompatible; after the onset of the twentieth century, domesticity faded as a trope of political desire in African-American literature. Although Hopkins continued to write stories that venerated the ideal black heroine, producing three serial novels from 1901 to 1904, she shifted her focus from the courtship story—or the romance formula—as the expressive medium of the reformist imperative of idealized domesticity to the courtship story as a frame for other popular formulaic plots of the classical mystery,[15] the western, and the psychological ghost story, that were gaining popularity on the pulp market. This is not to say that Hopkins abandoned her faith in fiction as a means of inciting social reform, for as Hazel Carby has explained, Hopkins was confident "of the possibility of narrative intervention in the political and social formation because she believed that fiction, as a cultural form, was of great historical and political significance."[16] John Cawelti would later designate such morally enhanced romantic stories "social melodramas."

However, rather than use her serial novels to affirm political desires not within her heroine's reach, like the other black women writers of this study, Hopkins used the heroine's entertaining adventures to repudiate racism. This shift in intentionality makes her three serial novels fundamentally different from the domestic novels, in a number of ways. First, the serial novels make the courtship formula marginal to the more dominant mystery formula, thereby transforming the marriage stories in these works into backdrops, respectively, for a murder mystery, a western adventure, and a psychological ghost story. Second, these novels do not transform the courtship story into an allegory of fulfilled political desire; rather, the modified courtship story is one of frustrated civil expectations. Third, by placing the serial novels within the white social milieu, Hopkins relinquished the formerly steadfast story of racial affirmation. Fourth, by shifting the focus of the story to both a white hero and a mulatta heroine (in *Hagar's Daughter* that heroine is unknowingly passing for white), the novel stages the courtship as a contest between a white hero (in *Of One Blood* that hero is passing for white) and a white villain for the possession of the mulatta heroine, in which the former's convictions of true love confront the latter's racist expedience of lust and greed. In this way the racist hegemony is initially personalized and seemingly alterable before Hopkins points out the persistence of nationally sanctioned racism.[17] Even after the hero and heroine defeat the villain(s), the racist domain remains, forcing the heroic couple to live outside the United States. Moreover, the closing marriage does not write itself into harmonious prosperity beyond the ending; the happy ending is conditional. Lastly, by relying on displacements of racial identity (in *Hagar's Daughter*), noncontemporality (in *Winona*), and foreign setting (in *Of One Blood*), the serials further undermine the conventional happy ending of the domestic genre, thereby emphasizing the failure of the U.S. civil sphere of Hopkins's epoch to sustain the ideal ending. Together these features suggest that with the onset of the twentieth century, the explicit repudiation of racism rather than political assertion in the plot of ideal family formation becomes the more urgent theme.[18] My focus is not to center the disruptions in the racial discourses in the serials,[19] but to discuss how Hopkins framed these discourses within Victorian ideologies of true love to enhance both black and white readers' racial sympathy.

Probably the most distinctive feature that all three serials share is their transformation of the polemic on racial equality and civil justice into tests of true love. In the black female domestic novels of the 1890s, the discourse of true love is sanctioned without excessive testing and the plot of social reform is a discrete activity rather than one with stated national consequences. By contrast, in each of Hopkins's serial novels the villain initiates a set of circumstances that challenges the emotional attachment between the heroine and her beloved by engaging their individual will power, personal integrity, and depth of love in a contest against the imperatives of racist conventions. This struggle is played out as the test of true love, a cultural practice with which the first readers of these novels would no doubt have been well acquainted.

Karen Lystra characterizes this cultural contest in *Searching the Heart* by describing the dominant, Victorian American courtship ritual as "elaborate emotional tests"[20]:

> Doubt about the choice of a mate was channeled in nineteenth-century courtship into elaborate emotional texts. These dramas of crisis and resolution took different forms but were more than random troubles in love's path. Women particularly took the materials of life at hand and shaped them into obstacles that men had to overcome to prove the depth and sincerity of their love. . . . While the individuals involved seemed only partially aware of their own complicity, the tests of courtship formed such a consistent pattern that they cannot be explained as mere coincidence. (p. 167)

Similarly, the 1903 African-American conduct manual *Golden Thoughts* strongly endorsed a "conscientious and judicious courtship." The manual's authors, themselves exemplars of the text they espouse, contended that "If young men and women are true to themselves, if they do not assume that which they do not possess, if they shun deceit, each may obtain a fair estimate of the other's character and disposition by means of a timely courtship" (p. 88). While *Golden Thoughts* does not employ a dramatic strategy for adjudging the integrity of premarital love, the manual does suggest an economic measure of masculine resolve in the section entitled "Menial Service the Test of True Worth." This section explains that "When a young man will do any kind of work, even though distasteful to him, rather than be idle, you may make up your mind that he possesses some quality worth having, and that in time he will amount to something" (p. 250). This mark of sound character as a sign of true love was a most fitting criterion for black courting couples, given their political and material conditions during the post-Reconstruction era. Indeed the suitor's willingness to perform menial labor seems a cultural variation of the dominant society's practice of testing true love, which Lystra recovers. Both works cite the importance of the courtship period for discerning the character of the beloved. *Golden Thoughts* admonishes that the courtship ought not be regarded as "only a pleasant pastime, or possibly what is worse, a period of flirtation. . . . If marriage is not to be a lottery, this is the time to be on the look-out. One must not keep one eye open for perfections, and the other closed to defects" (p. 88). As we expect, it was the female participant to whom the conduct manuals addressed their most serious admonitions, for the marriage market seldom offered women an opportunity to renegotiate an adverse exchange.

Lystra goes on to explain in *Searching the Heart* that at the close of the nineteenth century the discourse of true love was also a part of the process of bourgeois individuation in which the individual defined a distinct (albeit here an initially romantic) self:

> The romantic self was constructed in nineteenth-century American culture upon the distinction between social roles and an inner identity that transcended all roles the individual filled. . . . Though this romantic sense of personal identity was an historical creation, within its circle of belief, the self was regarded as something of an essence, antithetical to custom and society. (p. 30)

The cultural practice of testing true love among courting couples not only found expression in conduct manuals but dominated black and white women's nineteenth-century fiction as well. For it was the compassion of true love that motivated the hero-husband's endorsement of the heroine's ambitions in the public sphere, and it was true love that disavowed arbitrary social boundaries.

Hopkins drew on this construction of romantic integrity to repudiate the prohibition of interracial marriage in each of her serials. However, rather than have her serial heroines simply stage testing "dramas of crisis and resolution" in the contexts of courtship and matrimony (Lystra, p. 167), Hopkins entangled her heroines and heroes in interracial plots whose conflicts were initiated by villains. They precipitate a series of events that disunite the romantic pair. Thus what is important to observe is that Hopkins took the polemical, civil argument of racial equality and played it out as an interracial love story, knowing that her audience — black and white alike — was already at least theoretically sympathetic to the romantic fulfillment of a virtuous couple. Evoking that sympathy was each serial's strategy of intervention. By manipulating the plot so as to increase the story's pathos, the text attempts to regulate particularly the white reader's attitude toward the mulatta heroine and ultimately liberalize particularly that reader's racial outlook. Hence the serials do not make polemical discourse the dominant argument for interracial equality;

rather the demonstration of the nobility of the heroic couple's true love is the primary means for arousing the readers' sympathy. By drawing on Victorian constructions of true love, then, each serial places its readers into a conflict with predetermined meaning—they must either sanction the arbitrary racist conventions or the power of true love between the interracial couple. As we shall see, the primary argument of each serial, like the domestic novels discussed above, shifts from civil to domestic domain, as the racial conflict seeks closure with the harmonious resolution of interracial marriage.

In 1891 Hopkins acquired the copyright on the first three chapters of *Hagar's Daughter: A Story of Caste Prejudice*, eight years before she secured the copyright for *Contending Forces*.[21] The remaining thirty-four chapters of *Hagar's Daughter* were copyrighted in 1901, the year its serialized publication began in *The Colored American*. This chronology alone suggests reasons for the similarities between the two tales; in fact, *Hagar's Daughter* reads somewhat like an inversion of *Contending Forces*, with the former recasting the Eastern romantic mystery as a murder mystery with allusions to western adventure.[22] *Contending Forces* is set largely in a black social sphere; evolves from black narrative authority, presumably for a black audience; and begins by retelling the typically tragic, antebellum story of interracial love between the beautiful mulatta and her white husband. While *Hagar's Daughter* begins with a similar antebellum scenario, the novel relies on racial passing to set the story in a white social sphere, implying a white audience,[23] and retells another familiar tale of the tragic mulatta whose white lover comes too late to reclaim his beloved, much as in Charles Chesnutt's *The House Behind the Cedars*.[24] However, *Hagar's Daughter* was not published in a journal with a predominantly white readership but was serialized in *The Colored American*, whose title clearly indicates the racial identity of the majority of its readers. The novel's interventionary thematics of social reform imply correction in the attitudes of white readers, for the text bears special witness to the white hero's racist viewpoints. Despite the similarities between the two novels, serialization has significant impact on the narrative design of *Hagar's Daughter* as well as of Hopkins's other magazine fictions, necessitating "an increased emphasis on such narrative elements as suspense, action, adventure, complex plotting, multiple and false identities, and the use of disguise" (Carby, Introduction, p. xxxvi).[25]

While *Contending Forces* mounts an optimistic call for vigilant social protest, *Hagar's Daughter*, as the biblical allusion suggests, reflects the failure of racial optimism with the death of the heroine. The text displays a wealth of "narrative formulas of the sensational fictions of dime novels and story papers" to manipulate the plot line so as to extenuate her readers' sympathy for the distressed love of Jewel Bowen (alias Hagar's daughter) and the white Cuthbert Sumner as well as for the reaffirmed love of her interracial parents, the mulatta Hagar Sargent Enson and the white Ellis Enson (Carby, Introduction, p. xxxvi). What is key to the novel's strategy of social interventionism is its transformation of the protest polemic for racial equality and civil justice into generational tests of interracial true love between her parents and between

Jewel and Sumner, once a series of events disclose her racial identity. Put in Hopkins's words, the discourse of racial protest is presented as a contest for determining whether "beastly prejudice alone [should] separate [Sumner] from the woman pre-destined for [his] life-companion?"[26]

Prior to Sumner's learning of Jewel's background, he affirms racist conventions, explaining "the sum total of what Puritan New England philanthropy will allow" (p. 271):

> "I think that the knowledge of her origin [any attractive woman with black ancestry] would kill all desire in me," replied Sumner. "The mere thought of the grinning, toothless black hag that was her foreparent would forever rise between us. I am willing to allow the Negroes education, to see them acquire business, money, and social status within a certain environment. I am not averse even to their attaining political power. Farther than this, I am not prepared to go. . . . Ought we not, as Anglo-Saxons, keep the fountain head of our racial stream as unpoluted [sic] as possible?" (p. 271)

By contrast, Jewel's white father Enson claims a higher law in his reclamation of his mulatta wife Hagar and cautions Sumner by saying, "'You will learn one day that there is a higher law than that enacted by any earthly tribunal, and I believe that you will then find your nature nobler than you know'" (p. 271). Within a few days of Enson's admonition and after the disclosure of Jewel's ancestry he delivers his daughter's "pathetic note bidding [Sumner] farewell" (p. 281). The text reports that "Twenty-four hours passed and left Sumner as they found him, in mental torture. Then his good angel triumphed. He swore he would not give her up, and then he learned the power of prayer" (p. 282). Sumner immediately seeks Jewel only to learn that she and her family have gone to Europe. But surprisingly, he delays his search for Jewel: "He went home to his father for a brief time and then started for the Continent himself" (p. 282). After an unsuccessful search for her in Europe,

> Sumner returned to America and again sought the Bowen mansion. . . . He never paused until he reached the pretty little rustic town in Maryland that held his heart, his dove of peace. . . . He . . . wandered up the country road. . . . Suddenly with a great cry he stood still before a fair, slender shaft of polished cream-white marble,

> JEWEL, aged 21.
> "Not my will, but Thine be done!"

> He fell down with his face upon her grave. She had died abroad of Roman fever. . . .

> Cuthbert Sumner questioned wherein he had sinned and why he was so severely punished.
>   Then it was borne in upon him: the sin is the nation's. It must be washed out. (p. 283)

The text refuses to describe the process by which Sumner reverses his prior decision; neither does it characterize the vigilance of his search or the depth of his grief. What the text deems important is the moral, which is emphasized by the unalterability of Jewel's death.[27]

The failed romantic consummation aborts the story of ideal family formation but, nevertheless, preserves the allegorical link between the discourses of domesticity and liberation, namely racial equality, by evoking the alternative generic ending of exaggerated pathos for domestic fiction. This ending also occurs in Chesnutt's *The House Behind the Cedars*; for not long after the white George Tryon has rejected the mulatta heroine Rowena Walden, he finds himself "driven by an aching heart toward the same woman. . . . Custom was tyranny. Love was the only law" (p. 263). Like Sumner, Tryon is too late. Grief accentuates the interracial construction of Victorian love in the interventionary agendas of both works; their authors seem to have racialized and extenuated the viewpoint that the "romantic sense of personal identity . . . was regarded as something of an essence, antithetical to custom and society" (Lystra, p. 30).

Like *Hagar's Daughter*, *Winona* and *Of One Blood* also evolve as tests of true love; however, these latter serials are more explicit racial polemics although cast in highly symbolic format. Hopkins again relied on the popularity of the formula novels to entertain her readers with adventure and intrigue, while she manipulated the plot to incite the reader's sympathy for the virtuous mulatta heroine and scorn for those harboring racist viewpoints who threaten the heroine's happiness. Rather than transparently reveal her frustration with the increasingly hostile racial climate of her era, Hopkins again depended on discursive displacements.

Winona: A Tale of Negro Life in the South and Southwest is set prior to the Civil War, a time when the oppression of African Americans was legal and racial liberalism was strong. The novel is reminiscent of James Fenimore Cooper's 1841 novel *The Deerslayer*[28] and the 1855 idyllic ballad "The Song of Hiawatha" by Henry Wadsworth Longfellow, both of which were very popular and would probably have been familiar to Hopkins as well as her readers. This serial novel opens during the 1850s in a small, tranquil community of mostly whites and Indians along the Buffalo-Canadian border and draws on the formulaic format of the western dime novel, which by the turn of the century was a highly ritualized and colorful adventure "of transcendent heroism overcoming evil figures of authority" (Cawelti, pp. 214–15).[29] In hundreds of dime novels, as Christine Bold has explained in *Selling the Wild West*, the "hero is an Easterner who dresses up to go west, where he leads a group of people, all less skilled and less cultured than him, to the rescue of a female captive in battles against various enemies."[30] Like the dime novel and *The Deerslayer* as well, *Winona* relies on the suspense and adventure of a series of captures and escapes, hidden motives, and disguise to drive its complex plot to happy resoltuion. But the serial's similarity to *The Deerslayer* also intensifies its theme of oppression by transforming white people's cruel treatment of Indians into white Southerners' brutality of blacks. Hence

Winona invites an interrogation of turn-of-the-century so-called civilized attitudes about black people just as the earlier novel had attempted to do with respect to red people and the destruction of the wilderness.

The triangular love story of *Winona* again plots a struggle of good and evil intentions for the mulatta heroine who here is Winona. However, honorable love in this work has two faces: the white Warren Maxwell from England and the black Judah who has grown up with Winona. Similarly, the Southern Colonel Titus and his white overseer Bill Thomson serve as the story's dual villains. The story begins with Maxwell's search for the heir to the Carlingford fortune.[31] Soon after arriving at the border town he encounters two adolescents, the mulatta heroine Winona, and Judah, her adopted black brother. They are seeking aid for her injured white father, White Eagle (alias Henry Carlingford from England), whom they later determine has been murdered. The murderers kidnap, transport, and enslave Winona and Judah on a plantation near Kansas City, Missouri. Maxwell summons aid from John Brown and his army of "Free-State men" to launch a rescue mission in a series of "the battle[s]-royal."[32] By selecting a British gentleman to displace the white Eastern hero, Hopkins indirectly implicated all white Americans in racial prejudice and applauded England as a land where "neither their color nor race will be against [Winona and Judah]" (p. 311). Thus Maxwell revises Cuthbert Sumner in *Hagar's Daughter* whose heroism, to say nothing of his happiness, is undermined by his prejudicial racial attitudes.

In addition the text celebrates the Christian valor of the abolitionist Brown and his army, who in the novel rescue not only Winona and Juda but Maxwell as well[33]:

> It was a terrible struggle between the two great forces—Right and Wrong. Drunken with vile passions, the Rangers fought madly but in vain against the almost supernatural prowess of their opponents; like the old Spartans who braided their hair and advanced with songs and dancing to meet the enemy, the anti-slavery men advanced singing hymns and praising God. (p. 412)

The rescue missions largely displace the courtship story, with the exception of intermittent romantic flashes between Maxwell and Winona. For example, after rescuing Winona and Judah, Maxwell is captured by a mob intent on burning him alive. As he is tormented,

> Maxwell compressed his lips. Winona stared at him across the shadows of the dim old woods. "Be true," she whispered to the secret ear of his soul. With rapture he read aright the hopeless passion in her eyes when he left her. He knew now that he loved her. (p. 363)

Before the mob can carry out its intentions, he is rescued by Southern officials only to be thrown into prison where he is abused for several months, virtually becoming an invalid, while he awaits his execution by hanging. This particular incident conflates Maxwell with the real-life John Brown by having the fictive hero suffer a portion of Brown's fate. However, Winona relieves much of his suffering by disguising herself as a boy so that she can attend to Maxwell in prison. In risking recapture in this way she demonstrates her own heroism. The partial overlapping of Brown's fate onto Maxwell intensifies the latter's heroism.

After Maxwell's friends, particularly Winona and Judah, joined by Brown and his army mount a successful rescue of Maxwell, they escape to the original border town, with their Southern enemies, led by Colonel Titus, hot on their trail. During the escape Winona becomes a full-fledged soldier in this emancipatory army. She carries a rifle, rides a horse, and eventually is "in command of the homeguard" (p. 409). Poetic justice causes Titus to fall from a steep ledge. But before he dies he explains the mysterious events leading to White Eagle's death, who is, of course, the missing heir to the Carlingford estate. With Winona identified as its last legitimate heir, she, Maxwell, and Judah abandon the United States for sanctuary in Great Britain. For them this becomes home.

The antebellum setting for this novel gave Hopkins an opportunity to recover the abolitionist fervor and definitively relate the Civil War to the abolition of slavery, a relationship that would be effaced with much of the historiography of the twentieth century. The story elevates John Brown to a Christian hero, describing him as "pastor, guide and counsellor," as "a man of deep religious convictions; but mingled with austerity were perfect gentleness and self-renunciation which inspired love in every breast" (p. 374). In addition the novel venerates the valor of the representative black male in Judah who "had become a man" (p. 335) and not a brute, in contrast to the degeneration of the black male self, which Frederick Douglass describes in his 1845 narrative.[34] Indeed Judah's manhood is celebrated as "a living statue of a mighty Vulcan" (p. 323), who speaks "like a senator" (p. 310).[35]

> [Judah's] demeanor was well calculated to inspire admiration and trust. Something truly majestic—beyond his years—had developed in his character. Warren thought him a superb man, and watched him, fascinated by his voice, his language, and his expressive gestures. Slavery had not contaminated him. His life with White Eagle had planted refinement inbred. In him was the true expression of the innate nature of the Negro when given an opportunity equal with the white man. (p. 335)

In addition to censuring racial oppression, the text relies on Judah's perspective to critique the white sexual privilege of Maxwell:

> If they [Judah and Winona] had remained together in slavery, she would have been not one whit above him, but the freedom for which he had sighed had already brought its cares, its duties, its self-abnegation. He had hoped to work for her and a home in Canada; it had been the dream that had buoyed his heart with hope for weary days; the dream was shattered

now. He saw that the girl would not be satisfied with his humble love
. . . . The white man has the advantage in all things. Is it worth while
struggling against such forces? (p. 357)

Aware that he cannot compete with Maxwell's white male prestige, Judah is
on the verge of descending into bitterness. But before he does, the text calls
him literally to carry Maxwell in order to stage his last rescue. As a result,
"[h]e felt all his passionate jealousy die a sudden death as pity and compassion
stirred his heart for the sufferings of his rival" (p. 396). While John Brown
declares, "This is a holy war, and it's only just begun" (p. 419), Judah is less
optimistic. "Unconsciously he was groping for the solution of the great question of social equality" (p. 377). Ultimately, he resolves that "he will not fight
for the Stars and Stripes if war comes . . . " (p. 406).

With the rescue complete and the mystery solved, the novel is ready for its
romantic conclusion of marriage. Maxwell becomes keenly aware of his growing attachment to Winona:

> There are loves and loves; but Warren told himself that the love of the
> poor forsaken child before him was of the quality which we name celestial.
> All the beauty and strength of the man, and every endowment of tender-
> ness came upon him there as the power came upon Samson; and he regis-
> tered a promise before heaven that night. (p. 392)

This is not a love between a man and a woman, but a sentimental, spiritualized
attachment based on the dependency of a lovely child. While romantic desire
enhances the racial thematics, that desire does not achieve the liberational
integrity of the heroine's text in the earlier novels. Rather, interracial romance
displaces the text of female development in this novel.

Maxwell's near-death struggle to free Winona and Judah from slavery
makes him eligible for the racialized test of true love. He wins it by demonstrating that racial prejudice does not interfere with the expression of his
honorable love for Winona, but he does not actually claim the prize of Winona
as we would expect. In fact the novel tempts us with that expectation; for
with Maxwell safe, the liberation of Winona and Judah secured, and the
villain's deathbed confession, the novel ought to have advanced speedily to
the conventional happy ending in marriage. However, the marriage does not
occur within textual time, it is fated for the future.

Refusing to gratify her readers' expectations with the happy marriage of
Winona and Maxwell, Hopkins arrested her story with Maxwell's return to
England and the expatriation of Winona and Judah and their warm reception
into British aristocracy. In place of the expected ending, Hopkins repudiated
"American caste prejudice":

> [Winona and Maxwell] made not plans for the future. What necessity was
> there of making plans for the future? They knew what the future would
> be. They loved each other; they would marry sooner or later, after they
> reached England. . . . American caste prejudice would not touch them in

their home beyond the sea. . . . Judah never returned to America. After the news of John Brown's death had aroused the sympathies of all christendom for the slaves, he gave up all thoughts of returning to the land of his birth and entered the service of the Queen. His daring bravery and matchless courage brought its own reward; he was knighted; had honors and wealth heaped upon him, and finally married into one of the best families of the realm. . . . Winona celebrated in her letters . . . the wonders of her life in England. . . . She is a noble woman. (pp. 435–36)

Hopkins's last discursive displacement at the very end of the work exchanges the conventional happy ending of marriage with explicit confidence in the approach of freedom. But prior to discussing freedom's advance, there is a brief historical summary of "the subsequent fortunes of John Brown, and his sons and their trusty followers—a story of hardships, ruined homes and persecutions, and retribution to their persecutors" . . . (p. 435) and restated assurance that Winona is happy abroad, confident in herself and Maxwell's love:

She is fortified against misfortune now by her deep knowledge of life and its inevitable sorrows, by love. Greater joy than hers, no woman, she believes, has ever known. (p. 435)

We too must share that confidence, for the text situates the expected marriage in ellipses (* * *).

At this point the story abandons the small cast of white and black gentry in Britain and returns for closure to the folk—black and white—along the Buffalo-Canadian border. Here the characters anticipate freedom. An escaped bondwoman recalls "Winona's strange fortunes" as the prologue to "a short sermon on the fate of her race" (p. 436). The woman exclaims, "Glory to God, we's boun' to be free. . . . Somethin's gwine happen" (p. 436). While the story's historical context suggests the sermon's meaning as predictive of the Civil War, the first readers of this serial novel in 1902 no doubt read the sermon as divine sanctioning of civil liberty for African Americans with the Civil War as the most important providential sign.

Hopkins's last novel, *Of One Blood*, relies on both the passing strategies and masked character identities of *Hagar's Daughter*, the mystery plot of a ghost story, Ethiopian legend, the familiar triangular love story, and enough intrigue to keep even a late-twentieth-century reader engaged. Two specific cultural discourses of the nineteenth century—the psychological ghost story (arising from an increased interest in spiritualism, mesmerism, and psychological research) and Ethiopianism—charge Hopkins's attack on racism in which she unwrote the presumption of Western supremacy with biblical prophesy.[36] Hopkins's choice to unify her plot around a ghost story and Ethiopian legend becomes particularly meaningful when we are mindful that during the nineteenth century ghost stories by women were very prominent in popular literature and evolutionary biology dominated scientific discussions.[37] The discourse of Ethiopianism, a pre-modern version of black nationalism, also reflected increasing scientific interest in explaining the origins of mankind and civilization. Hopkins intersected Ethiopianism, a psychological ghost story, romantic love, and the historic dispossession of black American bondwomen to advance her didactic story about "the Ethiopian as the primal race" (p. 521) and the ancient African city of Meroë as the original site of Western culture.[38] In the words of Elizabeth Ammons, *Of One Blood* is "Hopkins's allegory about racism in the United States . . . [which] is both as simple and as complex as the system it excoriates" (p. 82).[39]

The opening chapter of the novel presents the angst-ridden, Harvard-educated, scientist-hero Reuel Briggs in a rented room in Cambridge, Massachusetts, during a raging storm. Although Briggs is passing presumably for white inasmuch as "It was rumored at first that he was of Italian birth, then they 'guessed' he was Japanese" (p. 444), his characterization clearly recalls probably the most famous black student at Harvard during the last years of the nineteenth century — William E. B. Du Bois.[40] Saturated with references to "supernatural phenomena or *mysticism*," "new discoveries in psychology," "things recorded under the name of divinations, inspirations, demoniacal possessions, apparitions, trances, ecstasies, miraculous healing and productions of disease, and occult powers possessed by peculiar individuals over persons and things" (pp. 442–43), *Of One Blood* seems to insinuate the work of William James in psychology, who was one of Du Bois's most esteemed and personally admired Harvard professors. An early proponent of psychology, James authored the two-volume treatise *The Principles of Psychology* in 1890 and his famous *Varieties of Religious Experience: A Study in Human Nature* in 1902.[41] His brother Henry was a master writer of psychological ghost stories, which is precisely the generic category of *Of One Blood*. His famous *The Turn of the Screw* also appeared in 1898. Given Hopkins's proximity and her erudition, she may have been aware of the Jameses' publications, which might have additionally fueled her interests in, using her own words, "the great field of new discoveries in psychology" (p. 442) that she projected onto her hero Briggs. Thus by recontextualizing Ammons's provocative contention that *Of One Blood* is an allegorical racial discourse with aspects of the intellectual life of late-nineteenth-century Cambridge, the novel's psychic allusions invoke not only Du Bois but William and Henry James as well.

Much like William James's characterization of "The Sick Soul" in *The Varieties of Religious Experience* that suffers fits of "nervous exhaustion" and is "tired of living" (*Varieties*, p. 128), Briggs possesses a "passionate, nervous temperament," an intense interest in "spiritualistic phenomena," and a preoccupation with suicide (*Of One Blood*, p. 444). Intimations of racial despair — poverty, ostracism, and solitude — further magnify his despondency (a despair that Søren Kierkegaard termed "the sickness unto death" and Freud later termed "the death instinct"[42]), bringing him to the brink of taking his own life (pp. 443, 442). While contemplating suicide, he discovers that he possesses the power of clairvoyance, which he immediately demonstrates with one of several visions:

> He fell into a dreamy state as he gazed for which he could not account. As he sent his earnest, penetrating gaze into the night, gradually the darkness and storm faded into tints of cream and rose and soft moist lips. Silhouetted against [t]he background of the lowering sky and waving branches, he [s]aw distinctly outlined a fair face. . . . (p. 445)

He concludes this particular excursion into the unknown by later explaining to his friend Aubrey Livingston (also presumably white) "that the wonders of a material world cannot approach those of the undiscovered country within ourselves—the hidden self lying quiescent in every human soul" (p. 448). In language remarkably similar to Du Bois's terminology in "Of Our Spiritual Strivings" in *The Souls of Black Folks*, Reuel explains that he understands the bond between individual human corporeality and enigmatic spirituality. This "gift of *duality*" (p. 447) fortifies Reuel's resolve to "go farther than M. Binet in *unveiling* the vast scheme of compensation and retribution carried about in the vast recesses of the human soul" (p. 448, emphasis added).[43]

Against the backdrop of a proliferation of references to psychic phenomena in the novel's early chapters, the mulatta heroine Dianthe Lusk mysteriously enters and recedes from Briggs's life at the close of "Hallow-eve," after he and his friends had been telling ghost stories (pp. 454, 455), much like the opening scene of Henry James's *The Turn of the Screw*. The next night she reappears, and Briggs draws on his formidable skill in psychic power to release her from a death-like trance induced by mesmerism. Almost immediately Dianthe's love rescues Reuel from extreme depression. Aubrey (who according to Ammons represents "the powerful white man who symbolizes the [racist] system" [p. 82]) becomes obsessed with Dianthe. Shortly after her marriage to Reuel and after his departure on a scientific expedition to Africa, Aubrey abducts and later murders Dianthe. What grants Aubrey power over Dianthe is his knowledge that she is black, knowledge that she herself could not disclose to Reuel due to amnesia but knowledge which he nevertheless already has. Had Reuel been honest with Dianthe about his racial identity and disclosed hers as well, he probably could have prevented her fate. As Ammons correctly observes, "there is a level at which Reuel, the black man, tragically abets the white man's evil by his silence—as Reuel in the end recognizes" (p. 82). Needless to say, this marriage in this macabre story cannot inspire a happy ending.

Further complicating the story's meaning is its disclosure at the end that the triangular love conflict is multiple incest due to the fact that Reuel, Aubrey, and Dianthe are siblings. Not only has the recurring theme of matrimonial harmony among spouses who possess sibling-like affinity, found in black women's domestic novels of the 1890s and Hopkins's own *Contending Forces*, gone awry in this novel, but in it also is played out a white/black struggle over the dominance of black women, a struggle that Du Bois in particular would comment on in a 1922 article in *The Crisis*.[44] Ammons points to "the figurative meaning of the incest of *Of One Blood*" as a hyperbolic racial allegory about racist strategies to frustrate the unity of the human family:

> Symbolically, it [incest] shows that the black woman is abused and killed by her white "brother" to keep her from union with her black "brother," whose reciprocal bond with her can, the jealous white brother knows, offer strength and the miracle of resurrection to black people in the racist United States (the mutual resuscitation we see between Dianthe and Reuel). To prevent such racial wholeness and healing, according to Hopkins's literally incredible but symbolically accurate plot, the white man will lie, steal, rape, commit incest, and kill. (p. 83)

Of One Blood's ending in the fantastic underground city of Telassar adds to the reader's uneasiness by making the acquisition of equal justice an even more remote possibility.[45] For this African wonderland of underground labyrinths seems in part like an external projection of Briggs's desire for suicidal release from his racial anguish.

The political optimism of the domestic novels of the 1890s is decidedly absent in this novel, making it even more somber than *Hagar's Daughter* and *Winona*. *Of One Blood* concludes with these words, "There [in Telassar] he [Briggs] spends his days teaching his people all that he has learned in years of contact with modern culture. United to Candace [his queen], his days glide peacefully by in good works; but the shadows of great sins darken his life . . . (p. 621). While the novel closes with him living peacefully if not happily, the tone and mood of the entire novel are grotesque, even morbid with three graphic deaths and Briggs's recurring bouts with suicidal despair. The only answer that the text poses to "the ubiquitous race question" (p. 584) is external to human agency. This answer negates the efficacy of social protest, promoted in *Contending Forces*, as a remedy for racial injustice. This last of Hopkins's novels asks "Where will ['the advance of mighty nations penetrating the dark, mysterious forests of his native land'] stop?" (p. 621). The answer is left to God:

> But none save Omnipotence can solve the problem.
> To our human intelligence these truths depicted in this feeble work may seem terrible, —even horrible. But who shall judge the handiwork of God, the Great Craftsman! Caste prejudice, race pride, boundless wealth, scintillating intellects refined by all the arts of the intellectual world, are but puppets in His hand, for His promises stand, and He will prove His words, "Of one blood have I made all races of men." (p. 621)

The racial optimism that dominates the 1890s novels and is evident in Hopkins's *Contending Forces* is initially mitigated in her first two serials and ultimately suspended in death-like dissolution in this last novel. The demise of this optimism makes her earlier references to "There is no death. Life is everlasting" (p. 464) necessary to preserve dispirited political desire for racial justice. Rather than reinvigorate the disheartened desire, the novel suspends it in hibernation. Much like Ralph Ellison's nameless hero of the *Invisible Man* (1952), Briggs resorts to a state of other-worldly suspension to await divine racial intervention.

In addition to this inscription of chronic racial despair, Hopkins's serial novels decenter the heroine's prominence. Both Jewel and Winona display inordinate courage, but in each case their fortitude is directed only toward the men they love. Hence these two heroines, in addition to Dianthe Lusk of the last novel, abandon the woman-centered discourse of female development. As fair, noble, and genuinely loving heroines who all have the proverbial drop of black blood, their function is to incite the sympathy of the reader for their racial plights. They are not intellectual heroines who inspire the reader with the wisdom of their viewpoints, like many of the prior heroines. In fact, the serial heroines seldom speak, perhaps in response to turn-of-the-century censure of literary heroines for "talk[ing] rather more brilliantly than is consistent with good manners" in an attempt "to show how clever they were, or undertaken to demonstrate that theirs was the superior sex."[46] Hopkins seems to have silenced the discourse of female agency, which was a very important feature of the 1890s domestic novels. Her reticence calls attention to dissolution of the "heroine's text" of black female authority as an effective pedagogical strategy for stimulating social reform during the early years of the twentieth century.

By the second decade of the twentieth century, the domestic story and household setting often became sites for staging the ultimate consequences of deteriorating race relations on black family life. The optimism reflected in the persistent depictions of ideal family formation in black women's post-Reconstruction domestic novels of the 1890s is generally replaced by the deformation of that ideal, as this excerpt from Angelina Weld Grimké's domestic drama *Rachel* (1916) suggests.

> Every year, we [black people] are having a harder time of it. In the South, they make it as impossible as they can for us to get an education. We're hemmed in on all sides. Our safeguard—the ballot—in most states, is taken away already, or is being taken away. Economically, in a few lines, we have a slight show—but at what a cost! In the North, they make a pretense of liberality: they give us the ballot and a good education, and they snuff us out. Each year, the problem just to live, gets more difficult to solve. How about these children—if we're fools enough to have any?[47]

8
Domestic Tragedy as Racial Protest

Quite automatically he arose and followed the path. Quite automatically he drew the branches aside and saw what he saw. Underneath those two terribly mutilated swinging bodies, lay a tiny unborn child, its head crushed in by a deliberate heel.

ANGELINA WELD GRIMKÉ, "Goldie" (1920)

Agnes Milton had taken a pillow off of my bed and smothered her child.

ANGELINA WELD GRIMKÉ, "The Closing Door" (1919)

Why — it would be more merciful — to strangle the little things at birth. And this nation — this white Christian nation — has deliberately set its curse upon the most beautiful — the most holy thing in life — motherhood Why — it — makes — you doubt — God!

ANGELINA WELD GRIMKÉ, *Rachel* (1920)

The corpus of works that Angelina Weld Grimké published during her lifetime is very small. Although she wrote a respectable number of poems, short stories, and dramas, she did not vigorously pursue their publication. While her talent as a poet received considerable endorsement, especially during the years of the Harlem Renaissance,[1] I direct my attention specifically to her short stories and dramas. It is there that the maternal discourses of desire become explicit and domestic configuration appears as an emphatic expressive mode, not for racial affirmation as in the post-Reconstruction domestic novels of the 1890s, but for racial protest. Grimké is clearly a minor, early-twentieth-century author whose writings lie largely just beyond the end of the post-Reconstruction era; however, her stories and dramas offer a significant cultural critique on the domestic novels of African-American women of that period.

Grimké's dramas and short stories illuminate two important aesthetic transitions in U.S. literary history in general and African-American literary history in particular. These works mark a point in both literary traditions where a "new horizon of expectations has achieved more general currency."[2] These works designate a point in U.S. literary culture where the growing social alienation that would later be identified as the modern condition intersects Victorian positivism, reflected in nineteenth-century literary sentimentality. In specifically black literary culture, Grimké's writings mark a place where the domestic plots of social optimism become outmoded, and explicit depictions of social alienation and racial protest commence to satisfy the expectations of twentieth-century black readers. Thus the self-affirming, maternal discourses of political desire in the works of her black female predecessors seem transformed into blues epics in Grimké's works.[3] Aligning these new aesthetic expectations against those of her black female predecessors, who relied on an ideal domestic polity in their novels, is also particularly revealing. For when these earlier writers persistently encountered more and more racist legislation and intimidation during the last decade of the nineteenth century and the first years of the next, as I previously discussed, they seem to have stopped writing idealized domestic fiction altogether.

Grimké's best known work is *Rachel*, a racial problem play, which was first staged in 1916 and published in 1920.[4] Arthur P. Davis has cited this play as "the first successful stage drama to have been written by a Negro."[5] Although *Rachel* seems to have been notably staged only three times, as Grimké's biographer Gloria T. Hull explains, Grimké intended for its presentation to serve as a strategy of intervention in racist hegemony by appealing to a sympathetic white audience with the utter hopelessness of the play's heroine, Rachel, who goes mad because of racial despair (Hull, p. 119).[6] Among the newspaper reviews, the *Washington Star* best described the play's sobering intentionality by writing that "The action progresses by way of episodes calculated to show the futility of individual effort on the part of the colored people, since no amount of effort is able to overcome the arrogance of the white race."[7] Grimké hoped that *Rachel* would attract the attention of a professional producer, and in 1919 there seems to have been talk of that possibility but to no avail (Hull, p. 119). The play's failure to secure professional staging probably prompted Grimké to publish the work in 1920 as a means of encouraging its widest possible dissemination.

Before analyzing *Rachel*, I focus briefly on the handbill for its original performance (Figure 6).[8] The handbill portrays the extreme resignation of the title character Rachel Loving. She wears a white dress and poses in the posture of exaggerated humble supplication, while indicting her intended audience with a desperate stare. It is important to note that this handbill is a part of a growing graphic tradition of social intervention that gave powerful visual representation to the changing racial climate in the United States.

Throughout the pages of many late-nineteenth- and early-twentieth-century black publications, like *The A.M.E. Church Review*, *The Colored American*, *Golden Thoughts*, and *The Crisis*, are compelling pictorial representations of African Americans at different moments of history and in various conditions. In *The Colored American* and *Golden Thoughts*, for example, there are emphatic depictions of racial optimism among African Americans. *The Colored American* is full of portraits of successful black Americans—men and women.

"RACHEL"

The Drama Committee
of the District of Columbia Branch
of the N. A. A. C. P.
—PRESENTS—

"RACHEL"

A Race Play in Three Acts by
Angelina Grimke
under direction of

NATHANIEL GUY

AT

Myrtilla Miner Normal School
Friday Eve., March 3rd and
Sat. Eve., March 4th, 8 P. M.

Tickets   -   75 and 50 Cts.

Tickets on Sale at Gray and Grays Drug Store 12th & U
Sts. N. W. after February 1st from 6 to 8 o'clock P. M.
All Seats Reserved.

PRINTED BY MURRAY BROS.

Figure 6. Handbill for Angelina Grimké's play "Rachel," 1916. Courtesy of the Moorland-Spingarn Research Center, Howard University.

The handsome photographs accompanying Hopkins's serial article "Famous Women of the Negro Race" (1902, discussed above) constitute merely one of many instances in which the pictorial detail complements the discourse. *Golden Thoughts* is as vigorous in its pictorial representation of the progress of African Americans in thirty-two illustrations, which are listed in the table of contents by page. Dr. Henry R. Butler explained the significance of the art work in his introduction to the manual:

> The art work is especially interesting and important. I wish to call the reader's attention to these illustrations. They are the work of colored artists, and the pictures are all of colored Americans, and it is a fact that the best of these pictures represent the inside home life of fully one-third of the ten million colored Americans. I entreat you to study these pictures as well as the reading matter; they tell their own story; they tell of the coming of a new aristocracy, a people powerful in strength, morals, culture, wealth and refinement.[9]

Two illustrations from the front matter of this work—"One-Room Cabin," presumably of the Reconstruction period (Figure 7) and "A Modern Home" of the new twentieth century (Figure 8)—emphasize the hard-won social progress of African Americans during this interval.

By contrast, the premier and subsequent volumes of *The Crisis* inaugurated in 1910, whose name clearly indicates the crisis in African-American society

Figure 7. "One-Room Cabin," from *Golden Thoughts,* 1903. Courtesy of the Afro-American Studies Resource Center, Howard University.

Figure 8. "A Modern Home," from *Golden Thoughts*, 1903. Courtesy of the Afro-American Studies Resource Center, Howard University.

caused by the resurgence of racism, especially lynching, reflect the loss of that optimism. In addition to a litany of lynching stories, a running count of victims, and hideous pictures of their bodies hanging from trees, the first volume depicts two woodcuts by John Henry Adams previously introduced (Figures 1 and 2, pages 16 and 17) that poignantly depict the lost hope of African Americans. The first illustration depicts a dignified black businessman with his equally dignified black female typist, and the second presents presumably the same businessman leaving the bank after having made a deposit. These two woodcuts labeled "1900" and "1910" appear on opposite pages and present the following captions: "1900" states, "The colored man that saves his money and buys a brick house will be universally respected by his white neighbors"; "1910" states, "New and dangerous species of Negro criminal lately discovered in Baltimore. He will be segregated in order to avoid lynching."[10] The racial texts of these two works reveal the frustration of African Americans whose dignity and work ethic were rewarded with racial prejudice, discrimination, and violence.

Like "1910," the portrait of the distressed Rachel has antecedents who lived in happier days when a young black woman joyously looked forward to marriage and motherhood. One such precursor is depicted in the photograph entitled "Purity" from *Golden Thoughts* (Figure 9). This photograph presents the ideal feminine innocence of a young black woman who is dressed like a turn-of-the-century bride, an image that makes the portrayal of Rachel's agony on the 1916 handbill even more compelling. Other precursors are the numerous heroines of black women's domestic novels of the 1890s who relied on the emancipatory thematics of ambition, personal virtue, and hard work for achieving prosperity. What is significant to note is that those novels and Grimké's *Rachel* exploit the domestic discourse to chronicle respectively the preservation and ultimately the deterioration of black Americans' collective dream of freedom as full U.S. citizens.

Rachel is set during the first decade of the twentieth century in a Northern city, where Rachel Loving lives happily with her mother and brother Tom.

Figure 9. "Purity," a photograph from *Golden Thoughts,* 1903. Courtesy of the Afro-American Studies Resource Center, Howard University.

Rachel wants nothing more than to be a mother. In fact, much of the play's emotional effusion concerns Rachel's maternal desire:

> (*With head still raised, after she has finished [singing to her piano accompaniment of Nevin's "Mighty Lak a Rose"], she closes her eyes. Half to herself and slowly [says,]* I think the loveliest thing of all the lovely things in this world is just (*almost in a whisper*) being a mother! (p. 134; Grimké's emphasis)

Rachel vicariously enacts this desire by caring for a small, orphaned black child. Her happiness, however, is sadly sobered one day when her mother informs Rachel and Tom that their father and half-brother were lynched ten years earlier in the South because the father wrote a newspaper article denouncing a white mob that had lynched an innocent black man. Knowledge of this event causes Rachel to view the children whom she so hopefully desires as potential victims of lynching. While she tries to adapt to the blight of racism, which she understands as a "curse upon the most beautiful—the most holy thing in life—motherhood" (p. 149), she and Tom have their professional aspirations dashed by employment discrimination. In addition, she witnesses the terrifying effects of increased racial victimization on small black school children, especially her own adopted child. Ultimately, the pressure of racial despair is too much for Rachel, for she slips into madness, imagining that she hears her unborn children appealing to her not to give them life in a racist society. At the end of the play she rejects John Strong's marriage proposal and renounces her great desire to be a mother as the expression of her personal outrage at racism.

Grimké began writing this play under other titles "as early as 1914 (and possibly before then), for she was circulating it in manuscript for criticism in January 1915" (Hull, p. 118).[11] A similar plot is recounted in Grimké's two short stories—"The Closing Door" and "Goldie"—which were solicited by and subsequently published in *The Birth Control Review*, respectively in 1919 and 1920. Like *Rachel*, these two stories have a long developmental history with several earlier versions cast from different narrative perspectives with various titles (Hull, p. 130).[12]

"The Closing Door" is also about an initially happy young black woman, Agnes Milton, who here is married. The story is told as flashback from the perspective of a teenage girl, Lucy, whom Agnes has adopted. Lucy recalls Agnes's bliss in learning that she was to be a mother. However, fearful that she is too happy, she goes about insisting that "'We must make no protestations of delight but go softly underneath the stars, lest God find . . . out'" (p. 261). She hopes that this sacrifice is sufficient for God who is indirectly characterized as capricious and perhaps even jealous of her happiness. Before Agnes's child is born, she learns that her favorite brother has been lynched, and like Rachel, she comes to the conclusion that she is "[a]n instrument . . . to bring children here . . . for the sport—the lust—of possibly orderly mobs" (pp. 274–75). Her despair compels her to pray for the death of her unborn child. But when her son is born healthy, she responds to the ironic failure of prayer by murdering him.[13]

"Goldie" is yet another story about an initially happy young black woman—Goldie—that is much more psychologically complex and aesthetically satisfying than the previous "The Closing Door." It is cast from the perspective of Victor Forrest, Goldie's adoring brother whom she has suddenly summoned to her home in a small, Southern black settlement. As he walks through a forest between the railway station and her home, his thoughts oscillate between anxious hopefulness and terrifying dread. Complicating his anxiety about racial violence is his probe of complex feelings for his sister, suggested in the analogy of his name, the almost impenetrable state of his mind, and his location. Seeking emotional clarity first, he acknowledges his guilt for not sending for his sister earlier, for he concludes that she married a man whom he repeatedly calls a "fathead" in order to free himself from that responsibility:

> Well, sisters . . . weren't above marrying and going off and leaving you high and dry—just like this.—Oh! of course, Cy was a good enough fellow . . .—no one could deny that—still, confound it all! How could Goldie prefer a fathead like Cy to him. Hm!—peeved yet, it seemed!—Well, he'd acknowledge it—he was peeved all right. . . . Peeved first, then what? . . .*Relief!*—Honest at last.—Relief! Think of it, he had felt relief when he learned he wasn't to be bothered, after all, with little, loyal, big-hearted Goldie.—*Bothered!* . . . A rotter, that's what he was, and a cad. (pp. 286–87)

An omniscient narrator mediates the exposure of the brother's complex feelings with the word "cad" to describe both his breached responsibility and latent jealousy, suggestive of an affection that exceeds the bounds of sibling love.[14] But before he has the opportunity to confront these feelings, he arrives at Goldie's home and finds that she and her husband have been lynched: "Underneath those two terribly mutilated swinging bodies, lay a tiny unborn child, its head crushed in by a deliberate heel" (p. 302). The story does not end here. Victor avenges his sister, her husband, and unborn child, instigating his own death at the hands of lynchers.

Grimké's best work of fiction is the novella "Jettisoned," published for the first time in her *Selected Works*. Probably at the advice of a sympathetic reviewer,[15] this work presents distressed motherhood but without the lynching scenario. Motherhood here is redefined and subsequently affirmed in an artificially constructed family. Briefly, this story recounts a few days in the life of Miss Lucy, an old black woman who is a domestic for a white family. She resides in a rooming house and befriends Mary Lou, a young black woman who lives down the hall. Miss Lucy is unaware that Mary Lou is slowly starving due to her refusal to accept racially exploitive work. On one evening Miss Lucy shares with Mary Lou her plans to visit her married daughter and her husband. But because her daughter is passing for white, the only way that

Miss Lucy can visit her is to pretend that she is the daughter's mammy.[16] That same evening a young black medical student, who lives in the same building, averts Mary Lou's suicide. The thankful Miss Lucy decides not to visit her daughter but to devote her maternal feelings to Mary Lou instead. Together with the student, they form a revised family. This story prompts me to speculate that had it not been for Grimké's obsession with rendering lynching in practically all of her stories and their attendant pathetic repudiations of motherhood, her writing might have had a broader creative plateau on which to develop.

Some time around 1920 Grimké returned to the theme of lynching in the writing of another play, *Mara*. She wrote numerous drafts of this play, and the complete version exists as a holograph of nearly 200 pages.[17] The absence of a typescript among her papers suggests that she did not attempt to stage or publish the play (Hull, p. 125). *Mara* concerns a black family, the Marstons, and their teenage daughter Mara. They live on a Southern estate walled off from the rest of the community in response to the prior murder of Mr. Marston's mother. However, the wall cannot keep out a lusting white man who rapes Mara on her eighteenth birthday. As a consequence, Mara goes mad. The outraged father avenges Mara, and the play ends as a white mob drags him and his wife from their home.

Grimké's preoccupation, indeed obsession, with lynching and tormented black maternity as her expression of racial protest is clearly evident in these works. Curious though, given Grimké's abolitionist family background and work on antilynching petitions (Hull, p. 131), is that none of her characters is engaged in the work of racial uplift and protest. Rather, they are most disconsolate. Her letter to *Atlantic Monthly* that accompanied her story "Blackness" recalls a catastrophic event that seems to have inspired her recurring lynching stories[18]:

> I am sending enclosed a story. It is not a pleasant one but it [is] based on fact. Several years ago, in Georgia, a colored woman quite naturally it would seem became wrought up, because her husband had been lynched. She threatened to bring some of the leaders to justice. The mob, made up of [?] and [?] white men determined to teach her a lesson. She was dragged out by them to a desolate part of the woods and the lesson began. First she was strung up by her feet to the limbs of a tree, next her clothes were saturated with kerosene oil, and then she was set afire. While the woman shrieked and writhed in agony, a man, who had brought with him a knife used in the butchering of animals, ripped her abdomen wide open. Her unborn child fell to the ground at her feet. It emitted one or two little cries but was soon silenced by brutal boots that crushed out the head. Death came at last to the poor woman. The lesson ended. (*Selected Works*, p. 417)

Evidently this event so severely affected Grimké that not only did she rewrite that story over and over again, but the activity of rewriting it seems to have been more important to her than her desire to see it in print or performed. To

explore this latter hypothesis, it is necessary to examine her works in relationship to some of the biographical details of Grimké's life, mindful of the persistent attention that lynching was receiving in African-American print media of
the first two decades of the twentieth century to secure support for the Dyer
Anti-Lynching Bill of 1922 (Hull, p. 131).[19]

Angelina Weld Grimké was the great niece of the famous white abolitionist
and suffrage sisters Sarah M. Grimké and Angelina Grimké Weld of South
Carolina and the daughter of their partly black nephew Archibald Henry
Grimké (who graduated from Harvard Law School in 1874) and his white
wife Sarah E. Stanley. In addition, her paternal uncle was the Reverend Francis Grimké, pastor of the famous Fifteenth Street Presbyterian Church in
Washington, D.C., whose wife Charlotte Forten Grimké was a well-known
educator and lesser-known writer. Less is known about Grimké's mother,
whom Archibald Grimké married in 1879 and whom the Boston *Sunday
Globe* in 1894 described as "'a white woman who belonged to one of the
best known families in this city'" (Hull, p. 108).[20] Due to her parents' early
separation, Grimké was raised by her father, to whom she was exceptionally
devoted and on whom she was extremely emotionally dependent (Hull, p.
115). He encouraged her writing, and evidently he sustained her faith in her
literary talent, probably making it not essential for her to maintain a public
audience. After his death in 1930 she left Washington, D.C. and relocated in
New York City until her death in 1958. During this interval she apparently
stopped writing (Hull, p. 149).

Another very significant biographical factor of Grimké's life—her homo-
eroticism—explicitly appears in the large number of her poems that have
only recently been published.[21] In the words of her editor Carolivia Herron,
Grimké's verse discloses a desperate "need to voice, to vent, to share—if only
on paper—what was pulsing within her, since it seems that sometimes she
could not even talk to the women she wanted, let alone anybody else."[22]
Herron goes on to explain that "it is clear that she [Grimké] decided to forgo
the expression of her lesbian desires in order to please her father" (p. 6).
"Clearly these poetic themes of sadness and void, longing and frustration," as
Hull has also explained, "relate directly to Grimké's convoluted life and
thwarted sexuality" (Hull, "Under the Days," p. 23).

By publishing the "The Closing Door" and "Goldie" in *The Birth Control
Review*, edited by the famous proponent of birth control Margaret Sanger,
Grimké clearly had a white, progressive, and largely female audience in mind
for her message of racial protest. This was an audience reminiscent of the
mid-nineteenth-century white female abolitionist readership to which Harriet
A. Jacobs had directed her slave narrative *Incidents in the Life of a Slave Girl*
(1861). Grimké similarly targeted this audience for *Rachel*, an intention that
she discussed in a letter, which I quote at length:

> Now my purpose was to show how a refined, sensitive, highly-strung
> girl, a dreamer and an idealist, the strongest instinct in whose nature is a
> love for children and a desire some day to be a mother herself—how, I

say, this girl would react to this force [of extreme racism, specifically the lynching of her favorite brother].

The majority of women, everywhere, although they are beginning to awaken from one of the most conservative elements of society. They are, therefore opposed to changes. For this reason and for sex reasons, the white women of this country are about the worst enemies with which the colored race has to contend. My belief was then that if I could find a vulnerable point in their amour, if I could reach their hearts, even if only a little, then perhaps instead of being active or passive enemies they might become, at least, less inimical and possibly friendly.

Did they have a vulnerable point and if so what was it? I believed it to be motherhood. Certainly all the noblest, finest, most sacred things in their lives converge about this. If anything can make all women sisters underneath their skins, it is motherhood. If, then, I could make the white women of this country see, feel, understand just what their prejudice and the prejudice of their fathers, brother, husbands, sons were having on the souls of the colored mothers everywhere, and upon the mothers what are to be, a great power to affect public opinion would be set free and the battle would be half won.[23]

By depicting black characters who live in clean, well-kept homes "with many evidences of taste and refinement about them," Grimké self-consciously asserted a counterargument to the pervasive stereotype of the "grinning, white-toothed, shiftless, carefree . . . chicken-stealing, watermelon eating, always . . . properly obsequious to a white skin" black.[24] However, in directing these works to a white audience, Grimké forfeits the posture of intraracial affirmation that was the principal source of inspiration in the post-Reconstruction domestic novels of her black female precursors. Embracing the protest mission also forced her to abandon the heartening depiction of maternity that empowers "Jettisoned." Similar to authors of antebellum slave narratives, who relied on repetitive and representative scenes of physical and psychological racial violence to incite the moral outrage of the abolitionists, Grimké relied on overstated pathos to awaken what she presumed to be the unique feminine sympathy of her intended white female audience. Unfortunately, the zeal of social activism among white women had turned from the plight of black people to their own sexual oppression; thus her appeal largely fell on deaf ears.

In the three domestic tragedies "The Closing Door," "Goldie," and *Rachel*, Grimké characterized three young, maternal, black women who largely reproduce one another precisely because each relies on the anguish of repudiated or devastated motherhood to give expression to racial protest. To emphasize the injustice of racism, Grimké repeatedly made her heroines child-like, excessively generous, good, gentle, and pure so as to underscore the inhumanity of racism that ruins their innocent lives. In Rachel Loving, as her surname suggests, Grimké gave her audience a "young, joyous and vital [woman], caring more to be a mother than anything else in this world," to use Grimké's own words.[25] Like Rachel Loving, Agnes Milton of "The Closing Door" venerates her anticipated motherhood by adopting an orphan. The maternal desire of

Goldie Harper of "Goldie" is characterized by her adoring older brother, who recalls that

> When Goldie was only a little thing and you asked her what she wanted most in all the world when she grew up, she had always answered: "Why, a little home—all my own—a cunning one—and young things in it and about."
> And if you asked her to explain, she had said:
> "Don't you *know*?—not *really*?"
> And, then, if you had suggested children, she had answered: Of course, all my own; and kittens and puppies and little fluffy chickens and ducks and little birds in my trees. . . . (p. 288)

While Rachel, Agnes, and Goldie are exemplars of maternal devotion, they do not duplicate the self-authorized black heroines of the domestic novels of the 1890s who in addition to motherly love also rely on intelligence, training, and personal fortitude to nurture their families. Grimké's heroines are clearly not proponents of an enlarged female sphere of professionalism or educated domesticity, nor are they outspoken advocates for racial advancement. Their diminutive size and puerile sexuality reflect the reduction of their ambitions to fit the constriction of their personal lives. They are meek, juvenile, and miniature mutations of the heroines of post-Reconstruction domestic novels. However, they are also early projections of new methods of characterization. For although Grimké's heroines are marked with effusive pathos, their fragmented physical portraits, loss of spiritual faith, and frequent repudiation of maternal desire suggest a hybridization of the nineteenth-century sentimental heroine and the modern alienated character who becomes pronounced during the decade of the 1920s.

While Grimké gushed maudlin effusion to accentuate her heroines' child-like innocence, purity, and gentle goodness, she critiqued their predecessors' expressions of spiritual piety. Unlike the heroines of the post-Reconstruction domestic novels, who live in fictive worlds defined by spiritual morality and poetic justice that is mediated by a caring God, Grimké's characters live in fictive worlds characterized by humiliating prejudice and racial violence. Her characters find little strength or direction in spiritual piety, religion, and church work, as do Meg, Iola, and Beryl, for example. Although God has not disappeared entirely in Grimké's stories and plays (as He would in later modernist works), God has undeniably lost divine judgment, power, and benevolence.

In "The Closing Door," for instance, Agnes is initially fearful of a frail, covetous deity. But after learning of her brother's lynching, she proclaims,

> "There is no more need for silence—in this house. God has found us out . . . I will give Him one more chance. Then, if He is not pitiful, then if He is not pitiful"—But she did not finish. She fell back upon her pillows. (p. 275)

Grimké's use of the word "pitiful" here suggests several meanings. The word implies that Agnes implores God's pity in her desperate prayers for the death of her unborn child. But God proves to be weak rather than almighty, in fact, pitiable Himself and thus deserving sympathy like Agnes herself. When the child is born strong and healthy, Agnes concludes that God has failed to offer her a most despondent form of pity. Consequently, she abandons her faith and disavows God, resolutely declaring to Lucy, "You thought *your* God was pitiful. . . . He—is—*not*" (p. 278; emphasis added). Ironically, pitiful is precisely what He is. After she murders her newborn son and becomes "blank, empty, a grey automation, a mere shell" (p. 256), her adopted daughter Lucy reports that she prayed for Agnes's death: "Night and day I have prayed since the same prayer—that God if he knows any pity at all may soon, soon, release the poor spent body of hers" (p. 256). Lucy's prayers also call attention once again to God's pathetic, contemptible condition, thus undercutting the premise of divine magnanimity.

In "Goldie" God has only a fleeting presence in Victor's memory as a reflection of Goldie's faith in His goodness and justice. However, the horrible events of the story rapidly erase that memory from his consciousness. By contrast, in *Rachel* spiritual faith is not simply an erased discourse but renounced—Rachel believes that God "has been mocking at her by implanting in her breast this desire for motherhood, and she swears by the most solemn oath of which she can think never to bring a child here to have its life blighted and ruined" (p. 416). Like Agnes, Rachel assumes the burden of correcting the improvident God by acting on behalf of herself and her child(ren). The play closes with Rachel quieting her crying unborn children with the assurance that she will allow them to remain happy beyond the reach of a racist society and a dubious God:

> I shall never—see—you—now. . . . But you are somewhere—and wherever you are you are mine! You are mine! All of you! Every bit of you! Even God can't take you away. . . . My little children!—No more need you come to me—weeping—weeping. You may be happy now—you are safe. Little weeping, voices, hush! hush! (p. 209)

For according to Grimké, "In her [Rachel's] anguish and despair at the knowledge [of race prejudice] she turns against God" and motherhood (p. 416). What is important to discern is that Rachel's loss of faith and her renunciation of motherhood are simultaneously expressions of racial protest and grievances about the impotence of divine justice.

In a larger social context Rachel's character is also a likely expression of the spiritual uncertainty that was rampant in the dominant society, exacerbated by the horrors of World War I and reflected in modernist literature. However, racial oppression and not modern angst is the explicit motivation for the failure of faith in Grimké's works. While Hopkins's hero Reuel Briggs at the end of *Of One Blood* believes that "none save Omnipotence can solve the

[race] problem" (p. 621), as he ventures into veritable hibernation, Grimké's characters are left without a place of retreat. Cut off from possibilities of domestic happiness, they struggle to survive. Their struggle and loss of faith are vigorously symbolized in the renunciation of motherhood and repudiation of domesticity, which in turn are the symbolic discourses for communicating racial protest in her writings.

Also indicative of the onset of modernism as a major force in literary production is Grimké's manner of portraying her characters. Immediately apparent is her reliance on what we now recognize as a prominent modern strategy of characterization to delete from her stories and plays the physical detail of the typically pretty if not beautiful sentimental heroine. While her black female predecessors of the post-Reconstruction period portrayed heroines with exacting physical detail, Grimké gave her audience fragmented portraits of her heroines. For example, aside from her being pregnant, all we know of Goldie's appearance is that her skin, hair, and eye color are all a light golden brown. The narrator of "The Closing Door" informs us that Agnes has wrinkles around her eyes from smiling and laughing too much. The narrator goes on to say that

> [Agnes] wasn't tall and she wasn't short; she wasn't stout and she wasn't thin. Her back was straight and her head high. She was rather graceful, I thought. In coloring she was Spanish or Italian. Her hair was not very long but it was soft and silky and black. Her features were not too sharp, her eyes clear and dark, a warm leaf brown in fact. Her mouth was really beautiful. This doesn't give her [sic] I find. It was the shining beauty and gayety [sic] of her soul that lighted up her whole body and somehow made her, and she was generally smiling or chuckling. (pp. 256–57)

By the narrator's own admission this portrait of Agnes is none too specific. When we examine Rachel's description, we find that she has tendrils that fall about her eyes, making her look "exactly like some one's pet poodle" (p. 126). Clearly, comely appearance is not tightly aligned to these heroines's virtue and ambitions, perhaps because they clearly do not live in an equitable social realm.

The shattering of their optimism assumes discursive dominance in each work, which is accentuated by the heroines' gentle, innocent, loving vulnerability and frail happiness that initially arises from the strength of their desire for motherhood. These traits heighten the piteous effects of their frustrated or devastated motherhood and transform failed maternal desire into racial protest. Whereas the post-Reconstruction heroines repeatedly use exuberant maternal discourses to sustain female self-definition and to express the expansion of their sexual, racial, and professional desires behind approbations of duty, Grimké's heroines dramatize the destruction of those ambitions. Her works insist that the modern black woman's sphere has dwindled to the denial of the one desire that is biologically designated—motherhood. Like the slave women before them, who practiced contraception, abortion, and infanticide as their rebellion against slavery,[26] Grimké's heroines protest racism by refusing to produce its victims.

Moreover, Grimké's heroines no longer live within supportive, optimistic communities, like their post-Reconstruction predecessors such as Tillman's Beryl Weston or Kelley-Hawkins's Meg. Grimké's heroines live on the margins of white communities, isolated in little intraracial enclaves. Her black characters, like those in Paul Laurence Dunbar's novel *The Sport of the Gods* (1901), become alienated from prior codes of social meaning and value formation. And like individuals who are infected with yet unnamed diseases, they claim the names of those known. By *no* means am I suggesting that racism was not a vicious social disease; clearly it was and continues to be. But because it was so visibly evident in Grimké's era, racial despair probably masked other personal anxieties, social problems, and changing cultural values. For instance, when her female characters renounce motherhood, racism precludes the allegation of self-elected spinsterhood associated with the "new woman." By exploring the historical, social, and biographical contexts of Grimké's repudiated maternal discourses, I suggest the likely presence of these conflicts besides those incited by racism that repeatedly surface in Grimké's works as ambivalence about motherhood.

The persistence of Grimké's discourse of maternal desire is immediately reminiscent of Harriet E. Wilson's focus in *Our Nig* (1859). For like Wilson, Grimké was raised without a mother; her mother not only was separated from her by distance as a young child but by death before Grimké was an adult. Although Grimké confided in her diary in 1903 that "she needed a mother . . . [but] was accustomed to the lack" (Hull, p. 127), her maternal longing seems both explicit and unrelenting. Both Wilson and Grimké fashioned their respective works around maternal discourses whose repetition intimates personal longing for and vicarious re-creation of the absent mother. Whereas in *Our Nig* Wilson sustains that discourse throughout the novel, in Grimké's writings mother love is a repeatedly and tragically aborted discourse. Grimké had her heroines deliberately fail to reproduce the heroic maternity that typified black women's antebellum narratives and the maternal confidence that characterized their post-Reconstruction domestic novels.

Grimké's preoccupation with tragic motherhood may have been her own unique way of addressing personal sexual anxieties as well as a thematic of racial protest. In an entry in her diary on September 10, 1903, at the age of twenty-three, she wrote, "I shall never know what it means to be a mother, for I shall never marry. I am through with love and the like forever" (Hull, p. 124). Although we might attribute her early rejection of motherhood and marriage to disappointment in love, Grimké remained true to this pledge. She never married and she never gave birth to a child. Instead she devoted her life to caring for her aging father (Hull, pp. 113–14). Grimké projected her own resolve onto her heroines' repudiation of motherhood, but their decisions evolve from protesting racism. Are her obsession with that theme and her own analogous behavior exclusively expressions of racial protest?

The new generation of white women coming into adult maturity at the turn of the century created a big commotion by discarding Victorian definitions of womanhood.[27] These post-Victorian or early modern women experienced sex-role discontent, which they acted out as challenges to patriarchal authority. For them it was not enough to enlarge the female sphere; they wanted to escape it altogether and share masculine prerogatives. They wanted the vote, sexual gratification, professional autonomy, and economic independence. While these white post-Victorian women searched for new roles that would be more satisfying than the roles that had oppressed their mothers and grandmothers, their black counterparts were largely struggling to survive in a racist society that denied them what the "new (white) woman" was eagerly casting off.

Late-nineteenth- and early-twentieth-century black women appropriated the various facsimiles of a racially refined ladyhood not because it was essentially their prerogative and clearly not because white society demanded such demeanor of them. Given the economic hardship of racist labor exploitation that the vast majority of black people faced at this time, behaving like ladies certainly did not mean that black women could expect relief from strenuous forms of wage labor. Such behavior also had little to do with deferring to black men as patriarchs. For although turn-of-the-century black America subscribed to male dominance, racism demanded a dialectical hegemony that routinely undermined black male privilege. And yet elite African Americans, whom Du Bois labeled "the talented tenth" (whose economic stability sustained intraracial communities that afforded more protective isolation from crude forms of racism than did the usual black community), enforced social codes that respected black patriarchal entitlement, as evidenced in the works of Anna Cooper, Gertrude Mossell, and Julia Coston. Notwithstanding their desire to be regarded as ladies in their own communities, the vast majority of black women probably adopted conventions of Victorian feminine deportment because they believed that this would grant them esteem, enhance their opportunities for personal advancement, and aid them in averting white people's verbal and physical attacks on their chastity.

By virtue of her father Archibald and her Uncle Francis, Grimké was a member of the educated black elite, and she was expected to be a lady in the strictest sense of the term. Unlike the majority of the mulattoes of "the talented tenth," though, Grimké's fair skin color was not so much an immediate product of the sexual abuses of slavery (although her paternal grandfather was a white slave owner) as of a legal interracial marriage. In addition, most of her formative years of adolescence and early adulthood were not spent ensconced in intraracial middle-class enclaves of church and school, like those found in Philadelphia and Washington, D.C., but in several Northern boarding schools where she was usually the only black student (Herron, p. 7). Moreover, spiritual piety seems not particularly consequential to the development of her character, although she "lived in an atmosphere of religious, feminist, political, and racial liberalism" (Hull, p. 110). All of these elements of Grimké's early life intimate the likelihood of her having experienced strong feelings of social marginality, alienation, and racial anxiety.

Grimké's educational background is also particularly significant when we recall the social climate at institutions of higher learning at the turn of the century, for it is here "[i]n college [that] many girls grew into 'new women'" (Filene, p. 26). While this observation pertains to white women, Grimké had much in common with the very small percentage of them who attended college between the decades of 1890 and 1910. She received her academic training almost exclusively in white institutions. The Carleton Academy in Northfield, Minnesota; Cushing Academy in Ashburnham, Massachusetts; and the Girls' Latin School in Boston provided her secondary education, which spanned the years 1895–98 (Hull, p. 115).[28] In 1902 she graduated from the Boston Normal School of Gymnastics, which was to become the Department of Hygiene of Wellesley College, and in the years 1904–10 she enrolled in Harvard summer school. In short, Grimké's educational as well as her professional experience as a teacher probably brought her into direct contact with the "new woman," for this woman was found in "colleges, professions and 'bachelor woman' apartments," exactly those places that Grimké found herself (Filene, p. 19).

When I cast Grimké's repeated depictions of repudiated black motherhood in her works against her personal background, I find that this preoccupation might have been aggravated not only by racism but by her social marginality and lesbianism as well. The personal ordeals of her parent's marital discord (producing her motherlessness), her own sexual frustration, and her sustained contact with women students who were very likely either "new girls" themselves or sympathizers probably exacerbated her misgivings about the presumed feminine fulfillment ascribed to marriage and motherhood.[29] While Grimké had a strict Victorian upbringing and inherited as well the African-American celebratory tradition of noble black motherhood, in all probability she was also aware of the radical "new women" who rejected motherhood and formed other types of domestic arrangements than the traditional family. I speculate that this celebratory tradition collided head on with Grimké's personal misgivings and sexual ambivalence about motherhood, causing her to idealize her fictive mothers and to depict their racist destruction as a more general social as well as personal protest. Hence Grimké's maternal thematics may very well be her public demonstration of racial protest and her extremely personal expression of frustrated sexual desire.

Herron is most emphatic in her psychological analysis of Grimké's recurring depictions of the racist devastation of black matrimony and motherhood as expressions of renounced heterosexuality. Referring to Grimké's play *Rachel*, Herron writes,

> Although Grimké attempts to justify . . . [a young woman's response to racism by forgoing motherhood], in terms of the cruelties that African Americans are forced to endure in the United States, it is probable that in this plot she is using a psychic energy that repudiates heterosexuality on a personal level to accentuate her passion for annihilating the marital and familial expectations in African-American culture. (p. 17)

While it is difficult to determine whether Grimké was repudiating heterosexuality as Herron contends, her preoccupation with this theme clearly suggests sexual conflict.

Rachel also reflects the changing sexual attitudes about professional vocation for women, couched in Rachel's brother Tom's protest on employment discrimination:

> Rachel is a graduate in Domestic Science; she was high in her class; most of the girls below her in rank have positions in the schools. I'm an electrical engineer—and I've tried steadily for several months—to practice my profession. It seems our educations aren't of much use to us: we aren't allowed to make good—because our skins are dark. . . . Their children shall grow up in hope; ours, in despair. . . . —God's justice, I suppose. (pp. 160–61)

Employment discrimination has barred Rachel from finding a teaching position in domestic science, which she no doubt planned to secure until she could practice that science in her own home as wife and mother. Rachel's training in domestic science or home economics reflects increasing gender conservatism of the twentieth century and the rise of professionalized domesticity in place of other less traditional professional occupations for women. Unlike her heroic predecessors—Lucille Delany, Meg Randal, and Beryl Weston, for instance— Rachel does not espouse lofty professional ambitions. While domestic science was a respectable female vocation, it sought to elevate housework by professionalizing all forms of household labor. The new science "served the traditionalists as a convenient weapon to keep woman 'in her place'" (Filene, p. 45).

Rachel also reveals changing attitudes about demonstrative sexual love. Near the end of the play, the following passionate scene occurs between Rachel and her suitor John Strong, her brother Tom's friend and her would-be husband, which requires extensive quotation. The scene begins as Rachel finishes playing a sad sentimental song on the piano and singing the words to John:

> (*A long pause. Then Strong goes to her and lifts her from the piano-stool. He puts one arm around her very tenderly and pushes her head back so he can look into her eyes. She shuts them, but is passive*).
>   Strong (*Gently*): Little girl, little girl, don't you know that suggestions— suggestions—like those you are sending yourself constantly—are wicked things? You, who are so gentle, so loving, so warm—(*Breaks off and crushes her to him. He kisses her many times. She does not resist, but in the midst of his caresses she breaks suddenly into convulsive laughter. He tries to hush the terrible sound with his mouth. . . . Strong picks her up bodily and carries her to the armchair. . . . He smoothes her hair back gently, and kisses her forehead—and then, slowly her mouth. She does not resist; simply sits there, with shut eyes, inert, limp*. (pp. 204–5; Grimké's emphasis)

Immediately following this scene, John proposes marriage and she responds:

Rachel: (*During Strong's speech life has come flooding back to her. Her eyes are shining; her face, eager. For a moment she is beautifully happy*). Oh! You're too good to me and mine [her brother], John. I—didn't dream any one—could be—so good. (*Leans forward and puts his big hand against her cheek and kisses it shyly.*) . . . Oh, yes! yes! yes! and take me quickly, John. Take me before I can think any more. You mustn't let me think, John. And you'll be good to me, won't you? (p. 206)

While we late-twentieth-century readers might not have recognized the romantic scenarios in black women's post-Reconstruction domestic novels in which love is depicted as social duty, we readily recognize the above as a modern love scene full of sexual passion. The repetitive kissing and caressing make this scene's deviation from the prior scenarios require little elaboration. Thus I leave to speculation the multiple meanings of Rachel's impassioned, somewhat hysterical, and repeated appeals for John to "take [her] quickly." But before any action transpires, Rachel's adopted son interrupts the sexual passion with his weeping caused by racially induced nightmares. His distress is Rachel's justification for electing spinsterhood. So while Rachel's response to the marriage proposal is cast as a fitting reaction to racial oppression, giving ultimate expression to the play's racial protest, it also reflects changing social attitudes about dramatizing erotic sexuality and a woman's choice to reject marriage.

Unlike the women authors of the post-Reconstruction domestic novels who retextualize segregation as their heroines' opportunity at comfortable self-management, Grimké emphatically presented the ultimate consequences of "separate but equal" as a travesty. The ethic of hard work and frugality that had been a central doctrine in the post-Reconstruction texts is found to be deficient by Grimké's early modern black characters because they find that working hard for success invites severe racial strife. Their fictive lives reflect real ones, as black people of Grimké's epoch reluctantly realized that Booker T. Washington's agenda of black economic self-sufficiency, deferred enfranchisement, and conciliation were failed strategies of racial advancement. Although Grimké's characters report that the North affords some relief from life-threatening racial assaults, they are painfully aware that racial prejudice, severe employment, and housing discrimination still circumscribe their lives and abort their hope of ever gaining a foothold on the ladder of self-propelled success.

While some of Grimké's characters seem successful in their struggle to make compromises with racism, her heroines refuse the effort. In "The Closing Door," for example, Lucy vainly tries to persuade Agnes that she need not fear for her child:

"Agnes," [Lucy] cried out. "Agnes! Your child will be born in the North. He need never go South."

"Yes," she said. "In the North. In the North—And have there been no lynchings in the North?" (p. 275)

In *Rachel* John shares his conciliatory strategy with Tom: "My philosophy—learned hard, is to make the best of everything you can, and go on" (p. 164). Later John tries to impress upon Rachel a similar fortitude: "You don't want to get morbid over these things, you know. I've tried your way. I know. Mine is the only sane one" (p. 169). Rachel accepts employment discrimination, but she proves unable to accommodate the capricious racial abuse of young black children, an abuse for which she holds God personally accountable.

Rachel, like most of Grimké's prose fiction, reaffirms the racial protest tradition, established with the antebellum slave narrative. This aesthetic would dominate the twentieth century undoubtedly because black people faced degrees of social oppression that approximated slavery. During the first decades of the twentieth century racism surged, laying to waste Booker T. Washington's agenda of black economic self-sufficiency. Thus the ideological ground on which to launch a new assault for black social advancement rapidly receded, causing wide-scale racial pessimism to surface. Chronic racial despair seems to have caused the demise of idealized domesticity in black women's fiction, as those authors in the prime of life (like Kelley-Hawkins, Johnson, and Tillman, who had been prolific writers of this fiction during the decade of the 1890s) ceased publishing it. As the counterhegemonic trope of domestic idealism subsided as an expression of political desire in black literature, the more familiar mode of racial protest reemerged, as Grimké's works demonstrate. Her particular medium, as Herron provocatively explains, is an early expression of the blues aesthetic in black literature:

> For the two major themes [in Grimké's works], the desire for romantic and sexual companionship and the desire for social and political equality for African Americans, give her work the import, if not the discrete form, of the blues—that musical and poetic cultural form which is the repository for African-American heroic anguish over love, lost love, and political disenfranchisement. (pp. 20–21)

Even in the more hopeful and better known novels of Grimké's contemporary Jessie Fauset, domesticity is a tenuous medium for instructing black people in responsible citizenship and personal ambition.

Fauset's 1924 novel *There Is Confusion* presents an upbeat domestic blues story about enduring racism with individual black heroism and sexual satisfaction.[30] At the novel's close the heroine Joanna Marshall Bye oversees her husband Peter's development of personal resolve in spite of racism, his "complete metamorphosis":

> Joanna was free.
> But Peter had to undergo a complete metamorphosis. He was a supersensitive colored man living among a host of indifferent white people. Not only had he to change in every particular his theory of how to maintain such a relationship, but indeed he had to decide what sort of relationship

> was worth maintaining. . . . Joanna, clever Joanna, helped him here. . . .
> Perhaps it is wrong to imply that Joanna had lost her ambition. She was
> still ambitious, only the field of her ambition lay without herself. It was
> Peter now whom she wished to succeed. (p. 291)

Joanna guides Peter's acquisition of racial pride, personal responsibility, and
assertive independence as the bases for defining his character and interpersonal
relationships. At the end of the novel, his greatness and by implication hers
too resides not in the "grand and noble purposes"[31] of working on an imposing
scale for racial uplift, as did that of their more optimistic post-Reconstruction
precursors like Iola and her husband Frank Latimer. For Joanna and Peter,
"Greatness is even in daily living" (Fauset, p. 297). Like Grimké's John Strong,
their heroism resides in surviving racism day by day with dignity and in continuing to strive for elusive freedom.

In the twentieth century, writers, critics, and scholars would define greatness for the African-American writer differently. The esteemed black writer of
the late 1960s was one who championed militant social protest and nationalism that venerated black folk solidarity rather than assimilation. Hence freedom for the celebrated black writer of this epoch would be more than a rite of
passage into the lifestyles of the white middle class.

Our late-twentieth-century historical perspective should temper the tempta-
tion to dismiss black women's domestic novels of the post-Reconstruction era
as naive dramatizations of a failed assimilationist strategy for securing a gendered citizenry. For during the mid-twentieth century this strategy of social
intervention reappeared. After the 1964 Civil Rights Act gave teeth to the
Fourteenth Amendment, black Americans again embraced the integrationist
zeal of their predecessors of the Reconstruction and post-Reconstruction eras.
During most of the 1960s integration and assimilation were once again *the*
social agendas of "colored" or Negro Americans. Diahanne Carroll's "The
Julia Show" integrated prime-time television, and her diminutive, plastic facsimile competed with the original "Barbie" doll. "Star Trek"'s Nichelle Nichols
treked throughout space in the starship "Enterprise" with surrogate, multi-
racial siblings. Sydney Poitier became a veritable one-man race show on the
"big screen." He dramatized the patriarchal frustration of black men in the
film version of Lorraine Hansberry's "A Raisin in the Sun," black/white male
bonding in "The Defiant Ones," the disavowal of presumed excessive black
male sexuality of the racist retrogressionist ideology in "A Patch of Blue," and
interracial marriage in "Guess Who's Coming to Dinner." In addition, the
broadly canonized James Baldwin depicted interracial (as well as homoerotic)
friendships in *Giovanni's Room* (1956) and *Another Country* (1960). But in
1968, with the death of Martin Luther King, Jr., and urban riots of that
summer, the integrationist optimism and its depiction in popular culture came
to an end. In its place appeared the resurgence of black nationalism and
emphatically explicit social protest, as African Americans of the Black Power
era voiced a resounding "No" to James Baldwin's question: "Do I really want

to be integrated into a burning house?"[32] Interestingly, the domestic trope emerges in Baldwin's question but as the repudiation of assimilation and the imminent destruction of the house.

Black expressive culture, indeed the collective political agenda of African Americans, seems to oscillate between two extremes: embracing or repudiating assimilation; redefining black identity or imitating white America; celebrating folk wisdom or bourgeois accomplishment. Only the process of redefinition is open to possibility, which is no doubt the reason why African Americans keep returning to self-naming. All of the other activities are already bound to the limitations of the social texts of historical representation and already inadequate for the liberational task. As soon as one extreme fails again, the culture oscillates, revising the other. Two of the extremes — promoting interracial similarity in the ideal domestic novels of post-Reconstruction black women and promoting interracial dissimilarity in writings of black nationalistic zeal — repeatedly play out the political anxieties of what seems an irreconcilable contest between racial binaries that Du Bois so aptly named the "double consciousness" of African Americans. If this conflict can be resolved, the winning strategy will no doubt consist of more than re-presentation of an oppressive past; it will figure a future that embraces the elusive freedom.

NOTES

Introduction

1. Zora Neale Hurston, *Their Eyes Were Watching God* (1937; Reprint. Urbana: University of Illinois Press, 1978), p. 37. For a discussion of black families in transition from slavery to freedom that relies on documents in the National Archives of the United States, see Ira Berlin, Steven F. Miller, and Leslie S. Rowland, "Afro-American Families in Transition from Slavery to Freedom" in *Black Women in United States History*, edited by Darlene Clark Hine, Vol. 1 (Brooklyn: Carlson Publishing Inc., 1990).

2. Rayford W. Logan, *The Betrayal of the Negro, From Rutherford B. Hayes to Woodrow Wilson* (New York: Collier, 1965), p. 11. The Progressive Era gained its name from the tremendous scientific, technological, and industrial advances as well as social reform occurring during it in the United States.

3. The card catalogue of the Library of Congress lists Amelia Johnson as the author of a third novel, *Martina Meriden; or, What is My Motive* (Philadelphia: American Baptist Publication Society, 1901). However, this novel seems no longer extant. I was directed to the Library of Congress by *Prologue: The Novels of Black American Women, 1891–1965* by Carole McAlpine Watson (Westport, Conn.: Greenwood Press, 1985). This work is very helpful for its chronology of obscure novels written by black American women.

4. Tillman's *Beryl Weston's Ambition* and *Clancy Street* were serialized in *The A.M.E. Church Review*. They are actually novellas, though I designate them as novels in order to categorize them collectively with the other extended domestic fictions written by black women of the post-Reconstruction period. With the exception of *Contending Forces*, Hopkins's novels were serialized in *The Colored American* magazine. Hopkins's *Hagar's Daughter* was published under her mother's name, Sarah Allen. Kelley-Hawkins's *Four Girls at Cottage City* was copyrighted in 1895, three years before its publication.

Miss Garrison's serial novel *A Ray of Light* was also published in *The A.M.E. Church Review* in 1889. I have not included this work in this book due to the fact that I cannot locate any biographical information on Garrison. Ann Allen Shockley's *Afro-American Women Writers 1746–1933* (Boston: G. K. Hall, 1988) includes Miss Garrison, though Schockley does not provide any documentation that Garrison was a black author.

For additional works by black women written from 1900 to 1920 see *Short Fiction by Black Women, 1900–1920*, edited by Elizabeth Ammons (New York: Oxford University Press, 1991).

5. This is Wilson J. Moses's term. While many scholars might contend that *feminism* is largely a twentieth-century term, given the woman-centered agency that these novels assert the term is politically appropriate. See Moses's "Domestic Feminism, Conservatism, Sex Roles, and Black Women's Clubs 1893–1896" in *Black Women in United States History: From Colonial Times Through the Nineteenth Century*, Vol. 3, edited by Darlene Clark Hine (Brooklyn: Carlson Publishing Inc., 1990), p. 964.

6. Professor and Mrs. J[ohn]. W[illiam]. Gibson, *Golden Thoughts on Chastity and Procreation*, with an Introduction by Dr. Henry R. Butler (Atlanta: J. L. Nichols and Co., 1903). I am greatly indebted to E. Ethelbert Miller for bringing this provocative work to my attention.

While *Golden Thoughts* is the most comprehensive, it is typical of other book-length black conduct manuals of the period. They include E. M. Woods, *The Negro in Etiquette: A Novelty* (St. Louis: Buxton and Skinner Printers, 1899), and Silas Floyd, *Floyd's Flowers, or Duty and Beauty for Colored Children* (Washington, D.C.: Hertel, Jenkins and Company, 1905).

7. See Paula Giddings, *When and Where I Enter: The Impact of Black Women on Race and Sex in America* (New York: Morrow, 1984), p. 136. Giddings also explains that "the club movement shattered the stereotypes of Black women," allowing them "to emerge in a new light" in the theatre, classical music, fine arts, and literature (pp. 136–37). Future references to this work appear parenthetically in the chapter. For another discussion of black women's organized reform movements, also see Dorothy Salem, *To Better Our World: Black Women in Organized Reform, 1890–1920* (Brooklyn: Carlson Publishing Inc., 1990).

8. Ammons makes her observation in pointing out "differences between the era in which [Harriet E.] Wilson published *Our Nig* [in 1859] and the one in which Harper brought out *Iola Leroy* [1892]." See Elizabeth Ammons, *Conflicting Stories: American Women Writers at the Turn into the Twentieth Century* (New York: Oxford University Press, 1991), p. 28.

9. The first thirty volumes of *The Schomburg Library of Nineteenth-Century Black Women Writers* were published in 1988 by Oxford University Press. The ten-volume supplement was published in 1991. Although I refer here specifically to the fictional works of this series, each volume has an excellent introduction. The series also includes Anna Cooper's *A Voice From the South* and Gertrude Mossell's *The Work of the Afro-American Woman*, to which I also refer throughout this book.

10. The term *first readers* is not meant to reference an homogenized readership but rather an actual audience that was likely to subscribe or have access to publications like *The A.M.E. Church Review* and *The Colored American*. Though theoretically conceived, such an audience would include the very small number of academically trained professionals, for example ministers, doctors, and teachers, as well as tradesmen and tradeswomen such as caterers, seamstresses, tailors, hairdressers, stenographers, typewriters (typists), and cobblers. For a characterization of the black middle class see Willard B. Gatewood, *The Aristocrats of Color: The Black Elite, 1880–1920* (Bloomington: University of Indiana Press, 1990), p. 191. I refer to this characterization in Chapter 5.

11. I quote Cathy N. Davidson here. She argues that the popularity of the early novel originated in its didactic intent: "Novels allowed for a means of entry into a

larger literary and intellectual world and a means of access to social and political events from which many readers (particularly women) would have been otherwise largely excluded." See *Revolution and the Word: The Rise of the Novel in America* (New York: Oxford University Press, 1986), p. 10. Future references to this work appear parenthetically in the chapter.

12. The words of Dr. Henry Butler, author of the Introduction to *Golden Thoughts*. At the turn of the century he was a physician and surgeon at Morris Brown College.

13. M[ikhail]. M. Bakhtin, *The Dialogic Imagination: Four Essays* (Austin: University of Texas Press, 1981), p. 39.

14. Joseph Allen Boone, *Tradition Counter Tradition: Love and the Form of Fiction* (Chicago: University of Chicago Press, 1987), p. 7.

15. John G. Cawelti, *Adventure, Mystery, and Romance: Formula Stories as Art and Popular Culture* (Chicago: University of Chicago Press, 1976), p. 41. Future references to this work appear parenthetically in the chapter.

16. Nina Baym, *Novels, Readers, and Reviewers: Responses to Fiction in Antebellum America* (Ithaca, N.Y.: Cornell University Press, 1984), p. 63. The Baym study specifically refers to antebellum readers of popular novels, who needless to say were white. She argues that the desire for pleasurable reading was endemic to the popular novelistic traditions of the nineteenth as well as the twentieth century. I apply her argument to black post-Reconstruction readers, who would have learned this reading expectation as well as other cultural practices from the dominant society.

17. The actual size of the readership for these novels is unknown. The number of copies for each edition and the breadth of their dissemination are difficult to determine. However, several of them went into second editions almost immediately after the first printing, which suggests their great popularity. The second edition of Kelley-Hawkins's *Megda* appeared in 1892, one year after the first edition (see Hite's introduction to the Oxford edition of *Megda*, p. xxviii). There were also two nineteenth-century editions of Harper's *Iola Leroy* (1892 and 1893). Tillman's two novellas were published in *The A.M.E. Church Review* in 1893 and 1898. According to Rayford Logan (see note 2), the circulation for *The Review* in 1889 was 2,800 (Logan, p. 321). Therefore I estimate that the circulation during the next decade was generally in that range. The Boston-based *The Colored American* advertised the publication of Hopkins's *Contending Forces* from 1900 to 1904 and published her three serial novels also during this period. The magazine had agents throughout the country, and by the end of 1901 the magazine boasted 100,000 readers, which is different from circulation figures (see Hazel V. Carby, *Reconstructing Womanhood: The Emergence of the Afro-American Woman Novelist* [New York: Oxford University Press, 1987], pp. 123–24). Despite the probably small number of copies per edition compared with even modest contemporary printing runs, the individual novels no doubt circulated widely among readers. A small circulation, like 2,800 for *The Review*, very likely sustained an actual readership many times that number, as the figure for *The Colored American* indicates.

18. Hans Robert Jauss, "Literary History as Challenge" in *Toward an Aesthetic of Reception* (Minneapolis: University of Minnesota Press, 1982), p. 25. Future references to this work appear parenthetically in the chapter.

19. In *Revolution and the Word* (see note 11), Davidson refers to Robert Escarpit's term *community assumptions* from his *Sociology of Literature* (London: Frank Cass, 1971). In *Adventure, Mystery, and Romance* (see note 15), Cawelti borrows a similar term, *network of assumptions*, from Raymond Durgnat's study of spy films ("Spies and Ideologies" in *Cinema*, March 1969, p. 8).

20. These are Mrs. E. D. E. N. Southworth's words from her novel *The Mother-in-Law* (1851). I excerpted the entire passage, including the alteration with the word "but," from Joseph Allen Boone, *Tradition Counter Tradition*, p. 17.

21. While Cawelti is analyzing the psychological relationship between the general category of formula fictions here and audiences who enjoy them, I am applying his argument specifically to the domestic novels of post-Reconstruction black women and their first readers. Cawelti argues that the formulas give expression to unconscious, repressed, or latent needs and desires. Moreover, he contends that "[p]ossibly one important difference between the mimetic and escapist impulses in literature is that mimetic literature tends toward the bringing of latent or hidden motives into the light of consciousness while escapist literature tends to construct new disguises or to confirm existing defenses against the confrontation of latent desires." I suggest that in the case of black people of the post-Reconstruction era, formulas also gave pleasurable expression to conscious political desires whose enactment was prohibited by the dominant society, while mimetic black literature enraged or frustrated them at their civil plight. See Cawelti, *Adventure, Mystery, and Romance*, p. 26.

22. Susan Winnett terms these texts "female narratologies." See her essay "Coming Unstrung: Women, Men, Narrative, and Principles of Pleasure" in *PMLA* 105, 3 (May 1990), pp. 505–18.

Just as there are works written by men that center a female character and female authority, there are works written by women that center the male figure and perspective. Works in which masculine values and patriarchal ambitions govern the characters' development and in which there is no critique of patriarchal values assert a male narratology; these are *male texts*. For example, Lucretia Newman Coleman's 1890 biographical novel *Poor Ben* and Katherine Tillman's 1905 short story "The Preacher at Hill Station" as well as her 1910 drama *Fifty Years of Freedom* are essentially male texts written by women authors. They endorse the patriarchal viewpoint that only men should have voiced public ambitions. This conservative viewpoint is generally absent in the domestic novels at the center of this book. Corresponding patriarchal or male texts by men include William Wells Brown's various editions of *Clotelle* and Charles Chesnutt's 1900 novel *The House Behind the Cedars*. Chesnutt's short stories featuring central female figures in his 1899 collections *The Conjure Woman* and *The Wife of His Youth* grant limited social agency to women; however, they are circumscribed by Western patriarchal hegemony. Interestingly, William E. B. Du Bois's 1911 novel *The Quest of the Silver Fleece* critiques the patriarchal discourse and asserts female authority and public ambition; therefore, this work can be considered a female text.

23. *Master narrative* is Fredric Jameson's term for the discursive "representational structure which allows the individual subject to conceive or imagine his or her lived relationship to transpersonal realities such as the social structure or the collective logic of History." See his *The Political Unconscious: Narrative as a Socially Symbolic Act* (Ithaca, N.Y.: Cornell University Press, 1981), p. 30.

24. Clifford Geertz, *The Interpretation of Cultures* (New York: Basic Books, 1973), p. 27.

25. Ellen Ross and Rayna Rapp, "Sex and Society: A Research Note from Social History and Anthropology" in *Powers of Desire: The Politics of Sexuality*, edited by Ann Snitow, Christine Stansell, and Sharon Thompson (New York: Monthly Review Press, 1983), p. 51.

26. Herbert G. Gutman, *The Black Family in Slavery and Freedom, 1750–1925*

(New York: Pantheon Books, 1976), pp. 531–32. Future references to this work appear parenthetically in the chapter.

27. This is Gutman's term for late-nineteenth-century white Southern conservatives.

28. For excellent discussions of the alleged and categorical immorality of all black people, see Bettina Aptheker, "Quest for Dignity: Black Women in the Professions, 1865–1900" in *Woman's Legacy: Essays on Race, Sex, and Class in American History* (Amherst: University of Massachusetts Press, 1981), pp. 89–110. Also see Paula Giddings, *When and Where I Enter*, pp. 17–135. For a discussion of the Bourbon rhetoric and the proponents of the retrogressionist argument, see Gutman, *The Black Family in Slavery and Freedom*, pp. 531–44; and Joel Williamson, *The Crucible of Race: Black-White Relations in the American South since Emancipation* (New York: Oxford University Press, 1984), pp. 111–39.

29. For historical surveys of the racial climate of the Reconstruction and post-Reconstruction eras see Logan, *The Betrayal of the Negro* and Williamson, *The Crucible of Race*, particularly pp. 1–79. For Logan's coinage of the terms *the nadir* and *the Dark Ages of recent American history* see *The Betrayal of the Negro*, p. 9.

30. For an excellent discussion of the evolution of the culture of African-American slavery see Sterling Stuckey, *Slave Culture: Nationalist Theory and the Foundations of Black America* (New York: Oxford University Press, 1987).

31. Nancy K. Miller, *The Heroine's Text: Reading in the French and English Novel, 1722–1782* (New York: Columbia University Press, 1980).

32. For an argument on the resistant story in the "heroine's text" see Molly Hite, *The Other Side of the Story: Structures and Strategies of Contemporary Feminist Narratives* (Ithaca, N.Y.: Cornell University Press, 1990), pp. 1–11. Quotation from page 5.

33. The characters of Johnson's *Clarence and Corinne* and *The Hazeley Family* are constructed without reference to race. The characters of Kelley-Hawkins's *Megda* are depicted in terms of skin color rather than race, although there is a reference to Cottage City as their vacation destination, which was a well-known black resort town. The characters of *Four Girls at Cottage City* are similarly depicted and candidly draw on the Cottage City setting.

34. The quoted portion is excerpted from the unpublished 1975 Harvard Ph.D. thesis *Aspects of Social Thought in the African Methodist Episcopal Church, 1884–1910*, by David Wood Wills, pp. 177–78. Future references appear parenthetically in the chapter.

This highly privatized agenda is in the foreground in Johnson's *The Hazeley Family*. For after Flora's aunt has trained her "according to her own idea of what constituted the education of a girl," Flora expresses the ambition of using it in order "to be of some use in the world" (pp. 6, 10). While she initially does not know just what to do, she knows that "it was to be something great and good, [and] she was confident, for small things did not enter into her conception of usefulness" (p. 11). Flora soon executes this ambition by "making [her] home just what [she] would like to have it" (pp. 48–49). And while "she had not yet attempted to influence her [brothers] by word . . . they soon noticed the new air of homeliness pervading the rooms, and consequently did not go out so much as had been their custom" (p. 52). Flora's act of usefulness "in the world," doing something "great and good" seems neither high-minded nor public. Unlike Iola, who "would like to do something of lasting service for the race" (Harper, p. 262), Flora's aspirations are reserved and homewardly directed. Rather than giving her lofty public aspiration, Johnson endorses Flora's humble objective of improving the quality of life within her own household. The text asserts that this is not a small endeavor. All noble women cannot possibly assume Iola's public ambition; there must be encouragement for the supportive roles that women like Flora can play in social advancement. Although Johnson promotes a conservative gender education for Flora, she does not censure those women who assume public posture. Rather, that part of her gender discourse is curiously silent, perhaps due to the desire to avoid contention or tacitly to sanction various roles of female activism.

35. My use of the term *self* here as well as throughout this study does not imply the pre-poststructural concept of a unified, self-conscious entity. I use "self" to underscore the ways in which the individual interacts with social conventions to construct a multi-faceted identity.

36. Rosetta Douglass Sprague's discussion of the relationship between intemperance and poverty is typical of such arguments. See her "What Role Is the Educated Negro Woman to Play in the Uplifting of Her Race?" in *Twentieth Century Negro Literature; or, a Cyclopedia of Thought on the Vital Topics Relating to the American Negro*, edited by D[aniel]. W. Culp (Toronto: J. N. Nichols and Co., 1902), p. 171.

37. Molly Hite uses this term in her introduction to the 1988 Oxford University Press edition of *Megda*, p. xxvii.

38. Nina Baym, "Women and the Republic: Emma Willard's Rhetoric of History" in *American Quarterly* 43, 1 (March 1991), p. 2. See also Davidson, *Revolution and the Word*, who explains that while female education from the Puritan epoch through the eighteenth century maintained feminine subordination, during the latter period proposals justified female education "as an education for potential mothers of men, for caretakers of future voters and citizens . . . " (pp. 62–63). Also see Barbara Welter, "The Cult of True Womanhood, 1820–1860" in *Dimity Convictions: The American Woman in the Nineteenth Century* (Athens: Ohio State University Press, 1976), pp. 3–41. The reformist ideology of motherhood remained pervasive in the twentieth century as well, as women declared themselves surrogate mothers in urban settlement work. Also see Hazel V. Carby, *Reconstructing Womanhood*, p. 108.

39. This is Gillian Brown's term for referring to the conflation of the nineteenth-century discourses of political reform and domesticity. See her *Domestic Individualism: Imagining Self in Nineteenth-Century America* (Berkeley: University of California Press, 1990), p. 17. Future references appear parenthetically in the chapter.

40. The term *racial* is often used instead of *interracial* in racialized discourse. I will use both terms as well as the term *racialized*; however, I will specifically use "inter-racial" when I want to stress the mediation of African-American and Western ideology in the discourses of race. This designation calls attention to the presumption of stan-dardized whiteness imprinted in such discourse.

Traditional usage of "racial" has presumed the normative standard of white. Thus, any reference to a racial signifier refers to nonwhite. In the nineteenth century east of the Mississippi, the racial signifier was usually black. The ideology of normative white-ness is also responsible for the assumption that references to any category of humans or human culture without the racial marker categorically means white. The assump-tion of normative whiteness complicates the racial discourses in novels like Kelley-Hawkins's *Megda* and *Four Girls at Cottage City* and Johnson's *Clarence and Corinne* and *The Hazeley Family*, in which their black authors deliberately erase or make self-contradictory the racial characteristics of the characters.

41. One important reason the family story was an important medium for communi-cating social uplift among African Americans is explained by Wilson J. Moses: "From Booker T. Washington to Marcus Garvey, the proponents of 'Negro Improvement'

argued that the proper way for black people to secure their fortune was by changing themselves rather than by attempting to change their environment." As a consequence, according to Moses, advocates for black improvement believed that African Americans could earn full U.S. citizenship by demonstrating that they practiced the genteel standard of Victorian sexual decorum. See Moses, "Domestic Feminism," pp. 959–71.

42. Giddings provides an excellent description in *When and Where I Enter* of the growing racial despair among African Americans of the post-Reconstruction era. Giddings's remarks refer specifically to Ida B. Wells's response to the Tennessee Supreme Court's reversal of her suit against the Chesapeake and Ohio Railroad. Giddings writes,

> For [Wells], it wasn't just the loss of the case, but the loss of faith that justice would ultimately prevail. "I feel shorn of that belief and utterly discouraged," she wrote in her diary. In hindsight, her despondency seems naive, but as late as the 1880s most Blacks still believed that racial injustice was the handiwork of the lowly, an aberration that could be successfully challenged. It was their faith in the "system" that steeled their determination to be worthy citizens despite the bitter experience of slavery and discrimination. With that faith, Afro-Americans—and not just the most privileged ones—were making substantial economic gains after the war. They were attending schools in droves. . . . But as the twentieth century drew nearer, that deeply rooted faith in justice began to be shaken. (pp. 23–24)

43. This is Carolivia Herron's term for what I call racial despair. See her introduction to *Selected Works of Angelina Weld Grimké* (New York: Oxford University Press, 1991), p. 5.

44. The woodcuts appear in *The Crisis* I, 4 (February 1911), pp. 18 and 19.

45. Here I am specifically referring to Fauset's *There Is Confusion* (1924; Reprint. Boston: Northeastern University Press, 1989), *Plum Bun* (1929; Reprint. Boston: Pandora Press, 1985), *The Chinaberry Tree* (New York: Frederick A. Stokes Co., 1931), and *Comedy: American Style* (New York: Frederick A. Stokes Co., 1933); as well to Larsen's *Quicksand* and *Passing* (1928 and 1929, respectively; Reprint. New Brunswick, N.J.: Rutgers University Press, 1985).

46. Most of Grimké's writings remained unpublished until the recent release of *Selected Works of Angelina Weld Grimké* (edited by Carolivia Herron [New York: Oxford University Press, 1991]). This edition is part of the ten-volume sequel to *The Schomburg Library of Nineteenth-Century Black Women Writers*.

I have located the following novels by black women authors published during the early twentieth century. They are Sarah Lee Brown Fleming, *Hope's Highway* (New York: Neale Publishing Co., 1918); Zara Wright, *Black and White Tangled Threads* and *Kenneth* (Chicago: Barnard & Miller, 1920); Lillian E. Wood, *Let My People Go* (Philadelphia: A.M.E. Book Concern, 1921); and Mary Etta Spencer, *The Resentment* (Philadelphia: A.M.E. Book Concern, 1921). None of these authors seems to have written more than two extended works, while Grimké wrote at least a half dozen.

I use Houston A. Baker Jr.'s concept of deformation of a prior text. See his *Modernism and the Harlem Renaissance* (Chicago: University of Chicago Press, 1987), pp. 49–51.

47. For excellent discussions on lynching and rape as racial terrorism see Bettina Aptheker, "Woman Suffrage and the Crusade against Lynching, 1890–1920" in *Wom-*

an's Legacy, pp. 53–76; and Paula Giddings, "To Sell My Life as Dearly as Possible: Ida B. Wells and the First Antilynching Campaign" in *When and Where I Enter*, pp. 17–32.

The dominant racial discourses of rape and lynching constitute what Aptheker terms "rape-lynching mythology" (Aptheker, p. 62). The "rape-lynching mythology" is the linchpin (no pun intended) in the mythology of race, which in turn, as Frankie Y. Bailey argues, is "a part of a larger myth of America." Bailey succinctly summarizes these latter embedded mythologies in *Out of the Woodpile: Black Characters in Crime and Detective Fiction* (Westport, Conn.: Greenwood Press, 1991):

> According to [the myth of America], from its inception, the United States was the realization of an "Anglo-Saxon" dream to "discover" and "conquer" a "brave new world." But there were "Calibans" in this "new world." These alien "others" . . . were perceived by whites as the "shapes of the Devil." They were the embodiment of the sin and savagery that white Christians strove to suppress within themselves. To survive and to achieve their "manifest destiny," the white settlers felt compelled to subjugate or to destroy these others. To justify their treatment of these nonwhites, the white settlers perpetuated and shaped to their own needs the racial mythology that they had acquired in their European homeland. This mythology of race revolved around two predominant themes—the savagery and the sexuality of nonwhites." (p. x)

48. See my introduction to *The Works of Katherine Davis Chapman Tillman* (New York: Oxford University Press, 1991), pp. 16–17.

49. See Joan R. Sherman's introduction to *Collected Black Women's Poetry* (New York: Oxford University Press, 1987), p. xxix. Further references appear parenthetically in the chapter.

50. Katherine D. Tillman, *Thirty Years of Freedom: A Drama in Four Acts* (Philadelphia: A.M.E. Book Concern, 1902), original pagination. Reprinted in the Oxford University Press edition of *The Works of Katherine Davis Chapman Tillman*, 1991.

51. Katherine D. Tillman, "The Preacher at Hill Station" in *The A.M.E. Church Review* XIX (January 1903), 634–43. Reprinted in *The Works of Katherine Davis Chapman Tillman*.

52. Katherine D. Tillman, *Fifty Years of Freedom; or from Cabin to Congress: A Drama in Five Acts* (Philadelphia: A.M.E. Book Concern, 1910), original pagination. Reprinted in *The Works of Katherine Davis Chapman Tillman*.

53. The contradiction is discussed in Introduction, Tillman's *Works*, pp. 51–52.

54. Elizabeth Ammons also comments on what she perceives as Hopkins's growing frustration in the context of the black female artist: "Whatever guarded optimism Hopkins might have felt about the future of the African-American woman artist at the time she wrote *Contending Forces* was gone by the time she wrote *Of One Blood*" (p. 84). Ammons adds that the economic conditions at the onset of the twentieth-century put black women artists in extreme distress. They had to survive before they could create, and often survival was difficult enough. See Ammons's *Conflicting Stories*, pp. 84–85.

55. Jane Tompkins uses this term to refer to the heuristic and didactic force of Stowe's *Uncle Tom's Cabin* as it manipulates social conventions and stereotypes so as to revise cultural formations. See her "Sentimental Power: *Uncle Tom's Cabin* and the Politics of Literary History" in *Sensational Designs: The Cultural Work of American Fiction, 1790–1860* (New York: Oxford University Press, 1987), pp. 122–46.

56. All three works are published by Oxford University Press.

57. I thank Hazel Carby for calling my attention to the correspondence between what I term "gendered political discourses" and the discourse of citizenship.

Chapter 1

1. While I refer particularly to the link between the abolitionist discourse of domestic reform and its post-Reconstruction counterpart, the reformist power of that story is also found in such contemporary works as Alice Walker's *The Color Purple* (1983) and *The Temple of My Familiar* (1989) as well as Toni Morrison's *The Bluest Eye* (1970) and *Beloved* (1987). Unlike these late-twentieth-century versions, however, the nineteenth-century domestic discourse was, despite its reformist agenda, fundamentally patriarchal.

Deborah E. McDowell (whom I paraphrase below) points out that although the integrity of the family—domesticity's most powerful convention—was a potent argument against slavery, domesticity itself as well as abolitionism and slavery was a patriarchal institution. Paternal property relations defined each institution. McDowell makes this very astute observation in the context of Frederick Douglass who, in the words of McDowell, "forged [an] unexamined connection between abolitionism and domesticity at the same moment that the link between slavery and feminism was 'being forged by various reform figures, including Douglass himself. . . .'" See Deborah E. McDowell, "In the First Place: Making Frederick Douglass and the Afro-American Narrative Tradition" in *Critical Essays on Frederick Douglass*, edited by William Andrews (New York: G. K. Hall, 1992), p. 200.

To elaborate a bit further, it was precisely white women's increasing awareness of their status as male property that instigated the activists among them to try to wrench domesticity from patriarchal control by using domestic discourse to transform the paternal into a feminist social dominance. However, by privileging their race, most of these women activists (the early women's rights' proponents, especially) seemed more interested in declaring themselves honorary white patriarchs than in extending self-ownership to black men and women. In other words, white women activists were generally not interested in reforming the white patriarchy, they merely wanted to claim its power.

2. Barbara Welter, "The Cult of True Womanhood: 1820–1860" in *Dimity Convictions: The American Woman in the Nineteenth Century* (Athens: Ohio State University Press, 1976), p. 41.

3. My argument is indebted to Gillian Brown's analysis of domestic politics in "Domestic Politics in *Uncle Tom's Cabin*" in *Domestic Individualism: Imagining Self in Nineteenth-Century America* (Berkeley: University of California Press, 1990), pp. 13–38. Future references to this work appear parenthetically in the chapter.

4. Harriet Beecher Stowe, *Uncle Tom's Cabin* (1851; Reprint. New York: Signet, 1966), p. 227.

5. I refer to Alan Kulikoff's anthropological definitions of household, domestic groups, and families. "A *household* . . . is a coresidence group that includes all who shared a 'proximity of sleeping arrangements'" or lived under the same roof. *Domestic groups* include kin and nonkin, living in the same or separate households, who share cooking, eating, child rearing, working, and other daily activities. Families are composed of people related by blood or marriage. See Kulikoff's "Beginnings of the Afro-American Family" in *Black Women in United States History*, Vol. 3, edited by Darlene Clark Hine (Brooklyn: Carlson Publishing Inc., 1990), p. 786.

6. Sherley Anne Williams's *Dessa Rose* (New York: Morrow, 1987) and Toni Morrison's *Beloved* (New York: Knopf, 1987) are especially sensitive to the way that slavers regarded slaves. Both writers employ specialized language associated with farm animals, particularly horses, to describe the slaves' biological functions and thereby illustrate how the ideology of slavery constructed the identities of slaves as beasts of burden.

7. Herbert G. Gutman, *The Black Family in Slavery and Freedom, 1750–1925* (New York: Pantheon Books, 1976), p. 275.

8. See Welter's "The Cult of True Womanhood" in *Dimity Convictions*.

9. Although Jones refers to recently freed slave women, these women shared a common lot with black women who were technically freed during the early part of the nineteenth century. See Jacqueline Jones, *Labor of Love, Labor of Sorrow: Black Women, Work, and the Family, from Slavery to the Present* (New York: Basic Books, 1985), p. 53. For another discussion on gender conventions and labor practices among free blacks see James Oliver Horton, "Freedom's Yoke: Gender Conventions among Antebellum Free Blacks" in *Black Women in United States History*, Vol. 2.

10. Dorothy Sterling, Ed., *We Are Your Sisters: Black Women in the Nineteenth Century* (New York: W. W. Norton, 1984), p. 87.

11. Sterling relied on letters written by free black people of the antebellum era to characterize their living conditions. Included among them are examples of indentures that place Frado's plight in Wilson's *Our Nig* in historical context, demonstrating that black children were frequently placed into indentured service due to the extreme poverty of their families.

12. Mary Helen Washington perceptively remarks in *Invented Lives* that "the male narrator [of the slave narrative] could write his tale as a reclamation of his manhood, but under the terms of white society's ideals of chastity and sexual ignorance for women Brent certainly cannot claim 'true' womanhood" (p. 4). For her excellent discussion on Jacobs's *Incidents in the Life of a Slave Girl* as well as other selected works by African-American women see her *Invented Lives: Narratives of Black Women, 1860–1960* (New York: Anchor, 1987). Future references to *Invented Lives* appear parenthetically in the chapter.

13. Although *Incidents* and *Our Nig* were published in 1861 and 1858, respectively, I refer to both as antebellum texts due to the fact that slavery was not abolished in the Confederate States until January 1, 1863.

14. See Jean Fagan Yellin, "*Written by Herself:* Harriet Jacobs's Slave Narrative" in *American Literature* 53 (November 1981), pp. 479–86. Also see the introduction and appendix in Yellin's edited edition of *Incidents in the Life of a Slave Girl* (Cambridge, Mass.: Harvard University Press, 1987). Future references to this edition of *Incidents* appear parenthetically in the chapter.

15. See Henry Louis Gates Jr.'s introduction to *Our Nig* (New York: Vintage, 1984), pp. xiii, xxx–xxxiv. Future references to this introduction and edition appear parenthetically in the chapter.

Barbara Christian also speculates about the obscurity of *Incidents* and *Our Nig*. In regard to *Our Nig* she explains that it

> did not cater to the accepted mores of the time. By emphasizing the racism . . . of her northern white mistress, by exposing racism in the North, as well as by ending her story with her desertion by her fugitive-slave husband, Frado, the protagonist of *Our Nig* questioned the progressive plat-

form of her time—that white northern women were the natural allies of blacks, that the North was not racist, that all Black men were devoted to the women of their race. . . . The disappearance of *Our Nig* . . . was also due to doubts raised about its authorship. Like *Incidents in the Life of a Slave Girl, Our Nig* was thought to have been written by a white woman because of its point of view and its excellent style.

See Barbara Christian, "African-American Women's Historical Novels," in *Wild Women in the Whirlwind*, edited by Joanne M. Braxton and Andree Nicola McLaughlin (New Brunswick, N.J.: Rutgers University Press, 1990), p. 331.

16. See note 14.

17. I borrow William Andrews's term *novelization of voice* from his essay "The Novelization of Voice in Early African American Narrative" in *PMLA* 105 (January 1990), pp. 23–34, to sustain the distinction between authorial voice and authorial-constructed autobiographical voice. Bakhtin was probably the first critic to use the concept "novelize" and other derivatives of the word in his *The Dialogic Imagination: Four Essays* (Austin: University of Texas Press, 1981). Further references to "the novelization of voice" appear parenthetically in the chapter.

18. Valerie Smith, Introduction, *Incidents in the Life of a Slave Girl* by Harriet A. Jacobs (1861; Reprint. New York: Oxford University Press, 1988), p. xxxi. Future references to this introduction appear parenthetically in the chapter.

19. Mary Helen Washington contends that Jacobs's "contemporary interpreters, Jean Fagan Yellin, Hazel Carby, Valerie Smith and Joanne Braxton have demonstrated conclusively Brent's struggle to resist the ideological implications of the sentimental novel and the cult of true womanhood." See *Invented Lives*, p. 6.

20. Mary Helen Washington's discussion of *Incidents* places the work in the tradition of slave narratives rather than that of domestic or sentimental novels. Washington cites the moment in *Incidents* when Jacobs expresses her outrage at having to be purchased in order to claim her freedom as the climax of the text. Washington also specifically refers to Jacobs's evocation of the rhetoric that Frederick Douglass employed in his 1845 narrative. Washington contends that feminist readings frequently overlook Jacobs's expression of this outrage. See *Invented Lives*, p. 10.

21. Frederick Douglass, *Narrative of the Life of Frederick Douglass*. (1845; Reprint. Garden City, N.Y.: Doubleday Dolphin, 1963), p. 56. Further references appear parenthetically in the chapter.

22. For a sustained discussion of the protesting voice of the outraged mother in black women's autobiographies, see Joanne M. Braxton, *Black Women Writing Autobiography: A Tradition within a Tradition* (Philadelphia: Temple University Press, 1989), pp. 1–39.

23. See Sherley Anne Williams's depiction of the sexual affair between the slave Nathan and his mistress Miz Lorraine in *Dessa Rose*, pp. 155–58. Also see Toni Morrison's reference to fellatio in *Beloved*, p. 108.

24. For more extended discussions of Douglass's relegation of abused sexuality to the female body, see Jenny Franchot, "The Punishment of Esther" in *Frederick Douglass: New Literary and Historical Essays*, edited by Eric J. Sundquist (New York: Cambridge University Press, 1990), pp. 141–65; and Deborah E. McDowell, "In the First Place: Making Frederick Douglass and the Afro-American Narrative Tradition" in *Critical Essays on Frederick Douglass*. For a discussion of Douglass's appropriation of the republican rhetoric of the "founding fathers," see James Olney, "The Founding

Fathers—Frederick Douglass and Booker T. Washington" in *Slavery and the Literary Imagination*, edited by Deborah E. McDowell and Arnold Rampersad (Baltimore: Johns Hopkins University Press, 1987).

25. Zora Neale Hurston, *Their Eyes Were Watching God* (1937; Reprint. Urbana: University of Illinois Press, 1978), p. 31.

26. My reading of *Incidents* builds on the foundation of the excellent introductions to the Harvard and Oxford University Press editions of this work by Jean Fagan Yellin and Valerie Smith, respectively, as well as on Mary Helen Washington's discussion in *Invented Lives*.

27. Gary Saul Morson, "Parody, History, and Metaparody" in *Rethinking Bakhtin: Extensions and Challenges*, edited by Gary Saul Morson and Caryl Emerson (Evanston: Northwestern University Press, 1989), p. 70. Further references appear parenthetically in the chapter.

28. Mag has already had a child out of wedlock. The father, however, was presumably white; thus, that was but a single social transgression. By marrying a black man Mag doubly challenges white patriarchal authority, disregarding both its sexual and its racial codes.

29. Molly Hite explains that women are presumed to be "'essentially' either prostitute or beloved—which is to say either financially or emotionally dependent, but not both. . . . A good woman is one who needs a man emotionally. Although she may also need his economic support to survive, this need must remain secondary, contingent, accidental. . . . On the other hand, a bad woman is one who needs—and cold-bloodedly uses—a man financially." See Molly Hite, *The Other Side of the Story: Structures and Strategies of Contemporary Feminist Narrative* (Ithaca, N.Y.: Cornell University Press, 1990), p. 24.

30. Jessica Benjamin, *The Bonds of Love: Psychoanalysis, Feminism, and the Problem of Domination* (New York: Pantheon, 1988), p. 41.

31. I am especially indebted here and immediately following to Morson's argument in "Parody, History, and Metaparody" in his *Rethinking Bakhtin*, p. 65. I recontextualize that argument to fit Wilson's title.

32. Texts like Edward Pendleton Kennedy's *Swallow Barn* (1832) and William Gilmore Simm's *The Sword and the Distaff* (1852), entitled *Woodcraft* in 1854.

33. See note 31 above.

34. Linda Hutcheon, "Modern Parody and Bakhtin" in *Rethinking Bakhtin*, pp. 87–88.

35. Beyond the purposes of this chapter is the identification and exploration of nineteenth-century parodied slave narratives, written by those sympathetic and not sympathetic to the abolitionist movement. Wilson's parody implies currency in such texts. See Morson, *Rethinking Bakhtin*, p. 73.

36. See Sandra Gilbert and Susan Gubar, *The Madwoman in the Attic: The Woman Writer and the Nineteenth-Century Literary Imagination* (New Haven, Conn.: Yale University Press, 1979), pp. 45–93.

37. See Judith Fetterly, *Provisions: A Reader from 19th-Century American Women* (Bloomington: University of Indiana Press, 1985), pp. 5–9. The quotation is taken from page 5.

38. See notes 36 and 37. Also see Ann D. Wood, "The 'Scribbling Women' and Fanny Fern: Why Women Wrote" in *American Quarterly* 23, 1 (Spring 1971), pp. 3–24. Also see Joanne Dobson, "The Hidden Hand: Subversion of Cultural Ideology in Three Mid-Nineteenth-Century American Women's Novels" in *American Quarterly* 38, 2 (Summer 1986), pp. 223–42.

39. Excerpt is from Alfred Habegger's discussion of the political implications of allegory that is particularly helpful to my understanding of *Our Nig* as well as other works by black women. He writes,

> Unlike realism, the literature of writers with some democratic freedom, allegory is the literature of exiles, prisoners, captives, or others who have no room to act in their society. . . . Allegory is one of many human artifacts expressing a sense of individual powerlessness.

See Alfred Habegger, *Gender, Fantasy, and Realism in American Literature* (New York: Columbia University Press, 1982), pp. 111–12.

40. A popular metaphor in works like Margaret Homan's *Bearing the Word: Language and Female Experience in Nineteenth-Century Women's Writing* (Chicago: University of Chicago Press, 1986) and Gilbert's and Gubar's *The Madwoman in the Attic*.

41. For a discussion of parody in black minstrelsy (which Baker regards as a particular case of "deformation of the master's form") see Houston A. Baker Jr.'s *Modernism and the Harlem Renaissance* (Chicago: University of Chicago Press, 1987), pp. 49–52, 56–57.

42. Authors of slave narratives usually affixed authenticating documents in the preface and/or appendix of their works in anticipation of challenges to the authenticity of their authorship.

43. Nathanial Hawthorne, *The Scarlet Letter* (New York: Norton, 1961). Further references appear parenthetically in the chapter.

44. Religious conversion was an important transformative event that granted self-authorization to an individual, negating the authority of masters and husbands for slaves and wives, respectively. William Andrews sees this form of female self-determinism as radical spiritual individualism. See William L. Andrews, *Sisters of the Spirit: Three Black Women's Autobiographies of the Nineteenth Century* (Bloomington: University of Indiana Press, 1986), pp. 2–3.

45. My students are habitually uneasy about the affinity between Frado and the Bellmont males. They note how often she is in their rooms, seeking comfort, or they are taking her to her room. I share their uneasiness, for a deleted sexuality seems to be looming in these episodes. Barbara Christian expresses similar concern in her introduction to *The Hazeley Family* by Amelia E. Johnson (New York: Oxford University Press, 1988), p. xxxv.

46. On page 25 Jack says, "She's real handsome and bright, and not very black, either." On page 47 James asks, "Is this that pretty little Nig, Jack writes to me about. . . ." On page 70 Jack asks, "Where are your curls, Fra. . . . Thought you were getting handsome, did she?"

Chapter 2

1. I am indebted to Hazel Carby for pointing out that nineteenth-century discourses of citizenship were inherently gendered. Our late-twentieth-century perspective obscures that fact.

2. See Angela Davis, *Women, Race, and Class* (New York: Vintage Books, 1983), pp. 87–88.

3. Turn-of-the-century black educator Fannie Barrier Williams achieved national prominence in 1892 when she "convinced the board of the World's Columbian Exposition in Chicago to give official representation to Negroes." She also remarked that she

was "constantly in receipt of letters from the still unprotected colored women of the South, begging [her] to find employment for their daughters according to their ability, as domestics or otherwise, to save them from going to the homes of the South as servants, as there is nothing to save them from dishonor and degradation" (p. 167). See "The Accusations Are False" by Fannie Barrier Williams in *Black Women in White America: A Documentary History*, edited by Gerda Lerner (New York: Vintage, 1973), pp. 166–69. Bettina Aptheker provides a compelling explanation for "[white] male presumption of the sexual accessibility of household workers" (p. 123). See her *Woman's Legacy: Essays on Race, Sex, and Class in American History* (Amherst: University of Massachusetts Press, 1981), pp. 122–28.

4. For an excellent discussion about the exploited labor of black domestic workers, see Bettina Aptheker, "Domestic Labor: Patterns in Black and White" in *Woman's Legacy*, pp. 111–28. Toni Morrison dramatizes the consequences of exploited black domesticity in her 1970 novel *The Bluest Eye*. Here she portrays the black domestic Pauline Breedlove's delight in her organizational skills and artistic talents as well as her vicarious authority in the household of her white employer, while she disparages her own home in which similar expression is frustrated.

5. Jacqueline Jones, *Labor of Love, Labor of Sorrow: Black Women, Work, and the Family from Slavery to the Present* (New York: Basic Books, 1985), p. 28.

6. Linda Perkins, "Black Women and Racial 'Uplift' Prior to Emancipation" in *The Black Woman Cross-Culturally*, edited by Filomina Chioma Steady (Cambridge, Mass.: Schenkman Books, Inc., 1981), p. 321.

7. See Thomas Webber, *Deep Like the Rivers: Education in the Slave Quarter Community, 1831–1865* (New York: W. W. Norton, 1978), p. 149.

8. See Deborah Gray White, *Ar'n't I a Woman: Female Slaves in the Plantation South* (New York: W. W. Norton, 1985), pp. 69–70. Future references to this work appear parenthetically in the chapter.

9. Susan A. Mann, "Slavery, Sharecropping, and Sexual Inequality" in *Signs: Journal of Women in Culture and Society* XIV, 4 (Sumner 1989), p. 798. Future references appear parenthetically in the chapter.

10. Barbara Omolade contends that

> the historical oppression of black women and men should have created social equality between them, but even after the end of slavery when the white patriarch receded, maleness and femaleness continued to be defined by patriarchal structures, with black men declaring wardship over black women. In the black community, the norm of manhood was patriarchal power; the norm of womanhood was adherence to it, though black men and women selected which aspects of these norms they would emphasize.

See Barbara Omolade, "Hearts of Darkness" in *Powers of Desire: The Politics of Sexuality*, edited by Ann Snitow, Christine Stansell, and Sharon Thompson (New York: Monthly Review Press, 1983), p. 361.

11. See E. Franklin Frazier, *The Negro Family in the United States* (Chicago: University of Chicago Press, 1966), pp. 367–68.

12. Evelyn Brooks-Higginbotham, "The Problem of Race in Women's History" in *Coming to Terms: Feminism, Theory, and Politics*, edited by Elizabeth Weed (New York: Routledge, 1989), pp. 122–33. Future references appear parenthetically in the chapter.

13. Joyce A. Ladner, "Racism and Tradition: Black Womanhood in Historical Per-

spective" in *The Black Woman Cross-Culturally*, p. 280. Future references appear parenthetically in the chapter.

14. "Though African immigrants did not bring a unified West African culture with them . . . they did share important beliefs about the nature of kinship" that bears on gender specificity. "They saw kinship as a principal way of ordering relations between individuals. Each person in the tribe was related to most others in the tribe. The male was father, son, and uncle; the female was mother, daughter, and aunt to many others." See Alan Kulikoff, "Beginnings of the Afro-American Family" in *Black Women in United States History*, Vol. 3, edited by Darlene Clark Hine (Brooklyn: Carlson Publishing Inc., 1990), p. 787.

15. See Daniel Patrick Moynihan, *Moynihan Report: The Case for National Action* (Washington, D.C., 1965).

16. Mary Church Terrell, for example, recalled that her father was very unhappy when she decided to work after graduation from Oberlin College: "In the South for nearly three hundred years 'real ladies' did not work, and my father was thoroughly imbued with that idea." Terrell explained that he wanted his daughter be a "lady" (p. 59). See Terrell's autobiography, *A Colored Woman in a White World* (Washington, D. C.: National Association of Colored Women's Clubs, Inc., 1968). Paula Giddings contends that Church Terrell's father disinherited her and refused to write to her for a year because she took a teaching job at Wilberforce. See Paula Giddings, *When and Where I Enter: The Impact of Black Women on Race and Sex in America* (New York: Morrow, 1984), pp. 109–10.

17. Lawrence W. Levine, *Black Culture and Black Consciousness: Afro-American Folk Thought from Slavery to Freedom* (New York: Oxford University Press, 1977), p. 138. Future references appear parenthetically in the chapter.

18. Steven Mintz and Susan Kellogg, *Domestic Revolutions: A Social History of American Family Life* (New York: The Free Press, 1988), p. 77. Future references appear parenthetically in the chapter.

19. The preference of female domestic labor among the black population no doubt was greatly influenced by the dominant society's division of labor in which, as Barbara Epstein explains,

> the male head of household was responsible for the economic support of the family and the wife and mother was responsible for housekeeping and caring for children. . . . A man's ability to support his wife and children adequately was central to the nineteenth-century middle-class notion of masculinity, and the corresponding notion of femininity revolved around a woman's reliance on her husband's support.

See Barbara Epstein, "Family, Sexual Morality, and Popular Movements" in Snitow, Stansell, and Thompson's *Powers of Desire: The Politics of Sexuality*, p. 119.

20. See Eugene Genovese, *Roll Jordan, Roll: The World the Slaves Made* (New York: Vintage Books, 1974), p. 490; Herbert G. Gutman, *The Black Family in Slavery and Freedom, 1750–1925* (New York: Random House, 1976), p. 168; E. Franklin Frazier, *The Negro Family in the United States* (Chicago: University of Chicago Press, 1966), p. 39; Jacqueline Jones, *Soldiers of Light and Love: Northern Teachers and the Georgia Blacks, 1865–1973* (Chapel Hill: University of North Carolina Press, 1980); and Evelyn Brooks, "The Women's Movement in the Black Baptist Church, 1880–1920," Ph.D. dissertation, University of Rochester, New York, 1984.

21. See Charles Valentine, "Deficit, Difference, and Bicultural Models of Afro-

American Behavior" in *Harvard Educational Review* 44 (May 1971), p. 144; also see Bonnie Thornton Dill, "The Dialectics of Black Womanhood," *Signs* 4 (Spring 1979), pp. 543–55.

22. For discussions of black women's access to academic education see Cynthia Neverdon-Morton, *Afro-American Women of the South and the Advancement of the Race, 1895–1925* (Knoxville: University of Tennessee Press, 1989), pp. 10–68. For discussions of the American Negro Academy (ANA) see Mary Helen Washington, *Invented Lives: Narratives of Black Women, 1860–1960* (New York: Anchor, 1987), p. xviii and note 5 on p. xxix, and Washington's introduction to the Oxford reprint of Anna Cooper's *A Voice From the South* (New York: Oxford University Press, 1988), pp. xl–xli. Washington cites Cooper's review of the opening meeting of the ANA in the *Southern Workman* in which she commented, "Its membership is confined to men." This comment refutes the viewpoint of Cooper's biographer Louise Daniel Hutchinson, who seems to interpret Cooper's attendance of the opening meeting of the ANA as the participation of an invited member. In referring to Cooper, Hutchinson writes, "An active member of the Oberlin Alumni Association . . . the American Negro Academy . . . " (pp. 106–7). Hutchinson goes on to write that "Anna Cooper was the only woman ever elected a member of the American Negro Academy . . . " (p. 109). See Louise Daniel Hutchinson, *Anna J. Cooper, a Voice From the South* (Washington, D.C.: Smithsonian Institution, 1981).

Historian Linda M. Perkins contends that when the nineteenth century came to a close, racial uplift was "synonymous with black women." She adds that the black senator John Mercer Langston from Virginia observed black women everywhere in the forefront in the "social, political, educational, moral, religious and material status" of the African American. Moreover, Perkins says that Du Bois similarly wrote that "after the war the sacrifice of Negro women for freedom and black uplift is one of the finest chapters in their history." "Yet, today," as Perkins comments, "this chapter is rarely found in black, women's or educational histories." See Linda Perkins, "The Impact of the 'Cult of True Womanhood' on the Education of Black Women" in *Journal of Social Issues* 39, 3 (1983), p. 25. This too is my observation. See my introduction to *The Works of Katherine Davis Chapman Tillman* (New York: Oxford University Press, 1990), pp. 5–6.

After considering Du Bois's position on female membership in the ANA and after reviewing Mary Helen Washington's very thoroughly researched description of Cooper's sustained interest in Du Bois's pan-Africanism (in her introduction to Cooper's *A Voice From the South*), I speculate that, as a young and impressionable member of the ANA, he was well aware of that organization's presumption of male privilege and probably was simply unwilling to question the sexist attitudes of its prominent members. According to David L. Lewis, one of Du Bois's biographers, when Du Bois became more influential in ANA and more explicitly supportive of female participation in racial uplift programs (as evident by his support of female participation in the second meeting of the Niagara Movement), he was frequently absent from meetings. Thus he could not exert his influence.

23. See Charles W. Chesnutt, "The Wife of His Youth" in *The Wife of His Youth and Other Stories* (1900; Reprint. Ann Arbor: University of Michigan Press, 1968), pp. 1–24.

24. Willard B. Gatewood, *The Aristocrats of Color: The Black Elite, 1880–1920* (Bloomington: University of Indiana Press, 1990), p. 27. Future references appear parenthetically in the chapter.

25. See Dickson D. Bruce, Jr., *Black American Writing from the Nadir: The Evolu-*

tion of a Literary Tradition, 1877–1915 (Baton Rouge: Louisiana State University Press, 1989), pp. 1–56, for a thorough discussion of the impact of Victorian culture and its mandate of gentility on the evolution of the literary tradition of African Americans. The quotation is taken from pages 19–20. Future references are given parenthetically in the chapter.

26. Similar patterns of character portraiture appear in *Hearts of Gold* (1896) by J. McHenry Jones and *The Sport of the Gods* (1902) by Paul Laurence Dunbar. However, William E. B. Du Bois's *The Quest of the Silver Fleece* (1911) reverses this practice by depicting the heroine as a comely dark-skinned woman who remains a member of the folk even after she has acquired higher education and broad cultural experience.

27. My colleague Tara Wallace has perceptively suggested that the fair-skinned husband is Ruth's mark of superior virtue and her material, indeed sexual, reward. While personal nobility allows Ruth to transcend color restrictions, the reward of the light-skinned husband reinscribes color privilege.

28. Pauline E. Hopkins, *Hagar's Daughter* in *Magazine Novels of Pauline Hopkins* (1901; Reprint. New York: Oxford University Press, 1988), p. 224 (emphasis in original).

29. In the excellent introduction to *The Magazine Novels of Pauline Hopkins*, Hazel Carby argues that Venus "evolves from being a black maid to becoming a heroine of the story" (p. xxxix). My reading of this character is more reserved. While disguised as a boy, Venus rescues her mistress and cancels the villains' plot. In this role she assumes the agency of a hero but not the narrative attention associated with a heroine. After the trial she rapidly recedes into the background. Her last words comment on her mistress' broken heart (p. 281).

30. See Barbara Welter, "The Cult of True Womanhood, 1820–1860" in *The Dimity Convictions: American Woman in the Nineteenth Century* (Athens: Ohio State University Press, 1976). Also see Carroll Smith-Rosenberg, *Disorderly Conduct: Visions of Gender in Victorian America* (New York: Oxford University Press, 1985), pp. 11–23, 109–29.

31. Wilson J. Moses, "Black Feminism versus Peasant Values" in *The Golden Age of Black Nationalism* (Hamden, Conn.: Archon Books, 1978), pp. 103–31.

32. For excellent histories of the national black women's clubs' movement, see "Defending Our Name" and "To Be a Woman, Sublime" in Paula Giddings's *When and Where I Enter*, pp. 95–118; and "Developing a National Organization of Afro-American Women" in Cynthia Neverdon-Morton's *Afro-American Women of the South and the Advancement of the Race, 1895–1925*, pp. 191–201.

33. Here I am especially highlighting Amelia Johnson's *Clarence and Corinne* and *The Hazeley Family* and Emma Dunham Kelley-Hawkins's *Megda* and *Four Girls at Cottage City*. However, I could mount a similar argument for the remaining seven novels. For excellent discussions of black women writers' use of the counter black stereotype see Barbara Christian, *Black Women Novelists: The Development of a Tradition, 1892–1976* (Westport, Conn.: Greenwood Press, 1980), pp. 1–62; and Hazel V. Carby, *Reconstructing Womanhood* (New York: Oxford University Press, 1987), pp. 19–33.

34. See for example, Nina Baym, *Woman's Fiction: A Guide to Novels by and about Women in America, 1820–1870* (Ithaca, N.Y.: Cornell University Press, 1976); Joanne Dobson, "The Hidden Hand: Subversion of Cultural Ideology in Three Mid-Nineteenth-Century American Women's Novels" in *American Quarterly* 38, 2 (Spring 1986); Janet Todd, *Sensibility: An Introduction* (New York: Methuen, 1986); Elaine Showalter, *A Literature of Their Own: British Women Novelists from Brontë to Les-*

sing (Princeton, N.J.: Princeton University Press, 1977); and Sandra Gilbert and Susan Gubar, *The Madwoman in the Attic: The Woman Writer and the Nineteenth Century Literary Imagination* (New Haven, Conn.: Yale University Press, 1979).

35. Joanne Dobson, "The Hidden Hand," pp. 333–35.

Nina Baym refers to Louisa May Alcott's *Little Women* (1869) to explain the future of women's fiction: "The story of feminine heroism now becomes a didactic instrument for little girls; as an adult genre, woman's fiction becomes gothic romance." See Nina Baym, *Woman's Fiction*, p. 296.

36. Susan K. Harris, *19th-Century American Women's Novels: Interpretive Strategies* (New York: Cambridge University Press, 1990), p. 200. By contrast to the exploratory novels of the mid-nineteenth century, Harris identifies what she terms the novels of an

> *exclusion* of possibility: first, in their thematic insistence on women's sub-mission to justified authority and, second, in their formal restriction of readers' interpretations, [the novels refuse] to countenance alternative points of view. . . . Overall, their assumption is that virtue in a woman consists of passivity, obedience to legitimate external authority, and self-abnegation. Apolitical, they do not question their society's power struc-tures; rather, they teach their readers how to accommodate themselves to the status quo. (pp. 199–200)

I strongly disagree that these early novels are apolitical, but argue that they were novels of dominant political consensus rather than those of resistance.

37. See Janet Todd's *Sensibility: An Introduction*, pp. 1–31.

38. Cathy R. Davidson, *Revolution and the Word: The Rise of the Novel in America* (New York: Oxford University Press, 1986), pp. 122–23. Future references appear parenthetically in the chapter.

39. I take a moment here to stress that realism is no less artificially constructed than sentimentality. "Realism," as Joseph Allen Boone succinctly explains, "is predicated on a series of narrative manipulations working to present . . . reality as stable, ordered, and trustworthy. . . . [These] 'technical elements of narrative . . . tended to impose the image of a stable, coherent, continuous, unequivocal, entirely decipherable uni-verse.'" See his *Tradition Counter Tradition: Love and the Form of Fiction* (Chicago: University of Chicago Press, 1987), p. 8.

40. See my discussion on male and female texts in the Introduction, pp. 8–9.

41. Wilson J. Moses, "Domestic Feminism, Conservatism, Sex Roles and Black Women's Clubs, 1893–1896" in *Black Women in United States History*, p. 969.

Chapter 3

1. Zora Neale Hurston, *Their Eyes Were Watching God* (1937; Reprint. Urbana: University of Illinois Press, 1978); Richard Wright, *Black Boy* (New York: Harper and Brothers, 1945). Further references to these works appear parenthetically in the chapter.

2. I borrow the terms *cover-plot* and *cover story* from Susan K. Harris's *19th-Century American Women Novels: Interpretative Strategies* (New York: Cambridge University Press, 1990). She regards both terms as variations of Nina Baym's "over-plot," discussed in her *Woman's Fiction: A Guide to Novels by and about Women in America, 1820–1870* (Ithaca, N.Y.: Cornell University Press, 1976). Harris defines cover-plot and cover story as "formulaic covering[s] . . . [for] disguis[ing] subversive discourse" in texts written by women and men (pp. 20–23). In women's texts, the

cover-plot is the conservative story of sanctioned patriarchal behavior and expectations for females that literally covers the radical story about the subversion of that patriarchal text.

Molly Hite explains the narrative closure of the romance plot as "dysphoric" and "euphoric." The former ending "resolve[s] the situation created by the sexual suscepti- bility of the protagonist by terminating her life" and the latter "resolve[s] the same situation by absorbing her into a conventionally happy marriage." See Molly Hite, *The Other Side of the Story: Structures and Strategies of Contemporary Feminist Narratives* (Ithaca, N.Y.: Cornell University Press, 1990), p. 5.

3. Susan Willis has presented a similar material analysis of Janie's relationship to her three husbands in *Specifying: Black Women Writing the American Experience* (Madison: University of Wisconsin Press, 1987). She writes that Killicks "regards his young wife as a mule . . . in [a] system of backbreaking rural labor [in which] women were expected to bear the burdens of field work as well as domestic toil" (p. 46). Willis goes on to explain that "Joe Starks represents the nascent black bourgeoisie" (p. 47). In describing Tea Cake, Willis contends that Janie "offers a utopian betrayal of history's dialectic" (p. 48). The difference between my discussion and Willis's is that I place the material analysis of Janie's three marriages into the context of antebellum, postbellum, and modern black gender constructions.

4. Mary Helen Washington, "The Darkened Eye Restored" in *Reading Black, Read- ing Feminist*, edited by Henry Louis Gates, Jr. (New York: Penguin Books, 1990), p. 39.

5. Peter G. Filene, *HIM/HER/SELF: Sex Roles in Modern America* (Baltimore: Johns Hopkins University Press, 1986), p. 35.

6. Richard Wright, "Between Laughter and Tears" in *New Masses* 5 (October 1937), pp. 22, 25.

7. Ralph Ellison, "Recent Negro Fiction" in *New Masses* 40, 6 (5 August 1941), pp. 22–26.

8. Arthur P. Davis, *From the Dark Tower: Afro-American Writers 1900–1960* (Washington, D.C.: Howard University Press, 1974), p. 117.

9. In her essay "On Richard Wright and Zora Neale Hurston," for example, June Jordan writes that "[Black aesthetic critic] Hoyt Fuller proposed the primary functions of Protest and Affirmation as basic to an appreciation of Black Art." Jordan goes on to write that, "Wright's *Native Son* [and I suggest *Black Boy* as well are] widely recognized as the prototypical Black protest novel." The black novels of affirmation receive less scholarly attention because the black aesthetic critics endorsed protest over affirmation. See June Jordan, "On Richard Wright and Zora Neale Hurston: Notes Toward a Balancing of Love and Hatred" in *Black World* (August 1974), pp. 4–8. Indeed, the number of times that Richard Wright's name is mentioned throughout *The Black Aesthetic*, edited by Addison Gayle, Jr. (New York: Anchor Doubleday, 1971), makes the book appear is if it were dedicated to him as well as to Gayle's deceased father. Such strong affinity between Wright and his commentators suggests that they shared a common vision.

I distinguish traditional criticism from the more recent criticism influenced by femi- nism, structuralism, and poststructuralism. Thus my use of the terms *traditional* and *recent* criticism designates the respective temporal frames of approximately the 1940s through the early 1970s and the 1980s to the present.

Also see Mary Helen Washington's foreword to the 1990 Harper and Row edition of *Their Eyes Were Watching God* (pp. vii–viii) for a summary of the novel's reception by black male writers and critics.

10. For example, see the influential studies of Hugh Gloster, *Negro Voices in Ameri-*

can Fiction (Chapel Hill: University of North Carolina Press, 1948), pp. 236–37; Robert A. Bone, *The Negro Novel in America* (New Haven, Conn.: Yale University Press, 1958), pp. 127–28; and David L. Littlejohn, *Black on White: A Critical Survey of Writing by American Negroes* (New York: Viking, 1966), pp. 63–64. These critics, among others, influenced a school of traditional criticism that adhered to the prevailing interpretative expectations of the Protest Era and the Black Arts movement.

For a discussion of the critical bias of traditional black literary scholarship regarding women's writing, here the novels of Jessie Fauset, see Deborah E. McDowell's introduction to *Plum Bun* (New Brunswick, N.J.: Rutgers University Press, 1990), pp. xii–xiii.

11. See Susan Winnett's "Coming Unstrung: Women, Men, Narrative, and Principles of Pleasure" in *PMLA* 105, 3 (May 1990) in which she interrogates the presumption of male pleasure in theories of narrative.

12. Ron Karenga, "Black Cultural Nationalism" in *The Black Aesthetic*, edited by Addison Gayle, Jr. (New York: Anchor Doubleday, 1971), p. 33.

13. Addison Gayle, Jr., Ed., *The Black Aesthetic*, p. xxii. Future references appear parenthetically in the chapter.

14. Richard Wright, "Blueprint for Negro Writing," originally published in *New Challenge II* (Fall 1937), pp. 53–65. Reprinted in *The Black Aesthetic*, edited by Addison Gayle, Jr.

15. James Baldwin's "Everybody's Protest Novel" and "Many Thousands Gone" were originally published in *The Partisan Review* 16 (June 1949), pp. 578–723, and 18 (November–December 1951), pp. 665–68, respectively. They were republished in *Notes of a Native Son* (Boston: Beacon Press, 1955). Ralph Ellison's "Richard Wright's Blues" was originally published in *Antioch Review* 5 (Summer 1945), pp. 198–211, and was reprinted in *Shadow and Act* (New York: Vintage Books, 1964), in which "Twentieth-Century Fiction and the Black Mask of Humanity" and "The World and the Jug" also appeared.

16. Pauline E. Hopkins, *Contending Forces* (1900; Reprint. New York: Oxford University Press, 1988), p. 151. Further references appear parenthetically in the chapter.

17. Hopkins here is referencing the pervasive racist viewpoint of her day that mulattoes were degenerates on the verge of extinction. Many black writers of this period responded to this allegation. For example, Sutton Griggs prompted his readers to question this viewpoint by having a mulatto heroine in his 1899 novel *Imperium in Imperio* commit suicide rather than reproduce other mixed children. See Arlene Elder's *The Hindered Hand: Cultural Implications of Early African-American Fiction* (Westport, Conn.: Greenwood Press, 1978), p. 75, for additional discussion.

Carby also addresses the polemical function of the mulatto character by arguing in *Reconstructing Womanhood* that

> historically the mulatto, as narrative figure, has two functions: as a vehicle for an exploration of the relationship between the races and . . . an expression of the relationship between the races. The figures of the mulatto should be understood and analyzed as a narrative device of mediation. . . . between white privilege and black lack of privilege. . . . In relation to the plot, the mulatta figure allowed for movement between two worlds, white and black, and acted as a literary displacement of the actual increasing separation of the races.

Hazel V. Carby, *Reconstructing Womanhood* (New York: Oxford University Press, 1987), pp. 89–90. The racialist discourse about the degeneration of the mulatto is a part of a larger effort of scientists like Benjamin Disraeli to explain the degeneration of great civilizations. See J. A. V. Chapple, *Science and Literature in the Nineteenth Century* (New York: Macmillan, 1986), pp. 122–24.

18. Although I refer here to Douglass's *Narrative of the Life of Frederick Douglass* (1845; Reprint. Garden City, N.Y.: Doubleday Dolphin, 1963), other prominent slave narratives also written by men seem to have used Douglass's text as a prototype. These include Henry Northrup's *Twelve Years a Slave* (1855; Reprinted in *Puttin' On Ole Massa*, edited by Gilbert Osofsky [New York: Harper and Row, 1969]), Henry Bibb's *Narrative of the Life and Adventures of Henry Bibb, an American Slave* (New York: Self-published, 1849) and William Wells Brown's *Narrative of William Wells Brown, A Fugitive Slave, Written by Himself* (1847; Reprint. Reading, Mass.: Addison-Wesley, 1969). Deborah Gray White surveys the male historiography of slavery and slave narratives in *Ar'n't I a Woman?: Female Slaves in the Plantation South* (New York: Norton, 1985), pp. 62–90. For another discussion of the construction of slave narratives, see William L. Andrews, *To Tell a Free Story: The First Century of Afro-American Autobiography, 1760–1865* (Urbana: University of Illinois Press, 1986), pp. 97–167.

19. This is Fredric Jameson's terminology. See *The Political Unconscious: Narrative as a Socially Symbolic Act* (Ithaca, N.Y.: Cornell University Press, 1981), p. 34. One very prominent discourse of the Western patriarchy depicts the Oedipus complex.

20. Robert B. Stepto, *From Behind the Veil: A Study of Afro-American Narrative* (Urbana: University of Illinois Press, 1979), p. 5. Further references appear parenthetically in the chapter.

21. Deborah McDowell has argued persuasively that Douglass's battle with Covey "serves to incarnate a critical/political view that equates resistance to power"; thus engendering a masculinist protocol of reading that denies black female characters heroic recognition. See Deborah E. McDowell, "In the First Place: Making Frederick Douglass and the Afro-American Narrative Tradition" in *Critical Essays on Frederick Douglass*, edited by William Andrews (New York: G. K. Hall, 1992), p. 205.

22. For a discussion about reading female slave narratives and proving the authenticity of Jacobs's narrative, see respectively Jean Fagan Yellin, "Texts and Contexts of Harriet Jacobs's *Incidents in the Life of a Slave Girl: Written by Herself*" in *The Slave's Narrative*, edited by Charles T. Davis and Henry Louis Gates, Jr. (New York: Oxford University Press, 1985); and Jean Fagan Yellin, "Written by Herself: Harriet Jacobs's Slave Narrative" in *American Literature* 53, 3 (November 1981), pp. 479–86.

23. Victoria Earle Matthews's *The Value of Race Literature: An Address* was delivered at and published by the First Congress of Colored Women of the United States on July 30, 1895 in Boston. Copy catalogued at Howard University's Moorland-Spingarn Research Center and reprinted with an afterward by Fred Miller Robinson in *The Massachusetts Review* 27 (Summer 1986), pp. 169–92. Further references to the original edition appear parenthetically in the chapter.

The call for this First Congress of Colored Women was precipitated by a notorious incident in which an Englishwoman, Florence Galgarnie, the Honorable Secretary of the Anti-Lynching Committee of London, received a letter from Mr. Jno. William Jacks and forwarded it to *The Woman's Era*, the publication of the Woman's Era Club of Boston. The letter alleged that "Out of some 200 [Negroes] in this vicinity it is doubtful if there are a dozen virtuous women or that number who are not daily thieving from the white people." The letter continued in this fashion. The meeting's specific agenda, then, was to address the slanderous attacks on black womanhood and the integrity of the race. Among the titles of papers read at this gathering, including "The Value of Race Literature," were others on racial issues: "Industrial Training," "Individual Work for Moral Training," and "Social Purity." In short, my point is that

Matthews's address was a part of the discourse of racial assertiveness rather than a tangential concern of the black intelligentsia or literary aesthetics.

At the conclusion of the convention, the Congress renamed itself the National Federation of Afro-American Women. It adjourned with the explicit desire to merge with the Washington Colored Women's League. See Wilson J. Moses, *The Golden Age of Black Nationalism* (Hamden, Conn.: Archon Books, 1978), pp. 114–19. Also see Beverly Guy-Sheftall, *Daughters of Sorrow: Attitudes toward Black Women, 1880–1920* (Brooklyn: Carlson Publishing Inc., 1990), pp. 15–28. Particularly interesting in her discussion are the excerpts from Richard T. Greener's account of the convention. Greener was the first black graduate of Harvard College (1870) and a prominent black lawyer in Boston (pp. 27–28).

24. Mrs. N[athan]. F. Mossell, "Life and Literature" in *The A.M.E. Church Review* 14 (January 1898), pp. 318–26.

25. Darwin T. Turner, Introduction to Charles W. Chesnutt's *The House Behind the Cedars* (New York: The Macmillan Company, 1969), p. viii.

26. Frances E. W. Harper, *Iola Leroy; Or, Shadows Uplifted* (1892; Reprint. Boston, Beacon Press, 1987).

27. Henry Louis Gates, Jr., *Signifying Monkey: A Theory of Afro-American Literary Criticism* (New York: Oxford University Press, 1989), p. 113.

28. Daniel Murray, "Bibliography of Negro Literature" in *The A.M.E. Church Review* 16 (July 1900), pp. 24–25.

29. Daniel Murray, "Bibliographia-Africania" in *The Voice of the Negro* III–IV (1906–1907), p. 187. I cannot help but wonder what intellectuals like Murray might have accomplished had they directed their considerable talents to less defensive scholarly enterprises.

30. I thank Vicki Arana for this description.

31. For example, in *Incidents in the Life of a Slave Girl*, Jacobs did not depict literacy and liberation as mutually related states of psychological and physical freedom. Twentieth-century women's slave novels, like *Kindred* by Octavia Butler (Garden City, N.Y.: Doubleday, 1979), *Beloved* by Toni Morrison (New York: Knopf, 1987), and *Dessa Rose* by Sherley Anne Williams (New York: Morrow, 1987), seem to follow Jacobs's lead.

32. Gillian Brown, *Domestic Individualism: Imagining Self in Nineteenth-Century America* (Berkeley: University of California Press, 1990), pp. 39, 45.

33. I am not implying that the male-female opposition is a relatively recent phenomenon. On the contrary, as Teresa de Laurentis explains,

> the picture of the world produced in mythical thought since the very beginning of culture would rest, first and foremost, on what we call biology. . . . In so doing the hero, the mythical subject, is constructed as human being and as male; he is the active principle of culture, the establisher of distinction, the creator of differences. Female is what is not susceptible to transformation, to life or death; she (it) is an element of plot-space, a topos, a resistance, matrix and matter.

Thus the ideological opposition of man as agent and woman as resistance is a classical one. See Teresa de Laurentis, *Alice Does-N'T: Feminism, Semiotics, Cinema* (Bloomington: University of Indiana Press, 1984), p. 119.

34. John A. Bouvier, *A Law Dictionary Adapted to the Constitution and Laws of the U.S.A.*, 3rd ed. (Philadelphia: T. and J. W. Johnson, 1848); 15th ed. (Philadelphia:

J. B. Lippincott, 1883); new ed. rev. Francis Rawle (Boston: Boston Book Co., 1897); and *Judicial and Statutory Definitions of Words and Phrases*, collected, edited, and compiled by members of the editorial staff of the National Reporter System (St. Paul, Minn.: West Publishing Co., 1904–5). Future references to these works appear parenthetically in the chapter.

35. Herbert G. Gutman, *The Black Family in Slavery and Freedom, 1750–1925* (New York: Random House, 1976), p. 275. Further references appear parenthetically in the chapter.

36. Jessie Bernard questioned the presumption of marriage as a free choice among the recently emancipated. She argued that civil and military laws were factors in imposing domestic order on "hundreds of thousands of freeman milling about . . . with equivocal family status" (p. 10). She went on to explain that while many state legislatures legalized slave marriages and military ordinances placed pressure on ex-slaves to adopt the marital practices of the dominant society, both efforts were consistently and severely undermined by two widely shared viewpoints among white people. Many of them believed that either polygamous relationships among black people was the norm or that black people were incapable of maintaining sexual constancy. Bernard observed that, whether largely a matter of personal choice or a choice reinforced by social regulations, the institutionalization of monogamic marriage among freeman "progressed to such an extent that the proportion of Negro infants borne in wedlock [during Reconstruction] rose markedly—so markedly, in fact, that such births became the 'normal' or 'expected thing'" (p. 13). See Jessie Bernard, *Marriage and Family among Negroes* (Englewood Cliffs, N.J.: Prentice-Hall, Inc., 1966).

Bernard provided no statistical evidence or speculation about the proportion of coerced marriages to those of free choice. Moreover, given the fluidity of what she termed an "almost undifferentiated mass [of freemen]," I find it difficult to believe that coerced marriages would have any duration or integrity, thus making it unlikely for them to contribute in any substantial way to the tremendous rise of so-called legitimate births of Negro infants in households with both a mother and a father. E. Franklin Frazier estimates illegitimate births among African Americans during the last decades of the nineteenth century to be between ten and twenty percent. See his *The Negro Family in the United States* (Chicago: University of Chicago Press, 1966), pp. 90–91. This evidence leads me to conclude that these marriages were largely the product of free choice, the argument that Herbert Gutman presents in his *The Black Family in Slavery and Freedom*.

37. I thank Barbara Johnson for calling my attention to the fact that the discourse of bourgeois domesticity forms the basis of the reactionary political rhetoric of many twentieth-century conservative partisan politicians.

38. Nancy Armstrong, *Desire and Domestic Fiction: A Political History of the Novel* (New York: Oxford University Press, 1987). Further references appear parenthetically in the chapter.

39. Jane Tompkins, *Sensational Designs: The Cultural Work of American Fiction 1790–1860* (New York: Oxford University Press, 1987). Further references appear parenthetically in the chapter.

40. In *Reconstructing Womanhood: The Emergence of the Afro-American Woman Novelist*, Hazel Carby clearly delineates these among other missions of her work:

> This book traces ["the dominant domestic ideologies and literary conventions of womanhood"] as they were adopted, adapted, and transformed to effectively represent the material conditions of black women, and explores

> how black women intellectuals reconstructed the sexual ideologies of the
> nineteenth century to produce an alternative discourse of black woman-
> hood. (p. 6)

She goes on to characterize her interpretative model for reading early black women's novels as the product of "understand[ing] not only the discourse and context in which they were produced but also the intellectual forms and practices of black women that preceded them" (pp. 6–7). Thus she places the writings of slave and free women into the context of "political lecturing, the politics of fiction, and a variety of essay, journalistic, and magazine writing" (p. 7).

41. The literary scholar, however, is more disposed to obscuring personal desire behind approbations of aesthetics. The mediation of authorial and scholarly aspirations in literary scholarship is conspicuously competitive; and unless there is affinity of mutual desire between text and scholar, the criticism is likely to be antagonistic, as traditional commentary on *Their Eyes* illustrates.

Chapter 4

1. David Wood Wills, *Aspects of Social Thought in the African Methodist Episcopal Church, 1884–1910*. Unpublished Ph.D. thesis, Harvard University, February 1975, p. 174.

2. Frances E. W. Harper, *Iola Leroy, Or Shadows Uplifted* (1892; Reprint. Boston: Beacon Press, 1987), pp. 262–63. Future references appear parenthetically in the chapter.

3. A[melia]. E. Johnson, *Clarence and Corinne; Or, God's Way* (1890; Reprint. New York: Oxford University Press, 1988); *The Hazeley Family* (1894; Reprint. New York: Oxford University Press, 1988). Further references appear parenthetically in the chapter.

4. Barbara Christian's introduction to *The Hazeley Family*, p. xxxi. Future references to this introduction appear parenthetically in the chapter.

5. See Carroll Smith-Rosenberg, "The New Woman and the New History" in *Feminist Studies* 3 (Fall 1975), pp. 185–98; Anne Firor Scott, "The 'New Woman'" in *The Southern Lady: From the Pedestal to Politics, 1830–1930* (Chicago: University of Chicago Press, 1970); and Peter G. Filene, "The End of the Victorian Era" in *HIM/HER/SELF: Sex Roles in Modern America* (Baltimore: Johns Hopkins University Press, 1986), pp. 18–23.

6. Here I provide a partial composite of two definitions of ideology that cultural anthropologist Clifford Geertz delineates in *The Interpretation of Cultures* (New York: Basic Books, 1973), pp. 196 and 197, respectively. Geertz defines "symbol," and thus "symbolic action," broadly as in "the sense of any physical, social, or cultural act or object that serves as the vehicle for a conception" (p. 206n).

7. I impose James Clifford's discussion of social performance on Geertz's definition of ideology. See James Clifford, "On Ethnographic Allegory" in *Writing Culture: The Poetics and Politics of Ethnography*, edited by James Clifford and George E. Marcus (Berkeley: University of California Press, 1986), p. 98. Future references appear parenthetically in the chapter.

8. This term is from Deborah E. McDowell's forthcoming book—*The Changing Same: Studies in Fiction by Black Women* (Bloomington: University of Indiana Press). I thank her for pointing out the need to resist an unproblematicized reading of political desire and intentionality in these novels. While I contend that their political self-consciousness arose largely from the extremely hostile racial climate of post-Recon-

struction United States, the novels' discursive strategies for effecting liberational resocialization are different and suggest varying degrees of success.

McDowell faces a similar problematic reading in *The Changing Same*. In the context
of her discussion on Kelley-Hawkins and Harper, McDowell writes:

> Lacking a critical vocabulary that could encompass these nineteenth-
> century writers, we have erred outlandishly in trying to fit them into a
> twentieth-century world picture. In our zeal to correct that error, however,
> we have remade these writers into aesthetic ideals and granted them an
> artistic and political self-consciousness that re-homogenizes them, albeit
> favorably so.

9. Fredric Jameson, *The Political Unconscious: Narrative as a Socially Symbolic
Act* (Ithaca, N.Y.: Cornell University Press, 1981), p. 67.

10. Wolfgang Iser, *The Act of Reading: A Theory of Aesthetic Response* (Baltimore:
Johns Hopkins University Press, 1978), p. 30. Iser has explained that

> The intended reader represents a concept of reconstruction, uncovering
> the historical dispositions of the reading public at which the author was
> aiming. . . . It is evident that no theory concerned with literary texts can
> make much headway without bringing in the reader, who now appears to
> have been promoted to the new frame of reference whenever the semantic
> and pragmatic potential of the text comes under scrutiny. The question is,
> what kind of reader? . . . We may call him, for want of a better term, the
> implied reader. He embodies all those predispositions necessary for a liter-
> ary work to exercise its effects—predispositions laid down, not by an
> empirical outside reality, but by the text itself. Consequently, the implied
> reader as a concept has his roots firmly planted in the structure of the
> text; he is a construct and in no way to be identified with any real reader.
> (p. 34)

11. See Hans Robert Jauss, "Literary History as Challenge" in *Toward an Aesthetic
of Reception* (Minneapolis: University of Minnesota Press, 1982).

12. I[rvin]. Garland Penn, *The Afro-American Press, and Its Editors* (Springfield,
Mass.: Willey & Co., 1891), pp. 424–26. Future references to this work appear
parenthetically in the chapter.

13. Hortense J. Spillers, Introduction to *Clarence and Corinne*, p. xxvii. Future
references to this introduction appear parenthetically in the chapter.

Whether to place one's fiction in a black or white social milieu was an especially
complex question for black writers of the late nineteenth and early twentieth century.
Arlene A. Elder refers to Paul Laurence Dunbar to illustrate this point:

> The portrait offered by Dunbar's biographers is that of a young man
> impaled on the horns of the same dilemma that threatened all the early
> African-American writers—whether to work within the cherished tradi-
> tions of the vast white audience or to risk having no audience at all. Sutton
> Griggs, for example, remained virtually unknown because he appealed
> almost exclusively to Black readers. (p. 105)

See Elder's *The Hindered Hand: Cultural Implications of Early African-American Fiction* (Westport, Conn.: Greenwood Press, 1978). Amelia Johnson, Emma Kelley-

Hawkins, and Pauline Hopkins responded to this dilemma by partly or entirely silencing race thematics, which I discuss later in this chapter.

14. By referring to Penn's account of selected reviews of the novel, Spillers explains that Johnson's contemporaries regarded her novel as race literature, that is, as literature committed to subverting racial prejudice despite its racial neutrality.

15. Alice Walker, "If the Present Looks Like the Past, What Does the Future Look Like?" in *In Search of Our Mother's Garden* (New York: Harcourt Brace Jovanovich, 1983), p. 301.

16. All four excerpts come from white newspapers. However, as part of the society that published Johnson's novel, the readers of *The American Baptist* are an example of a targeted, virtually ideal first readership.

17. Peter Brooks, *Reading for the Plot: Design and Intention in Literature* (New York: Vintage, 1985), p. 12. Future references appear parenthetically in the chapter.

18. Audre Lorde, "The Uses of the Erotic" in *Sister Outsider* (Trumansburg, N.Y.: The Crossing Press, 1984), pp. 55, 59. Lorde defines the erotic as "a resource within each of us that lies in a deeply female and spiritual plane" (p. 53). She goes on to indicate the erotic as a particular female characteristic. However, I qualify Lorde's designation so as to suggest that behavior in general and the erotic in particular has been subjected to binary opposition that separates artificially feminine and masculine aspects of human nature. While patriarchal society encourages men and women to repress traits that lie external to their constructed sexual identities, females and males possess both aspects. Future references appear parenthetically in the chapter.

19. This phrase is part of the title of her famous essay: "The Uses of the Erotic: Erotic as Power." See the preceding note.

20. Henry Louis Gates, Jr., "TV's Black World Turns—but Stays Unreal" in the Arts and Leisure section of *The New York Times* (Sunday, November 12, 1989), p. 40.

21. I am grateful to Jennifer Jordan for calling my attention to Pam.

22. I draw on the distinction that Roland Barthes maintains between *representation* and *figuration* in *The Pleasure in the Text* (New York: Hill and Wang, 1975), pp. 57–58.

23. Deborah McDowell's argument about the response of traditional scholars of African-American literature to the works of Jessie Fauset in her essay "The Neglected Dimension of Jessie Redmon Fauset" is applicable here (and I paraphrase and extend her argument), for it reestablished two reading patterns for approaching black women's works. On the one hand, if the works address middle-class ambitions, they are seen as politically naive and simplistic. On the other hand, if the works are seen as fictive counterstereotypes, they are aesthetic failures. In either case, if they are mentioned in the scholarship at all, they become markers on an historical time line between great male master texts. These patterns were so widespread they can be found in virtually any study on black literature published from 1931, when Vernon Loggins's *The Negro Author: His Development in America to 1900* (New York: Columbia University Press) appeared, throughout the 1970s.

McDowell illustrates the application of this pattern to Jessie Fauset's novels. She writes,

> Robert Bone, for example, whose work on the black novel has influenced a number of critics, groups Fauset with the writers he classifies as "the Rear Guard." . . . Unlike the Harlem School, the members of the Rear Guard drew their source material from the Negro middle class in their efforts "to orient Negro art toward white opinion" and "to apprise edu-

cated whites of the existence of respectable Negroes" [*The Negro Novel in America* (New Haven, Conn.: Yale University Press, 1958), pp. 97, 65, respectively]. . . . David Littlejohn likewise makes short shrift of her work, likens her novels to "vapidly genteel lace curtain romances" [*Black on White: A Critical Survey of Writing by American Negroes* (New York: Viking, 1966), pp. 50–51].

See Deborah E. McDowell, "The Neglected Dimension of Jessie Redmon Fauset" in *Conjuring: Black Women, Fiction, and Literary Tradition*, edited by Marjorie Pryse and Hortense J. Spillers (Bloomington: University of Indiana Press, 1985), pp. 86–104.

24. See Susan Winnett's essay "Coming Unstrung: Women, Men, Narrative, and Principles of Pleasure" in *PMLA* 105, 3 (May 1990) in which she interrogates the presumption of male pleasure in theories of narrative.

25. Winnett critiques the masculine pleasure that covertly directs Brooks's discussion of desire in texts. She refers to his narrative theory as "male narratology."

26. I use Ann Ardis's term for describing how the British "New Woman" novelists transcended traditional literary realism in their narratives to envision a world that addressed their desires. While these novelists used this strategy to reject the bourgeois patriarchy, black women novelists of the post-Reconstruction era used a similar one to reject white hegemony and reform the female sphere. See Ann Ardis, *New Women, New Novels: Feminism and Early Modernism* (New Brunswick, N.J.: Rutgers University Press, 1990), p. 3.

27. The context of the discussion for this quotation is an analysis of realism in two Spike Lee films, "School Daze" and "Do the Right Thing." See Wahneema Lubiano, "But Compared to What?" in *Black American Literature Forum* 25, 2 (Summer 1991), p. 262.

28. Wilson J. Moses, "Domestic Feminism, Conservatism, Sex Roles, and Black Women's Clubs, 1893–1896" in *Black Women in United States History*, Vol. 3, edited by Darlene Clark Hine (Brooklyn: Carlson Publishing, Inc., 1990), pp. 963–64. Future references appear parenthetically in the chapter.

29. Professor and Mrs. J[ohn]. W. Gibson, *Golden Thoughts on Chastity and Procreation*, with an Introduction by Dr. Henry R. Bulter (Atlanta: J. L. Nichols and Co., 1903).

30. Dickson D. Bruce, Jr., *Black American Writing From the Nadir* (Baton Rouge: Louisiana State University Press, 1989), p. 32. Future references appear parenthetically in the chapter. The quotation in the passage is from William T. Alexander's *History of the Colored Race in America* (Kansas City, Mo.: Palmetto Publishing Co., 1887; Reprint. New York: Negro Universities Press, 1968), p. 20.

31. For a discussion distinguishing romantic and sentimental love, see William Leach, *True Love and Perfect Union: The Feminist Reform of Sex and Society* (New York: Basic Books, Inc., 1980), pp. 101–12. For a discussion of the relationship between romantic love and narcissism, see Elaine Hoffman Baruch, *Women, Love, and Power: Literary and Psychoanalytic Perspectives* (New York: New York University Press, 1991), p. 88.

32. Jessie Redmon Fauset, *There Is Confusion* (1924; Reprint. Boston: Northeastern University Press, 1989), p. 18. Future references appear parenthetically in the chapter.

33. Emma Dunham Kelley-Hawkins, *Megda* (1891; Reprint. New York: Oxford University Press, 1988). Future references appear parenthetically in the chapter.

34. Charles Chesnutt, *The Marrow of Tradition* (1901; Reprint. Ann Arbor: University of Michigan Press, 1969).

35. The novel is reprinted in *The Works of Katherine Davis Chapman Tillman*, edited by Claudia Tate (1893; Reprint. New York: Oxford University Press, 1991).

36. The coincidence that Beryl is traveling to Tennessee, the state that had overturned integrated railway travel and paved the way to the Supreme Court decision of *Plessy v. Ferguson*, suggests subversive intentionality on Tillman's part.

37. The date of the Emancipation Proclamation was January 1, 1863. If the stranger was seven years old when he was sold from his mother, and he is approximately twenty-seven when the story begins, his birth would have been around 1855. If he hasn't seen her in twenty years, that is, since right before the Emancipation, the story would be set around the mid 1880s.

38. These authors represent those on the reading list of my first undergraduate course on what was then termed "Negro Literature" at the University of Michigan in the fall of 1968, and also on the list of my first graduate-credit course in Afro-American literature at Harvard University in the spring of 1970.

39. For an excellent discussion of the frustrated patriarchal privilege of black men, see Paula Giddings, *When and Where I Enter: The Impact of Black Women on Race and Sex in America* (New York: Morrow, 1984), pp. 58–64.

40. These are the respective expressions of Valerie Smith and Deborah McDowell. Both refer specifically to Frederick Douglass's condemnation of slavery; however, they are equally applicable to writers, like Richard Wright, who experienced racism as the negation of their participation in Western patriarchy. See Valerie Smith, *Self-Discovery and Authority in Afro-American Narrative* (Cambridge, Mass.: Harvard University Press, 1987), p. 20; and Deborah E. McDowell, "In the First Place: Making Frederick Douglass and the Afro-American Narrative Tradition" in *Critical Essays on Frederick Douglass*, edited by William Andrews (New York: G. K. Hall, 1992), p. 200.

41. Kelley-Hawkins's picture, appearing in the frontispiece of *Megda*, presents a woman who would be labeled a light-skinned mulatta by those readers who knew her racial identity. She would probably be called white by those who did not know her racial background. Thus, unlike Molly Hite, I contend that white readers would not have automatically assumed Kelley-Hawkins to be black. See Hite's introduction to *Megda*, p. xxviii. The reviews of Johnson's first novel, *Clarence and Corinne* (which Penn and Scruggs summarize), identify her as black.

42. Paul Laurence Dunbar also wrote several novels featuring the white milieu: *The Uncalled* (1898; Reprint. Westport, Conn.: Negro Universities Press, 1969), *The Love of Landry* (1900; Reprint. Westport, Conn.: Negro Universities Press, 1970), and *The Fanatics* (1901; Reprint. New York: Negro Universities Press, 1971).

43. For claims that early black women's fiction is nonpolitical, see Vernon Loggins, *The Negro Author*, pp. 211, 245–47, and 342–44; Hugh M. Gloster, *Negro Voices in American Fiction* (Chapel Hill: University of North Carolina Press, 1948), pp. 30–31, 33–34, 131–39, and 141–46; Robert A. Bone, *The Negro Novel in America*, pp. 31–32 and 101–6.

44. Bell Hooks, *Ain't I a Woman: Black Women and Feminism* (Boston: South End Press, 1981), p. 138.

45. Robert C. Toll, *Blacking Up: The Minstrel Show in Nineteenth-Century America* (New York: Oxford University Press, 1974), pp. 68–69.

46. While I suggest that there are other aspects about Jem that encode race, Barbara Christian notes Jem's name as "provid[ing] the only hint of blackness in the novel." See Christian's introduction to *The Hazeley Family*, p. xxxvi.

47. See Deborah E. McDowell's introduction to *Four Girls at Cottage City* (1898; Reprint. New York: Oxford University Press, 1988), p. xxviii.

48. This characteristic is reminiscent of the bushy hair in *Clarence and Corinne*, a subject often given literary attention in black women's writing. See for example Katherine Tillman's "When Mandy Combs Her Head" in *The Works of Katherine Davis Chapman Tillman* and Ntozake Shange's, *Nappy Edges* (New York: St. Martin's Press, 1978).

49. Paul Smith, *Discerning the Subject* (Minneapolis: University of Minnesota Press, 1988), pp. xxx–xxxi. Future references appear parenthetically in the chapter.

50. See Wills's *Aspects of Social Thought* (p. 176) for a discussion of *The A.M.E. Church Review* articles about advice on "how the wife could communicate her troubles to her husband without offending him with her unpleasantness."

Chapter 5

1. Surveys of real-life black exemplars published during the 1890s and at the turn of the century appeared in works like I[rvin]. Garland Penn's *The Negro Press and Its Editors* (1891), William Simmon's *Men of Mark* (1887), Monroe A. Majors's *Noted Negro Women* (1893), Lewis A. Scruggs's *Women of Distinction* (1893), *The A.M.E. Church Review* (1884–1916), and *The Colored American* magazine, (1900–1910).

2. Ellen K. Rothman, *Hands and Hearts: A History of Courtship in America* (Cambridge, Mass.: Harvard University Press, 1987), pp. 186–91.

3. Frances E. W. Harper, *Iola Leroy, Or Shadows Uplifted* (1892; Reprint. Boston: Beacon Press, 1987), p. 266. Future references appear parenthetically in the chapter.

4. A[melia]. E. Johnson, *The Hazeley Family* (1894; Reprint. New York: Oxford University Press, 1988), p. 189. Future references appear parenthetically in the chapter.

5. Katherine Davis Chapman Tillman, *Beryl Weston's Ambition: The Story of an Afro-American Girl's Life* (1893; Reprint. New York: Oxford University Press, 1991), p. 245. Future references appear parenthetically in the chapter.

6. Susan Winnett, "Coming Unstrung: Women, Men, Narrative, and Principles of Pleasure" in *PMLA* 105, 3 (May 1990), p. 512. Future references appear parenthetically in the chapter.

7. While many historical studies draw a distinct line between the racial conservatism of Washington and the militancy of Du Bois, the positions of these two during the 1890s were probably not that categorically distinct. For example, Washington's "Atlanta Compromise" address, as historian Wilson J. Moses contends, was "fairly liberal" when measured against the general attitudes of the black bourgeoisie of the day. Moses explains that the "speech was a masterpiece of double talk and did not involve—as Washington himself reminded Edna D. Cheney [a Bostonian liberal]—the renunciation of any of the Afro-American's rights. Nor does the speech seem conservative," Moses adds, "when compared to the position of the American Negro Academy in whose bosoms the Talented Tenth philosophy first quickened." See Moses's *The Golden Age of Black Nationalism* (Hamden, Conn.: Archon Books, 1978), pp. 123–25.

8. Frederick Douglass, *Narrative in the Life of Frederick Douglass* (1845; Reprint. Garden City, N.Y.: Doubleday Dolphin, 1963), p. 122.

9. Booker T. Washington, *Up from Slavery* in *Three Negro Classics* (1901; Reprint. New York: Avon Books, 1965). Further references appear parenthetically in the chapter.

10. Gillian Brown, *Domestic Individualism: Imagining Self in Nineteenth-Century America* (Berkeley: University of California Press, 1990), p. 4.

11. Another instance in which political meaning is invested in a domestic situation concerns the famous incident in which President Theodore Roosevelt invited Booker T. Washington to dinner. See Joel Williamson, *The Crucible of Race: Black-White Relations in The American South since Emancipation* (New York: Oxford University Press, 1984), pp. 350–51.

12. William E. B. Du Bois, *The Souls of Black Folk* in *Three Negro Classics* (1903; Reprint. New York: Avon Books, 1965), p. 219.

13. Du Bois's feminized denigration of masculine authority seems an early example of the discourse of black male emasculation that became prominent in the racial discourse of the twentieth century. In addition, the equation between the lack of political authority and emasculation explains why male self-assertion becomes more readily eroticized than politicized, producing "macho" power instead of civil power.

14. Pauline E. Hopkins, *Contending Forces: A Romance Illustrative of Negro Life North and South* (1900; Reprint. New York: Oxford University Press, 1988), pp. 244–45. Future references appear parenthetically in the chapter.

15. Other black women writers who explicitly addressed the politicization of black womanhood include Josephine Turpin Washington, Rosetta D. Sprague, Mary Church Terrell, and Rosa D. Bowser. For example see Washington's introduction to *Women of Distinction: Remarkable in Works and Invincible in Character* by Lewis Arthur Scruggs (Raleigh, N.C.: by the author, 1893). Sprague, Terrell, and Bowser engage in a literary dialogue in answer to the question, "What Role Is the Educated Negro Woman to Play in the Uplifting of Her Race?," solicited by D[aniel]. W. Culp for his edited volume *Twentieth-Century Negro Literature; or A Cyclopedia of Thought on the Vital Topics Relating to the American Negro* (Toronto: J. L. Nichols & Co., 1902).

16. See Anna J. Cooper, *A Voice From the South* (1892; Reprint. New York: Oxford University Press, 1988) and Mrs. N. F. Mossell, *The Work of the Afro-American Woman* (1894; Reprint. New York: Oxford University Press, 1988).

Another important "race woman" was Ida B. Wells-Barnett. Almost singlehandedly she launched a national campaign against lynching. See Hazel V. Carby's *Reconstructing Womanhood: The Emergence of the Afro-American Novelist* (New York: Oxford University Press, 1987), pp. 3–19. Also see Wells (-Barnett)'s *The Reason Why: The Colored American Is Not in the World's Columbian Exposition* (1893: Reprinted in *Selected Works of Ida B. Wells-Barnett*, compiled by Trudier Harris [New York: Oxford University Press, 1991]) for her analysis of the racial politics of her era.

17. Joanne M. Braxton, Introduction to *The Work of the Afro-American Woman* by Mrs. N. F. Mossell, p. xxviii.

18. Victoria Earle (Matthews) published *Aunt Lindy: A Story Founded on Real Life* in *The A.M.E. Church Review 5* (January 1889), pp. 246–50. It was reissued as a single work in 1893 by J. J. Little & Company, Astor Place, New York City.

19. *Expressive culture* is a term that Houston A. Baker, Jr., coins in *Blues, Ideology, and Afro-American Literature: A Vernacular Theory* (Chicago: University of Chicago Press, 1984).

20. Frances Harper was the other woman whom Cooper referenced in this passage.

21. In instances like this one, Cooper's use of the word *man* and its derivatives is generic and not gender specific, as it was soon to become in most social exchange; for example, the previous excerpt from Du Bois's writing illustrates such specificity.

22. Another instance of Cooper's use of the generic masculine.

23. Here I refer to Hazel Carby's argument about the political engagement of particularly black women writers of the post-Reconstruction era who used their writing to engender social reform. See Carby, *Reconstructing Womanhood*, pp. 6–7.

24. Katherine Tillman, for example, makes explicit reference to the new woman in her Sunday School drama *Fifty Years of Freedom* (1910). For a discussion of the new (white) woman see Anne Firor Scott's "The 'New Woman'" in her *The Southern Lady: From Pedestal to Politics, 1830–1930* (Chicago: University of Chicago Press, 1970), pp. 212–33 and her "What, Then, Is the American: This New Woman?" in *Journal of American History* 65 (December 1978), pp. 679–703; Peter G. Filene, *HIM/HER/ SELF: Sex Roles in Modern America* (Baltimore: Johns Hopkins University Press, 1986), pp. 18–46; Carrol Smith-Rosenberg, "The New Woman and the New History" in *Feminist Studies* 3 (Fall 1975), pp. 185–98.

25. Following is a summary of the antebellum gender argument that is elaborated upon in the Introduction. Although West African societies, from which the slaves were kidnapped, were gendered societies, slavery eroded their indigenous gender constructions by removing sex-role distinctions. Female slaves, like their male counterparts, worked in the fields and in the house, performed difficult physical as well as less strenuous tasks. Hence the institution of slavery did not support consistent gender constructions for New World Africans in general and female Africans in particular.

26. Nancy Armstrong, *Desire and Domestic Fiction: A Political History of the Novel* (New York: Oxford University Press, 1987). Future references appear parenthetically in the chapter.

27. Charles W. Chesnutt, *The House Behind the Cedars* (1901; Reprint. Macmillan, 1969), p. 250.

28. Harriet A. Jacobs, *Incidents in the Life of a Slave Girl* (1861; Reprint. Cambridge, Mass.: Harvard University Press, 1987 [Jean Fagan Yellin, Ed.]), pp. 196–97. Future references appear parenthetically in the chapter.

29. David Wood Wills, *Aspects of Social Thought in the African Methodist Episcopal Church, 1884–1910*. Unpublished Ph.D. thesis, Harvard University, February 1975, p. 3.

30. *The Oxford English Dictionary*, 2nd ed., prepared by J. A. Simpson and E. S. C. Weiner (London: Clarendon Press, 1989) designates the nineteenth century as the period for coining the popular expressions "to spend the honeymoon," "honeymooners," and "honeymooning" (Vol. 7, p. 354).

31. See Carby's discussion on rethinking black historiography of the late nineteenth century, which foregrounds her discussion of black female activism, in "Woman's Era" in *Reconstructing Womanhood*, pp. 3–19.

32. Nancy Armstrong and Leonard Tennenhouse, Eds., *The Ideology of Conduct: Essays on Literature in the History of Sexuality* (New York: Methuen, 1986).

33. Wells signed her columns "Iola." See Bettina Aptheker, *Woman's Legacy: Essays on Race, Sex, and Class in American History* (Amherst: University of Massachusetts Press, 1981), p. 68. Also see Giddings, *When and Where I Enter: The Impact of Black Women on Race and Sex in America* (New York: Morrow, 1984), pp. 24, 30.

34. See William L. Andrews, *Sisters of the Spirit: Three Black Women's Autobiographies of the Nineteenth Century* (Bloomington: University of Indiana Press, 1986), pp. 16–22.

35. May Miller Sullivan, who graduated from Howard University in 1920, corroborates this policy. According to her, female instructors were to notify the Board of Education of impending marriage plans. If they did not retire from teaching voluntarily immediately after marriage, they were compelled to do so (interview on January 19, 1989, at Miller Sullivan's home in Washington, D.C.). Also see Louise Daniel Hutchinson, *Anna Cooper: A Voice From the South* (Washington, D.C.: Smithsonian Institution, 1981), p. 49. Here she writes that until 1923 married women were required by law to retire from teaching. As a result a large "spinster" teacher population arose. In

1890–91, for example, the District of Columbia employed 265 black teachers, 225 of whom were female.

36. Elizabeth Ammons argues that Harper's "*Iola Leroy* is a parable about surviving rape" (p. 31), contending that Harper speaks in reticent code to communicate Iola's having suffered the sexual abuse—rape—that typified the condition of enslaved women. While Ammons's reading is credible, especially given the routine sexual abuse of young bondwomen and Iola's circulation among several owners, I would have been more convinced if, in addition to referring to the general dialect coding that appears on the opening pages of the novel, Ammons had cited specific textual evidence or implications of Iola's violated sexual condition. See Elizabeth Ammons, *Conflicting Stories: American Women Writers at the Turn into the Twentieth Century* (New York: Oxford University Press, 1991), pp. 310–31. Hazel Carby presents such evidence in a provocative close textual reading of rape in the whipping scene of Grace Montfort in *Contending Forces*. See her *Reconstructing Womanhood*, p. 132.

37. Ammons similarly argues in *Conflicting Stories* that *Contending Forces* is a fable about a woman's will to survive rape. Ammons presents this interpretation in the context of Sappho as a black woman in hiding, and as a writer who "has been brutally silenced by the systematic exercise of white sexual terrorism" (p. 80). Ammons's selection of novels is unified around the identifies of the central female figures as women artists. While it is possible to regard the creation of self as an artistic enterprise, I read such plots of female self-development within a political context of self-authority instead.

38. This is the term that Yellin uses in her introduction to the Harvard edition of Harriet A. Jacobs's *Incidents in the Life of a Slave Girl*, p. xxxi.

39. Sappho was an early classical author and the most famous colonist of the isle of Lesbos during the sixth century B.C. She was reputed by her contemporaries to have been a greater poet than Homer and was called the Tenth Muse. However, her work was scorned because of her homosexuality, and by the eighth century A.D. only fragments of her large corpus of poetry survived early Christian book burning. See Barbara W. Walker, Ed., *The Woman's Encyclopedia of Myths and Secrets* (New York: Harper and Row, 1983), pp. 535–36, 890.

Chapter 6

1. No doubt Hopkins was responding to the patriarchal argument against the higher education of women that was based on the increased celibacy among white women who graduated from private colleges like Smith, Wellesley, and Mount Holyoke and at public university systems like the Universities of Michigan at the turn of the century.

2. See note 35 in Chapter 5 about the teaching restrictions placed on married women whose husbands were alive.

3. Willard B. Gatewood, *The Aristocrats of Color: The Black Elite 1880–1920* (Bloomington: University of Indiana Press, 1990), p. 191. Future references appear parenthetically in the chapter.

4. In *When and Where I Enter: The Impact of Black Women on Race and Sex in America* (New York: Morrow, 1984), Paula Giddings characterizes Wells-Barnett's response to such criticism:

> [M]en often criticized women who took the initiative, as Ida Wells-Barnett discovered. The now familiar accusation of Black women "emasculating"

Black men also discouraged her from going to the scene of a lynching in 1909. "I had been accused," she wrote, "by some of our men of jumping ahead of them and doing work without giving them a chance." (pp. 117–18)

Mary Helen Washington further comments on the presumption of male privilege at the turn of the century. In her excellent introduction to the Oxford edition of Anna Cooper's *A Voice From the South* (1892; Reprint. New York: Oxford University Press, 1988) and in Part II of Washington's *Invented Lives* (New York: Anchor, 1987), she describes the intellectual sexism of Hopkins's black male contemporaries, an attitude that was not restricted to men. Further references to *A Voice From the South* appear parenthetically in the chapter.

5. The topic of higher education for women circulated widely at virtually all levels of black society. One such exchange appeared in *Twentieth Century Negro Literature* (Toronto: J. L. Nichols & Co., 1902 [D[aniel]. W. Culp, Ed.]). Five prominent black women addressed the question: "What Role Is the Educated Negro Woman to Play in the Uplifting of Her Race?" The women were Mary B. Talbert (the former assistant principal of Little Rock, Arkansas, High School), Rosetta Douglass Sprague (Frederick Douglass's daughter), Mary Church Terrell (the first president of the National Association of Colored Women), Rosa D. Bowser (member of the Executive Board of the Southern Federation of Colored Women and Chairman of the Standing Committee of Domestic Economy for the Hampton Conference, among other activist organizations), and Sarah Dudley Pettey (general secretary of the Woman's Home and Foreign Missionary Society of the A.M.E. Zion Church). Each woman was married and signed her paper with the title "Mrs.," probably to demonstrate that higher education had not distracted her from the home, which Talbert defined as the "greatest field for effective work" of "the educated Negro woman" (p. 170).

6. Josephine Turpin Washington, Introduction to *Women of Distinction: Remarkable in Works and Invincible in Character*, Lewis Arthur Scruggs, Ed. (Raleigh, N.C.: Self-published, 1893), p. xi. Future references appear parenthetically in the chapter.

7. Linda M. Perkins, "The Impact of the 'Cult of True Womanhood' on the Education of Black Women" in *The Journal of Social Issues* 39, 3 (1983), pp. 17–28. Even though antebellum black people shared the desire for educational advancement, by 1863 "every southern state had laws that prohibited the education of slaves, and in many instances free blacks as well" (p. 19). Perkins further explains that the "decades of the 1830s and 1840s in which free blacks sought access to educational institutions in the North paralleled the founding of seminaries for white women" (p. 19).

8. Eric Foner, *Reconstruction: America's Unfinished Revolution, 1863–1877* (New York: Harper & Row, 1988), p. 96. Foner also cites a report from a Mississippi Freemen's Bureau agent to illustrate the intensity of their passion for education. The agent recounts that in 1865 "when he informed a gathering of 3,000 freedmen that they were to have the advantages of schools and education, their joy knew no bounds. They fairly jumped and shouted in gladness" (p. 96). Lest we regard the term *freedmen* as sex specific rather than generic, Foner chronicles similar desire among black women. He reports, for example, that "a Northern correspondent in 1873 found adults as well as children crowding Vicksburg schools and . . . that 'female negro-servants make it a condition before accepting a situation, that they should have permission to attend the night-schools'" (p. 366).

Linda Perkins cites another interesting example that illustrates the nonspecificity of gender in the support of intraracial higher education, concerning Fanny Jackson Coppin. In 1860 she received a scholarship from the A.M.E. Church, under the auspices of Bishop Daniel Payne, to attend Oberlin College (which in 1833 admitted both women and blacks on an equal basis with white men). Perkins argues that

> This financial assistance is not insignificant when one remembers that when Fanny Jackson Coppin entered Oberlin in 1860, no black women in the nation had a college degree and very few black men attempted higher education. Bishop Payne's enthusiasm and support for Coppin's education contrasts with the debates on the danger of higher education that surrounded the question of education for white women [and I add would make problematic the higher education of black women at the close of the nineteenth century].

See Perkins, "The Impact of the 'Cult of True Womanhood' on the Education of Black Women," p. 20.

9. For an excellent discussion of conservative and liberal gender attitudes among African Americans (especially males), focused on black women's access to the public domains of voting, preaching, and teaching, see Beverly Guy-Sheftall, "Books, Brooms, Bibles, and Ballots: Black Women and the Public Sphere" in *Daughters of Sorrow: Attitudes toward Black Women, 1880–1920* (Brooklyn: Carlson Publishing, Inc., 1990), pp. 91–159.

10. Perkins explains that by 1890 there were only 30 black women with baccalaureate degrees, while over 300 black men and 2,500 white women held that degree. In addition, the employment opportunities for educated black men were greater than those for their female counterparts. See Perkins, "The Impact of the 'Cult of True Womanhood,'" p. 23.

The two basic questions regarding the appropriateness of higher education circulated in black society as well: whether higher education distracts a woman's attention from her domestic expectation and duties and whether the intellectual concentration needed to acquire that education imperils "the physical force requisite for motherhood" (*Golden Thoughts*, p. 79). *Golden Thoughts* promoted equality in education for men and women, and it also refuted the alleged physiological and social restrictions obstructing women's access to higher education. See Professor and Mrs. Gibson, *Golden Thoughts On Chastity and Procreation* (Atlanta: J. L. Nichols and Co., 1903), pp. 78–83.

11. Mrs. N. F. Mossell, *The Work of the Afro-American Woman* (1894; Reprint. New York: Oxford University Press, 1988), pp. 9–10. Future references appear parenthetically in the chapter.

12. Blanche Glassman Hersh, *The Slavery of Sex: Feminist-Abolitionists in America* (Urbana: University of Illinois Press, 1978), pp. 3, 157.

13. Fannie Jackson Coppin, the first black woman to receive a college degree, headed the oldest black private high school in the nation from 1869 to 1901. After she was forced to retire, the school had black male leadership. Mary Jane Patterson, who was Coppin's assistant principal from 1865 to 1869, was appointed principal of M Street School in 1869. She was removed several years later, according to Perkins, so that a black man could head the institution. Cooper served as principal of the M Street School from 1901 to 1906. When she was replaced for "her refusal to adhere to the inferior curriculum prescribed for black students," the school was thereafter headed by a black man. See Perkins, "The Impact of the 'Cult of True Womanhood,'" pp. 24–25.

14. For detail on this biographical episode see Hutchinson, *Anna J. Cooper: A Voice From the South* (Washington, D.C.: Smithsonian Institution, 1981), p. 22.

15. For a biography of Julia Ringwood Coston, see Lewis Arthur Scruggs's *Women of Distinction* (Raleigh, N.C.: Self-published, 1893), pp. 141–43, and Monroe A. Majors's *Noted Negro Women: Their Triumphs and Activities* (1893; Reprint. Nashville, Tenn.: Fisk University Library Negro Collection, 1971), pp. 251–58. Future references to both of these works appear parenthetically in the chapter.

16. Ella Wright-Pleasant, "Beautiful Woman!" in *The A.M.E. Church Review* 16 (October 1900), pp. 171–72.

17. See note 25 in Chapter 2.

18. Jacqueline Jones explains in *Labor of Love, Labor of Sorrow: Black Women, Work, and the Family from Slavery to the Present* (New York: Basic Books, 1985), "Imbalance of sex-ratio in favor of females [characterized] . . . the black population in southern cities" and towns during the late nineteenth century (pp. 113, 96). For although the ideal expectation for young black women was marriage, the disproportionately large black female population in the South seems to have required parents to regard the aspirations for their sons and daughters differently by the first decades of the twentieth century (p. 96). Jones explains that black girls usually attended normal school in larger numbers than boys, and girls remained in school longer (p. 96). Without some education the vast numbers of black women for whom there were no husbands, given the demography, were consigned to domestic service and laundry work. Washing clothes on a scrub board was backbreaking work for which black women received starvation wages, and domestic work was even worse because not only did it pay pitifully low salaries but those so employed were frequently sexually compromised by the white males of the household in which they worked. Herbert Gutman also maintains in *The Black Family in Slavery and Freedom 1750–1925* (New York: Random House, 1977) that the same demography generally prevailed in the North, as "[a]dult [black] women significantly outnumbered adult men" (p. 450).

19. Pauline E. Hopkins, *Contending Forces: A Romance Illustrative of Negro Life North and South* (1900; Reprint. New York: Oxford University Press, 1988). Both *Contending Forces* and *Iola Leroy, or Shadow Uplifted* (1892; Reprint. New York: Oxford University Press, 1988) revise the conventions of sentimental fiction in order to produce a fiction of racial protest in which idealized black characters conflate their moral outrage against racial prejudice with the author's direct social commentary. Also like *Iola Leroy*, *Contending Forces* depicts romantic love not as exalted passion or as expressions of amorous platitudes, as the term *sentimental* implies to traditional scholars, but as the lovers' mutual commitment to dedicating their lives to working for racial advancement. Marriage arises, in both texts, from emotional integrity and not from a woman's need to secure her social or economic security. Hence both novels validate gainful employment for women as a means for developing personal autonomy, moral fiber, and economic solvency, as well as for promoting a greater possibility for their matrimonial happiness. However, neither text moves the heroine's racial or personal ambitions beyond the threshold of marriage to depict their effects on their personal lives and communities. By entitling Iola's speech the "Education of Mothers," Harper carefully places educated womanhood within the confines of marriage and motherhood. Ultimately, these novels make their advocacy of female autonomy less controversial by giving expression to unrealized desire. For a very perceptive discussion of *Iola Leroy* and *Contending Forces*, see Mary Helen Washington's *Invented Lives*, pp. 74–86.

Here she refers to specific instances of racial antagonism and patriarchal presumption that surface in Hopkins's short stories but that are suppressed in *Contending Forces*.

20. Hazel V. Carby, *Reconstructing Womanhood* (New York: Oxford University Press, 1987), p. 142.

21. I would add the industrial world as well, for black people were denied employment in all but menial jobs.

22. Here Hopkins specifically dramatized the debates on contemporaneous social issues—industrial versus academic education, the epidemic of lynchings and rapes, and the necessity for black men to claim their voting rights as the most effective means of fighting racism—as masculine activities.

23. Iola Leroy is the only heroine of these eleven novels who speaks at a mixed meeting of social uplift. I suggest that Hopkins here, as most of her sister writers would also, attempted to assuage the growing conservatism of black gender prescriptions that are characterized in the first part of this chapter.

24. Carby mounts a similar argument, pointing out what I earlier termed "frustrated patriarchal desire" in writings by contemporaneous black males. She writes that

> The most significant absence of social forces through which Hopkins delineated her characters was the black fathers. The father was a narrative figure who mediated patriarchal control over women. In Hopkins's text, as in most by nineteenth-century black women, patriarchal control was exercised and mediated through the figures of white men who denied political, social, and economic patriarchal power to black men. [The absence of the Smith father] thus confirmed the denial of patriarchal power to black men, but in this space Hopkins created alternative figures of black men constructed in peer relations, as brothers or as potential partner/ husbands. . . . *Contending Forces* posed but did not explore the possibility of utopian relations between men and women.

See *Reconstructing Womanhood*, p. 143.

25. Mrs. Willis's character portrait is somewhat evocative of Josephine St. Pierre Ruffin. Lewis Scruggs writes in *Women of Distinction*, "Since the death of her husband Mrs. Ruffin has been more than ever active in the charities and philanthropies which fill so large a place in the life of the true Boston Woman" (p. 147). Ruffin was very active in the women's clubs movement until she was denied admission to the General Federation of Women's Clubs convention in Milwaukee in 1889, while serving as a delegate. She founded the Woman's Era Club of Boston in 1894. In July of 1895 she organized the First National Conference of Colored Women of America, at which Victoria Earle Matthews presented the address, "The Value of Race Literature." The Conference gave rise to the founding of the National Federation of Afro-American Women with Ruffin as president, which in 1896 merged with the Washington-based National Colored Women's League to form the National Association of Colored Women's Clubs of America with Mary Church Terrell as president. See Cynthia Neverdon-Morton, "Developing a National Organization of Afro-American Women" in *Afro-American Women of the South and the Advancement of the Race, 1895–1925* (Knoxville: University of Tennessee Press, 1989).

26. Here too Hopkins seems to have sanctioned the viewpoint, summarized in the first part of this chapter, that males deserve primary consideration in opportunities for higher education.

27. Mrs. Willis evokes the image of the caricatured (inauthentic) "progressive

woman" that Josephine Turpin Washington identified in her introduction to *Women of Distinction* by Lewis A. Scruggs.

28. In his excellent introduction to the Schomburg Library volume of *Contending Forces* (New York: Oxford University Press, 1988), pp. xxxii–xxxiii, Richard Yarborough briefly refers to the allegation that black women were unchaste, whose refutation is the subtext of that novel. Yarborough refers to the responses that this allegation drew from Nannie H. Burroughs, Josephine Silone-Yates, Mary Church Terrell, and Fannie Barrier Williams in addition to Hopkins, who termed it "a most malicious slander, and outrage against a worthy class of citizens." He also explains that refuting this charge gave rise in 1895 to the formation of the National Federation of Afro-American Women in Boston. For more discussion on its formation see note 23 in Chapter 3.

Carby places this allegation into an imperial discourse in which she draws parallels between the prevalence of rape of black women and the oppression of female slaves. She explains that Hopkins concentrated on presenting the history of "the black female body as colonized by white male power and practices. . . . The link between economic/political power and economic/sexual power was firmly established in the battle for control over women's bodies." See *Reconstructing Womanhood*, p. 144.

29. Mrs. Willis's remarks become particularly meaningful when placed in the context of Alexander Crummell's promotion of Victorian morality on the grounds that "in West Africa, every female is a virgin to the day of her marriage," and that "the harlot class is unknown in all their tribes." Crummell was the first president of the American Negro Academy and a principal influence on the career of Du Bois. See Wilson J. Moses, *The Golden Age of Black Nationalism* (Hamden, Conn.: Archon Books, 1978), p. 140.

30. Fredric Jameson, *The Political Unconscious: Narrative as a Socially Symbolic Act* (Ithaca, N.Y.: Cornell University Press, 1981), p. 10.

31. Yarborough also notes Hopkins's ambivalence toward Mrs. Willis. He writes,

> obviously attracted to this woman's strength of mind and forthright feminism, Hopkins seems somewhat unsettled, however, by the extraordinary extent of Willis's driving ambition. . . . Like Sappho, Hopkins never resolves her feelings toward Willis, a powerful figure who captures the author's imagination to a greater extent than her small role in the novel might indicate.

See Richard Yarborough's introduction to the Oxford edition of *Contending Forces*, p. xl. Further references to this introduction appear parenthetically in the chapter.

32. Bakhtin discusses the plasticity of the novel in "Epic and Novel" in *The Dialogic Imagination* (Austin: University of Texas Press, 1981), pp. 7–8. For a discussion of Bakhtin's theory on the plasticity of the novel in which the genre both asserts and subverts the traditional marriage, see also Joseph Allen Boone, *Tradition Counter Tradition: Love and the Form of Fiction* (Chicago: University of Chicago Press, 1987).

33. We should not underestimate the significance of this opportunity for married women. As the writers discussed in the first part of this chapter emphatically explain, black gender rites severely restricted the activity of married women to the home.

34. Ellen K. Rothman, *Hands and Hearts: A History of Courtship in America* (Cambridge, Mass.: Harvard University Press, 1987), p. 107.

35. Karen Lystra, *Searching the Heart: Women, Men, and Romantic Love in Nineteenth-Century America* (New York: Oxford University Press, 1989), p. 42.

36. For an excellent discussion of black people's rebuttal to white society's allegation of excessive black sexuality, see Chapters 4 and 5 ("Defending Our Name" and "To Be a Woman, Sublime") in *When and Where I Enter* by Paula Giddings.

37. Frances E. W. Harper, *Iola Leroy* (1892; Reprint. Boston: Beacon Press, 1988), p. 266.

38. Emma Kelley-Hawkins, *Megda* (1891; Reprint. New York: Oxford University Press, 1988), pp. 370–71.

39. Katherine Davis Chapman Tillman, *Beryl Weston's Ambition* (1893; Reprint. New York: Oxford University Press, 1991), p. 232.

40. Mrs. A. E. Johnson, *Clarence and Corinne* (1890) and *The Hazeley Family* (1894) (both Reprint. New York: Oxford University Press, 1988). Quotation is from page 182 in *The Hazeley Family*. Future references appear parenthetically in the chapter.

41. Due to the fact that male privilege in black culture was not an absolutely empowering masculine discourse, courtships and marriages of sibling affinity more successfully implied a blurring of gender distinctions, thus suggesting relative gender equality, in black texts than in corresponding white texts.

Sibling affinity was a prevalent fictive discourse in the nineteenth century, as Joseph Allen Boone explains in *Tradition Counter Tradition*, his study of three centuries of British and Anglo-American marriage or domestic novels. He explains that "the ideal of falling in love with one's 'duplicate' image, rather than with a 'contrast,' was an increasingly familiar part of the discourse of nineteenth-century romantic ideology . . . " (p. 11). While "likeness" included "moral affinity, spiritual harmony, mental compatibility," it did not include gender (p. 11).

42. Steven Mintz and Susan Kellogg, *Domestic Revolutions: A Social History of American Family Life* (New York: The Free Press, 1988), p. 117.

43. While the phrase *compassionate marriage* does not appear in popular currency until 1925, the ideology making that term appropriate moved into social exchange at the turn of the century. See Mintz and Kellogg, *Domestic Revolutions*, pp. 114–15.

44. In the 1890s companionate marriage revised the Victorian model arising from compassion and duty. As Steven Seidman explains,

> A new type of marriage was evolving that highlighted love and companionship as the principal conjugal bond. Furthermore, love was thought to be anchored in mutual sexual attraction and gratification. Sex was not merely a sign of love but its origin, underpinning and essential ingredient.

See Seidman's *Romantic Longings: Love in America, 1839–1980* (New York: Routledge, 1991), p. 73.

45. Leonard I. Sweet, Ed., *The Evangelical Tradition in America* (Macon, Ga.: Mercer University Press, 1984), p. 59.

46. Lydia Maria Child, *The Mother's Book* (1831; Reprint. New York: Arno Press, 1969), p. 91. Future references appear parenthetically in the chapter.

47. The works that turn-of-the-century black activists promoted were those that emphasized exemplary moral behavior; they severely denounced what *Golden Thoughts* designates as "romance-reading," namely those works that not only create "false and unreal ideas of life," but that give "descriptions of love-scenes, of thrilling, romantic episodes which find echo in the girl's [and boy's] physical system and tend to create an abnormal excitement of her [or his] organs of sex, which she recognizes only as a pleasurable emotion, with no comprehension of the physical origin of the evil effects" (Gibson, p. 94).

48. Katherine D. Tillman, *Clancy Street* (1898; Reprint. New York: Oxford University Press, 1991), p. 256. Future references appear parenthetically in the chapter.

49. These are titles of actual serials of the period.

50. See Deborah McDowell's excellent introduction to *Four Girls at Cottage City* (Reprint. New York: Oxford University Press, 1988), pp. xxxiii–xxxiv.

51. During the nineteenth century, converted women seized moral and spiritual authority as divinely appointed messengers to address an ever broadening range of social problems—abolition of slavery, temperance, suffrage, and settlement work—as well as to define themselves. The powerful force of evangelicalism also charged women's domestic fictions with additional social power as their heroines relied on spiritual validation to reform their own lives, those of family members, of friends, and ultimately of the community at large. By the middle of the nineteenth century religious enthusiasm, as historian Nancy A. Hewitt explains, became a "powerful force in many women's lives and, for a few, provided the impetus to demand fundamental social change" and enabled some of them "in the face of male censure and social restrictions . . . to formulate and maintain a female-oriented social critique and a feminist politics." See Nancy A. Hewitt, "The Perimeters of Women's Power in American Religion" in *The Evangelical Tradition in America* (Macon, Ga.: Mercer University Press, 1984), p. 256.

52. Dana Nelson Salvino, "The Word in Black and White: Ideologies of Race and Literacy in Antebellum America" in *Reading in America: Literature and Social History*, edited by Cathy N. Davidson (Baltimore: Johns Hopkins University Press, 1989), p. 143.

53. Her new name references the famous classical poet Sappho, who lived on the isle of Lesbos during the sixth century B.C. Sappho was reputed by her contemporaries to have been greater than Homer and was called the Tenth Muse. However, her work was scorned because of her homosexuality, and by the eighth century only fragments of her large corpus of poetry survived early Christian book burning. See Barbara G. Walker, Ed., *The Woman's Encyclopedia of Myths and Secrets* (New York: Harper and Row, 1983), pp. 535–36, 890. Also see Elizabeth Ammons's *Conflicting Stories: American Women Writers at the Turn into the Twentieth Century* (New York: Oxford University Press, 1991), pp. 79–80, for an excellent discussion of Sappho's assertion of self-definition.

54. Hopkins's *Hagar's Daughter*, in which the heroine is unknowingly passing for white, dramatizes a courtship in passionate ardor probably because the presumably white heroine does not have to bear the burden of stereotyped excessive sexuality. Although this courtship is consummated in marriage, the marriage is annulled when the heroine's true racial identity is disclosed.

55. Nina Baym, *Woman's Fiction: A Guide to Novels Written by and about Women in America, 1820–1870* (Ithaca, N.Y.: Cornell University Press, 1976), pp. 11–21.

56. In Harper's *Iola Leroy*, Kelley-Hawkins's *Megda*, and Hopkins's *Contending Forces* as well as her three serial novels, the heroine's father is dead for practically all of each story. In Tillman's *Beryl Weston* and *Clancy Street* and in Johnson's *The Hazeley Family*, the fathers are usually away at work. In Johnson's *Clarence and Corinne*, the father is a drunkard who deserts his children and eventually dies. In Kelley-Hawkins's *Four Girls*, the story focuses on late adolescents outside the supervision of parental authority.

57. Emma Kelley-Hawkins, *Four Girls at Cottage City* (1898; Reprint. New York: Oxford University Press, 1988). Future references appear parenthetically in the chapter.

58. See Deborah McDowell, Introduction to *Four Girls at Cottage City* (Reprint. New York: Oxford University Press, 1988), pp. xxxiii–xxxv.

59. This is Elizabeth Ammons's term used in her essay "Stowe's Dream of the Mother-Savior: *Uncle Tom's Cabin* and American Women Writers before the 1920s" in *New Essays on Uncle Tom's Cabin*, Eric Sundquist, Ed. (New York: Cambridge University Press, 1986).

60. Religion is only a marginal concern in Hopkins's *Contending Forces* and is of virtually no consequence in her serial novels. Harper and Tillman generally presumed the spiritual reverence of their heroines. Tillman's Caroline Waters in *Clancy Street* reinforces her own nobility with her conversion, which is duplicated throughout her family, and Tillman's Beryl Weston in *Beryl Weston's Ambition* dedicates herself to strengthening her spiritual resolve. Johnson emphasizes conversion for all of her characters, enabling them to place their trust in "God's way[s]," a phrase that she frequently repeats in her novels. The fact that both Johnson and Tillman were married to ministers no doubt influenced the prominence of religion in their novels.

Chapter 7

1. In addition to "The Value of Race Literature," Victoria Earle (Matthews), experimented with literary realism in the novella "Aunt Lindy," first published in *The A.M.E. Church Review* (January 1889) and later reissued in pamphlet form by the A.M.E. Book Concern (1893). Octavia Albert authored *The House of Bondage* in 1890. This work is based on oral life narratives of former female slaves, which Albert collected, and has been reissued as a part of the Oxford edition of *The Schomburg Library of Nineteenth-Century Black Women Writers* (1988).

2. Katherine Davis Chapman Tillman, *Beryl Weston's Ambition: The Life of an Afro-American Girl* (1893; Reprint. New York: Oxford University Press, 1991). Beryl's father exemplifies the members of the National Negro Business League, organized by Booker T. Washington. The organization was composed of African Americans who were making significant economic gains throughout the South by transforming their labor into business enterprises. However, with the resurgence of the economic terrorism of lynching and rape, Washington's strategy for black advancement failed. Future references to this work appear parenthetically in the chapter.

3. Frances E. W. Harper, *Iola Leroy, or Shadows Uplifted* (1892; Reprint. Boston: Beacon Press, 1987), p. 256. Future references appear parenthetically in the chapter.

4. Professor and Mrs. J. W. Gibson, *Golden Thoughts on Chastity and Procreation* (Atlanta: J. L. Nichols and Co., 1903). Future references appear parenthetically in the chapter.

5. Julia Ward Howe, *Reminiscences* (1899; Reprint. New York: Negro Universities Press, 1969).

6. Emma Kelley-Hawkins, *Megda* (1891; Reprint. New York: Oxford University Press, 1988), p. 394. Future references appear parenthetically in the chapter.

7. See note 35 in Chapter 5.

8. Katherine Davis Chapman Tillman, *Clancy Street* (1898; Reprint. New York: Oxford University Press, 1991), pp. 251, 254. Future references appear parenthetically in the chapter.

9. Hortense Spillers, Introduction to *Clarence and Corinne*, p. xxxv.

10. Washington writes in his autobiography *Up from Slavery* that there were "ten million Negroes inhabiting this country, who themselves or whose ancestors went

through *the school of American slavery*" (emphasis added). Although the autobiography was published after *Clancy Street*, I suspect that this was an often-repeated phrase in Washington's public addresses that was reported in newspapers of the day. See Booker T. Washington, *Up from Slavery* in *Three Negro Classics* (1901; Reprint. New York: Avon Books, 1965), p. 37.

11. I have modified Ann Douglas's term *domestication of death*, which she employs in *The Feminization of American Culture* (New York: Knoff, 1977). Lynette Carpenter and Wendy K. Kolmar explain that the "domestication of death" in the nineteenth-century United States encouraged mourners to see heaven as an extension of this world in the most literal terms. See Carpenter and Kolmar, *Haunting the House of Fiction* (Knoxville: University of Tennessee Press, 1991), p. 8.

12. Harriet B. Stowe, *Uncle Tom's Cabin* (1851; Reprint. New York: Signet, 1966), pp. 311, 319.

13. From the antebellum period until the Civil Rights Law of 1964, Southern states' laws prohibited interracial marriage. These laws directly encouraged illicit sex between white men and black women, however. First, they created a climate in which white men considered black women sexual prey. Second, even in cases where an interracial couple had genuine feelings that would have produced marriage, the laws prohibited such legitimation. While intraracial premarital sex could be remedied somewhat with marriage, the laws against intermarriage throughout the South automatically and irreversibly condemned the black woman in a racially mixed liaison to the ranks of the fallen woman.

14. Dickson D. Bruce, Jr., *Black American Writing from the Nadir* (Baton Rouge: Louisiana State University Press, 1989), p. 32.

15. Edgar Allan Poe was the creator of the classical mystery formula during the 1840s. The formula features an unsolved crime, motivated by hidden guilt, within a family circle. The plot evolves as the detective untangles the clues in order to discern the motive for the crime and thus its perpetrator. The formula affirms bourgeois values due to the facts that the crime is always solved and justice is always served. See John G. Cawelti, *Adventure, Mystery, and Romance: Formula Stories as Art and Popular Culture* (Chicago: University of Chicago Press, 1976), pp. 102–5. Also see Ernest Mandel, *Delightful Murder: A Social History of the Crime Story* (Minneapolis: University of Minnesota Press, 1984), p. 47.

16. As evidence, Carby cites Hopkins's preface to *Contending Forces*. See Hazel V. Carby, *Reconstructing Womanhood* (New York: Oxford University Press, 1987), p. 128.

17. In Carby's introduction to the 1988 Oxford edition of Hopkins's *Magazine Novels*, she explains that "in *Hagar's Daughter* and *Winona* [and I add *Of One Blood*, although the characters are both knowingly and unknowingly passing] the white world is represented directly through white villains as individual figures of greed [and lust] who symbolize the power of the white society to oppress" (p. xxxvii). Future references to this introduction appear parenthetically in the chapter. This theme similarly appears at the close of Chesnutt's *The House Behind the Cedars*; however, he does not depict individuals as personally responsible for racial oppression. His perspective creates the tone of impersonal detachment, as his reviewers note. Referring to those reviews (in *Cleveland Plain Dealer* and *Pittsburgh Post*), Arlene A. Elder explains that

> The reason for Chesnutt's dispassionate tone, as [his] critics realized is that the "tragedy which inevitably comes is no one's fault in particular." "All concerned, white, black, and the most unfortunate of all, the 'white

negroes' are the victims of their environment, the inheritors of feelings and prejudices for which the author does not hold them responsible, and from which sons of each class endeavor to free themselves.

See Elder's *The Hindered Hand: The Cultural Implications of Early African-American Literature* (Westport, Conn.: Greenwood Press, 1978), p. 175.

18. Carby presents a sustained argument in *Reconstructing Womanhood* on how Hopkins's novels attempted to enter and disrupt the discourse of imperialism by presenting "an alternative historical interpretation of the relationship between white and black through an engagement with the concepts that structured the racist discourse" (p. 134). By focusing on generational family histories, Carby illustrates that Hopkins's novels repeatedly insisted that the "degradation of race was not the result of degeneration through amalgamation but a consequence of an abuse of power; [in other words] it was the use of brutality against a subordinate group that was defined as and equated with savagery" (p. 134). Carby goes on to explain that Hopkins represented this "generational history across a century to situate the contemporary reassertion of the doctrine of white supremacy within a framework that demythologized the American story of [democratic] origins" (p. 141).

19. This is one of Carby's objectives in *Reconstructing Womanhood*.

20. Karen Lystra, *Searching the Heart: Women, Men, and Romantic Love in the Nineteenth-Century America* (New York: Oxford University Press, 1989), p. 166. Future references appear parenthetically in the chapter.

21. See the note on the first page of the novel in *The Colored American* II, 5 (March 1901), p. 337. The final chapters were published in January and March, 1902.

22. The novel's climax pivots on Detective Benson's discovery of the real murderer of a woman, thus freeing Sumner from the crime. The murder mystery is enhanced with allusions to the western. Described as "a Western girl. . . . [who] had been brought up on a ranch," Jewel carried and knew how to shoot a pistol "with deadly effect" (p. 210). (Jewel's actions are reminiscent of those of Ida Wells-Barnett, who was reputed to have packed a pistol for her self-defense.) Jewel's adoptive father Zenas Bowen, the newly elected senator from California, is described as an elderly man of dark complexion . . . with a decidedly Western air" (p. 76). "He had the hair and skin of an Indian" (p. 81). His character portrayal duplicates the ideal of the Western frontiersman of the early dime novels. See "The Voice of the Fiction Factory in Dime and Pulp Westerns," in *Selling the Wild West* by Christine Bold (Bloomington: University of Indiana Press, 1987), pp. 10–17.

23. Other narrative features suggest a targeted white audience. These include the failure of the text to critique the reward of a lifetime of menial labor that Venus's grandmother receives for finding a large bag of money in the Treasury Building and the references to Sumner's loyal black servant as a "buck."

24. *The House Behind the Cedars* was initially serialized in *Self Culture Magazine* XI (August 1900)–XII (February 1901), shortly before the appearance of *Hagar's Daughter*. The complete novel was reissued in 1901 by Houghton, Mifflin and Company. Future citations refer to the 1969 Macmillan edition; they appear parenthetically in the chapter.

25. In discussing *Contending Forces* and Hopkins's intention to recall the "'fire and romance' of negro history [that] had been unrecognized by Anglo-Saxons," Vernon Loggins provided a gender-specific and ahistorical assessment in which he contended that she "tried to crowd enough fire and romance for forty books into one four-hundred-page volume." That estimation prompts me, for one, to speculate what he

might have said about her serial novels, which make the plot of *Contending Forces* seem economical. Loggins is typical of early- to mid-twentieth-century scholars of African-American literature who isolate black women's writing from other cultural products and contexts. See Vernon Loggins, *The Negro Author: His Development in America to 1900* (New York: Columbia University Press, 1931), p. 326.

By contrast, Carby places Hopkins's serial novels into the categories of the popular formulas of the dime novel and story papers of Hopkins's day. Carby specifically refers to the mystery formula of "Black Tom the Negro Detective." I extend Carby's categorization of these serials to include two other formulas that were gaining popularity at the turn of the century—the western and the ghost or monster story. See Carby's introduction to *The Magazine Novels of Pauline Hopkins*, pp. xxxviii–xxxix.

26. Pauline E. Hopkins, *Hagar's Daughter* (1901; Reprint. *Magazine Novels of Pauline Hopkins*. New York: Oxford University Press, 1988), pp. 270–71. Future references appear parenthetically in the chapter.

27. Carby explains this shift from personal to national as "Hopkins's rejection of a return to an acceptable moral order at the end of her tale that a simple 'happy ending' would have imposed. Hopkins's refusal to resolve *Hagar's Daughter* within the terms of the popular conventions that structured her narrative is," Carby argues, "symptomatic of the tension between her political and didactic intent and the desire to write popular fiction" (Carby, Introduction, p. xlii).

28. The last of the Leatherstocking Tales *The Deerslayer* is a meandering story that Cawelti describes as full of "chases and captures, escapes and pursuits, in which the [hero] finally succeeds in rescuing his companions from the threat of death or torture at the hands of savage Indians." See Cawelti, *Adventure, Mystery, and Romance*, p. 203.

29. While Carby places *Hagar's Daughter* within the dime novel tradition by referring to its first appearance with the Old Cap. Collier Library series of detective fictions of the 1880s, she does not extend this application to Hopkins's other serials to illustrate how they draw on the formulaic formats of the western and the ghost story that were also very popular by the late nineteenth and early twentieth century. See *Reconstructing Womanhood*, pp. 149–50.

I extend Carby's discussion of the dime novel tradition to demonstrate how all of Hopkins's serials are a part of that tradition. Hopkins revised the conventional easy social resolution of the dime novels by drawing on the formula's tactic of disguise to dramatize racial polemics in the form of the story's romantic plot. She adapted the formula for racial discourse in the hope of using popular fiction to intervene in racist creeds and to give expression as well to her own despair about the worsening interracial social conditions.

30. The western dime novel was first made famous by Edward S. Ellis and Beadle and Company's *Seth Jones; or, The Captives of the Frontier* (1860) and subsequently by Edward L. Wheeler's *Deadwood Dick on Deck, or Calamity Jane, the Heroine of Whoop-up* (1878). This latter work especially established the western formulaic plot that can be traced back to James Fenimore Cooper's Leatherstocking Tales. However, in Cooper's entertaining but socially complex novels, "the encounter between civilization and wilderness, East and West, settled society and lawless openness" was the problematicized presumption of the divine destiny of Euro-Americans (Cawelti, p. 193). While Cooper dealt with social conflict, the dime novels replaced the social interrogation with "ritualistic adventure" and escapist entertainment, erasing all moral ambiguities by displacing, first, the frontiersman hero with a rugged Eastern genteel hero and, second, social controversy with predictable harmonious endings (Bold,

p. 10). A principal factor producing this form of reductivism in the dime novels was that the frontier was closed at the time of their production, while during Cooper's era there was still the possibility of reforming the conquest of the West. For discussions on the evolution of the western dime novel, see Christine Bold, *Selling the Wild West*, pp. 10–18; and Cawelti, pp. 192–215. Future references to Bold's *Selling the Wild West* appear parenthetically in the chapter.

31. The search for missing heirs was a typical plot in formula fiction for it provided the occasion for entertaining adventure: the detective's search, villainy, and happy resolution. See Cawelti, p. 196. In addition, the typical Eastern origin of the hero, which both Cawelti and Bold characterize, is exaggerated in the case of Maxwell. See also Bold, *Selling the Wild West*, p. 13.

32. Pauline E. Hopkins, *Winona: A Tale of Negro Life in the South and Southwest* (1902; Reprint. New York: Oxford University Press, 1988), pp. 324–25. Future references appear parenthetically in the chapter.

33. John Brown was hung for treason for the attack on Harper's Ferry in West Virginia in 1859.

34. This section seems to allude to Douglass's reference to working under Covey in Chapter X of *The Narrative of the Life of Frederick Douglass* (1845; Reprint. Garden City, N.Y.: Doubleday Dolphin, 1963), pp. 66, 68. He writes:

> Mr. Covey succeeded in breaking me. I was broken in body, soul, and spirit. . . . the dark night of slavery closed in upon me; and behold a man transformed into a brute."

Later Douglass explains, "You have seen how a man was made a slave; you shall see how a slave was made a man." At this point he recalls his fight with Covey.

35. Judah's heroic character and formidable physical strength recall two predecessors: Madison Washington in Frederick Douglass's 1853 novel *The Heroic Slave* and Jerome in William Wells Brown's 1867 novel *Clotelle; or The Colored Heroine*. In addition, Judah's senatorial eloquence, which characterizes his self-esteem, is part of the prescription of genteel eloquence for the dime novel hero.

36. Peter Penzoldt explains that the psychological ghost story arises from "the findings of modern psychiatry and psychoanalysis" during the last decades of the nineteenth century (p. 53). The most famous of these stories "describe cases of neurosis, where the person concerned has retained a child's magical conception of the universe beyond the age at which it usually disappears," which incite a series of events whose explanation seems only to lie in the supernatural (p. 54). See Peter Penzoldt, *The Supernatural in Fiction* (New York: Humanities Press, 1965), pp. 53–57.

Ethiopianism was a persistent theme in nineteenth-century African-American writing. Ethiopianism (in the form of direct and indirect biblical references) enabled New World Africans to regard their oppression as a part of a divine plan for the broad and unified development of civilization. This tradition finds expression, for example, in the sermons of Alexander Crummell, in Daniel Payne's 1862 oration "To the Colored People of the United States," in Harper's poem "Ethiopia," in Dunbar's "Ode to Ethiopia," in many of the works of Du Bois (for example "The Conservation of Races" [1897]), and in Langston Hughes's "The Negro Speaks of Rivers." See Wilson J. Moses's *The Golden Age of Black Nationalism* (Hamden, Conn.: Archon Books, 1978), pp. 156–69.

37. As Carpenter and Kolmar explain, "The ghost story was one of several nineteenth-century popular genres dominated by women writers" (pp. 6–7). Ghost stories

by women, they add, are full of dispossessed women and children whose visitations impart warnings frequently about "the dangers of domesticity." See *Haunting the House of Fiction*, p. 14.

38. Pauline E. Hopkins, *Of One Blood: or, The Hidden Self* (1903; Reprint. *Magazine Novels of Pauline Hopkins*. New York: Oxford University Press, 1988), pp. 520–21. Future references appear parenthetically in the chapter.

39. Ammons reads *Of One Blood* as an allegory of the black American woman artist. Hers is a very provocative and appropriate reading, which I extend (but not in terms of the theme of woman as artist) so as to contextualize Briggs's interest in psychic phenomena and to direct special attention to the novel's implications of social justice for African Americans at the beginning of the new century. See *Conflicting Stories* (New York: Oxford University Press, 1991), pp. 81–85.

40. Pauline Hopkins spent most of her life in the Boston-Cambridge area, where she worked as a stenographer. Hence it is not surprising that she would portray the heroes of both *Contending Forces* and *Of One Blood* as Harvard graduates who evoke Du Bois and would set both novels in Cambridge. See her autobiographical sketch in *The Colored American* 2 (January 1901), pp. 218–19.

Du Bois attended Harvard from 1888–92, entering as a junior with a B.A. from Fisk University. He graduated from Harvard, B.A., cum laude with a major in philosophy in 1890. From 1890–92 he was a fellow in Harvard's graduate school, receiving the M.A. in history in 1891 and the Ph.D. in 1896. From 1888–92 he "carried on lively social intercourse with a group of [colored] professional men, students, white collar workers and upper servants." These were circles in which Hopkins was likely to have circulated or been aware of. See *The Autobiography of W. E. B. Du Bois* (New York: International Publishers Co., 1968), p. 137.

41. William James was "Pragmatism's leading exponent [who] defend[ed] his belief that the evidence for God lies primarily in inner personal experiences rather than in abstract philosophical systems." This statement appears on the cover of the 1961 Collier edition of *The Varieties of Religious Experience*. There are many similarities between James's discussions on psychic and spiritual phenomena and those in Hopkins's *Of One Blood*, suggesting that she may have been familiar with that work.

42. In *The Sickness unto Death: A Christian Psychological Exposition for Edification and Awakening* (Copenhagen, 1849), Danish philosopher Søren Kierkegaard depicted a precursor to James's "sick soul." Freud would also provide a detailed description of this struggle between the instincts for self-preservation and death, which he respectively named Eros and Tantalos in *Beyond the Pleasure Principle* (1920) and *Civilization and Its Discontents* (1930).

In her short story "The Mystery Within Us" (1900), Hopkins presented a character much like Briggs on the brink of suicide until he discovers within him the life force of another who has transcended the finality of death. See *Short Fiction by Black Women, 1900–1920*, collected with an introduction by Elizabeth Ammons (New York: Oxford University Press, 1991), pp. 21–26.

43. I suggest that the teachings of James helped to stimulate Du Bois's interest in the psychological characteristics—the soul—of different human races, which he later combined with his racialized version of Hegelian dialectics—*Volksgeistian*. Du Bois executed these theories in "The Conservation of Races," originally published in 1897 as a pamphlet by the American Negro Academy and "Strivings of the Negro People," published in *Atlantic Monthly* 80 (1897), pp. 194–98. That latter argument presented the famous paragraph "After the Egyptian and Indian . . . the Negro is a sort of seventh son, born with a veil, and gifted with second-sight. . . . One ever feels his

two-ness, — an American, a Negro; two souls, two thoughts, two unreconciled striv-ings; two warring ideals in one dark body . . . " (p. 194). The two articles form the basis of the first chapter, "Of Our Spiritual Striving," in *The Souls of Black Folk*, published in 1903. Du Bois wrote in his autobiography that "it was [William] James with his pragmatism and Albert Bushnell Hart with his research method, that turned me back from . . . philosophic speculation, to the social sciences as the field . . . which would apply to my program for the Negro" (p. 148). See *The Autobiography of W. E. B. Du Bois*. For a summary discussion of Du Bois's racialization of Hegelian dialectics, see Joel Williamson's *The Crucible of Race* (New York: Oxford University Press, 1984), pp. 397–413.

Hopkins's allusion to M. Binet seems to refer to an essay entitled "Alterations of Personality," published in The International Scientific Series in 1896 or 1897. See James, *The Varieties of Religious Experiences*, p. 192.

44. Du Bois made a strikingly similar observation about how sexism and racism interconnect. Referring to an article by Norman Angell in *The Freeman*, Du Bois contends that Angell

> reveals an astonishing attitude of mind in higher quarters than we had hitherto looked to see it. To the ordinary American or Englishman, we have always realized, the race question is at bottom simply a matter of ownership of women; white men want the right to own and use all women, colored and white, and they resent the intrusion of colored men in this domain. This, as we have said has long been the attitude of the ordinary white man, but we had scarcely thought to see this attitude illustrated in an article by Norman Angell.

See Du Bois, "Opinion of W. E. B. Du Bois" in *The Crisis* 23, 5 (March 1922), pp. 199–200. Irene Diggs also refers to this commentary in her essay "Du Bois, and Women: A Short Story of Black Women" in *Current Bibliography on African Affairs* 7, 3 (Summer 1974), p. 260.

45. This city is reminiscent of the black underground of Imperio in Sutton Griggs's 1899 novel *Imperium in Imperio*. Imperium is a secret, national, radical society com-posed of educated black people dedicated to addressing and hopefully rectifying the racism of the post-Reconstruction period. With the archeological digs in Northern Africa and the Middle East drawing a great deal of attention and intellectual inquiry, as well as the circulation of the motif of the underground in works like Lewis Carroll's *Alice in Wonderland*, the underground was a fascinating setting that had emancipatory, historical, and political significance for writers like Griggs and Hopkins.

46. Unsigned article in the Women's Department of *The A.M.E. Church Review* XVI (October 1900), p. 173.

47. Angelina Weld Grimké, *Rachel* (1920; Reprint. New York: Oxford University Press, 1991), p. 167.

Chapter 8

1. When Grimké eventually turned from writing stories and plays about lynching at middle-age, she increasingly concentrated on poetry. Fortunately for her, poetry was in vogue, for these were the years of the Harlem Renaissance. As a consequence many of her poems were published in the Renaissance journals and anthologies, such as *The Crisis* and *Opportunity*, as well as in *The New Negro*, edited by Alain Locke; *Caroling Dusk*, edited by Countee Cullen; and *Ebony and Topaz*, edited by Charles S. Johnson.

The most complete listing of Grimké's previously published and unpublished works is in the selected bibliography of *Selected Works of Angelina Weld Grimké*, edited by Carolivia Herron (New York: Oxford University Press, 1991), pp. 442–45. Future references to Grimké's works published in this volume are cited parenthetically in the chapter.

2. Hans Robert Jauss, "Literary History as Challenge" in *Toward an Aesthetic of Reception* (Minneapolis: University of Minnesota Press, 1982), p. 26.

3. My reference to the blues aesthetic in Grimké's stories draws on the excellent introduction to *Selected Works of Angelina Weld Grimké* by Carolivia Herron, pp. 20–21. Herron contends that Grimké's "unflinching descriptions of the violence of lynching" foreshadow depictions of violence that "were unknown in African-American fictional literature prior to the work of Richard Wright" (p. 21).

4. *Rachel* was "first staged in Washington on March 3–4, 1916, under the auspices of the Drama Committee of the District of Columbia branch of the N.A.A.C.P." See Gloria T. Hull, *Color, Sex and Poetry: Three Women Writers of the Harlem Renaissance* (Bloomington: University of Indiana Press, 1987), p. 119. Future references to this critical work appear parenthetically in the chapter. *Rachel: A Play in Three Acts* was originally published in 1920 in Boston by The Cornhill Company (Reprinted in *The Schomburg Library of Nineteenth-Century Black Women Writers*. New York: Oxford University Press, 1991).

5. Arthur P. Davis, *From the Dark Tower: Afro-American Writers 1900–1960* (Washington, D.C.: Howard University Press, 1974), pp. 7, 58. For a summary discussion of *Rachel*'s reception at the time of its first performances, see Robert J. Fehrenbach, "Angelina Grimké's *Rachel*" in *Wild Women in the Whirlwind*, Joanne M. Braxton and Andrée Nicola McLaughlin, Eds. (New Brunswick, N.J.: Rutgers University Press, 1990), pp. 89–106. For a survey of Grimké's works published prior to *The Schomburg Library*, see Jeanne-Marie A. Miller, "Angelina Weld Grimké: Playwright and Poet" in *C.L.A. Journal* 21 (1978), 513–24.

6. For Grimké's discussion of her reasons for writing *Rachel*, see "'Rachel': The Play of the Month, The Reason and Synopsis by the Author." Reprinted in *Selected Works*, pp. 413–18. I incorporate parts of this discussion in my examination of *The Closing Door* and *Goldie* later in this chapter.

7. See *Washington [D.C.] Star* (5 December 1920). For a list of newspaper reviews of *Rachel* see the selected bibliography in *Selected Works*, p. 446.

8. The handbill is a part of Grimké's collection housed in the Moorland-Spingarn Research Center, Howard University.

9. Henry R. Butler, Introduction to *Golden Thoughts on Chastity and Procreation* by Professor and Mrs. J[ohn]. W. Gibson (Atlanta: J. L. Nichols and Co., 1903), p. 4.

10. See *The Crisis* I, 4 (February 1911), pp. 18 and 19. Graphic depictions of the changing conditions of black life became very prominent in the publications of the New Negro Renaissance of the 1920s. At this time the depictions became celebratory, thus reembracing the racial optimism of the Reconstruction and early post-Reconstruction eras.

11. Carolivia Herron explains that *Rachel* was also called *The Pervert, The Daughter*, and *Blessed Are the Barren*. See her introduction to *Selected Works*, p. 17.

12. The terrifying plot of lynching also occurs in "Blackness" and "Black Is, as Black Does," the latter of which was originally published in *The Colored American* 1 (August 1900), pp. 160–63. "Blackness" was not published until the publication of *Selected Works of Angelina Weld Grimké*. It is difficult to determine just how long many of Grimké's works remained in manuscript before appearing in print due to the fact that she was not aggressive in having them published, and the holographs and typescripts

of her works are usually not dated. The early versions of Grimké's stories are collected in her papers at Howard University's Moorland-Spingarn Research Center.

13. The plot of maternal infanticide foreshadows Toni Morrison's *Beloved*, an observation that Herron also makes. See her introduction to *Selected Works*, p. 21.

14. This allusion is reminiscent of the double plots of incest in Hopkins's *Of One Blood*.

15. Lillie Buffum Chace Wyman wrote a review of *Rachel* that appeared in the April 1921 issue of *The Journal of Negro History*. This review is reprinted in *Selected Works*, pp. 447–49. Wyman wrote a letter to Grimké in which she "entreat[ed her] to leave out . . . consideration of the lynching horror. . . ." See Hull's *Color, Sex, and Poetry*, p. 132.

16. This scenario is reminiscent of the short story "Her Virginia Mammy" in *The Wife of His Youth* (1899) by Charles Chesnutt.

17. Angelina Grimké's papers are housed at the Moorland-Spingarn Research Center of Howard University. Also see Hull, *Color, Sex, and Poetry*, p. 124.

18. "Blackness" was evidently rejected inasmuch as it remained unpublished until the issuance of her *Selected Works*.

19. Hull adds that Grimké's concern with antilynching work began in 1899 when at the age of nineteen, "she collected signatures for an anti-lynching petition" (Hull, p. 131).

20. Gatewood contends that Archibald Grimké's marriage to Sarah Stanley was "denounced by her father, a minister in Indiana" but he does not cite the source of his information. See Willard B. Gatewood, *The Aristocrats of Color* (Bloomington: University of Indiana Press, 1990), p. 178.

21. Grimké's diaries as well as the recollection of people who knew her as a teacher also corroborate this viewpoint. During my interview with May Miller Sullivan on January 8, 1989, she recalled that while she was a student at "M" Street High School there was a great deal of talk about an intimate relationship between Grimké and Mary (Mamie) Burrill who also taught there.

22. Gloria T. Hull, "Under the Days: The Buried Life and Poetry of Angelina Weld Grimké" in *Conditions 5*, II, 2 (Autumn 1979), p. 22. Future references appear parenthetically in the chapter as "Under the Days."

23. Undated correspondence from Angelina W. Grimké at the address of 1415 Corcoran Street, N.W., Washington, D.C. Portions of this letter are incorporated into "'Rachel': The Play of the Month, The Reason and Synopsis by the Author" which is reprinted in *Selected Works*, p. 413–16.

24. The quoted material is taken from the letter in note 23.

25. Grimké, "'Rachel,' The Play of the Month: The Reason and Synopsis by the Author," in *Selected Works*, p. 415.

26. The novelization of this rebellion is depicted in Toni Morrison's *Beloved* (1987) with Sethe's murder of Beloved and attempted murder of her other children, as well as in Sherley Anne Williams's *Dessa Rose* (1987) with the enslaved Dessa's and Kane's reluctance to have a child.

27. Peter B. Filene, *HIM/HER/SELF: Sex Roles in Modern America* (Baltimore: Johns Hopkins University Press, 1986), p. 19. Future references appear parenthetically in the chapter.

28. I am curious about the number of schools she attended during this period—one for each year. But I can only speculate.

29. Although only a small minority of "new women" genuinely seem to have wanted careers, economic independence, and sexual freedom, and a still smaller number actu-

ally dared to challenge marriage conventions, the legend of the few who did circulated widely. In contrast to this radical constituency, the vast majority of new women "preserv[ed] a large part of their traditional role" (p. 27):

> Even if they were training to teach other women's children and to manage other women's housekeeping, they were simply putting femininity on a vocational basis. . . . It is hard to say whether domestic science meant artful entrapment on a neo-Victorian pedestal or genuine emancipation from the corset of angelic ladyhood." (pp. 27, 46)

See the respective pages in Filene, *HIM/HER/SELF*.

Nevertheless, these new women were transforming the Victorian ideal of motherhood, "which [had] sentimentalized the woman as a pious and virtuous figure, the guardian of domestic morality" into a new womanly ideal who expected personal, professional, and sexual gratification" (p. 114). Also see Steven Mintz and Susan Kellogg, *Domestic Revolutions: A Social History of American Family Life* (New York: The Free Press, 1988).

30. Jessie Redmon Fauset, *There is Confusion* (New York: Boni & Liveright, Inc., 1924; Reprint. Boston: Northeastern University Press, 1989). Future references appear parenthetically in the chapter.

31. Frances E. W. Harper, *Iola Leroy, or Shadows Uplifted* (1892; Reprint. Boston: Beacon Press, 1988), p. 271.

32. James Baldwin, *The Fire Next Time* (1962; Reprint. New York: Dell Publishing Co., 1970), p. 127.

SELECTED BIBLIOGRAPHY

Albert, Octavia. *The House of Bondage: or Charlotte Brooks and Other Slaves*. 1890; Reprint. New York: Oxford University Press, 1988.

Ammons, Elizabeth. *Conflicting Stories: American Women Writers at the Turn into the Twentieth Century*. New York: Oxford University Press, 1991.

Ammons, Elizabeth. *Short Fiction by Black Women, 1900–1920*. New York: Oxford University Press, 1991.

Andrews, William. "The Novelization of Voice in Early African American Narrative" in *PMLA* 105 (January 1990).

Andrews, William. *Sisters of the Spirit: Three Black Women's Autobiographies of the Nineteenth Century*. Bloomington: University of Indiana Press, 1986.

Andrews, William L. *To Tell a Free Story: The First Century of Afro-American Autobiography, 1760–1865*. Urbana: University of Illinois Press, 1986.

Aptheker, Bettina. *Woman's Legacy: Essays on Race, Sex, and Class in American History*. Amherst: University of Massachusetts Press, 1981.

Ardis, Ann. *New Women, New Novels: Feminism and Early Modernism*. New Brunswick, N.J.: Rutgers University Press, 1990.

Armstrong, Nancy. *Desire and Domestic Fiction: A Political History of the Novel*. New York: Oxford University Press, 1987.

Armstrong, Nancy and Leonard Tennenhouse, Eds. *The Ideology of Conduct: Essays on Literature and the History of Sexuality*. New York: Methuen, 1986.

Bailey, Frankie Y. *Out of the Woodpile: Black Characters in Crime and Detective Fiction*. Westport, Conn.: Greenwood Press, 1991.

Baker, Jr., Houston A. *Blues, Ideology, and Afro-American Literature*. Chicago: University of Chicago Press, 1984.

Baker, Jr., Houston A. *Modernism and the Harlem Renaissance*. Chicago: University of Chicago Press, 1987.

Bakhtin, M[ikhail]. M. *The Dialogic Imagination: Four Essays*. Austin: University of Texas Press, 1981.

Baldwin, James. "Everybody's Protest Novel" in *The Partisan Review* 16 (June 1949). Reprinted in *Notes of a Native Son*. Boston: Beacon Press, 1955.

Baldwin, James. "Many Thousands Gone" in *The Partisan Review* 18 (November-December 1951). Reprinted in *Notes of a Native Son*. Boston: Beacon Press, 1955.

281

Baruch, Elaine Hoffman. *Women, Love, and Power: Literary and Psychoanalytic Perspectives*. New York: New York University Press, 1991.

Baym, Nina. *Novels, Readers, and Reviewers: Responses to Fiction in Antebellum America*. Ithaca, N.Y.: Cornell University Press, 1984.

Baym, Nina. *Woman's Fiction: A Guide to Novels by and about Women in America, 1820–1870*. Ithaca, N.Y.: Cornell University Press, 1976.

Baym, Nina. "Women and the Republic: Emma Willard's Rhetoric of History" in *American Quarterly* 43, 1 (March 1991).

Benjamin, Jessica. *The Bonds of Love: Psychoanalysis, Feminism, and the Problem of Domination*. New York: Pantheon, 1988.

Berlin, Ira, Steven F. Miller, and Leslie S. Rowland. "Afro-American Families in Transition from Slavery to Freedom" in *Black Women in United States History*. Edited by Darlene Clark Hind. Brooklyn: Carlson Publishing Inc., 1990.

Bernard, Jessie. *Marriage and Family Among the Negroes*. Englewood Cliffs, N.J.: Prentice-Hall, 1966.

Bold, Christine. *Selling the Wild West: Popular Western Fiction, 1860 to 1960*. Bloomington: University of Indiana Press, 1987.

Bone, Robert A. *The Negro Novel in America*. New Haven, Conn.: Yale University Press, 1958.

Boone, Joseph Allen. *Tradition Counter Tradition: Love and the Form of Fiction*. Chicago: University of Chicago Press, 1987.

Bouvier, John A. *A Law Dictionary Adapted to the Constitution and Laws of the U.S.A.* 3rd ed. Philadelphia: T. and J. W. Johnson, 1848; 15th ed. Philadelphia: J. B. Lippincott, 1883; new ed. rev. Francis Rawle. Boston Book Co., 1897.

Braxton, Joanne M. *Black Women Writing Autobiography: A Tradition within a Tradition*. Philadelphia: Temple University Press, 1989.

Braxton, Joanne M. Introduction to *The Work of the Afro-American Woman* by Mrs. N[athan]. F. Mossell. 1894; Reprint. New York: Oxford University Press, 1988.

Brooks, Peter. *Reading for the Plot: Design and Intention in Literature*. New York: Vintage, 1985.

Brooks-Higginbotham, Evelyn. "The Problem of Race in Women's History" in *Coming to Terms: Feminism, Theory, and Politics*. Edited by Elizabeth Weed. New York: Routledge, 1989.

Brown, Gillian. *Domestic Individualism: Imagining Self in Nineteenth–Century America*. Berkeley: University of California Press, 1990.

Brown, William Wells. *Clotelle*. 1853; Reprint. New York: Collier Books, 1970.

Bruce, Jr., Dickson D. *Black American Writing from the Nadir: The Evolution of a Literary Tradition, 1877–1915*. Baton Rouge: Louisiana State University Press, 1989.

Butler, Octavia. *Kindred*. Garden City, N.Y.: Doubleday, 1979.

Carby, Hazel V. *Reconstructing Womanhood: The Emergence of the Afro-American Woman Novelist*. New York: Oxford University Press, 1987.

Carpenter, Lynette and Wendy K. Kolmar. *Haunting the House of Fiction: Perspectives on Ghost Stories by American Women*. Knoxville: University of Tennessee Press, 1991.

Cawelti, John G. *Adventure, Mystery, and Romance: Formula Stories as Art and Popular Culture*. Chicago: University of Chicago Press, 1976.

Chesnutt, Charles W. *The Wife of His Youth and Other Stories*. 1900; Reprint. Ann Arbor: University of Michigan Press, 1968.

Chesnutt, Charles W. *The House Behind the Cedars* in *Self Culture Magazine* XI (August 1900)–XII (February 1901); Reprint. Boston: Houghton Mifflin and Company, 1900; Reprint. New York: Macmillan, 1969.

Chesnutt, Charles W. *The Conjure Woman*. 1899; Reprint. Ann Arbor: University of Michigan Press, 1969.

Child, Lydia Maria. *The Mother's Book*. Boston: Carter and Hendee, 1831; Reprint. New York: Arno Press, 1972.

Christian, Barbara. "African-American Women's Historical Novels" in *Wild Women in the Whirlwind: Afro-American Culture and the Contemporary Literary Renaissance*. Edited by Joanne M. Braxton and Andrée Nicola McLaughlin. New Brunswick, N.J.: Rutgers University Press, 1990.

Christian, Barbara. *Black Women Novelists: The Development of a Tradition 1892–1976*. Westport, Conn.: Greenwood Press, 1980.

Christian, Barbara. Introduction to *The Hazeley Family* by Mrs. A. E. Johnson. New York: Oxford University Press, 1990.

Clifford, James. *The Predicament of Culture: Twentieth-Century Ethnography, Literature, and Art*. Cambridge, Mass.: Harvard University Press, 1988.

Clifford, James. "On Ethnographic Allegory" in *Writing Culture: The Poetics and Politics of Ethnography*. Edited by James Clifford and George E. Marcus. Berkeley: University of California Press, 1986.

Coleman, Lucretia Newman. *Poor Ben*. Philadelphia: The Sunday School Union of the A.M.E. Church, 1890.

Cooper, Anna J. *A Voice From the South*. 1892; Reprint. New York: Oxford University Press, 1988.

Culp, D[aniel]. W., Ed. *Twentieth-Century Negro Literature; or, a Cyclopedia of Thought on the Vital Topics Relating to the American Negro*. Toronto: J. L. Nichols & Co., 1902.

Davidson, Cathy N. *Revolution and the Word: The Rise of the Novel in America*. New York: Oxford University Press, 1986.

Davis, Angela. *Women, Race, and Class*. New York: Vintage Books, 1983.

Davis, Arthur P. *From the Dark Tower: Afro-American Writers 1900–1960*. Washington, D.C.: Howard University Press, 1974.

de Laurentis, Teresa. *Alice Does-N'T: Feminism, Semiotics, Cinema*. Bloomington: University of Indiana Press, 1984.

Diggs, Irene. "Du Bois, and Women: A Short Story of Black Women" in *Current Bibliography on African Affairs* 7, 3 (Summer 1974).

Dill, Bonnie Thornton. "The Dialectics of Black Womanhood" in *Signs* 4 (Spring 1979).

Dobson, Joanne. "The Hidden Hand: Subversion of Cultural Ideology in Three Mid-Nineteenth-Century American Women's Novels" in *American Quarterly* 38, 2 (Spring 1986).

Douglass, Frederick. *Narrative of the Life of Frederick Douglass*. 1845; Reprint. Garden City, N.Y.: Doubleday Dolphin, 1963.

Du Bois, William E. B. *The Autobiography of W. E. B. Du Bois*. New York: International Publishers Co., 1968.

Du Bois, William E. B. "Opinions of W. E. B. Du Bois" in *The Crisis* 23, 5 (March 1922).

Du Bois, William E. B. *The Quest of the Silver Fleece*. 1911; Reprint. Boston: Northeastern University, 1989.

Du Bois, William E. B. *The Souls of Black Folk* in *Three Negro Classics*. 1903; Reprint. New York: Avon Books, 1965.

Du Bois, William E. B. "Strivings of the Negro People" in *Atlantic Monthly* 80 (1897).

Dunbar, Paul Laurence. *The Sport of the Gods.* 1901; Reprint. New York: Dodd, Mead & Company, 1981.

Editorial Staff of the National Reporter System. *Judicial and Statutory Definitions of Words and Phrases.* St. Paul, Minn.: West Publishing Co., 1904–5.

Elder, Arlene. *The Hindered Hand: Cultural Implications of Early African-American Fiction.* Westport, Conn.: Greenwood Press, 1978.

Ellison, Ralph. "Recent Negro Fiction" in *New Masses* 40, 6 (5 August 1941).

Epstein, Barbara. "Family, Sexual Morality, and Popular Movements" in *Powers of Desire: The Politics of Sexuality.* Edited by Ann Snitow, Christine Stansell, and Sharon Thompson. New York: Monthly Review Press, 1983.

Fauset, Jessie R. *There Is Confusion.* 1924; Reprint. Boston: Northeastern University Press, 1989.

Fehrenbach, Robert J. "Angelina Grimké's *Rachel* in *Wild Women in the Whirlwind.* Edited by Joanne M. Braxton and Andrée Nicola McLaughlin. New Brunswick, N.J.: Rutgers University Press, 1990.

Fetterly, Judith. *Provisions: A Reader from 19th-Century American Women.* Bloomington: University of Indiana Press, 1985.

Filene, Peter G. *HIM/HER/SELF: Sex Roles in Modern America.* Baltimore: Johns Hopkins University Press, 1986.

Franchot, Jenny. "The Punishment of Esther" in *Frederick Douglass: New Literary and Historical Essays.* Edited by Eric J. Sundquist. New York: Cambridge University Press, 1990.

Foner, Eric. *Reconstruction: America's Unfinished Revolution, 1863–1877.* New York: Harper and Row, 1988.

Frazier, E. Franklin. *The Negro Family in the United States.* Chicago: University of Chicago Press, 1966.

Gates, Jr., Henry Louis, General Ed. *The Schomburg Library of Nineteenth-Century Black Women Writers.* New York: Oxford University Press, 1988, 1991.

Gates, Jr., Henry Louis. *Signifying Money: A Theory of Afro-American Literary Criticism.* New York: Oxford University Press, 1989.

Gates, Jr., Henry Louis. "TV's Black World Turns—But Stays Unreal" in the Arts and Leisure section of *The New York Times* (Sunday, November 12, 1989), p. 40.

Gatewood, Willard B. *The Aristocrats of Color: The Black Elite, 1880–1920.* Bloomington: University of Indiana Press, 1990.

Gayle, Jr., Addison, Ed. *The Black Aesthetic.* New York: Anchor Doubleday, 1971.

Geertz, Clifford. *The Interpretation of Cultures.* New York: Basic Books, 1973.

Genovese, Eugene. *Roll Jordan, Roll: The World the Slaves Made.* New York: Vintage Books, 1974.

Gibson, Professor and Mrs. J[ohn]. W. *Golden Thoughts of Chastity and Procreation,* with an Introduction by Dr. Henry R. Butler. Atlanta: J. L. Nichols and Co., 1903.

Giddings, Paula. *When and Where I Enter: The Impact of Black Women on Race and Sex in America.* New York: Morrow, 1984.

Gilbert, Sandra and Susan Gubar. *The Madwoman in the Attic: The Woman Writer and the Nineteenth-Century Literary Imagination.* New Haven, Conn.: Yale University Press, 1979.

Gloster, Hugh. *Negro Voices in American Fiction.* Chapel Hill: University of North Carolina Press, 1948.

Griggs, Sutton. *Imperium in Imperio.* 1899; Reprint. New York: Arno Press, 1969.

Grimké, Angelina Weld. *Rachel: A Play in Three Acts*. Boston: The Cornhill Co., 1920; Reprint. New York: Oxford University Press, 1991.

Gutman, Herbert G. *The Black Family in Slavery and Freedom, 1750–1925*. New York: Pantheon Books, 1976.

Guy-Sheftall, Beverly. *Daughters of Sorrow: Attitudes towards Black Women, 1880–1920*. Brooklyn: Carlson Publishing Inc., 1990.

Harper, Frances E. W. *Iola Leroy, or Shadows Uplifted*. 1892; Reprint New York: Oxford University Press, 1988. Reprint. Boston: Beacon Press, 1987.

Harris, Susan K. *19th-Century American Women's Novels: Interpretive Strategies*. New York: Cambridge University Press, 1990.

Hawthorne, Nathaniel. *The Scarlet Letter*. 1850; Reprint. New York: W. W. Norton, 1961.

Herron, Carolivia. Introduction to *Selected Works of Angelina Weld Grimké*. New York: Oxford University Press, 1991.

Hersh, Blanche Glassman. *The Slavery of Sex: Feminist-Abolitionists in America*. Urbana: University of Illinois Press, 1978.

Hewitt, Nancy A. "The Perimeters of Women's Power in American Religion" in *The Evangelical Tradition in America*. Macon, Ga.: Mercer University Press, 1984.

Hite, Molly. Introduction to *Megda*. 1891; Reprint. New York: Oxford University Press, 1988.

Hite, Molly. *The Other Side of the Story: Structures and Strategies of Contemporary Feminist Narratives*. Ithaca, N.Y.: Cornell University Press, 1990.

Homans, Margaret. *Bearing the Word: Language and Female Experience in Nineteenth-Century Women's Writing*. Chicago: University of Chicago Press, 1986.

Hooks, Bell. *Ain't I a Woman: Black Women and Feminism*. Boston: South End Press, 1981.

Hopkins, Pauline E. *Contending Forces: A Romance Illustrative of Negro Life North and South*. 1900; Reprint. New York: Oxford University Press, 1988.

Hopkins, Pauline E. *Hagar's Daughter: A Story of Southern Caste Prejudice*. 1901; Reprinted in *Magazine Novels of Pauline Hopkins*. New York: Oxford University Press, 1988.

Hopkins, Pauline E. *Of One Blood; or, The Hidden Self*. 1903; Reprinted in *Magazine Novels of Pauline Hopkins*. New York: Oxford University Press, 1988.

Hopkins, Pauline E. *Winona: A Tale of Negro Life in the South and Southwest*. 1902; Reprinted in *Magazine Novels of Pauline Hopkins*. New York: Oxford University Press, 1988.

Horton, James Oliver. "Freedom's Yoke: Gender Conventions among Antebellum Free Blacks" in *Black Women in United States History*, Vol. 2. Edited by Darlene Clark Hine. Brooklyn: Carlson Publishing Inc., 1990.

Howe, Julia Ward. *Reminiscences*. 1899; Reprint. New York: Oxford University Press, 1988.

Hull, Gloria T. *Color, Sex and Poetry: Three Women Writers of the Harlem Renaissance*. Bloomington: University of Indiana Press, 1987.

Hull, Gloria T. "Under the Days: The Buried Life and Poetry of Angelina Weld Grimké" in *Conditions 5*, II, 2 (Autumn 1979).

Hurston, Zora Neale. *Their Eyes Were Watching God*. 1937; Reprint. Urbana: University of Illinois Press, 1978.

Hutcheon, Linda. "Modern Parody and Bakhtin" in *Rethinking Bakhtin: Extensions and Challenges*. Edited by Gary Saul Morson and Caryl Emerson. Evanston, Ill.: Northwestern University Press, 1989.

Hutchinson, Louise Daniel. *Anna J. Cooper, a Voice From the South*. Washington, D.C.: Smithsonian Institution, 1981.

Iser, Wolfgang. *The Act of Reading: A Theory of Aesthetic Response*. Baltimore: Johns Hopkins University Press, 1978.

Jacobs, Harriet A. *Incidents in the Life of a Slave Girl*. 1861; Reprint (edited by Jean Fagan Yellin). Cambridge, Mass.: Harvard University Press, 1987.

James, William. *The Varieties of Religious Experience: A Study in Human Nature*. 1902; Reprint. New York: Collier, 1961.

Jameson, Fredric. *The Political Unconscious: Narrative as a Socially Symbolic Act*. Ithaca, N.Y.: Cornell University Press, 1981.

Jauss, Hans Robert. "Literary History as Challenge" in *Toward an Aesthetic of Reception*. Minneapolis: University of Minnesota Press, 1982.

Johnson, Mrs. A[melia]. E. *Clarence and Corinne; or, God's Way*. 1890; Reprint. New York: Oxford University Press, 1988.

Johnson, Mrs. A[melia]. E. *The Hazeley Family*. 1894; Reprint. New York: Oxford University Press, 1988.

Jones, Jacqueline. *Labor of Love, Labor of Sorrow: Black Women, Work, and the Family from Slavery to the Present*. New York: Basic Books, 1985.

Jones, Jacqueline. *Soldiers of Light and Love: Northern Teachers and Georgia Blacks, 1865–1973*. Chapel Hill: University of North Carolina Press, 1980.

Jones, J. McHenry. *Hearts of Gold: A Novel*. 1896; Reprint. College Park, Md.: McGrath, 1969.

Jordan, June. "On Richard Wright and Zora Neale Hurston: Notes Toward a Balancing of Love and Hatred" in *Black World* (August 1974).

Karenga, Ron. "Black Cultural Nationalism" in *The Black Aesthetic*. Edited by Addison Gayle, Jr. New York: Anchor Doubleday, 1971.

Kelley-Hawkins, Emma. *Four Girls at Cottage City*. 1898 [1895]; Reprint. New York: Oxford University Press, 1988.

Kelley-Hawkins, Emma. *Megda*. 1891; Reprint. New York: Oxford University Press, 1988.

Kulikoff, Alan. "Beginnings of the Afro-American Family" in *Black Women in United States History*, Vol. 3. Edited by Darlene Clark Hine. Brooklyn: Carlson Publishing Inc., 1990.

Ladner, Joyce A. "Racism and Tradition: Black Womanhood in Historical Perspective" in *The Black Woman Cross-Culturally*. Edited by Filomina Chioma Steady. Cambridge, Mass.: Schenkman Books, Inc., 1981.

Leach, William. *True Love and Perfect Union: The Feminist Reform of Sex and Society*. New York: Basic Books, Inc., 1980.

Levine, Lawrence W. *Black Culture and Black Consciousness: Afro-American Folk Thought from Slavery to Freedom*. New York: Oxford University Press, 1977.

Littlejohn, David L. *Black on White: A Critical Survey of Writing by American Negroes*. New York: Viking, 1966.

Logan, Rayford W. *The Betrayal of the Negro, from Rutherford B. Hayes to Woodrow Wilson*. New York: Collier, 1965.

Loggins, Vernon. *The Negro Author: His Development in America to 1900*. New York: Columbia University Press, 1931.

Lorde, Audre. "The Uses of the Erotic: The Erotic as Power." 1978; Reprinted in *Sister Outsider*. Trumansburg, N.Y.: The Crossing Press, 1984.

Lubiano, Wahneema. "But Compared to What?" in *Black American Literature Forum* 25, 2 (Summer 1991).

Lystra, Karen. *Searching the Heart: Women, Men, and Romantic Love in Nineteenth-Century America*. New York: Oxford University Press, 1989.

Majors, Monroe A. *Noted Negro Women: Their Triumphs and Activities*. 1893; Reprint. Nashville, Tenn.: Fisk University Library Negro Collection, 1971.

Mandel, Ernest. *Delightful Murder: A Social History of the Crime Story*. Minneapolis: University of Minnesota Press, 1984.

Mann, Susan A. "Slavery, Sharecropping, and Sexual Inequality" in *Signs* 14, 4 (Summer 1989).

Marshall, Paule. *Brown Girl, Brownstones*. 1958; Reprint. New York: Avon, 1970.

Matthews, Victoria Earle. *Aunt Lindy: A Story Founded on Real Life*. 1889; Reprint. New York: J. J. Little, 1893.

Matthews, Victoria Earle. "The Value of Race Literature: An Address." 1895; Reprinted in *The Massachusetts Review* 27 (Summer 1986).

McDowell, Deborah E. "In the First Place: Making Frederick Douglass and the Afro-American Narrative Tradition" in *Critical Essays on Frederick Douglass*. Edited by William Andrews. New York: G. K. Hall, 1992.

McDowell, Deborah E. Introduction to *Four Girls at Cottage City* by Emma Kelley-Hawkins. 1898; Reprint. New York: Oxford University Press, 1988.

McDowell, Deborah E. Introduction to *Plum Bun* by Jessie Fauset. 1929; Reprint. New Brunswick, N.J.: Rutgers University Press, 1990. pp. xii–xiii.

McDowell, Deborah E. "The Neglected Dimension of Jessie Redmon Fauset" in *Conjuring: Black Women, Fiction, and Literary Tradition*. Edited by Marjorie Pryse and Hortense J. Spillers. Bloomington: University of Indiana Press, 1985.

Miller, Nancy K. *The Heroine's Text: Reading in the French and English Novel, 1722–1782*. New York: Columbia University Press, 1980.

Mintz, Steven and Susan Kellogg. *Domestic Revolutions: A Social History of American Family Life*. New York: The Free Press, 1988.

Morson, Gary Saul. "Parody, History, and Metaparody" in *Rethinking Bakhtin: Extensions and Challenges*. Edited by Gary Saul Morson and Caryl Emerson. Evanston, Ill.: Northwestern University Press, 1989.

Morrison, Toni. *Beloved*. New York: Knopf, 1987.

Morrison, Toni. *The Bluest Eye*. New York: Knopf, 1970.

Moses, Wilson J. "Domestic Feminism, Conservatism, Sex Roles, and Black Women's Clubs, 1893–1896" in *Black Women in United States History: From Colonial Times Through the Nineteenth Century*. Vol. 3. Edited by Darlene Clark Hine. Brooklyn: Carlson Publishing Inc., 1990.

Moses, Wilson J. *The Golden Age of Black Nationalism*. Hamden, Conn.: Archon Books, 1978.

Mossell, Mrs. N[athan]. F. "Life and Literature" in *The A.M.E. Church Review* 14 (January 1898).

Mossell, Mrs. N[athan]. F. *The Work of the Afro-American Woman*. 1908 [1894]; Reprint. New York: Oxford University Press, 1988.

Moynihan, Daniel Patrick. *Moynihan Report: The Case for National Action*. Washington, D.C.: 1965.

Murray, Daniel. "Bibliography of Negro Literature" in *The A.M.E. Church Review* 16 (July 1900).

Murray, Daniel. "Bibliographia-Africania" in *The Voice of the Negro* III–IV (1906–1907).

Neverdon-Morton, Cynthia. *Afro-American Woman of the South and the Advancement of the Race, 1895–1925*. Knoxville: University of Tennessee Press, 1989.

Olney, James. "The Founding Fathers—Frederick Douglass and Booker T. Washington" in *Slavery and the Literary Imagination*. Edited by Deborah E. McDowell and Arnold Rampersad. Baltimore: Johns Hopkins University Press, 1987.

Omolade, Barbara. "Hearts of Darkness" in *Powers of Desire: The Politics of Sexuality*. Edited by Ann Snitow, Christine Stansell, and Sharon Thompson. New York: Monthly Review Press, 1983.

Penn, I[rvin]. Garland. *The Afro-American Press, and Its Editors*. Springfield, Mass.: Willey & Co., 1891.

Penzoldt, Peter. *The Supernatural in Fiction*. New York: Humanities Press, 1965.

Perkins, Linda. "Black Women and Racial 'Uplift' Prior to Emancipation" in *The Black Woman Cross-Culturally*. Edited by Filomina Chioma Steady. Cambridge, Mass.: Schenkman Books, Inc., 1981.

Perkins, Linda. "The Impact of the 'Cult of True Womanhood' on the Education of Black Women" in *Journal of Social Issues* 39, 3 (1983).

Petry, Ann. *The Street*. 1946; Reprint. Boston: Beacon, 1985.

Ross, Ellen and Rayna Rapp. "Sex and Society: A Research Note from Social History and Anthropology" in *Powers of Desire: The Politics of Sexuality*. Edited by Ann Snitow, Christine Stansell, and Sharon Thompson. New York: Monthly Review Press, 1983.

Rothman, Ellen K. *Hands and Hearts: A History of Courtship in America*. Cambridge, Mass.: Harvard University Press, 1987.

Salem, Dorothy. *To Better Our World: Black Women in Organized Reform, 1890–1920*. Brooklyn: Carlson Publishing Inc., 1990.

Salvino, Dana Nelson. "The Word in Black and White: Ideologies of Race and Literacy in Antebellum America" in *Reading in America: Literature and Social History*. Edited by Cathy N. Davidson. Baltimore: Johns Hopkins University Press, 1989.

Scott, Anne Firor. "The 'New Woman'" in *The Southern Lady: From Pedestal to Politics, 1830–1930*. Chicago: University of Chicago Press, 1970.

Scott, Anne Firor. "What, Then, Is the American: This New Woman?" in *Journal of American History* 65 (December 1978).

Scruggs, Lewis A. *Women of Distinction: Remarkable in Works and Invincible in Character*. Raleigh, N.C.: Self-published, 1893.

Seidman, Steven. *Romantic Longings: Love in America, 1839–1980*. New York: Routledge, 1991.

Shange, Ntozake. *Nappy Edges*. New York: St. Martin's Press, 1978.

Sherman, Joan R. Introduction to *Collected Black Women's Poetry*. New York: Oxford University Press, 1987.

Shockley, Ann Allen. *Afro-American Women Writers, 1746–1933*. Boston: G. K. Hall, 1988.

Showalter, Elaine. *A Literature of Their Own: British Women Novelists from Brontë to Lessing*. Princeton, N.J.: Princeton University Press, 1977.

Smith, Paul. *Discerning the Subject*. Minneapolis: University of Minnesota, 1988.

Smith, Valerie. Introduction to *Incidents in the Life of a Slave Girl* by Harriet A. Jacobs. 1861; Reprint. New York: Oxford University Press, 1988.

Smith, Valerie. *Self-Discovery and Authority in Afro-American Narrative*. Cambridge, Mass.: Harvard University Press, 1987.

Smith-Rosenberg, Carroll. *Disorderly Conduct: Visions of Gender in Victorian America*. New York: Oxford University Press, 1985.

Smith-Rosenberg, Carroll. "The New Woman and the New History" in *Feminist Studies* 3 (Fall 1975).

Spillers, Hortense. Introduction to *Clarence and Corinne* by Mrs. A[melia]. E. Johnson. 1890; Reprint. New York: Oxford University Press, 1988.

Stepto, Robert B. *From Behind the Veil: A Study of Afro-American Narrative*. Urbana: University of Illinois Press, 1979.

Sterling, Dorothy, Ed. *We Are Your Sisters: Black Women in the Nineteenth Century*. New York: W. W. Norton, 1984.

Stevenson, Brenda. Introduction to *The Journals of Charlotte Forten Grimké*. New York: Oxford University Press, 1988.

Stowe, Harriet B. *Uncle Tom's Cabin*. 1851; Reprint. New York: Signet, 1966.

Stuckey, Sterling. *Slave Culture: Nationalist Theory and the Foundations of Black America*. New York: Oxford University Press, 1987.

Sweet, Leonard I., Ed. *The Evangelical Tradition in America*. Macon, Ga.: Mercer University Press, 1984.

Tate, Claudia. Introduction to *The Works of Katherine Chapman Davis Tillman*. New York: Oxford University Press, 1991.

Terrell, Mary Church. *A Colored Woman in a White World*. Washington, D.C.: National Association of Colored Women's Clubs, Inc., 1968.

Tillman, Katherine Davis Chapman. *Beryl Weston's Ambition: The Story of an Afro-American Girl's Life*. 1893; Reprinted in *The Works of Katherine Davis Chapman Tillman*. New York: Oxford University Press, 1991.

Tillman, Katherine Davis Chapman. *Clancy Street*. 1898; Reprinted in *The Works of Katherine Davis Chapman Tillman*. New York: Oxford University Press, 1991.

Tillman, Katherine Davis Chapman. *Fifty Years of Freedom; or from Cabin to Congress: A Drama in Five Acts*. 1910; Reprinted in *The Works of Katherine Davis Chapman Tillman*. New York: Oxford University Press, 1991.

Tillman, Katherine Davis Chapman. "The Preacher at Hill Station." 1903; Reprinted in *The Works of Katherine Davis Chapman Tillman*. New York: Oxford University Press, 1991.

Todd, Janet. *Sensibility: An Introduction*. New York: Methuen, 1986.

Toll, Robert C. *Blacking Up: The Minstrel Show in Nineteenth-Century America*. New York: Oxford University Press, 1974.

Tompkins, Jane. *Sensational Designs: The Cultural Work of American Fiction, 1790–1860*. New York: Oxford University Press, 1987.

Turner, Darwin T. "Afro-American Literary Critics: An Introduction" in *The Black Aesthetic*. Edited by Addison Gayle, Jr. New York: Anchor, 1971.

Turner, Darwin T. Introduction to *House Behind the Cedars* by Charles Chesnutt. Toronto: Macmillan Co., 1969.

Unsigned. Article in Women's Department in *The A.M.E. Church Review* 16 (October 1900).

Walker, Alice. *The Color Purple*. New York: Harcourt Brace Jovanovich, 1983.

Walker, Alice. "If the Present Looks Like the Past, What Does the Future Look Like?" in *In Search of Our Mother's Garden*. New York: Harcourt Brace Jovanovich, 1983.

Walker, Alice. *The Temple of My Familiar*. New York: Harcourt Brace Jovanovich, 1989.

Walker, Barbara W., Ed. *The Woman's Encyclopedia of Myths and Secrets*. New York: Harper and Row, 1983.

Washington, Booker T. *A New Negro for a New Century*. Chicago: American Publishing House, 1900.

Washington, Booker T. *Up from Slavery* in *Three Negro Classics*. 1901; Reprint. New York: Avon Books, 1965.

Washington, Josephine Turpin. Introduction to *Women of Distinction: Remarkable in Works and Invincible in Character*. Edited by Lewis Arthur Scruggs. Raleigh, N.C.: Self-published, 1893.

Washington, Mary Helen. "The Darkened Eye Restored" in *Reading Black, Reading Feminist*. Edited by Henry Louis Gates, Jr. New York: Penguin Books, 1990.

Washington, Mary Helen. *Invented Lives: Narratives of Black Women, 1860–1960*. New York: Anchor, 1987.

Watson, Carole McAlpine. *Prologue: The Novels of Black American Women, 1891–1965*. Westport, Conn.: Greenwood Press, 1985.

Wells-Barnett, Ida. *The Reason Why The Colored American Is Not in the World's Exposition*. 1893; Reprint. New York: Oxford University Press, 1991.

Welter, Barbara. "The Cult of True Womanhood, 1820–1860" in *Dimity Convictions: The American Woman in the Nineteenth Century*. Athens: Ohio State University Press, 1976.

White, Deborah Gray. *Ar'n't I a Woman: Female Slaves in the Plantation South*. New York: W. W. Norton, 1985.

Williams, Fannie Barrier. "The Accusations Are False" in *Black Women in White America*. Edited by Gerda Lerner. New York: Vintage, 1973.

Williams, Sherley Anne. *Dessa Rose*. New York: Morrow, 1987.

Williamson, Joel. *The Crucible of Race: Black-White Relations in the American South since Emancipation*. New York: Oxford University Press, 1984.

Wills, David Wood. *Aspects of Social Thought in the African Methodist Episcopal Church, 1884–1910*. Unpublished Ph.D. thesis, Harvard University, February 1975.

Wilson, Harriet E. *Our Nig; or, Sketches from the Life of a Free Black*. 1859; Reprint. New York: Vintage, 1984.

Winnett, Susan. "Coming Unstrung: Women, Men, Narrative, and Principles of Pleasure" in *PMLA* 105, 3 (May 1990), pp. 505–18.

Wood, Ann D. *The Feminization of American Culture*. New York: Knopf, 1977.

Wood, Ann D. "The 'Scribbling Women' and Fanny Fern: Why Women Wrote" in *American Quarterly* 23, 1 (Spring 1971).

Wright, Richard. "Between Laughter and Tears" in *New Masses* 5 (October 1937).

Wright, Richard. *Black Boy*. New York: Harper and Brothers, 1945.

Wright, Richard. "Blueprint for Negro Writing." 1937; Reprinted in *The Black Aesthetic*. Edited by Addison Gayle, Jr. New York: Anchor Doubleday, 1971.

Wright-Pleasant, Ella. "Beautiful Woman!" in *The A.M.E. Church Review* 16 (October 1900), pp. 171–72.

Yarborough, Richard. Introduction to *Contending Forces*. 1900; Reprint. New York: Oxford University Press, 1988.

Yellin, Jean Fagan, Ed. *Incident in the Life of a Slave Girl*. Cambridge, Mass.: Harvard University Press, 1987.

Yellin, Jean Fagan. "Texts and Contexts of Harriet Jacobs's *Incidents in the Life of a Slave Girl*" in *The Slave's Narrative*, edited by Charles T. Davis and Henry Louis Gates, Jr. New York: Oxford University Press, 1985.

Yellin, Jean Fagan. "*Written by Herself*: Harriet Jacobs's Slave Narrative" in *American Literature* 53, 3 (November 1981).

INDEX

Abolitionism: in Douglass's work, 27–29, 239n.1; in Hopkins's work, 200–203, 274n.33; in Jacobs's work, 24–26, 28, 30; racial hypocrisy of abolitionists, 48–49; in Stowe's work, 23–24; in Wilson's work, 24–26, 48–49. *See also* Slavery
Adams, John Henry, 213
Aesthetic reception theory, 6
African Americans. *See* Blacks; *and headings beginning with Black*
Albert, Octavia, 181, 270n.1
Alcott, Louisa May, 179, 248n.35
Allegory, 101–2, 109–10, 243n.39
A.M.E. Church Review, The, 84, 210, 232n.10, 233n.17, 259n.1, 259n.50, 270n.1
American Baptist, The, 103–4, 256n.16
Ammons, Elizabeth, 4, 205, 206–7, 232n.8, 238n.54, 262nn.36–37, 270n.59, 275n.39
Andrews, William, 241n.17, 243n.44, 251n.18
Angell, Norman, 276n.44
Antebellum period: abolitionism during, 23–26; blacks during, 11; free blacks during, 24–26, 32–50, 59, 240n.9; gender constructions of the black female, 52–59; in Jacobs's work, 24–32, 49–50; novels of, compared with post-Reconstruction novels, 86–87; in Stowe's work, 20, 23–

24; in Wilson's work, 24–26, 32–50. *See also* Slavery
Aptheker, Bettina, 237–38n.47, 244n.3
Ardis, Ann, 257n.26
Armstrong, Nancy, 93, 95, 138, 139, 142, 143–44
Audience. *See* Readership

Bailey, Frankie Y., 238n.47
Baker, Houston A., Jr., 237n.46
Bakhtin, Mikhail M., 5, 165, 241n.17, 267n.32
Baldwin, James, 79, 117, 229–30
Barthes, Roland, 106, 256n.22
Baym, Nina, 6, 65, 66, 233n.16, 248n.35, 248n.2
Benjamin, Jessica, 36
Bernard, Jessie, 253n.36
Bibb, Henry, 251n.18
Black Arts movement, 78–80, 89, 92, 250n.10
Black heroines: as agents of racial desire, 121–23; and black bourgeois individuation, 138–44; and black womanhood, 131–34; characteristics of, 8, 11, 69, 94, 97–102, 127–28, 137, 214; as "charming lady," 97, 98–99; in Grimké's work, 219–23; in Hopkins's work, 195–96, 208; as independent, spunky women, 179; as professional women, 13, 185, 187–88, 267n.31, 275n.40; and racial discourse, 193–96; realistic portrayal